# PRESIDENTS AND THEIR JUSTICES

**Douglas Clouatre**

**University Press of America,® Inc.**
**Lanham · Boulder · New York · Toronto · Plymouth, UK**

4501 Forbes Boulevard
Suite 200
Lanham, Maryland 20706
UPA Acquisitions Department (301) 459-3366

Estover Road
Plymouth PL6 7PY
United Kingdom


Printed in the United States of America
British Library Cataloging in Publication Information Available

Library of Congress Control Number: 2010935138
ISBN: 978-0-7618-5373-2 (paperback : alk. paper)
eISBN: 978-0-7618-5374-9

™ The paper used in this publication meets the minimum requirements of American National Standard for Information Sciences—Permanence of Paper for Printed Library Materials, ANSI Z39.48-1992

# Contents

## Section Three: Failed Successes: Failed Presidents Choose Great Justices

## Introduction

A comparison of the presidencies of Harry Truman and Herbert Hoover would draw the inevitable conclusion that Truman was a more successful chief executive than Hoover. Explanations for Truman's success and Hoover's failures would range from the ideological to the psychological but a consensus exists among historians and laymen alike that Truman's administration bordered on greatness while Hoover's approached failure.

Yet a full examination of Truman and Hoover's records might lead to different conclusions about success and failure. One portion of that record, Supreme Court appointments, would lead to a drastically different conclusion. Hoover's three appointees included two great justices while Truman's four appointees included three abject failures. On this single issue Hoover's instincts and actions were far beyond Truman's, raising an interesting question about the perception of presidential administrations. If Hoover proved more effective in his Court nominees than Truman or other presidential successes including Jackson, Jefferson, Polk, Wilson and Kennedy, how might other presidents, dismissed as failures, be compared to their brethren?

Supreme Court appointments are unpredictable events. Justices retire at their own discretion without regard to politics, party or convenience. Once chosen a just can fulfill a president's ideals or reject them. Justices also serve far beyond a presidential term, influencing the political system and the president's legacy. Judicial nominations are rarely used to measure presidential success, with observers of the office focusing on domestic and foreign policies over which presidents exert greater control. Yet the Supreme Court's importance in advancing or inhibiting a president's agenda is hard to overstate. A handful of great presidents, Jefferson, Jackson, Lincoln, Theodore Roosevelt, Franklin Roosevelt and Ronald Reagan faced hostile Supreme Courts to different degrees. Occasionally these courts acted to directly halt a president's legislative momentum by striking down laws, other times the courts interpret laws so as to dilute their effect. Presidential success can be tied directly to his ability to replace hostile judges with compliant ones and to receive the Court's imprimatur on the most controversial policies.

Studying the effect of Supreme Court nominations on presidential success represents a new approach to ranking presidents on a rising scale. Taking a single set of decisions and separating them from thousands of other decisions made over four to eight years then highlighting the effect of those decisions is the focus of this work. A president's success at appointing justices goes beyond making ideologically compatible selections and includes choosing competent and influential judges who can work with colleagues and build coalitions. Unlike cabinet or subcabinet appointments, Court justices cannot be removed if found to be lacking and with life tenure a poor choice can serve as a reminder of a president's failure in the appointment process.

By 2005 thirty seven presidents had appointed Supreme Court justices with varying degrees of success. Part of that success was serendipity with some presidents such as William Howard Taft able to appoint six justices within four years while others such as James Monroe were able to make a single selection in eight years. Untimely death, poor working conditions, sudden shifts in the political winds also contributed to the success or failure of a president's selections.

In surveying presidential and judicial scholars on a single subject, a president's Supreme Court nominees, this work hopes to raise questions and offer new avenues of research into the work of administrations and the effect of justices on presidential legacy.

Few books get done without a considerable and competent supporting staff and this work was no different. My deepest appreciation to those who helped me in writing, editing, formatting and psychoanalyzing Amy Erickson, Danica Reutzel, Stacy Bauer, Jessica Epting and Peggy Woodruff. I also cannot forget Smedley, Smedlina and Sludgepump, without them I would be nothing or at least a lot less funny.

# Section 1

# Great Presidents, Great Justices

*Few presidents are ranked among the great administrations, their achievements noted in an era they dominated. Of those greats a few also selected justices who excelled and added to the presidential legacy.*

## Chapter 1

# Presidential and Judicial Rankings past and present

Ranking prominent figures has become a cottage industry. Media outlets ranging from ESPN to C Span have used experts and the public to rank everyone from sports figures to presidents. Among the earliest of these rankings were those of presidents. In 1948 Arthur Schlesinger Sr. surveyed historians and presidential experts and ranked presidents from great, near great, average, below average and failure. His son, Arthur Schlesinger Jr. offered his own survey in 1962, updating rankings and adding two recent presidents. Other rankings have followed including a 1982 Chicago Tribune survey, two recent polls by C Span in 1999 and 2009, a survey from the Federalist Society and Wall Street Journal and another from Marist University. Though spread over six decades, the surveys had remarkably similar results at the top and bottom of the rankings. Abraham Lincoln, George Washington and Franklin Roosevelt are firmly entrenched at the top of the surveys while Warren Harding, Ulysses Grant and James Buchanan have settled into the bottom spots. The surveys rated presidential success according to broad categories of success in domestic and foreign policy, success necessarily interpreted by each participant producing certain biases reflected in the results.

An early observer of presidential rankings, Thomas Bailey, noted the partisan biases in rankings composed mostly of Democrats as the experts tended to rate Democrat presidents higher than Republicans. Bailey offered several explanations for the bias including an institutional bias with Democrats favoring a strong presidency while Republicans operated low key, more restrained administrations. The bias toward action caused raters to place Republicans at the lower end of the scale. Bailey also scrutinized the participants in both Schlesinger polls, noting many had been active in Democrat campaigns and administration and included such partisans as Justice Felix Frankfurter, who enjoyed a close relationship with Franklin Roosevelt.[1]

Additional biases were time based, as twentieth century presidents enjoyed greater power and higher expectations of their performance. Twentieth century presidents enjoyed tools that exceeded the authority of their nineteenth century predecessors. George H.W. Bush's single term offered greater opportunity for national and international achievement than enjoyed by any two term nineteenth century president. Successful nineteenth century presidents could list far fewer achievements than mere average twentieth century presidents, lowering their ranking.

The popularity of the Schlesinger and subsequent presidential polls led to broader surveys focusing on other institutions of government. Federal judges are the longest serving members of the national government beyond a few members of Congress who manage to withstand the electoral tides for decades. The most influential of these are Supreme Court justices.

Ranking of justices predated the Schlesinger polls but were based on individual assessments rather than a systematic survey of experts. The early raters included prominent lawyers, law professors and a former justice. Charles Evans Hughes produced a list of greats in 1927 followed by Dean Roscoe Pound in 1938 and Professor John Frank in 1958. One sitting justice, Felix Frankfurter, offered his own assessment of judicial greats in 1957. In the late seventies and early eighties two Court observers, Bernard Schwartz in 1979 and James Hambleton in 1983 offered their own list of greats which built upon the rankings of their predecessors. In 1997 Schwartz updated his list to include ten greatest and ten worst justices.[2]

The most systematic ranking of justices came in 1972 with a poll by Blaustein and Mersky ranking justices through Thurgood Marshall. A subsequent poll conducted in 2004 added eight justices to the mix while producing results similar to the 1972 survey. Blaustein and Mersky surveyed sixty six political scientists, historians and law professors and produced a list of twelve great justices, fifteen near greats, fifty five average and six below average or failed justices. The results resembled their predecessors' with a major exception, Roger Taney was listed among the greats joining John Marshall, Story, Holmes, Hughes, Brandeis and Cardozo.[3]

An early 1990s survey of hundreds of lawyers, judges, political scientist and law students rated the greatest justices, leaving most justices unrated and offering a truncated view of the Court's history. The results resembled those of previous surveys though William Rehnquist achieved greater recognition among law students.[4]

Presidential and Supreme Court surveys offered a general look at both institutions and those who served. Yet the executive and judicial branches are inexorably tied together as presidents choose judges they believe will advance their agenda far beyond the presidential term. Supreme Court nominations offer the greatest opportunity for legal and political influence as a single vote can produce dramatic shifts in policy or deciding a presidential election.

A few presidents are honored with eras named after them including Jackson, Franklin Roosevelt and Ronald Reagan. Most presidents either serve under the shadow of a famous predecessor or in an undefined period. Escaping this obscurity is the wish of most of the men who spend their adult lives seeking the presidency and judicial appointments offer that opportunity. Even presidential greats can enjoy an enhanced legacy as their Court appointments influence public policy decades after the end of the presidential term.

Abraham Lincoln and Franklin Roosevelt appointed justices who continued writing opinions thirty years after the president's death. Thus a measure of presidential greatness must include analysis of that president's Supreme Court appointments. Ranking presidents based solely on their Supreme Court appointment opens new avenues of analysis of administrations while gauging presidential success.

## The Survey

In spring and summer of 2005, surveys were distributed to political scientists, historians, judges, lawyers and other Court experts seeking their rankings of presidents based on a single criterion, their Supreme Court appointments. Fifty four responses were gathered, a number resembling that of the Blaustein and Mersky sampling of sixty five experts. The total number of participants was smaller than those of other Supreme Court rankings including Pederson and Provizer. Yet many surveys ask a narrower question such as listing great justices, deepening the pool of experts. The larger question of ranking presidents based on Supreme Court nomination demands greater expertise across the entire history of the Supreme Court.[5]

The survey results were tabulated producing a ranking from one to thirty seven with a ranking of five as highest and a ranking of one as the lowest. The averages were arranged according to different categories including number of justices appointed, appointment of chief justices, appointment of a majority of justices by a single president, party of appointing president and the standard deviations of the rankings. The survey results were compared to the rankings of presidential administrations and three categories were created, administration greats that also achieved greatness in their Court appointments, administration greats that were ranked below average for the appointments and failed or average presidents who were ranked near or above average for their Court appointments. This work examines those presidencies and their nominations along those three categories. The survey results are found in table one.

## The Surprises

Table One contains the full list of all presidents ranked according to their Supreme Court appointments. The rankings include the expected of Franklin Roosevelt and Abraham Lincoln among the greats but also some surprises. Among the top five, Herbert Hoover's ratings may be the most extraordinary and unexpected. Blamed for the Great Depression, Hoover's presidency was relegated to the mediocrity category but his legacy of Court appointments placed him among the top five of all presidents. Among the next ten, Calvin Coolidge was nestled beside Ronald Reagan, who temporarily revived Silent Cal's reputation during the 1980s. Another mediocrity, William Howard Taft, ranked twelfth while Richard Nixon, one of the lowest ranked twentieth century administrations rose to fourteenth based on his four Court appointments.

Andrew Jackson ranked among the near greats for his administration. His rank dropped to an average rating in the survey, just above the mean score and one slot below Gerald Ford. With four of his six Court appointees participating in the Dred Scot decision, the political legacy of the Dred Scott ruling placed him squarely among the mediocrities. Thomas Jefferson and Harry Truman fared even worse. The third president, bested by John Marshall in his war against the judiciary, was ranked twenty third, and squeezed between Millard Fillmore and Benjamin Harrison. Harry Truman fell to twenty seventh place, just above George H.W. Bush, for the rating of worst twentieth century president based on Supreme Court appointments. Truman's ranking resulted from three of his four justices being labeled as failures.

Table One

## Presidential rankings based on Supreme Court appointments

Averages

| | | | |
|---|---|---|---|
| Franklin Roosevelt | 4.63 | Warren Harding | 3.13 |
| John Adams | 4.59 | Grover Cleveland | 3.11 |
| Dwight Eisenhower | 4.04 | John Kennedy | 3.08 |
| George Washington | 3.94 | Millard Fillmore | 2.96 |
| Herbert Hoover | 3.93 | Thomas Jefferson | 2.91 |
| Theodore Roosevelt | 3.91 | Benjamin Harrison | 2.76 |
| James Madison | 3.89 | Harry Truman | 2.7 |
| Abraham Lincoln | 3.85 | George Bush | 2.68 |
| Woodrow Wilson | 3.79 | James Monroe | 2.61 |
| Ronald Reagan | 3.67 | James Polk | 2.56 |
| Calvin Coolidge | 3.43 | Martin Van Buren | 2.52 |
| William Howard Taft | 3.41 | Chester Arthur | 2.51 |
| Rutherford Hayes | 3.38 | James Garfield | 2.47 |

| | | | |
|---|---|---|---|
| Richard Nixon | 3.29 | William McKinley | 2.41 |
| Lyndon Johnson | 3.29 | Franklin Pierce | 2.4 |
| Gerald Ford | 3.25 | John Tyler | 2.4 |
| Andrew Jackson | 3.2 | John Quincy Adams | 2.38 |
| Bill Clinton | 3.17 | James Buchanan | 2.29 |
| Ulysses Grant | 3.17 | | |
| | | Mean | 3.18 |

Included among the top ten in the survey were five presidents rated as greats for the administrations. Among the bottom half are three presidents ranked among the greats or near greats including Harry Truman, James Polk and John Kennedy. Two consensus presidential failures, Warren Harding and Ulysses Grant are ranked near or above average for their Court nominations.

There are several possible explanations for the deviation in the two set of rankings. Among these are the types of justices appointed and the number of justices appointed. Presidents who appoint chiefs are more likely to achieve an above average ranking.

## Table Two

## Presidents who appointed Chief Justices

| | |
|---|---|
| John Adams | 4.59 |
| Dwight Eisenhower | 4.04 |
| George Washington | 3.94 |
| Herbert Hoover | 3.93 |
| Abraham Lincoln | 3.85 |
| Woodrow Wilson | 3.79 |
| Ronald Reagan | 3.67 |
| William Howard Taft | 3.41 |
| Richard Nixon | 3.29 |
| Andrew Jackson | 3.2 |
| Ulysses Grant | 3.17 |
| Warren Harding | 3.13 |
| Grover Cleveland | 3.11 |
| Harry Truman | 2.7 |
| Average | 3.63 |

Appointing a chief justice would be expected to enhance a president's rankings. Fourteen presidents appointed chief justices and thirteen of those were rated above average.[6] Among those presidents, five of them had administrations that were ranked as low average or failures including Herbert Hoover, William Howard Taft, Richard Nixon, Warren Harding and Ulysses Grant. Yet for some presidents their chief justice selections were not ranked among the great justices. Neither of George Washington's two appointed chief justices, John Jay or Oliver Ellsworth were ranked among the great justices in other surveys. The same was true of Roger Taney, Salmon Chase, Edward White, Harlan Stone, Warren Burger and William Rehnquist, all appointed by presidents in the top half of the survey but rarely ranked among the great justices for their career. Only Harlan Stone was rated among the greats in the Blaustein and Mersky survey but was not mentioned within that category for the other surveys. Only three chief justices, John Marshall, Earl Warren and Charles Evans Hughes were ranked as great justices in multiple surveys, suggesting that chief justices may play a smaller role in determining whether a president's Court appointments will be gauged as great. Contrarily Harry Truman appointed the only chief justice, Fred Vinson, who would be labeled a failure in the Blaustein and Mersky Poll, one of three failures chosen by Truman.

Appointing a majority of justices is another indicator of presidential success, enhancing the president's influence over the Court and improving the chances of choosing a great justice. Six presidents appointed at least a majority of the Supreme Court. All of the six were ranked among the top half in the survey, with four of the six among the ten greatest. The presidents were spread across party lines, three Republicans, two Democrats and the unaffiliated Washington while three were twentieth century presidents, two nineteenth and one eighteenth. The six presidents shared one characteristic in that all appointed a chief justice, another indicator of presidential greatness in Supreme Court appointments.[7]

## Table Three

## Majority Appointment

| | |
|---|---|
| Franklin Roosevelt | 4.63 |
| Dwight Eisenhower | 4.04 |
| George Washington | 3.94 |
| Abraham Lincoln | 3.85 |
| William H. Taft | 3.41 |
| Andrew Jackson | 3.2 |
| | |
| Average | 3.845 |

Among the six on the list, two presidents, Franklin Roosevelt and George Washington made nine appointments. Washington filled the six member Court, replacing three justices who resigned while Roosevelt replaced seven of the nine justices, reconstructing a Court once hostile to his agenda to one that advanced it at every opportunity. The other presidents made between five and six appointments with Taft managing six selections in a single term, a record for a one term president.

If appointing a majority of justices enhanced a president's legacy, appointing a single justice may harm a president's ranking.

## Table Four

## Single Appointment

| | |
|---|---|
| Calvin Coolidge | 3.43 |
| Gerald Ford | 3.25 |
| Millard Fillmore | 2.96 |
| James Monroe | 2.61 |
| James Garfield | 2.47 |
| William McKinley | 2.41 |
| John Tyler | 2.4 |
| Franklin Pierce | 2.4 |
| John Quincy Adams | 2.38 |
| James Buchanan | 2.29 |
| | |
| Average | 2.66 |

Presidents with a single Court appointment ranked near the bottom in the survey including the six lowest ranked presidents in the survey. Only two presidents who appointed a single justice, Calvin Coolidge and Gerald Ford ranked above average in the survey even as their administrations were ranked as average or below average. Yet other factors may contribute to these low rankings as only one of the presidents, James Monroe served two terms and only three presidents, Monroe, Coolidge and McKinley won reelection or were returned to office by the voters. Four of the presidents, Tyler, Fillmore, Pierce and Buchanan were among the antebellum failures usually blamed for the events leading to the Civil War. These failures may have partially transferred to their rankings.

Another contributing factor to the rankings is the average length of term for the presidents' justices. Extended tenures offer greater opportunities for influence and achievement while short tenures can consign a justice to obscurity because of a lack of opinion writing opportunity. Table five lists the average term for each president's appointments and includes a correlation coefficient measuring the importance of longevity on a president's ranking.

## Table Five

## Average Longevity of Justices

| | | | |
|---|---|---|---|
| James Madison | 29 | F. Roosevelt | 15.1 |
| Andrew Jackson | 27.17 | James Polk | 14.5 |
| John Tyler | 27 | Grover Cleveland | 14 |
| Wm. McKinley | 27 | Lyndon Johnson | 14 |
| John Adams | 23.33 | B. Harrison | 12.25 |
| James Buchanan | 23 | Warren Harding | 12.25 |
| Thomas Jefferson | 22 | T Roosevelt | 11.67 |
| Calvin Coolidge | 21 | Ulysses Grant | 11.5 |
| Abraham Lincoln | 20.8 | Herbert Hoover | 10.67 |
| Rutherford Hayes | 20.5 | William Taft | 10 |
| James Monroe | 20 | G Washington | 8.9 |
| Woodrow Wilson | 18.67 | Harry Truman | 8.75 |
| D. Eisenhower | 18 | Franklin Pierce | 8 |
| Martin van Buren | 17 | James Garfield | 8 |
| John Kennedy | 17 | Millard Fillmore | 6 |
| Chester Arthur | 16 | John Q Adams | 2 |
| F. Roosevelt | 15.1 | | |

correlation = .115

The correlation coefficient of .11, suggests a weak relationship between longevity and rankings. A glance at the top and bottom of the list reveal that among the presidents whose justices served the longer tenure, only three, John Adams, James Madison and Abraham Lincoln were listed among the great presidents in the survey while Andrew Jackson was ranked as average and William McKinley and John Tyler were among the ten worst for their Court appointments. Among the bottom ten for Court tenure were three presidents ranked as great, Washington, Theodore Roosevelt and Herbert Hoover. These three were mixed among presidents ranked as failures including John Quincy Adams and Franklin Pierce.

A president's rejected nominations for the Court could also explain the deviation between the ranking for an administration and the ranking for Supreme Court appointments. Difficult nominations may lead to a president choosing a less capable but easily confirmable nominee. Table Six lists the twelve presidents who suffered a rejected Court nominee. Of the dozen, only four ranked in the bottom half of the results while another four ranked among the top ten. Among these were George Washington, Ronald Reagan and Herbert Hoover, who were able to recover from a defeated Court nomination and appoint high quality justices who raised their rankings. The worst among these was John Tyler, who saw five of his nominees rejected, most of any president and a record of futility that undermined his entire administration.

## Table Six

## Rejected Appointments

| | |
|---|---|
| G Washington | 4.04 |
| Herbert Hoover | 3.93 |
| James Madison | 3.89 |
| Ronald Reagan | 3.67 |
| Richard Nixon | 3.29 |
| Lyndon Johnson | 3.29 |
| Andrew Jackson | 3.2 |
| Grover Cleveland | 3.11 |
| James Polk | 2.56 |
| John Tyler | 2.4 |
| James Buchanan | 2.29 |
| | |
| Average | 3.25 |

## Potential Biases

One of the dangers of surveying a select group of experts is the potential for bias based on partisanship or the influence of the president's administration influencing the ranking of their Court nominations. Bailey argued that the Schlesinger polls of 1948 and 1962 were biased in favor of Democrats as most of the survey takers were Democrats. Examining this bias required comparing average rankings for Democrat and Republican presidents.

Though the two party system of Republicans and Democrats did not begin until the 1856 election, the Democrat Party elected presidents starting in 1828. George Washington and John Adams are considered the only true Federalist presidents while James Monroe and John Quincy Adams presided over a one party country, making political labeling problematic. In addition Millard Fillmore, the only Whig president to appoint a justice and John Tyler, a Democrat elected as a Whig vice president, were also excluded. Eleven Democrats and seventeen Republican presidents from the nineteenth and twentieth century were included. Democrats earned a mean score of 3.02 while Republican presidents earned a mean score of 3.27 suggesting any bias favored Republicans over Democrats, contrary to findings in ratings of presidential administrations. This is best represented among those ranked as great with five Republicans, T. Roosevelt, Lincoln, Eisenhower, Hoover and Reagan among the top ten while only two Democrats F. Roosevelt and Woodrow Wilson enjoyed that status. At the same time, Democrats represent the overwhelming majority in terms of failed presidents with only William McKinley and Chester Arthur are listed among the ten failures and five Democrat presidents sink to that level.

## Table Seven

## Partisan division of ratings

| Democrats | | Republicans | |
|---|---|---|---|
| F. Roosevelt | 4.65 | D. Eisenhower | 4.04 |
| Woodrow Wilson | 3.79 | Herbert Hoover | 3.91 |
| Lyndon Johnson | 3.29 | T Roosevelt | 3.91 |
| Andrew Jackson | 3.18 | Abraham Lincoln | 3.87 |
| Grover Cleveland | 3.17 | Ronald Reagan | 3.67 |
| Bill Clinton | 3.17 | Rutherford Hayes | 3.57 |
| John Kennedy | 3.08 | Calvin Coolidge | 3.46 |
| James Polk | 2.70 | William Taft | 3.42 |
| Martin Van Buren | 2.65 | Richard Nixon | 3.29 |
| James Buchanan | 2.52 | Gerald Ford | 3.25 |
| Franklin Pierce | 2.52 | Ulysses Grant | 3.22 |
| John Tyler | 2.52 | Warren Harding | 3.13 |
| | | B. Harrison | 2.74 |
| Mean | 3.02 | George Bush | 2.67 |
| | | Chester Arthur | 2.61 |
| | | Wm. McKinley | 2.48 |
| | | James Garfield | 2.48 |
| | | Mean | 3.27 |

Another measure of bias in ratings is the perception a president is overrated or underrated in a survey. Recent presidents are the most difficult to rate, partisan precluding a consensus while history has yet to unravel and "score" their achievements. Among recent presidents, John Kennedy, evokes the most heated discussion about overrated presidents. Kennedy's shortened administration is frequently listed among the near greats even as his presidency lacked the serial achievements of other presidents ranked in the same category. The C span rankings of presidents asked participants to list the most overrated presidents with Kennedy and Ronald Reagan taking the top two spots.

A more systematic measure of over or underrated presidents is the standard deviation of scores. The larger the standard deviation of a president's rankings the greater the spread or disagreement among participants, suggesting a lack of consensus with high rankings seen as overrating a president's Court appointments while low rankings underrate those selections.

Andrew Jackson's rankings received the largest standard deviations, possibly a reaction to Jackson's ranking among the great administrations and his justices' involvement in the Dred Scott decision. Reagan's standard deviation placed him second while Lincoln's ratings placed him in a surprising third. Reagan's position may be explained in that all four of his appointees were on the Court at the time of the survey, their rulings still evoking controversy including the Bush v. Gore decision. Lincoln's position as third, may be explained by the radically different justices he selected including the arch conservative Stephen Field and the more moderate Samuel Miller, both usually ranked among the greats. Lincoln's other choices were controversial, Salmon Chase, or obscure, Noah Swayne, likely producing starkly different rankings.

## Table Eight

## Standard Deviation

| | | | |
|---|---|---|---|
| Andrew Jackson | 1.23 | George Bush | 0.76 |
| Ronald Reagan | 1.05 | Calvin Coolidge | 0.76 |
| Abraham Lincoln | 0.98 | James Buchanan | 0.74 |
| T Roosevelt | 0.92 | Herbert Hoover | 0.72 |
| Millard Fillmore | 0.87 | Rutherford Hayes | 0.72 |
| D. Eisenhower | 0.87 | Richard Nixon | 0.71 |
| Warren Harding | 0.86 | Grover Cleveland | 0.70 |
| James Madison | 0.84 | Ulysses Grant | 0.70 |
| Lyndon Johnson | 0.84 | Chester Arthur | 0.68 |
| Franklin Pierce | 0.83 | James Polk | 0.68 |
| Harry Truman | 0.83 | Martin van Buren | 0.63 |
| Gerald Ford | 0.80 | Wm. McKinley | 0.61 |
| G Washington | 0.80 | James Monroe | 0.60 |
| John Q Adams | 0.80 | F.Roosevelt | 0.55 |

| | | | |
|---|---|---|---|
| John Tyler | 0.80 | B. Harrison | 0.55 |
| Woodrow Wilson | 0.78 | John Kennedy | 0.49 |
| Bill Clinton | 0.77 | John Adams | 0.48 |
| James Garfield | 0.77 | Thomas Jefferson | 0.43 |
| William Taft | 0.76 | | |

At the lower end of the standard deviation scale was Thomas Jefferson, participants enjoying a consensus in their assessment of his appointments. Just above Jefferson was his old enemy John Adams, his choice of John Marshall another source of consensus though in this case participants agreeing to the greatness of his choice. Rounding out the bottom five was two below average presidents, John Kennedy and Benjamin Harrison, and the highest ranked president, Franklin Roosevelt, participants mainly in agreement in their rankings.

A thumbnail analysis of the findings also discounts systematic bias. Ranking a president on a single criterion, Supreme Court appointments, raises the possibility that a survey participant will be influenced by the president's administration, a rating based on factors other than Court appointments. If participants were wholly affected by their view of a presidential administration, then results of the Court survey would closely resemble results of presidential administration surveys. The Court survey results, though, differed in its rankings of several presidents.

Among the top half of presidents in the Supreme Court survey, seven were ranked as average or below average for their administrations. Two of the five greats, John Adams and Herbert Hoover, are ranked among the average or below average for their administrations. Calvin Coolidge and Richard Nixon suffer below average to near failure administration ratings but are among the top fifteen for the Court appointments. Warren Harding and Ulysses Grant, usually battling for the title of worst presidential administration, have their stock rise based on Court appointments with Grant ranked nineteenth and Harding twentieth, both above Kennedy (22), Jefferson (24), Truman (26) and Polk (29), all four presidents perennially rated among the greatest or near greatest administrations.

## The Plan of the Book

The differences between the rankings of administrations and a president's Court appointments are the focus of the remainder of this work. Fifteen presidents and their Court appointments are examined based on their survey rankings. The presidents are divided into three categories, great president who are recognized for their greatness in Court nominations, great presidents who failed in their Court nominations and failed or below average presidents who made extraordinary Court appointments.

The presidents were chosen on a comparison of their rankings in the Court survey and an average of rankings in four recent presidential surveys, Schlesinger 1996, Intercollegiate Studies Institute 1998, C Span 1999 and Wall Street Journal/Federalist Society 2002. The ratings for presidents were averaged across the four surveys producing a list which was compared to the Court survey. Presidents whose Court survey rankings were ten above or ten below their administration rankings were chosen for analysis, the deviation in the ratings requiring examination. Analyzing the careers of each justice appointed will offer some explanation as to the president's ranking and how his Court nominations added or subtracted from the presidential legacy thus creating the ranking deviations.

## Notes

1. Bailey, Thomas, *Presidential Greatness* (New York: Appleton Century Croft, 1966) 25-30.

2. Abraham, Henry, *Justices, Presidents and Senators* (New York: Rowman and Littlefield, 2008) 373-376.

3. Blaustein, Albert and Roy Mersky, *The First One Hundred Justices* (Hamden CT: Archon Books, 1978)

4. Pederson, William and Norman Provizer, *Great Justices of the Supreme Court* (New York:Peter Lang, 1993)

5. Each of the following participated in the survey: Henry Abraham, , David Atkinson, University of Missouri, Judith Baer Texas A&M University, Nancy Baker,New Mexico State University, Michael Benedict, Ohio State University, Bruce Buchanan, University of Texas, Milton Cantor, University of Massachusetts, Douglas Clouatre, Mid Plains Community College, Timothy Cole University of Maine, Richard Collins University of Colorado School of Law, George Crawford University of Florida, Christopher Curtis Iowa State University, Byron Danes Brigham Young University, George Dennison University of Montana, Robert Divine University of Texas, George Edwards Texas A&M University James Ely Jr. Vanderbilt University School of Law, John Fliter Kansas State University, Paul Finkelman University of Tulsa School of Law, Michael Genovese Marymount University, Sheldon Goldman University of Massachusetts, Joel Goldstein St. Louis University School of Law, Sally Hadden Florida State University, Robert Howard Georgia State University, Karen Hult Virginia Tech University, Robert Ireland University of Kentucky Carolyn Johnson University of Kansas, Douglas Kmiec Pepperdine University, Harold Krent Illinois Institute of Technology, William Lasser Clemson University, James Lopach University of Montana, George Lovell University of Washington, Judge Michael McConnell Tenth Circuit Court of Appeals, Forrest McDonald University of Alabama emeritus, J. Mitchell Pickerill Washington State University, Michael Ross Loyola University John Scheb University of

Tennessee, Bill Schreckhise University of Arkansas, Howard Schweber University of Wisconsin Kevin Scott Texas Tech University, Charles Shipan University of Iowa, Brooks Simpson Arizona State University, Don Songer University of South Carolina, Otis Stephens University of Tennessee, Isaac Unah University of North Carolina, Glynn Wolar Mid Plains Community College, David Yalof University of Connecticut, Tinsley Yarbrough East Carolina University

6. George Washington appointed three chief justices, John Jay, John Rutledge and Oliver Ellsworth.George W. Bush appointed Chief Justice John Roberts after the survey results had been calculated and he was not included in the survey

7. Lincoln was included among the group.Though he appointed five justices on what would become a ten member Court, Justice Catron's death in 1865 and the subsequent reduction of the Court to nine justices made the five Lincoln appointees a majority of the institution until 1873.

# Chapter 2

# George Washington (4) Franklin Roosevelt (1)

*Multiple Supreme Court appointments are considered a major opportunity for a president to change the institution. Nine Supreme Court appointments, an opportunity create a new Court, were available to only two presidents, George Washington and Franklin Roosevelt. Washington built a newly created institution, choosing those who had constructed the republic. Roosevelt moved the Court away from a conservative economic rights agenda. Both men's choices proved beneficial to the Court and placed them among the greats.*

## Washington and Roosevelt

Two giants of the American presidency, George Washington and Franklin Roosevelt, presided over very different administrations. As the first chief executive Washington set traditions by creating an independent and limited office. Roosevelt was a smasher of traditions, his third term breaking one of Washington's most enduring legacies, while leading the country through economic and foreign policy crises. Washington brought into his administration the most talented and outspoken leaders of his time. Roosevelt was less astute in his appointments, rarely choosing those with opposing views and creating a tangle of bureaucracy as he piled agency on top of agency.

Both men set the standard for the office with Washington's presidency restrained, dignified and independent. Roosevelt sought and created an aggrandized office, placing the chief executive at the top of the government pyramid. When confronted with opposition Roosevelt sought to dominate those who opposed his policies. Upset with the Court's rulings and frustrated by no vacancies during his first term, Roosevelt proposed increasing the size of the Court to fifteen. The proposal would have startled Washington, who preferred a balanced government able to preserve the new republic.

Both presidents made nine appointments to the Court, the most of any chief executive. Under the 1789 Judiciary Act, Washington filled six vacancies for the new Supreme Court. During his two terms three additional vacancies opened giving him nine total appointments. Washington faced the task of creating an institution lacking history or a tradition. He chose qualified jurists from a relatively small pool, selecting men who were committed to a Federalist concept of government while striking a regional balance in a political culture obsessed with state citizenship.

## John Jay

John Jay will be recalled by students of early American history as the namesake of the oft mentioned but rarely understood Jay Treaty. Jay was the first Chief Justice of the United States who, unlike George Washington, left a less visible imprint on the office he was the first to occupy.

A New Yorker, Jay was a lawyer by trade, revolutionary by circumstance. One of the leaders of the Continental Congress he later served as Chief Justice of New York State and was forced to flee approaching British troops.[1] His temperament impressed many and led to his election as president of the Continental Congress. A mostly ceremonial position lacking real power, the Congress' president mainly negotiated with its members to aid the war effort.[2] Jay worked with General Washington in funding the war effort and shared the general's distrust of Congress and its inability to put the country's fiscal house in order.[3]

Though unsuccessful in molding the Congress into an efficient legislature, Jay's efforts earned him Washington's respect. He was appointed consul to Spain, joining John Adams and Benjamin Franklin in negotiating the end of the war.[4] Their success at reaching beneficial terms from the most powerful nation in Europe testified to their skills. Jay later served as foreign minister under the Articles of Confederation.[5] Even with his experience and dedication to the revolution, Jay was not chosen as a constitutional convention delegate. After the convention Jay joined Alexander Hamilton and James Madison in arguing for ratification in a series of published editorials. Ill health and New York political intrigue limited his contribution to five articles in what became the Federalist Papers.[6]

After ratification Jay was appointed the first Chief Justice of the United States. By late 1789 a six member Court was in place but lacking cases the justices immediately adjourned for the circuit duties.[7]

Jay served as chief justice for five years, his deepest imprint concerning questions of the political role of the Court. France's controversial ambassador to the United States, Edward Genet, provoked a constitutional dispute by recruiting Americans to fight the British and outfitted ships in American ports for action against the Royal Navy. [8] Washington believed Genet's actions violated the American neutrality act and asked the Court for its opinion. Jay refused, stating foreign affairs were the specific province of the executive branch and any opinion the Court issued would be purely advisory, violating the case or controversy clause.[9]

Jay ignored the self imposed restraints when appointed to head a negotiating team sent to Britain to settle property disputes with the British. The subsequent Jay Treaty excited controversy and cast doubts on the political neutrality of the chief justice.[10]

Jay dabbled in New York politics, resigning as a justice to campaign for the New York governorship, a decision that would horrify any modern day justice. [11] After his tenure as New York governor ended Jay was offered the chief justice's post during the waning days of the John Adams Administration. His refusal allowed Adams to appoint John Marshall as chief justice, possibly Jay's greatest contribution to the founding of the republic.

## John Blair

John Blair was the prototypical public servant sought by the framers. Blair graduated from William and Mary College, serving as a colonial then state judge and following in the footsteps of his father and grandfather.[12] A member of the Virginia constitutional convention delegation, Blair had little impact on the debate but successfully lobbied the Virginia ratification convention to approve the constitution.

After the convention, Blair briefly returned to the Virginia Court of Appeals before elevation to the Supreme Court. Blair became a critic of circuit riding, mandated by the 1789 Judiciary Act. Justice Iredell the most vociferous in his opposition to riding circuit in Georgia and the Carolinas, spurring Blair to offer to alternate circuits with Iredell and temporarily solve the problem.[13]

His quiet pose, though, came to an abrupt halt during the controversy over Revolutionary War pensions. Faced with escalating claims Congress delegated the issue to the judiciary. The circuit courts were ordered to settle the pension claims though Congress maintained discretion in overturning the courts' decisions. [14] The justices rebelled against this additional political task and in *Hayburn's Case*, Blair, Justice James Wilson and District Judge Richard Peters ruled the pension law violated Article III. [15] Stung by the ruling, Congress rescinded the law and avoided a constitutional crisis if it had challenged the courts' authority to refuse to enforce the pension claims.

Blair served six years, resigning in protest of circuit riding. His low key personality belied his influence within the institution and his role in the early formation of judicial review.

## John Rutledge

John Rutledge was a rare justice whose tenure on the Supreme Court was the low point of his political career. A member of the South Carolina gentry, he had been a political and military leader in the south during the Revolutionary War. His courage and skill during the battle for Charleston earned him respect from his neighbors and he was one of four South Carolina delegates to the constitutional convention. Rutledge would be the most influential of the four as he fought to protect his state's export and slave driven economy.

The South Carolinian deflected moral arguments about slavery and focused the convention's attention on the economic necessity for a slave based work force.[16] In addition to protecting slavery, Rutledge lobbied for a single rather than multiple executive, life tenure for judges and a two chambered legislature. Rutledge also argued for a several constricted federal judiciary, composed only of a national supreme court. Under Rutledge's plan all state and federal cases would be decided by state courts with a national court enjoying appellate jurisdiction over the decisions. Fortunately for the federal judiciary, Rutledge's plan was overwhelmingly rejected by the convention.[17]

Rutledge was one of the original six and the first justice to resign from the Supreme Court in March 1791. Returning to South Carolina he served as Chief Justice of the state Supreme Court but his tenure was cut short by John Jay's resignation.[18] Rutledge lobbied for the position even as South Carolina politics ruined his candidacy. Anger over the Jay Treaty placed Rutledge in the untenable position of denouncing the administration while seeking a position from the president. His public break with Washington came after his recess appointment as chief justice, Rutledge's words scorched the ears of Federalist senators who rejected his appointment after a bitter debate that had grave consequences for the jittery Chief Justice. Depressed by the death of his wife and uncertain finances, Rutledge twice attempted suicide by drowning.[19] His erratic behavior doomed his political career and he became the only justice nominated by recess appointment and later rejected by the Senate. With the political pressures diminished, Rutledge lived for several more years in his beloved South Carolina, the shine off his legacy.[20]

## James Wilson

Born in Scotland, James Wilson traveled to the colonies in his youth. He was a protégé of John Dickinson, whose writings raised the tax issue as the main rift between the colonists and British homeland.[21] Dickinson was more moderate, refusing to call for immediate independence and passed his caution to Wilson, who represented Pennsylvania in the Continental Congress and was a late supporter of independence.[22]

As war raged, Wilson practiced law in Philadelphia and served on the state's constitutional convention. The delegates split over the basic issues of representation and power for the government branches. Their disagreements spilled into the streets and included an attack on Wilson's house that ended in a shootout and a death.[23]

A delegate to the constitutional convention, Wilson argued for a strong national system, promoting political and economic stability while protecting the nation from foreign threats. Wilson countered states' rights' arguments that sovereignty was vested in state government, instead finding that sovereignty was retained by the people who then delegated sovereignty to the national government. Wilson's democratic ideals and belief in the wisdom of the people were unusual for a Federalist, most of whom distrusted ordinary citizens. He sought to mix the centralized power of a strong national government with democracy, a combination that drew opposition from both sides in the convention.[24]

Later Wilson retreated from his purist views, acquiescing in the undemocratic Electoral College and agreeing that state legislatures should be vested with the authority to choose presidential electors. He successfully argued for a democratically elected House of Representatives and vested it with the authority to choose a president in the event of an electoral deadlock. Wilson also fought off property qualifications for federal voters by delegating voter qualifications to state governments. Wilson believed regular elections allowed the people to check the national government more effectively than institutions such as Congress or the judiciary.[25]

Wilson's contribution to the convention is overshadowed by luminaries including George Washington, James Madison and Alexander Hamilton even though Madison was the only one of the group who matched Wilson's influence. Unfortunately for Wilson, many of his contemporaries enjoyed political careers of historical renown while Wilson served in the obscure Supreme Court, dying at an early age and soon forgotten.

Appointed to the Court in 1790, Wilson used the decisions as a platform for expressing his democratic philosophy in *Chisholm v. Georgia*.[26] Chisholm sued the state of Georgia over money owed, relying on Article III and its diversity of citizenship clause. Georgia claimed sovereign immunity, the ancient legal doctrine precluding citizens from suing their government without its permission. Under the American doctrine, Chisholm could only sue Georgia in its courts. The dispute triggered a debate among the justices over the origins and exercise of sovereignty.

Wilson began his Chisholm opinion declaring the case was of "uncommon magnitude" and stating Georgia's claim of immunity from lawsuit "soars so high."[27] The justice ruled states were subordinate to the people because they were created by the people and claims of state sovereignty separate from the people was a perversion of the natural order denying citizens' God given rights to self government.[28] Wilson stirred the ire of states' rights politicians by declaring "Georgia is not a sovereign state" because the people did not surrender their sovereign rights to the state or its government.[29] Wilson dismissed state sovereign immunity as unworkable, noting laws could be made only with the consent of the governed, ultimately placing sovereignty in their hands.[30]

The four justices in the Chisholm majority were swiftly enveloped in a political firestorm as states' rights politician accepted Wilson's challenge and ratified the Eleventh Amendment to specifically overrule Chisholm. The decision marked the crest of Wilson's judicial career as his financial problems undermined his work and legacy.

A man of considerable talents in philosophy, politics and law, Wilson proved inept in financial matters. The justice speculated in western lands, borrowing millions of dollars with the belief land values would rise as settlers moved west. War in Europe froze credit, land values collapsed and when Wilson was unable to pay his debt, he was cast into prison. His annual circuit duties were overshadowed by debt collectors who sought his imprisonment. Wilson was jailed in 1798, the financial and professional pleasures sapping his strength and leading to his death in that same year at age fifty.

## William Cushing

Ranked as one of the more inconsequential justices ever to serve, William Cushing began as a British judge in Massachusetts and after the Revolution rose to chief justice of the state high court. Cushing later presided at the trial of Daniel Shays, who led the rebellion bearing his name. [31]

Cushing was an outspoken proponent of the new national government and presided over the state's ratification convention, answering anti federalist arguments. Once the constitution was ratified, Cushing enjoyed the honor as one of the first presidential electors, casting his vote for George Washington. Later that year Washington appointed him as one of the original six justices and later asked Cushing to accept the chief justice's position after the John Rutledge fiasco. Cushing refused, claiming ill health even though he served another fifteen years as justice.[32]

Justice Cushing offered few opinions of note though he was a proponent of judicial review in *Ware v. Hylton*[33] and *Cooper v. Telfair.* [34] Under the Treaty of Paris, the British could collect debts from the states without government interference. The Virginia legislature bristled at aiding a former enemy and passed a convoluted law allowing debtors to pay the state pennies on the dollars, thus preventing the British from collecting. [35] Ware challenged the law after being blocked from collecting a debt and in a sweeping opinion Justice Chase struck down the law. Cushing concurred, offering a textual analysis and noting the words of the treaty forbade state interference in debt collection, thus making the Virginia law unconstitutional.[36]

In Cooper the Georgia legislature passed a law banishing British loyalists, requiring each to surrender property to the state and specifically naming those affected by the law. Basil Cooper, banished to Jamaica, challenged the statute as an unconstitutional Bill of Attainder, imposing a legislative punishment on citizens without benefit of a trial. Four justices upheld the law with only a few paragraphs written between them. In a two line opinion Cushing ignored the Bill of Attainder question and upheld the Georgia law, ruling the law violated no part of the constitution but noting that courts retained the authority to strike down a state law deemed unconstitutional.[37]

Cushing also offered his views on state sovereign immunity in Chisholm. His opinion has been compared poorly to his colleagues' who composed wordy treatises focusing on high concepts of natural law and sovereignty. Cushing preferred the simpler approach of reading Article III and its explicit granting of federal court jurisdiction over cases where individuals were suing states.

The last of Washington's original six nominees to leave the Court, Cushing has suffered history's neglect. He played an insignificant role in the Marshall Court, composing no opinions of interest and simply following the chief justice while maintaining a low profile as the Jefferson Administration launched a political war against the judiciary. He retired in 1810, the longest serving of the Washington justices.

## James Iredell

The early Supreme Court was not considered by all of its members as a plum position. The pay was low for those who were otherwise wealthy enough to earn a law degree, thus prompting one of Washington's first choices, Robert Harrison, to decline the appointment. Washington then selected a leader of the North Carolina ratification movement, James Iredell. The future justice argued for ratification during the cranky North Carolina convention, which repeatedly rejected the document until faced with isolation after its adoption in 1788. A new convention was called and ratification quickly followed.[38]

One of the original six, Iredell authored two notable opinions. In Chisholm, Iredell's meandering opinion raised technical issues ignoring constitutional text while arguing for immunity. The justice claimed neither Article III nor the 1789 Judiciary Act granted federal courts jurisdiction in Chisholm's case. He relied on British precedents rather than the constitutional text in arguing for state sovereign immunity.[39]

In *Calder v. Bull*, Iredell and Justice Samuel Chase debated application of the Ex Post Facto Clause in a complicated estate case. [40] Iredell laid out a theory of constitutional interpretation that was the forerunner of textualism. According to Iredell, justices should narrowly interpret the document and defer to Congress and the executive rather than relying on natural law. Justice Chase's Calder opinion favored a natural law interpretation ruling the Ex Post Facto Clause did not apply to civil cases ignoring the constitution did not draw a distinction between the two forms of disputes.[41]

Iredell's textualism sharpened the legal debate over the role of judges in applying the constitution, making him a charter members of the originalist school of legal thought.[42] Iredell's contributions ended with early death at age forty eight, the justice exhausted by circuit riding duties.

## Thomas Johnson

Short tenures on the early Supreme Court were not unusual as boredom and health problems caused several resignations and deaths during the institution's first quarter century. Thomas Johnson was a casualty of the former, disgust with circuit riding ending his judicial career after a year.

A native of Maryland, Johnson served in the first and second Continental Congresses and suggested George Washington as leader of the revolutionary army. But after this single act of greatness he receded from the scene, returning to Maryland and serving as governor from 1777 to 1779. After the war Johnson was appointed to the state high court, serving until Washington tapped him in 1791 for the Supreme Court. Johnson delayed his arrival in Philadelphia, joining the Court in August 1792. A homebody who preferred to remain in Maryland, Johnson rebelled at his circuit writing duties, resigning in 1793 without leaving a mark on the institution.[43]

## William Patterson

Rarely do presidents personally witness their Supreme Court nominees in action. As president of the constitutional convention, George Washington took measure of the men he later appointed to high office. Sitting through the seemingly unending debate over representation in the new Congress, Washington was impressed by the New Jersey delegate, William Patterson. A former state legislator, Patterson attended the constitution convention, leading the small delegates in proposing a bicameral legislature with equal representation.[44]

Patterson was opposed by Virginia delegate John Randolph who proposed a legislature based on population, diminishing small state influence. Backed by large states including Pennsylvania, North Carolina, Massachusetts and New York, Randolph's plan became the focus of debate over the new Congress. Patterson represented the small states, warning the convention that the small states would leave the convention. Through June and July 1787 the debate raged and after a melding of the Virginia and New Jersey plans was a bicameral Congress established.[45]

After ratification, Patterson was elected New Jersey governor then Senator. Patterson worked with Senator and future justice, Oliver Ellsworth, in writing the 1789 Judiciary Act which created the first federal court system.

Patterson also worked with Alexander Hamilton to pay war debts and strengthen the republic's credit. Patterson fought to dispel conspiracy theories that paying the debt rewarded speculators who realized sizable profits once the debt was repaid. Patterson and Hamilton wanted the debt paid in full to attract European credit to the republic and to build the nation. Patterson pushed the bill through the Senate after lengthy debate and a grand compromise that moved the national capital to the Potomac shores.[46]

Thomas Johnson's resignation opened a seat for Patterson. The Federalist senator defended presidential foreign power, joining *Ware v. Hylton* which ruled states could not interfere with enforcement of a treaty.[47] During the Adams Administration Patterson stringently enforced the Alien and Sedition Acts, which threatened his immediate future and dulled his legacy.

When Congressman Matthew Lyon was charged with violating the act for criticizing the administration, Patterson presided at the trial. The justice rejected Lyon's claim the act violated the First Amendment's speech clause then used his jury instruction to prod jurors toward a conviction. After a guilty verdict, the justice sentenced Lyons to four months in prison.[48]

The same year Lyons was convicted, John Adams was defeated for reelection, ending Federalist domination of the government. The Jeffersonian majority immediately took aim at the Federalist judiciary but Patterson was protected as John Marshall and Samuel Chase proved to be more inviting targets. Patterson ingratiated himself with the Jeffersonians in *Stuart v. Laird*, upholding the congressional repeal of the 1801 Judiciary Act.[49] The Jeffersonians had cancelled the Court's 1801 term for fear the justices would strike the law but Patterson calmed those fears. Patterson served another three years, struck down during the despised circuit riding in 1804 and presenting Jefferson an opportunity to pack the Court.

## Samuel Chase

Impeachment may well be the quickest avenue to political immortality in the United States. Andrew Johnson and Bill Clinton are known by schoolchildren for being the only impeached presidents. Samuel Chase was rescued from the obscurity suffered by his contemporaries with his impeachment and Senate trial.

A leader of the revolution in Maryland Chase organized protests against the Stamp and Intolerable Acts then signed the Declaration of Independence while expressing concerns about breaking from Britain. Jealous of his success members of the Maryland Assembly charged him with creating a flour shortage in the state. Chase was acquitted but the taint of the accusations made Washington hesitate at appointing Chase to replace Justice Blair.[50]

The political controversies swirling around Chase overshadowed his legal achievements including his powerful opinion in *Calder v. Bull*. In Calder Chase ruled the Ex Post Facto Clause applied only to criminal not to civil cases.[51] Chase reached this conclusion through a broad interpretation of the clause and the common law definition of Ex Post Facto. Chase was an activist judge, seeking to use the judiciary as a protector of property. Adhering to the formal text of the constitution would limit judges in overturning laws attacking property rights. Under this theory, judges might choose to overturn laws considered unjust. Justice Iredell dissented from Chase's natural law philosophy, arguing judges were limited in their decisions by the plain wording of the text of the constitution.

Though joined in Calder, the debate over liberal construction versus strict construction of the constitution continues into the modern Court, taken up by Chase's and Iredell's successors.[52]

An unapologetic partisan, Chase reveled in the controversies provoked by the Alien and Sedition Acts. He presided in the trials of John Fries and James Callendar and used his position as a forum for promoting Federalist policies.

Fries led the rebellion against an Adams' Administration land tax imposed to fund a larger army during the French war scare. His first trial before Justice Iredell ended in a conviction, which was overturned, and his retrial was heard in Chase's courtroom. During the trial chase was curt toward Fries' counsel and pushed the jury hard to convict him.[53]

James Callendar was a "journalist" who savaged John Adams and was charged under the Alien and Sedition Acts. Callendar was found guilty after Chase slanted his jury instructions against him. Both the Fries and Callendar trials were exhibits in Chase's Senate impeachment trial as evidence of his partisanship and lack of judicial temperament.[54]

A third set of charges accused Chase of politicizing his comments to grand juries, including criticism of Jefferson's repeal of the 1801 Judiciary Act. While Chase's comments were considered impolitic, criticism of other branches is not generally considered an impeachable offense.

The Senate trial lasted three weeks, Chase and his counsel arguing the charges were political in nature, the vote on removing Chase was based on whether senators believed in the wisdom of impeachment as a tool to tame judges. The majority of senators chose to acquit Chase, with only one charge receiving a majority, far short of the two thirds necessary.[55]

Chase's acquittal removed impeachment as a political tool to curb judicial independence but it effectively silenced Federalist justices as Chase served out the remainder of his tenure quietly. But in mounting a defense for his job, Justice Chase established the tradition of judicial independence critical to the separation of powers.

## Oliver Ellsworth

Rutledge's successor as chief justice proved to be more of a political judge and better known for his resignation than his career as chief justice. Oliver Ellsworth rose from a Calvinist family in Connecticut to a series of ever more important positions. A lawyer, state judge and member of the Continental Congress, Ellsworth also served in the constitutional convention. He was among the delegates negotiating a bicameral legislature and was part of the important Committee of Detail polishing the document into its final form. Ellsworth pushed for ratification in his state then was appointed by the Connecticut state legislature to serve in the U.S. Senate.[56] In Philadelphia he was the closest thing to a majority leader in the Senate, as he shepherded important bills through the chamber, including the 1789 Judiciary Act, written with aid of his convention colleague, Senator William Paterson.[57] Rutledge's defeat in the Senate made Washington more circumspect in his appointments. The president asked Patrick Henry but the Revolutionary firebrand had become more conservative in his old age and preferred making money to service on a weak court. Ellsworth was his second choice and was easily confirmed under senatorial courtesy.

Ellsworth was immediately thrust in the middle of the Jay Treaty debate. Opponents of the treaty demanded the Washington Administration provide detailed information on treaty negotiations before the House of Representatives would appropriate money to enforce it. Ellsworth rushed to Washington's defense with unseemly haste, producing an opinion upholding Washington's claim of executive privilege, denying documents be sent to Congress. Ellsworth's opinion was considered advisory rather than authoritative and heightened suspicions he was a Federalist partisan.[58]

Ellsworth's involvement in the Jay Treaty debate was only one of his many forays into political. The chief savaged those who wanted war with Britain and warned of excessive French influence over American government.[59] At the request of the Adams Administration he declared the Alien and Sedition Acts constitutional. Ellsworth served Adams as chief negotiator in ending the French-American naval war.[60] During the negotiations, Ellsworth pled ill health when missing Court sessions and in five years as Chief Justice presided at only the 1799 Court term. Ellsworth used the same excuse for resigning in late 1800 likely recognizing the difficult road that lay ahead as the new Jefferson Administration took aim at the Federalist judiciary.[61] Ellsworth's departure presented an opportunity for Adams, who eventually settled on his Secretary of State, John Marshall, as the next chief justice. Starting with Marshall, the Supreme Court would become an institution men strived to join rather than begged to escape.

Next to Justice Rutledge, Ellsworth might have been Washington's most disappointing appointee. The chief justice was more a politician than judge, an ineffective and absent leader who allowed the institution to flounder.

## Washington's Court Legacy

George Washington's political legacy to the American republic is frequently forgotten in a modern age of telegenic politicians and glib media personalities. His calm rectitude, lack of overweening zest for power and unshakable judgment set a standard few of his successors could meet. In choosing a Supreme Court, he lacked the resources available to future presidents including a federal judiciary with experienced judges prepared for promotion to the high court. Washington had the advantage of close contact with the leading political minds of the age as they wrestled with political doctrines during the writing of the constitution and its ratification in the states. From these he found men supportive of the new constitution and federal power and placed them in a position to influence the republic.

Of his ten selections, James Iredell, James Wilson and Samuel Chase had the broadest impact on the judiciary. Both Iredell and Wilson framed many of the constitutional arguments that would divide the court and the country in the future. Iredell and Chase offered differing approaches to judging, a textualist method opposed to a natural rights method. John Jay, John Blair, William Paterson and William Cushing were stable judges whose contribution was limited to their circuit duties or to aiding the Republic in the political arena. Only John Rutledge could be considered a failure, his mental illness condemning him to a quiet life in South Carolina rather than one on the Court.

## The Roosevelt Court

Franklin Roosevelt used unprecedented presidential power to fight the Great Depression, creating a host of new agencies and programs in order to battle against the twin evils of unemployment and deflation. A federal minimum wage, labor laws, price and supply controls were implemented as national economic planning became the buzzword in Washington. While the president dominated a Democrat Congress, he struggled to convince the judiciary of the constitutionality of his revolution. By 1934 New Deal policies were being challenged in court setting the stage for a clash between branches that would develop into a constitutional crisis.

## Hugo Black

After his reelection Roosevelt challenged a Supreme Court that had struck down major portions of his New Deal including labor laws and the National Recovery Act. Proposing to swell the size of the Court to fifteen, Roosevelt stared down the justices, who eventually surrendered in the West Coast Hotel and Laughlin cases, accepting the bases of New Deal policy. Justice Van Devanter's resignation in spring 1937 created a vacancy quickly filled by Alabama Senator Hugo Black. After his confirmation Black faced questions about his temperament based on past membership in the Ku Klux Klan, forcing him to defend his record in a national radio broadcast. [62]

Black entered the Court angry at the federal judiciary's resistance to the New Deal. Contemptuous of complicated arguments and legal standards, the self taught Black favored a simpler, absolutist approach to constitutional rights including speech, press and the exercise of religion. For much of his career Black argued alone, gaining some support from Justice Douglas but occupying the Court's left fringe.

Black also crusaded for total incorporation of the entire Bill of Rights. His views attracted few votes though as he pushed for total incorporation his colleagues settled on a process of selective incorporation on a case by case basis.

During the 1940s, Black dissented in incorporation cases. *In Adamson v. California* and *Betts v. Brady*, he critiqued Justice Frankfurter's order liberty approach to incorporation, preferring an immediate application of all rights.[63] Chief Justice Earl Warren's appointment sped the pace of incorporation and after Frankfurter's retirement the Court applied much of the Bill of Rights to the states during the 1960s. Black joined in the process in *Gideon v. Wainwright* overturning *Betts v. Brady*, which had limited access to counsel for indigent defendants. After Gideon, indigent defendants would be guaranteed some form of counsel before being put on trial.[64]

Black had more success in speech cases, striking limits on proselytizing in the Jehovah's Witnesses cases. *In Martin v. Struthers* Black struck local regulations of book sellers and those distributing religious pamphlets. Martin was one in a series of cases that reinterpreted speech rights to limit government in restricting speech rights.[65] He joined the second Opelika case and Murdock, overturning a year old precedent and granting greater speech rights to minority groups.

But in 1944 Black composed a decision he would regret through his career. In *Korematsu v. United States*, he Black upheld the forced imprisonment of Japanese Americans under a military plan to prevent military sabotage and spying during the Pacific war. Ignoring the clear racial implications of the order, Black found that the national security threat overrode the constitutional concerns of race based government policies.[66] Korematsu would draw dissent from the left wing, Justice Murphy, and the right wing, Roberts and Stone, of the Roosevelt Court and was subsequently recognized as ignoring basic civil liberties under the guise of national security.

By the time of the Vinson Court, Black was established as the leader of the Court's civil libertarian wing. In 1949 he single handedly brought separation of church and state to the forefront of the Court's agenda by applying the First Amendment's Establishment Clause to the states *in Everson v. Board of Education.*[67]

In Everson Black used Thomas Jefferson's letter to the Danbury Baptist Association calling for a separation of church and state, to argue for limiting church and state cooperation. Black used a secular purpose test to uphold a New Jersey policy of funding transportation for parochial students. He ruled the state had a secular purpose of providing safe travel to students which was unconnected to religion and resembled police and fire protection of a church.[68]

The Everson opinion attracted four dissenters but little public controversy as Black had upheld church state cooperation. His opinion *in Engel v. Vitale* continued to stir controversy four decades after it was decided. In Engel Black overturned a nondenominational prayer used to start each school day in New York. Black ruled the prayer to be an establishment of religion and warned of the dangers of government imposed religious worship and the alleged poisonous effect on any religion favored by government.[69]

Black's striving for a separation of church and state has been attributed to his Alabama background, including a personal dislike of the Catholic Church.

During his speech on the Klan controversy, Black implied a Catholic conspiracy was to blame for his problems, warning the church would suffer for opposing his nomination.[70] The separation of church and state stirred emotions long after Black died and his doctrine has been chipped at by successor courts.

Black's efforts to create new constitutional doctrines were occasionally interrupted by efforts to eliminate old doctrines. In *Ferguson v. Skrupa* Black overturned Kansas Court of Appeals decision striking a ban on non lawyers engaging in debt adjustment. Black found the law was rationally related to a legitimate end and in a brief opinion stamped out one of the last vestiges of economic due process he had battled since his time in the Senate.[71] Skrupa represented the old New Dealer's final victory over the hated liberty to contract that had been used against New Deal policies.

Black's greatest achievement came in overturning the southern tradition of segregation. Notwithstanding his Alabama roots, the justice despised the second class citizenship imposed on blacks under the south's apartheid system.

In Korematsu Black recognized race as a discrete and insular category requiring strict scrutiny by the courts. During the Stone and Vinson Court, the justices struck white primaries and segregated law and graduate schools. As the debate over race turned toward public schools, Black expressed frustration at the slow pace of integration and pushed for immediate desegregation of schools.

Justice Black joined *Brown v. Board of Education* breaking the constitutional logjam on segregation though Black's frustration grew as southern judges followed Felix Frankfurter's doctrine of integrating at "all deliberate speed." By 1969 integration had lagged and Black took it upon himself to call for immediate integration in *Alexander v. Holmes County School Board.*[72] During the conference discussion of Alexander, Black announced he would dissent from any opinion allowing further delay. Though angered at the justice's ultimatum, Black's threat served the purpose of ending "all deliberate speed" even as integration efforts were sped by the threat of withdrawal of federal funds if dual school districts continued.[73]

Alexander represented Black's final victory over his old adversary, Felix Frankfurter, who left the Court in 1962. The two justices battled for two decades as Black's absolutist philosophy was challenged by Frankfurter's nuanced approach. The conflict was sparked in *Bridges v. California* where a state judge had held a newspaper in contempt for criticizing judicial decisions. Justice Frankfurter was initially assigned the opinion upholding the judge's injunction with Black dissenting, but Chief Justice Hughes and Justice McReynolds retirements followed by a vote switch by Justice Murphy placed Black in the majority. His opinion striking the injunction was an early victory for his First Amendment philosophy. His majority lost, Frankfurter bristled at having his leadership challenged by the Alabama lawyer.[74]

The battle between Black's simple arguments and Frankfurter's professorial disquisitions soon descended into personal disputes. When Justice Owen Roberts retired, Black objected to Chief Justice Stone's letter of regret that included lofty assessments of Roberts' career and expressing regret for his retirement.

Later Justice Jackson and Black tangled over Black's participation in a case argued by his former law partner. The dispute went public after Harlan Stone's death as both justices angled for the center chair. The two men battled in the media, Black relying on friendly columnists as surrogates to attack Jackson and Jackson sending letters to Congress and the president in a more direct effort. Truman responded by appointing Fred Vinson as chief, a decision favored by neither Jackson nor Black. The two justices would patch up their differences on a superficial level though only Jackson's death in 1954 prevented any further eruptions.

The split between Black and Frankfurter ended with Frankfurter's retirement in 1962 but Black soon split with his old ally, William Douglas, whose three divorces, Black believed, had injured the Court's reputation. Black clashed with Chief Justice Warren, declaring in a television interview the Court should have been named the Black Court rather than the Warren Court. Warren responded good-naturedly, remarking that Black could not "un-ring a bell." [75]

As the justice aged he retreated from past positions. The proponent of immediate school desegregation suddenly resisted his colleagues' integrationist impulses. He dissented in *Harper v. Virginia*, which used the Twenty Fourth Amendment to strike down the poll tax for state elections.[76] He dissented in the Douglas privacy opinion striking down a Connecticut law banning birth control[77] and upheld convictions of civil rights demonstrators, declaring their protests were not speech but action and not covered under his absolutist approach to free speech.[78] Black later accepted limits on speech.[79] When questioned about Black's growing conservatism Chief Justice Warren remarked the justice's change of heart was based on a desire to be buried in Alabama, tailoring his views to reflect the conservatism of his home state.[80]

Black's changing philosophy was noticeable in his final term. He rejected the claim that illegitimacy was a protected class under the Equal Protection Clause,[81] wrote a concurring opinion upholding constitutionality of the death penalty[82] and applied the brakes to mandated integration of public facilities including swimming pools.[83]

Yet Black held firm to a belief in absolute press rights.[84] When the Nixon Administration prevented the New York Times and the Washington Post from publishing classified information about the Vietnam War, Black authored the opinion banning all prior restraint against the press, arguing that the public's right to know exceeded the government's interest in protecting national security.[85] The New York Times case would be Black's last as he would die before the start of the 1971 term. Even after his death Black attracted controversy, the Court deluged with letters to the justice after the 1973 *Roe v. Wade* decision, complaining Black supported the opinion.[86]

## Stanley Reed

Lone dissents by justices provoke widely disparate reactions. For those who agree with the dissent, the justice is a modern day Jeremiah, crying out to an uninterested world while those disapproving dismiss the dissent as the rambling of a justice out of touch with society. Justice John Marshall Harlan's dissent in *Plessy v. Ferguson* is usually placed in the former category while Franklin Roosevelt's second appointee, Stanley Reed, barely escaped infamy after pulling his dissent in Brown v. Board of Education.

In 1938 an ailing George Sutherland retired from the Court removing the most intellectual and influential of the remaining judicial conservatives. That term would be the last that a conservative heavyweight would occupy a seat until the arrival of Justice Scalia in 1986. Roosevelt selected Reed from the Justice Department the first of three to serve from that position and the least memorable.

Reed had struggled as solicitor general fighting for the New Deal before a hostile and suspicious Supreme Court. His victories, such as the Gold Clause cases, were few while defeats accrued. A major defeat came *in Humphrey's Executor v. U.S.* as the Court curbed presidential removal powers [87] The justices also struck down critical portions of the National Industrial Recovery Act (NIRA), handing Reed and Roosevelt two more defeats. The losses for Reed continued into 1936 as the justices struck the Guffey Coal Act and the first Agricultural Adjustment Act. A lone victory came when he convinced the justices to uphold the Tennessee Valley Authority.[88]

Few lawyers with Reed's record could retain the confidence of their client but he was saved when Roosevelt turned his ire on the justices. His 1936 landslide reelection emboldened the president to propose a Court "reform" plan adding six justices to "aid" the enfeebled justices with their duties. The plan may have provoked the "switch in time that saved nine" as Charles Evans Hughes and Owen Roberts provided the key votes upholding federal labor and state minimum wage laws spring 1937. The victor in both cases, Reed became the toast of the Washington legal community.[89]

Joining the Court in 1938, Reed assumed the role of conservative New Dealer favoring economic legislation while suspicious of civil rights and liberties claims. A southerner, Reed became the Court spokesmen in racial cases, forced to administer the bitter medicine of integration to his home region.

An early opportunity came in *Smith v. Allwright*, overturning the white primary. [90] The Texas Democrat Party banned black voters in its primary and claimed its actions were private rather than state action. The Court unanimously struck the primary, ruling that in one party southern states the primary served as the general election and thus represented state action. Justice Frankfurter was assigned the opinion but Justice Jackson wrote Chief Justice Stone warning that southern Democrats would rebel against an opinion written by an Austrian Jew. Jackson suggested southerners would be more accepting of Smith if it was authored by Reed, a fellow southerner. Stone agreed, Frankfurter did not protest and Reed was assigned the opinion, though his roots did not make the decision more palatable to southerners.[91]

Reed also earned the assignment in two contentious criminal justice and incorporation cases, though the concurring and dissenting justices overshadowed his opinion. The failed execution of Willie Francis prompted a second attempt and an appeal against the execution on Eighth Amendment grounds. In *Louisiana v. Resweber* Reed upheld the second execution as constitutional though his opinion convinced only a single justice. Instead Justice Frankfurter and Burton sniped at each over the scope and meaning of the eighth amendment including its application to state governments.[92]

Four years later Reed was again in the eye of the storm as Justices Black and Frankfurter took aim at each other in *Adamson v. California.* Reed rejected Adamson's argument the Fifth Amendment's self incrimination clause applied to the states. Reed's opinion, though, was forgotten in the *sturm und drang* over the incorporation of rights as Black, Douglas, Murphy and Rutledge calling for immediate incorporation while Frankfurter and Jackson favored a case by case method.[93]

Amidst the turmoil, Reed delivered another bitter pill to southerners in *Morgan v. Virginia.* Reed struck a Virginia law segregating interstate bus travel, finding the state had improperly regulated interstate commerce, avoiding the contentious issue of segregation and the equal protection clause. Reed managed a unanimous opinion as Justices Black and Frankfurter agreed.[94]

As the communist threat became a political issue, Reed supported the government in its investigations and prosecutions of Communist Party leaders.[95] But his support of the anticommunist movement placed him in a difficult position in 1950. Reed was called as a character witness for Alger Hiss's during his perjury trial, placing Reed in the uncomfortable position of testifying for a man later proved to be a communist spy. His decision to testify on behalf of a spy cast a pall over Reed's judgment, particularly his admission he had recommended Hiss for a high level State Department position.[96]

Reed's legacy, though, was threatened as the justices considered separate but equal facilities in public schools. During the first Brown v. Board of Education argument Reed favored upholding the doctrine created in *Plessy v. Ferguson*, producing a deadlock on the cases and reargument. The arrival of Chief Justice Warren saw eight justices line up behind the new chief in favor of striking segregated schools.[97]

Reed was the lone holdout, working on his dissent in the fall and winter of 1953. Warren sought unanimity and pressured Reed by isolating him while gathering his colleagues' votes. The chief then applied the soft touch to Reed, using lunches with Justice Harold Burton to prod the Kentuckian toward joining the unanimous decision. Warren focused on the integrity of the institution and how a solo dissent could undermine the legitimacy of the Court's decision. Reed wavered from his polished dissent and prodded by his colleagues and clerks eventually joined Brown.[98]

After Brown, Reed receded into the background, regularly voting with Justice Frankfurter, seemingly waiting for a Democrat president to appoint his successor even as the justice's health declined. Eisenhower's reelection foreclosed the possibility and in early 1957 Reed retired. His judicial career did not end as Reed continued serving as a federal judge, hearing cases in districts where case backlogs delayed trials. Reed died in 1980 at age ninety six the last of the Roosevelt justices.

## Felix Frankfurter

The Roosevelt Court moved constitutional law in a leftward direction, favoring individual rights over government and labor and workers over business. Yet among the Roosevelt justices, Felix Frankfurter moved to the right, favoring restraint over activism and challenging his fellow Roosevelt appointees. A native of Vienna, Frankfurter was a lawyer and law professor who had earned his liberal spurs fighting to free the murderers Sacco and Vanzetti. During the 1930s he advised Roosevelt and befriended Justice Benjamin Cardozo, replacing him in 1938.[99]

Frankfurter disappointed those who expected him to transform the Court into a liberal bastion. Instead the justice preaching judicial restraint, a mantra he adopted in the 1920s as a student of Holmes and Brandeis. Frankfurter's shift right combined with lecturing tone he adopted, treating his colleagues like students in a Harvard law seminars, infuriated the other Roosevelt justices. Frankfurter's twenty three year career was marked with personal disputes including accusations of perfidious and unprofessional behavior. Frankfurter and Justice Hugo Black jockeyed for influence and after Chief Justice Hughes's 1941 retirement open warfare broke out among the justices.[100]

Frankfurter scored early victories in his call for judicial restraint including *Minersville School District v. Gobitis*. Frankfurter upheld a Pennsylvania law requiring students to salute the flag, rejecting Black's free speech arguments. Frankfurter composed a patriotic ode to the country as war approached, though Gobitis would not be overturned three years later in *West Virginia v. Barnette*, the opinion provoking a Frankfurter dissent. The dissent irritated his colleagues as Frankfurter reminded readers he was a member of "the most vilified and persecuted minority in history" a claim of exceptionalism rarely made by a justice.[101]

Frankfurter's defeat in Barnette triggered a rearguard fight as he fought against the wholesale incorporation of rights to apply to state governments. Since the Civil War and passage of the Fourteenth Amendment, the justices had debated whether state governments had to abide by the same rules as the federal government. For two decades the justices had inched toward applying some rights to state governments culminating with a Cardozo opinion setting the standard of rights that protected ordered liberty, an approach Frankfurter adopted.

Justice Black sought immediate incorporation of all rights, setting the stage as the old law professor bested the old senator through much of the 1940s and 1950s. *In Wolf v. Colorado* Frankfurter joined a majority of justices applying the Fourth Amendment's prohibition against search and seizure to the states but refusing to apply the enforcement mechanism known as the exclusionary rule to the states. [102] Black dissented, favoring incorporation. In *Adamson v. California*, Frankfurter concurred in the ruling that the right to self incrimination did not apply to state trials.[103] Black dissented, arguing again for total incorporation. In 1952, the *Rochin v. California* case had Frankfurter add his own twist to the incorporation debate, finding any state action that "shocks the conscience of the community" would be forbidden under the constitution. [104] The vague standard provided little guidance and was one in a series of tests created and discarded during the incorporation debate.[105]

While Frankfurter and Black shared nearly identical New Deal economic and political ideologies, their battles over incorporation focused on constitutional procedure and Court influence. Frankfurter was distressed by Black's challenge to his intellectual leadership of the Court much more than the justice's activist philosophy which he shared with justices William Douglas, Frank Murphy and Wiley Rutledge. Frankfurter warned his colleagues their activism resembled that of the 1930s Court which had struck down New Deal laws, remaining true to his restraintist beliefs from his law school years. But he was swimming against a legal tide that emphasized civil rights and liberties even at the expense of a restrained judiciary.

Black and his allies favored absolute adherence to the First Amendment speech clause and in the 1942 term they overruled recent speech cases producing a Frankfurter dissent in the twin cases *of Jones v. Opelika* and *Murdock v. Pennsylvania.*[106] He criticized the majority for striking down permit laws requiring those selling or distributing material to pay a license fee. As the forties progressed Frankfurter led the dissenters in *Saia v. New York*, which struck down a sound truck ordinance and concurred in *Kovacs v. Cooper* upholding a similar ordinance.

Among his more controversial opinions was *Beauharnais v. Illinois* where Frankfurter upheld a criminal libel law that punished any speech that held any group of people in contempt or derision.[107] Frankfurter dismissed claims the law violated free speech provoking dissents from two reliable allies Justices Reed and Jackson. In addition to criminal libel, Frankfurter joined decisions upholding prosecutions of communist party members and approved of contempt citations for those refusing to testify before congressional committees.[108] In each he took the familiar line that it was best for judges to defer to elected officials in their decision making.

The tug of war between Black and Frankfurter and his allies changed during the 1950s as each side tried to attract the votes of the Eisenhower justices. Black gained allies in Chief Justice Earl Warren and Justice William Brennan. Frankfurter struggled to attract the votes of John Harlan, Charles Whittaker and Potter Stewart. Whittaker was a special case, a man overwhelmed by his job, dependent upon prescription drugs and nearly driven to the asylum by Frankfurter's lobbying. By the late 1950s, Frankfurter found himself on the losing side, dissenting as his Wolf decision was overturned in *Mapp v. Ohio* and the Exclusionary Rule applied to the states.[109]

The most contentious issue during Frankfurter's final years was the desire by some justices to engage the Court in legislative redistricting. In *Colgrove v. Green* Frankfurter warned the Court to avoid the political thicket of redistricting, leaving such decisions to the political branches.[110] In 1960, though, the justice retreated, writing for a unanimous Court striking down a blatantly racial gerrymandering scheme.[111] In 1962 *Baker v. Carr* raised the question whether judges could order the Tennessee legislature to redraw state legislative boundaries in order to equalize the vote. Frankfurter immediately began working the wavering justices, including Tom Clark, Potter Stewart and Charles Whittaker. His aggressive tactics saw him lose Clark and Stewart's vote in Baker and Whittaker's vote forever as the justice suffered a nervous breakdown. The Herculanean effort destroyed Frankfurter's health as he suffered a stroke in the middle of the debate and never returned to the Court.[112]

## Lies, Damned Lies and William O. Douglas

Few autobiographies of Washington politicians are known for their dedication to truth or objectivity, but Justice William O. Douglas' political autobiography would put others to shame. Douglas lost his father at an early age and lived under a domineering mother. According to Douglas his youth was consumed by twin battles against polio and poverty, both claims intended to portray him as a man of the people even though they were false.[113]

Douglas was part of the New Deal cadre entering Washington on Franklin Roosevelt's coattails. He was hired as an assistant to the chairman of the new Securities and Exchange Commission (SEC), Joseph Kennedy, another man fond of embellishing his successes. When Kennedy became ambassador to the United Kingdom, Douglas assumed the chairmanship and from there was nominated to the Supreme Court after Justice Brandeis' retirement.[114]

Only thirty nine at his appointment, Douglas saw the Court as a stepping stone to the presidency. He sought the 1940 Democrat vice presidential nomination with little effect but in 1944 was on Roosevelt's short list, along with Harry Truman, for the vice presidency. In 1948 Truman offered Douglas the vice presidential nomination but the justice refused, preferring the top spot on the ticket and convinced Truman had little chance of winning.[115]

If Douglas' ambitions pointed him to the presidency, his personal life was more chaotic. The justice struggled to compartmentalize his personal, professional and public lives, nurturing the image of a man of the people who used his lofty perch for the benefit of the common man while acquiring the reputation as an inconsiderate boss prone to tantrums. Court personnel, his staff and clerks learned to keep their distance and ignored the frequent "firings" of those who dared cross him.[116]

Cursed with a roving eye, Douglas seized advantage of his prominence to attract women, his four marriages embarrassing the Court and pushing the Justice to the edge of financial catastrophe. Estranged from his family—his children did not inform of his first wife's death-he used and abused women throughout his life. His excessive womanizing and drinking is recalled in his former stomping grounds of Goose Prairie and Yakima, Washington where the mention of his name causes locals to curl their lips in disgust.[117]

Outside the Court Douglas was a man on the go, his world travels documented by his travel books which were also a source of desperately needed income.[118] The books lacked the gravitas of the monographs published by his predecessors and were quickly forgotten. As his troubles mounted, Douglas disengaged from his job as personal issues distracted him and disputes with his colleagues ended friendships. His extended vacations to Goose Prairie, Washington, where he lacked a phone, burnished his image as a part time justice whose brilliance allowed him to work much less than his colleagues.[119]

The personal controversies caught up with Douglas in the 1970s as members of Congress led by Congressman Gerald Ford mounted an impeachment effort with the aid of the Nixon White House. Evidence of impeachable crimes was thin and when referred to the Democrat dominated House Judiciary Committee, the effort petered out.[120]

The controversies would come later with Douglas' best opinions produced during the first two decades of his tenure. Douglas joined some of the conservative civil liberties opinions of the Hughes era including Gobitis and Chaplinsky but earned his liberal credentials during the Stone Court. *In Murdock v. Pennsylvania*, he overturned a local ordinance limiting distribution of religious literature.[121] In *Skinner v. Oklahoma* he struck a habitual criminal sterilization law, providing some of the initial grounding for the procreation right created in the Griswold decision.[122] Douglas explained his move to left as driven by *O'Malley v. Woodrough*, where the Court ruled federal judges were covered under the federal income tax. According to Douglas Woodrough made him a taxpaying citizen and entitled him to speak his mind.[123]

His most consequential ruling ended strict judicial oversight of administrative decisions. At the end of the nineteenth century the Court asserted review authority over decisions made by state and federal regulatory commissions. *In Smyth v. Ames* the first Justice Harlan ruled judges could use due process guarantees to ensure regulations provided a proper return on investment for railroads. Smyth became the means for conservative judges to protect corporate rights and profits. In *FPC v. Hope Natural Gas Co.* Douglas overturned Smyth, ruling judges were not qualified to determine fairness in regulation. Hope would later be modified by the Administrative Procedures Act, setting limits on regulatory schemes.[124]

Hope was one in a series of cases unraveling precedents favoring economic rights. Douglas performed the same feat in *Williamson v. Lee Optical*, upholding an Oklahoma law limiting glasses repair to optometrists and ophthalmologists.[125]

But Douglas was not without his conservative moments. In *Screws v. United States* Douglas weakened Section 1983 of federal law that allowed prosecution of state officials for violating civil rights laws.[126] In *Zorach v. Clauson* Douglas performed a U Turn on the Establishment clause upholding a voluntary program for students to attend religious classes during the school day.[127] Douglas then penned a phrase that would haunt his career, declaring that "We are a religious people whose institutions presuppose a Supreme Being," and that government "accommodates the public service to their spiritual needs," while the constitution did not force government to "show a callous indifference to religious groups."[128] The opinion clashed with the two year old McCollum opinion while Douglas changed his mind in the Walz case when he decried the Court upholding property tax exemption for churches.[129]

By the late 1950s Douglas was a predictable liberal vote. In 1958 he recognized a right to travel in *Kent v. Dulles*.[130] Kent was denied a passport because of his communist political beliefs and challenged the decision as a violation of his liberty right to travel. Douglas agreed, stating the right to travel was a liberty the government could not restrict for political or personal belief.[131]

In *Monroe v. Pape*, Douglas revived the 1871 Civil Rights Act, better known as the Ku Klux Act. Douglas ruled the act could be used against the state but not the city of Chicago, which was the target of the lawsuit. Though Pape lost his suit against Chicago, the decision paved the path for future lawsuits.[132]

But *Griswold v. Connecticut* drew scorn from his critics as he struck a state law banning the sale or distribution of contraceptives.[133] The justice wrote for five of his colleagues, though most felt compelled to distance themselves from his confused dissertation on penumbras and emanations. According to Douglas, the right to procreate was part of a right to privacy which emanating from the First, Fourth, Fifth and Eighth Amendments.[134] Lacking clear constitutional grounds, Douglas' right to privacy floated in an ethereal constitutional limbo where it was rescued with the Roe v. Wade decision.

When Roe was decided in 1973, Douglas was no longer part of a dominant liberal majority but rather a curiosity from an era dimming in the popular memory, a justice with quaint views who received less applause each year. The author of Griswold was relegated to a concurring opinion that enshrined loafing as a constitutional right.[135] His concurrence was one in a series of decisions exhibiting increasingly odd behavior. Appearing more disinterested in his work, Douglas became a parody, seemingly obsessed with dissents and irritating his colleagues with peculiar arguments.[136]

Douglas' final years were spent fighting off the despised Nixon administration and the Nixon justices. One success came in *Nixon v. United States* as the Court forced the president to turn over tapes of White House conversations and ended Nixon's presidency. But Douglas had little time to celebrate. Struck down by a stroke at the start of 1975, he hung onto his seat even as it was obvious he was unable to serve as a full time justice.

With Douglas mentally incapacitated, his colleagues secretly took away his vote, refusing to allow him to cast the decisive vote in a five to four decision. The 1974 term was hampered by the rescheduling of several arguments where Douglas' vote might affect the outcome. It was not until November 1975 that he finally left, a sigh of relief echoing among the brethren.[137] A mediocre member of the Court, at best, Douglas' presence likely hastened the Court's leftward movement, expressing his views in separate opinions and in conference and forcing the Court to confront issues they preferred to ignore.

## Frank Murphy

Defeated politicians have always had a place in presidential administrations. Loyalty to a president's cause is usually returned with a position, sometimes high, sometimes obscure. Frank Murphy was such a politician. Elected Detroit mayor in 1930, Murphy exhibited a gift for self promotion and dreamy thinking. As mayor he initiated a citywide relief program to fight the depression. The result was near bankruptcy for the city but easy reelection for Murphy in 1932. The beleaguered city was saved by the New Deal and the federal government taking responsibility for relief. By this time Murphy had left Detroit for a position as high commissioner of the Philippines.[138]

Many politicians would have gauged the appointment as a demotion but Murphy seized the opportunity to implement an East Asian form of the New Deal. Murphy initiated public works, health projects and relief programs for the Filipinos, making him popular among the ordinary people but unpopular among the elite.[139]

Murphy also clashed with another outsized personality on the islands, General Douglas MacArthur, who sought the position of high commissioner and launched a campaign to have him recalled. Murphy outmaneuvered MacArthur, convincing Roosevelt to keep him in place.[140]

Murphy's time in the Far East was cut short by domestic political concerns, including Roosevelt's need for a strong gubernatorial candidate in Michigan. Republicans seized control of the state legislature in 1934, sending shockwaves through the White House which feared losing the industrial Midwest. Murphy's return as a gubernatorial candidate may or may not have aided Roosevelt, who did not need Michigan's electoral votes to win in 1936, but Murphy was elected, winning a two year term, putting his political ineptitude on public display. In 1937 Michigan workers seized factories in a series of sit in strikes intended to force owners into collective bargaining. Murphy refused to use force against the strikers, appearing to favor the occupation of private property. His reputation tarnished as the state descended toward anarchy, Murphy joined the ranks of the unemployed after the 1938 election.[141]

Murphy's election defeat was rewarded by a promotion to be United States Attorney General. Murphy served little more than a year and was known for his politicized prosecution that drew scorn from his successor, Robert Jackson.

When Justice Butler succumbed in late 1939, Murphy was promoted to the Court. Murphy soon realized he was out of place in the Court's monastic setting.[142]

Murphy wobbled in his early years, influenced by the intimidating Chief Justice Hughes, exhibiting little of the liberal ideas he would express in the latter years of his career. Murphy joined the Gobitis decision upholding prosecution of Jehovah's Witnesses for refusal to salute the flag. In *Thornhill v. Alabama,* Murphy struck an Alabama ban on labor picketing but left open the possibility of bans on picketing if they prevented violence, a reversal of his 1937 position on strikes.[143]

Murphy introduced "fighting words" into the American lexicon. *In Chaplinsky v. New Hampshire*, Murphy agreed certain words provoked violence and their users could be prosecuted. Chaplinsky would be the sole instance of such words but represented another deviation from Murphy's strong support of speech rights. [144]

By 1943 the Roosevelt Court was in place and Murphy joined the four member liberal bloc in overturning Opelika and Barnette. Murphy switched his vote in Barnette and voted to overrule Gobitis.[145] Murphy dissented in Korematsu, questioning the wisdom of Japanese internment while decrying the "legalization of racism" and describing internment as "utterly revolting," strong words used to reject his political patron.[146]

Murphy was also at the fringes of the incorporation debate. He joined Justice Black's dissent in *Betts v. Brady* arguing for state financed counsels in serious felony cases.[147] In Adamson Murphy joined Justice Rutledge's opinion seeking incorporation of rights beyond those found in the constitution.

The sole Catholic on the Court Murphy was criticized by the church for his vote in *McCullom v. Board of Education* striking down a "release time" policy where students participated in religious classes in public schools.[148] Murphy was accused of rejecting his religious conviction and supporting a strict separation of church and state.[149]

Murphy's health declined during the 1940s, his playboy lifestyle dangerous for a man in his fifties. Admitted to a Detroit hospital in summer 1949, Murphy suffered a heart attack, pulling down the curtain on the Roosevelt Court.

## James Byrnes

Government czars became a controversy during the twenty first century but one of the first czars was the wartime czar, James Byrnes who earlier served as a Supreme Court justice. A South Carolinian in the tradition of Pitchfork Benjamin Tillman, Byrnes was a congressman and elected to the Senate in 1930 after a bitter battle with the incumbent Coleman Livingston Blease. [150]

Byrnes' political star rose after Franklin Roosevelt's 1932 election victory. With the South dominated by racist demagogues, Byrnes was a friendly face and rational mind, becoming Roosevelt's right hand man in the Senate. Two Court retirements in 1941, that of Charles Evans Hughes and James McReynolds offered the president three appointments. The first two came with Harlan Stone being promoted to chief justice and Robert Jackson to fill Stone's seat. Finally Byrnes was nominated to replace McReynolds. The balance of the three choices, Jackson the liberal, Stone the moderate and Byrnes the conservative Democrat, ensured easy confirmation.[151]

Reaching the Court in summer 1941 as war approached, Byrnes preferred the hustle and bustle of politics to the Court's political isolation. Entreating the president to allow him back into his inner circle, Byrnes pushed to become a war administrator after the Pearl Harbor attack. In the fall of 1942 as the military effort stalled and the Democrats suffered a stinging midterm defeat, Roosevelt relented, appointing Byrnes to a top White House position.

Byrnes reorganized the war effort, appointing competent directors for the war effort including Jesse Jones who clashed with Vice President Henry Wallace. Byrnes earned Roosevelt and his successor's gratitude and served at Truman's secretary of state.[152]

Byrnes molded postwar foreign policy then returned to his native South Carolina as governor to challenge public school integration. His obstructionism in the face of Court mandated integration stained his legacy and with his retirement in 1955 it appeared his political influence had vanished. Byrnes remained a potent political force as he moved his state and region toward the Republican Party in defiance of tradition and his predecessors. Byrnes died in 1972 the White House flag flown at half staff, a rare honor for a politician much less one out of office for seventeen years. [153]

Byrnes single year as a justice marked him as a failure, a ranking not reflective of his abilities. As a junior justice Byrnes managed a single memorable opinion, *Edwards v. California* where he struck a California "anti Okie" law prohibiting indigents from entering the state. [154] California feared an influx of poor into the state but Byrnes dismissed those concerns, finding that interstate travel was considered interstate commerce under congressional authority. Edwards prompted concurrences by Justices Douglas and Jackson, both of whom wanted travel recognized as a privilege and immunity of national citizenship. The same argument would be used in the 1960s and 1970s as the Court struck down residency requirements under state welfare laws.[155]

## "Solicitor General for Life" Robert Jackson

Robert Jackson's appointment represented the end of an era of self taught justices as Jackson would be the last justice without a law degree. A Democrat in Republican upper New York, Jackson joined the Roosevelt Justice Department tax division in 1934 and prosecuted former Treasury Secretary Andrew Mellon for tax fraud.[156]

Jackson was slavishly devoted to Roosevelt, admitting in congressional testimony the Court packing that the plan was an effort to dilute conservative votes.[157] As justices departed and were replaced by members of the Justice Department, Jackson advanced swiftly, replacing Stanley Reed and earning the title of "Solicitor General for Life" from Louis Brandeis.[158] When Attorney General Frank Murphy was promoted Jackson succeeded him, though not without controversy.

Upon becoming attorney general, Jackson halted prosecution of Spanish Loyalist recruiters, claiming they were political, delivering a slap at his old boss, which Murphy would not forget.[159] In 1941 Jackson was promoted to the Supreme Court, Roosevelt offering him the position of associate justice while implicitly promising to promote Jackson to chief justice after Harlan Stone's retirement.

During the war years, Jackson was the quintessential New Deal justice, favoring federal power in economic rights cases and the individual in civil liberties cases. In *West Virginia v. Barnette*, Jackson composed an ode to religious freedom, striking down the state requirement that all children salute the American flag. Jackson's reputation as a wordsmith was built on his Barnette opinion, his "constitutional constellation" phrase quoted by civil libertarians long after his death. [160]

Jackson also hammered the final nail in the coffin of the old Commerce Clause definitions in *Wickard v. Filburn.* Filburn was fined under the second Agricultural Adjustment Act for growing two acres of wheat beyond his assigned allotment. In his appeal, he argued the two acres of wheat was for personal consumption and could not affect interstate commerce. Jackson dug up Chief Justice Hughes' close and substantial effect doctrine for intrastate commerce and found the combined effect of thousands of farmers growing thousands of extra acres was intrastate commerce that would affect interstate commerce. Wickard significantly broadened congressional commerce power to include minor activity whose cumulative effect would be substantial.[161]

With Barnette and Wickard Jackson brought the commerce clause into the twentieth century. The remainder of his career though became bogged down in the personal disputes plaguing the Stone Court. A firm believer in judicial restraint, Jackson clashed with Justice Black's activist views and professional disagreements soon descended into personal disputes. The 1945 Jewell Ridge case began the feud with Black as Jackson composed a memo criticizing Black for participating in a case argued by Black's old law partner, irking the senior justice.[162]

Harlan Stone's death deepened the wound as Jackson expected to be promoted to the center chair but carefully leaked news stories from Justice Black torpedoed his candidacy. Jackson overreacted, sending letters of protest to the president and the Congress. Disgusted with the public fight, Truman selected Treasury Secretary Fred Vinson rather than Jackson as chief.[163] Angered by the experience, Jackson returned to the Court from Nuremberg in 1946 and dismissed claims of a split between him and Black.

Jackson had conducted his fight for the center chair from Germany where he served as chief U.S. prosecutor for the Nuremberg trials. His appointment by

Truman infuriated Chief Justice Stone and some justices who were coped with a larger workload.[164]

Jackson's Nuremberg duties did little to enhance his legacy. He became embroiled in disputes with the Soviet and French delegations then was embarrassed by Hermann Goering when the justice cross examined the former head of the Luftwaffe. Jackson lost his composure, unable to pin down Goering on Nazi crimes.[165] More central, the trials changed Jackson's perspective on civil liberties. Exposed to the Nazi regime, Jackson became obsessed with radicals and demagogues believing that if the Weimar government had acted sooner to suppress the Nazis, the movement would not have risen to power.

In 1950 the Court heard the appeal of Communist Party officials prosecuted for teaching communism. Jackson concurred in *Dennis v. United States*, the former prosecutor warned that allowing instruction communism and the overthrow of government was the first step toward revolution, requiring government action. Jackson's concurrence was a closing argument against a creeping totalitarianism and its threat to the American system. [166]

Dennis was on step in Jackson's transformation from civil libertarian to cold warrior. When Arthur Terminiello's speech attracted a violent crowd of demonstrators, Chicago police arrested him for inciting a riot.[167] Justice Douglas struck down the conviction as a restriction on free speech, provoking a vehement dissent from Jackson that ran for over twenty pages. He warned that allowing extremists to dominate public discourse was "convert(ing) the constitutional Bill of Rights into a suicide pact."[168]

Jackson dissented in *Saia v. New York* as the Court struck an ordinance limiting sound trucks. [169] He concurred *in Kovacs v. Cooper* when a majority upheld a similar sound ordinance. [170] Jackson was the lone dissenter *in Kunz v. New York*, arguing in favor of a New York City ordinance that prevent speech ridiculing or denouncing religion. [171] In *Feiner v. New York*, Jackson agreed that police could detain a speaker for creating a disturbance, thus weakening the Terminiello decision. [172] By 1951 the justice who had written Barnette had been transformed into a disciple of limited speech rights when that speech threatened national security or local order.

Jackson also doubted the liberal approach to integration. Though joining Court opinions integrating law schools and graduate schools, Jackson worried aloud about his colleagues' push to integrated secondary and elementary schools. Jackson was torn by the immorality of the system and the difficulties in enforcing integration. He doubted segregation was unconstitutional under the Fourteenth Amendment but was open to other arguments. In the first *Brown v. Board* arguments, Jackson expressing concerns with enforcement issues and sought reargument. The new chief justice Earl Warren assuaged some of Jackson's concerns. But as the Brown decision was reaching its climax Jackson suffered a serious heart attack. His physical condition ended his efforts to influence Warren's opinion and after a visit from the chief justice at the hospital, Jackson joined Brown without comment. Rising from his sick bed when Brown was read, his presence would be one of his last acts as justice, a second heart fatal heart attack occurring in September, 1954.[173]

Robert Jackson was the prototypical New Dealer, supporting the Roosevelt Administration during its battles with the Supreme Court. His later career would place him in opposition to the dominant liberal philosophy of the era, making him a controversial figure and one whose legacy is outshined by others. Yet his memorable opinions and witticisms are a reminder of his career which added to Roosevelt's Court legacy.[174]

## Chief Justice Stone

In 1941 Justice Harlan Stone became the second associate justice promoted to chief. Initially appointed by Republican Calvin Coolidge in 1925, Stone's unswerving support of the New Deal earned him Franklin Roosevelt's trust. With war approaching, Roosevelt made the political decision to choose Republicans for high level positions, choosing Henry Stimson as War Secretary and Frank Knox for Navy Secretary. Stone's promotion rounded out his bipartisanship but Roosevelt's choice would prove a disaster.

Stone's moment of triumph, his promotion to chief justice, became his time of troubles. The Roosevelt justices, intelligent and egotistical, had been contained by Chief Justice Hughes' strong hand. Hughes had used his presence and reputation to limit debate, intimidating his new colleagues and offering the image of a united Court. Stone loosened the constraints, seeking to convince rather than force his colleagues into agreement and producing long conferences that embittered the justices.

During the 1930s Stone had generally supported New Deal laws but had joined the Court in two cases striking down the National Industrial Recovery Act on non delegation grounds. In 1944 he repented for this apostasy in *Yakus v. United States*.[175] During World War II the Office of Price Administration (OPA) was given the task of preventing wartime inflation by setting fair prices. Congress' vague command to the executive was challenged by Yakus as an unconstitutional delegation of legislative power to the executive branch. Yakus' argument was based on the basic constitutional assumption that each branch's powers could not be given to another branch without violating the separation of powers doctrine.

Stone rejected Yakus' arguments, ruling Congress had given sufficient standards to the OPA by requiring it set "fair and equitable" prices.[176] Yakus removed the nondelegation doctrine as an impediment to executive law making, granting considerable authority to the branch to make and enforce laws.

Chief Justice Stone found that following Charles Evans Hughes as chief was a nearly impossible task. Hughes had awed his Roosevelt colleagues, maintaining order during the late 1930s even as he was outvoted by the dominant Roosevelt majority. Stone proved unable to guide his colleagues, having chafed under Hughes' tight control of the conference he opened up debate which led to chaos and fractures. Stone's five years as chief justice has been blamed for a permanent rise in the number of separate opinions by justices, the multitude of concurring and dissenting opinions fracturing decisions and making public what had been private disagreements.

The battle over Justice Roberts' retirement letter further undermined Stone's control as did Justice Jackson's decision to act as prosecutor at the Nuremberg War Crimes Trials. Stone fumed at Jackson's sabbatical, the added work and tension resulting in his slow physical decline and death in April 1946, Stone suffering a stroke in the midst of reading an opinion and being led off the bench by his colleagues only to die a few hours later.

## Wiley Rutledge

After Justice Byrnes' resignation in 1942, Roosevelt made his ninth and final appointment, Wiley Rutledge. Serving on the D.C. Court of appeals, Rutledge was an expert on the burgeoning administrative law field and authored his most compelling opinions on the issue. Replacing the conservative Byrnes with the liberal Rutledge produced an electrifying effect on the Court. Rutledge provided the fifth vote in the in speech cases including Jones v. Opelika and Murdock v. Pennsylvania as the Roosevelt majority flexed its muscles and began rewriting First Amendment law. [177] The new justice also joined the Korematsu decision, a significant retreat from the Court's expansion of civil liberties and the major deviation for Rutledge in his usual support for racial equality. In explaining his Korematsu vote, Rutledge argued that basic rights were less protected during times of crisis.[178]

After Korematsu Rutledge staked a position on the Court' left fringe. In Adamson v. California he dissented from Justice Reed's ruling that the right from self incrimination was not incorporated through the Fourteenth Amendment. While Justices Black and Douglas arguing for total incorporation of rights through the Fourteenth Amendment, Rutledge, joined by Justice Murphy, sought a broader definition of due process seeking to incorporate rights not explicitly found in the constitution. Rutledge's approach would have granted judges broad discretion in ruling certain courtroom procedures violated an amorphous definition of due process. [179]

Serving seven years Rutledge produced a sparse record when compared to the other Roosevelt appointees. His influence was strongest on issues of administrative law though he managed a few memorable civil liberties cases including *Thomas v. Collins*. In Collins a Texas state judge issued an injunction to prevent Thomas from addressing a union meeting. The judge acted according to a Texas law limiting union organizing even as Thomas claimed the law violated his First Amendment rights. Rutledge ruled the right to organize was part of the right to associate under the First Amendment, dismissing the claim that Collins' speech represented a clear and present danger and adding his own interpretation to the oft changed doctrine. [180]

Among his administrative law opinion was a dissent in *Yakus v. United States*. To curb wartime inflation Congress created the Office of Price Administration (OPA) and delegated it broad authority to ensure price stability through economic regulation. When Yakus was convicted of violating an OPA directive, he appealed, claiming the OPA violated his due process rights and exercised legislative powers improperly delegated to the president.[181]

Though six justices upheld OPA Rutledge dissent, arguing Yakus was denied access due process because of an absence of hearings or appeals for the administrative decision. Rutledge denied the OPA had been delegated legislative powers, an argument taken up by Justice Roberts, who returned to his pre 1937 roots in arguing Congress had not provided sufficient standards for the OPA and granted it excessive legislative authority. The two dissents exhibited the growing gulf between the Roosevelt justices and their predecessors..[182]

The National Labor Relations Act and the National Labor Relations Board (NLRB) were created to settle labor disputes and protect the right of collective bargaining. In *NLRB v. Hearst Publications*, Rutledge backed the board when it ruled newspaper carriers were regular employees of the Hearst Newspaper Syndicate and must be granted equal bargaining rights.[183] According to Rutledge when Congress passed the act it intended to create large bargaining units to strengthen unions. Allowing business to exclude a large number of employees would undermine union bargaining power and defeat that congressional intent. The Hearst case was another labor victory at the hands of the Roosevelt majority, which regularly favored unions over business.[184]

The reign of the Roosevelt liberals came to a sudden end in the summer of 1949 as Justice Murphy was struck down by a heart attack in July while Rutledge suffered the same fate in September, eliminating the two left fringe justices of the liberal bloc. Rutledge's six years as a justice limited his influence and contributed less to Roosevelt's legacy than Hugo Black and William Douglas.[185]

## Notes

1. Stahr, Walter, *John Jay* (New York: Hambledon and London, 2006), 82-84.

2. Stahr, 94

3 Stahr 109-112

4. McCullough, David, *John Adams* (New York: Simon and Schuster, 2001), 275, 278-279.

5. Stahr 197

6. Rossiter, Clinton, ed. *The Federalist Papers* (NY: Mentor Books, 1961)

7. Schwartz, Bernard, *History of the Supreme Court* (New York: Oxford University Press, 1996), 18.

8. Schwartz, 25; Smith, Richard Norton, *Patriarch* (New York: Houghton Mifflin, 1993), 171.

9. Smith, 173

10. In 1877 five justices participated in the Electoral Commission that chose a president; in 1943 Justice Roberts participated in an investigation of the Pearl Harbor attacks; in 1946 Justice Jackson served as a prosecutor in the Nuremberg War Crimes Trial; in 1964 Chief Justice Warren headed the investigation of John Kennedy's assassination.

11. Three justices would follow his dubious example. Charles Evan Hughes resigned his seat in 1916 to run for president, Justice Byrnes resigned to oversee the war effort in 1942 and Justice Goldberg resigned to be a U.N. Ambassador then later ran for the New York Governorship in 1970

12. Holt, Wythe"John Blair"in *Seriatim* ed. Scott Douglas Gerber (New York: New York University Press, 1998), 156-157.

13. Holt, 167

14. Holt, 173

15. 2 U.S. 409 (1792)

16. Bowen, Catherine Drinker, *Miracle at Philadelphia* (New York: Back Bay Book, 1986), 201-202.

17. Haw, James "John Rutledge" in *Seriatim* ed. Scott Douglas Gerber (New York: New York University Press, 1998), 79-80.

18. Abraham, Henry, *Justices, Presidents and Senators* ( New York: Rowman and Littlefield, 2008), 58-59.

19. Haw, 86—88

20. Abraham, 59

21. Smith, Page, *James Wilson* (Chapel Hill: University of North Carolina Press, 1956), 28.

22. Smith, 83

23. Smith, 44

24. Hall, Mark David, *The Political and Legal Philosophy of James Wilson* (Columbia, MO: University of Missouri Press, 1997), 150-151.

25. Hall, 129

26. 2 U.S. 419 (1793)

27. 2 U.S. 419, 454

28 . 2 U.S. 419, 456

29. 2 U.S. 419, 458

30. 2 U.S. 419, 459

31. Gerber, Scott Douglas, "Deconstructing William Cushing"in *Seriatim*ed. Scott Douglas Gerber (New York: New York University Press, 1998), 111.

32. Gerber, 114

33. 3 U.S. 199 (1796)

34. 4 U.S.14(1800)

35. Gerber,116
36. 3 U.S. 199, 284 (1796)
37. 4 U.S.14, 19 (1800)
38. Whichard, Willard, "James Iredell" in *Seriatim* ed, Scott Douglas Gerber (New York: New York University Press, 1998), 208-210.
39. 2 U.S. 419, 446-447
40. 3 U.S. 386 (1798)
41. Bork, Robert, *The Tempting of America* (New York: Free Press, 1990), 20.
42. Whichard, 215
43. Johnson, Herbert Alan,"Thomas Johnson" in Leon Friedman and Fred Israel *The Justices of the United States Supreme Court* 1789-1969 (New York: Chelsea House Publishing, 1969), 156-158; Marcus, Maeva "ThomasJohnson" in ed. Melvin Urofsky *The Supreme Court Justices* (New York: Garland Publishing, 1994),271.
44. O'Connor, John, *William Patterson* (New Jersey: Princeton University Press, 1979) 145-146.
45. Rossiter, Clinton, *The Grand Convention* (New York: The MacMillan Co, 1966), 190-193.
46. O'Connor, 174
47. 3 U.S. 199 (1796)
48. O'Connor, 244-245
49. 5 U.S. 299 (1803); Degnan, Daniel, "William Paterson"in *Seriatim* ed. Scott Douglas Gerber (New York: New York University Press, 1998), 248.
50. Elsmere, Jane *Justice Samuel Chase* (Muncie IN.: Janevar Publishing, 1980), 19-21.
51. 3 U.S. 386 (1798) Chase's interpretation of the Ex Post Facto Clause continued to be cited during the Court's third century, see Justice Breyer's opinion in *Stogner v. California* 539 U.S. 607, 610-612 (2003)
52. Bork, 20. Robert Bork mentioned Chase's opinion in Calder as the first example of activism by a Supreme Court justice.
53. Newman, Paul Douglas, *Fries Rebellion* (Philadelphia: University of Pennsylvania Press, 2004), 173.
54. Presser, Stephen, "The Verdict on Samuel Chase" in *Seriatim* ed. Scott David Gerber (New York: New York University Press, 1998) 264-265. Callendar proved an equal opportunity slanderer, breaking the Sally Hemmings rumor about Jefferson during the 1804 election.
55. Rehnquist, William, *Grand Inquests* (New York: Harper Perennial, 1999), 104-105
56. Casto, William, "Oliver Ellsworth"in *Seriatim* ed. Scott David Gerber (New York: New York University Press, 1998), 293.
57. Brown, William, *The Life of Oliver Ellsworth* (New York: MacMillan and Co, 1905), 188-191.

58. Casto, 302

59. Brown, 240

60 .Brown, 273

61. Casto, 313

62. McKenna, Marian Franklin, *Roosevelt and the Great Constitutional War* (New York: Fordham University Press, 2002), 539-544. During the height of the Court battle, Senator Hugo Black offered a constitutional amendment requiring Supreme Court justices to stand for national election.

63. The focus of Black's ire were the 1873 Slaughterhouse Cases where the Court refused to apply the Bill of Rights to the states and eviscerated the Fourteenth Amendment's Privileges and Immunities Clause. This made the Due Process Clause the only means by which the Court could incorporate the Bill of Rights.Black sought to revive privileges and immunities but failed.

64. 372 U.S. 335 (1963)

65. 319 U.S. 141 (1943)

66. 323 U.S. 214 (1944) 224

67. 330 U.S. 1 (1947)

68. 330 U.S. 1, 26.Black alludes to Chief Justice Waite's opinion in *Reynolds v. U.S.* 98 U.S. 145, 164 (1878) in which Waite references theletter. While the term separation of church and state has been used in modern times to limit religion in the public square, Waite used it to uphold a federalban on polygamy in Utah territory.

69. 370 U.S. 421 (1962) 436

70. Hamburger, Philip, *Separation of Church and State* (Harvard University Press, 2004), 430-432.

71. 372 U.S. 726 (1963)

72. 396 U.S. 19 (1969)

73. Newman, 601. "If anyone writes, I dissent," was the threat.

74. 314 U.S. 252 (1941); Wiecek, William, *The Birth of the Modern Constitution* (London: Cambridge University Press, 2006), 156-158.

75. Schwartz, Bernard, *Super Chief* (New York: New York University Press, 1983), 629.

76. 383 U.S. 663 (1966) In dissent, Black argued the Court stretched the Equal Protection Clause too far.The justice reminded his colleagues that the clause had been used to protect wealthy economic interests and was now being used to protect the poor.In his own way Black was accusing the Court of returning to the period of substantive due process and equal protection, a philosophy he had fought against during the 1930s.

77. *Griswold v. Connecticut* 381 U.S. 479, 524 (1965). Black's dissent sounded more like a declaration of independence from his more liberal colleagues.He criticized both Douglas' vague opinion and Justice Goldberg's arguments for the Ninth Amendment.Black compared Griswold to the substantive

due process cases including Lochner, *Coppage v. Kansas, Adkins v. Children's Hospital and Burns Bakery.*

78. *Adderley v. Florida* 385 U.S. 39 (1967)

79. *Cohen v. California* 403 U.S. 15 (1971) Black dissented when Justice Harlan struck Cohen's conviction for wearing a jacket bearing the words "Fuck the Draft" printed on the back.Black argued it was not a free speech issue.

80. Newman, Roger,*Hugo Black* ( New York:Pantheon Books,1994).

81. *Labine v. Vincent* 401 U.S. 532 (1971). Just four years earlier, the Court placed illegitimacy in the same constitutional class as race and ethnicity, making it nearly impossible for states to treat illegitimate children differently than children born with married parents, *Levy v. Louisiana* 391 U.S. 68 (1968). Levy had been authored by Justice Douglas, a further sign of their split.

82. *McGautha v. California* 402 U.S. 183 (1971). In a brief concurring opinion, Black made clear that the country's tradition and his literal reading of the constitution included the government using capital punishment.

83. *Palmer v. Thompson* 403 U.S. 217 (1971). Speaking for five justices, Black upheld the decision of the city of Jackson, Mississippi to close all municipalswimming pools after being ordered to integrate the pools.According to-Black, by closing all pools the city was treating everyone the same, all thatwas required by the constitution.

84. *Ginzburg v. Goldwater* 396 U.S. 1049 (1970) Barry Goldwater sued Ginzburg for libel winning and receiving one dollar in compensation. The court upheld the verdict but Black dissented arguing no public official could ever sue for libel.

85. *New York Times v. United States* 403 U.S. 713 (1971).In a final joining of the pair of justices, William Douglas joined Black's concurring opinion while Black joined Douglas'.

86. Woodward, Bob and Scott Armstrong *The Brethren* New York; Avon Books 1979 283

87. 295 U.S. 602 (1935)

88. Fassett, 112-118 passimThe successful case came in *Ashwander v. TVA* 297 U.S. 288 (1936)

89. Black, Conrad, *Franklin Delano Roosevelt* (New York: Public Affairs Press, 2005), 414.

90 *Smith v. Allwright* 321 U.S. 649 (1944)

91. Fassett, 362

92. 329 U.S. 459, 467, 473(1947) Justice Frankfurter concurred arguing against abroad reading of the Eighth Amendment. Justice Burton argued a second attempt at executing Willie Francis was cruel and unusual punishment.

93. 332 U.S. 46 (1947)

94. 328 U.S. 373 (1946)

95. See *Dennis v. United States* 341 U.S. 494 (1951)

96. Fassett, 451; O'Connor, 454-455. For a detailed examination of the Hiss case and the role of Washington elites in defending him see Tanenhaus, Sam, *Whittaker Chambers* (New York: Random House, 2002), 374-375.

97. Fassett, 571

98. Kluger, Richard *Simple Justice* (New York: Alfred Knopf, 1975), 874-875, 882.

99. Wiecek, 89

100. Simon, 127-128

101. 310 U.S. 586 (1940)

102. 338 U.S. 25 (1949)

103. 332 U.S. 45 (1947)

104. 342 U.S. 165 (1952)

105. 342 U.S. 165, 173 (1952)

106. 319 U.S. 105 (1943)

107. 343 U.S. 250 (1952)

108. *Dennis v. United States* 341 U.S. 494, 517 (1951); *Watkins v. U.S.* 354 U.S. 178 (1957); *Barenblatt v. U.S.* 360 U.S. 109 (1959)

109. 367 U.S. 643, 673

110. 328 U.S. 549 (1946)

111. *Gomillion v. Lightfoot* 364 U.S. 339 (1960)

112. Frankfurter's obsession with decorum continued even as he was carried from his office as he wanted his shoes located to accompany him to the hospital, Schwartz 427.

113. Murphy, Bruce Allen, *Wild Bill* (New York: Random House, 2003), 475- 477.

114. Abraham, 225-226

115. Simon, James, *Independent Journey* (New York: Harper and Row, 1980), 274

116. Simon, 351-352

117. Murphy, 407- 410; The author had several conversations with locals whose characterization of Douglas would be inappropriate for this work.

118. Murphy, 465

119. Woodward and Armstrong, 63

120. Murphy, 434-435

121. 319 U.S. 105 (1943)

122. 316 U.S. 535 (1942)

123. 307 U.S. 277 (1939); Murphy, 183

124. 320 U.S. 591 (1944)

125. 348 U.S. 483 (1955)

126. 325 U.S. 91 (1945)

127. 343 U.S. 306 (1952)

128. 343 U.S. 306, 315

129. *Walz v. Tax Commissioner* 397 U.S. 664 (1970)

130. 357 U.S. 116 (1958)

131. 357 U.S. 116, 126

132. 365 U.S. 167 (1961) 191

133. 381 U.S. 479 (1965)

134. 381 U.S. 479, 485

135. *Roe v. Wade* 410 U.S. 113, 209 (1973)

136. *Sierra Club v. Morton* 405 U.S. 727 (1972) Douglas compared ships and corporations, all inanimate objects given the right to sue, with trees, rivers, rocks and the air, arguing the latter should also be able to file suit to prevent environmental degradation.He could find no other justice to agree, *DeFunis v. Odegaard* 416 U.S. 312 (1974). In the first affirmative action case to reachthe Supreme Court, the justices declared the issue moot, thus sidestepping thecontroversy. But Douglas refused to ignore the issue, dissenting anddeclaring that "any state-sponsored preference to one race over another inthat competition is in my view 'invidious' and violative of the Establishment Clause," 344-345. Oddly enough, Douglas did not believe the law school admissions policy in Defunis was unconstitutional but his statement wentagainst his previous support for affirmative action and the beliefs of many of his like-minded colleagues including Justices Brennan and Marshall.

137. Douglas' odd behavior would continue during the lengthy illness preceding his death.In the second volume of his autobiography he composed a list of four outstanding justices that included Samuel Chase, Samuel Miller, Louis Brandeis and Peter Daniel, the last being a pro slavery zealot who served in the Taney Court and joined the Dred Scott decision. Douglas, William, *The Court Years* (New York:Random House,1980), 355-356.

138. Howard, J. Woodford, *Mr. Justice Murphy* (Princeton N.J.: Princeton University Press, 1968), 50-51.

139. Howard, 68

140. Manchester, William, *American Caesar* (New York: Random House, 1978), 177, 181-182

141. Howard 160

142. Howard, 219-220

143. 310 U.S. 88,106 (1940) According to Murphy, mass picketing was more likely to lead to violence and could be banned.

144. 315 U.S. 568 (1942)

145. Howard, 288-289

146. 323 U.S. 214, 243(1944)

147. 316 U.S. 455, 475 (1942)

148. 333 U.S. 203 (1948)

149. Howard 452

150. Robertson, David,*Sly and Able*(New York:WW Norton,1994), 534.

151. Abraham, 184

152. McCullough, David, *Truman* ( New York: Simon and Schuster, 1992), 368

153. Robertson, 547

154. 314 U.S. 160 (1941). Of all the criticisms of Byrnes as a justice it could not be said that he was a slow writer as Edward required only thirty four days between argument and decision, a near record for a constitutional case,.

155. *Shapiro v. Thompson* 394 U.S. 618 (1969), struck down state residency requirements for receiving welfare benefits.

156. Gerhart, Eugene, *America's Advocate: Robert Jackson* ( New York: Bobbs Merrill, 1958), 74-75; Cannadine, David, *Mellon* (New York: Alfred Knopf, 2008), 533-535.

157. McKenna, 361-362.

158. Gerhart, 109-111

159. Howard, 212-214

160. 319 U.S. 624, 643 (1943) .Jackson wrote "If there is any fixed star in our constitutional constellation, it is that no official, high of petty, can prescribe what shall be orthodox in politics, nationalism, religion, or other matters of opinion of force citizens to confess by word or act their faith therein."

161. 317 U.S. 111 (1942)

162. Simon 160-161; Gerhart 251-253; Wiecek 415-416

163. Simon 166-169; Gerhart 262-263; Wiecek 418-420

164. Stone called Nuremberg a "high grade lynching party." Gerhart 436

165. Simon 162-165; Gerhart 396-399

166. 341 U.S. 464 (1951) 565-566, 573-575;Wiecek, 109

167. *Terminiello v. Chicago* 337 U.S. 1 (1949)

168. 337 U.S. 1, 37

169. 334 U.S. 558 (1948)

170. 336 U.S. 77 (1949)

171. 340 U.S. 290 (1951)

172. 340 U.S. 315 (1951)

173. Wiecek, 689 Jackson's doubts about integration would be recalled some eighteen years after his death.During the Brown debate, Jackson's had one of his clerks compose an argument supporting continued school segregation. That clerk, William Rehnquist, would later be appointed to the Court and his memo arguing against the Brown decision would be used against him during his confirmation.

174. One such witticism was that the Court was not the last body to hear a case because the justices were infallible but rather the justices were infallible because they were last.

175. 321 U.S. 414(1944)

176. 321 U.S. 414, 425

177. 316 U.S. 584 (1942); 319 U.S. 103 (1943)

178. Ferren, John, *Salt of the Earth* (Chapel Hill: University of North Carolina Press, 2004), 245. See also Rutledge's concurring opinion in *Hirabayashi v. United States* 320 U.S. 81 (1943)

179. 332 U.S. 46 (1947)

180. 323 U.S. 516 (1945)

181. *Yakus v. United States* 321 U.S. 414 (1944)

182. 321 U.S. 414, 460-461

183. 322 U.S. 111 (1944)

184. Ferren, 281-282

185. Ferren, 419-421

# Chapter 3

# Abraham Lincoln (8) Theodore Roosevelt (6) Ronald Reagan (10)

Three Republican presidents, Abraham Lincoln, Theodore Roosevelt and Ronald Reagan are consensus greats or near greats when ranking their administrations. Recognized for success in domestic and foreign policy, the trio of presidents also succeeded in choosing justices of extraordinary ability. Those justices placed the three men within the ranks of greats based on Supreme Court appointments.

Three Republican presidents, Abraham Lincoln, Theodore Roosevelt and Ronald Reagan, rated among the greatest for the administrations' achievements and shared high rankings for their Supreme Court appointments. Lincoln's achievements as president, binding the nation together during its most dangerous period, far outweighed his success at transforming the Supreme Court from an institution dominated by narrow sectional interest into one representing all regions. While Lincoln sought justices who supported his war policies, he appointed men whose rulings helped industrialize the country. His influence carried far beyond his administration as Justice Field remained on the Court until 1897 and a new generation of corporate lawyers influenced the law into the 1930s.

The industrial revolution prompted by the Civil War and continuing through the nineteenth century was a point of contention for Theodore Roosevelt. Born of the progressive movement Roosevelt suffered from a populist suspicion of everything big. Bent on splitting the vast business monopolies that dominated the era, Roosevelt used antitrust prosecutions to break up monopolies while passing the first consumer laws guaranteeing food and drug purity. Roosevelt chose three justices for the Court, determined to find men to uphold his forays into economic regulation and dilute conservative votes. Roosevelt's success was limited to his first selection, Oliver Wendell Holmes.

The economic battles of the early twentieth century had receded into history when Ronald Reagan entered office. Much like Lincoln and Roosevelt, he faced a Supreme Court that had overreached and alienated key groups. The federal judiciary had seized administrative authority over school districts, hospitals and prisons, grasping legislative and executive power to control taxes and spending to achieve egalitarian ends.[1] The Reagan Administration sought to check this judicial activism, utilizing a systematic process to identify conservative judges who would enforce the Reagan agenda.

## Lincoln

Facing the greatest political crisis since the American Revolution, Abraham Lincoln ignored the Supreme Court and its pro slavery majority for the first year of his term. When Chief Justice Taney sought to curb executive power in Ex Parte Merryman, Lincoln ignored the decision, reducing the Supreme Court to a political backwater enjoying little influence and suffering from a shortage of justices.

The deaths of Justices Daniel and McLean and Justice Campbell's resignation left a rump Court, its prestige damaged by the Dred Scott decision, its voice drowned out by the rumble of impending war. After Congress passed the 1862 Judiciary Act redrawing circuit boundaries to provide greater Midwest representation to the detriment of southern circuits, Lincoln filled the three vacancies.

To replace Justice McLean Lincoln selected Ohioan Noah Swayne, who McLean had suggested as his replacement. From Iowa, Lincoln chose Samuel Miller, a medical doctor and a lawyer who was also the first justice from west of the Mississippi. Finally the president appointed his old campaign manager, David Davis. The three Lincoln justices would bolster the Union bloc which included Justices Grier and Wayne, two Jacksonian nationalists who eschewed their Democrat colleagues. The Lincoln appointees would rise to four in 1863 as Congress created a tenth circuit on the west coast and Lincoln chose a War Democrat, Stephen Field of California. Chief Justice Taney's death in October 1864 capped off Lincoln's Court appointments as he chose former Treasury Secretary Salmon Chase as the fifth chief justice. [2]

## Noah Swayne

Lincoln's selection of Noah Swayne was a political appointment intended to keep Ohio in the Republican column by appointing one of its favorite sons to the Court.[3] Swayne overestimated his influence and abilities, seeking the Court's center chair after the deaths of Roger Taney and Salmon Chase. His memorable opinions were limited to the obscure Contract Clause where he staked an extreme position favoring contract rights over other rights.

The 1857 Depression struck hard at western towns which borrowed heavily to fund railroad construction in their communities. As town teetered on the edge of default, bondholders took them to court, claiming a refusal to pay interest and principal violated the ban on state abrogation of contracts. In a series of cases Swayne revived the Contract Clause as a protection of economic rights.

In *Gelpecke v. Dubuque* the Dubuque city council ignored the city charter and state constitution in voting to fund railroad bonds. During the economic depression, the city refused to pay claiming the council's decision to issue the bonds was illegal and the city's taxpayers should not be expected to pay when the council violated the state constitution.[4]

In Gelpecke Swayne ruled for the bondholders, ruling their railroad investments were made with the belief the city council was acting legally. Bondholders would not be expected to bear the brunt of the council's bad decision, instead Dubuque would have to repay the bonds. Swayne ignored an Iowa Supreme Court decision, interpreting the state constitution as banning Dubuque's borrowing. The overruling of the state high court was a deviation from constitutional doctrine as the Court deferred to state court interpretations of state constitutions.[5]

*In Butz v. Muscatine*, Swayne further eroded the scope of state constitutions. In Butz, Swayne ruled the city of Muscatine could impose taxes above one percent of assessed property value. The Iowa constitution limited city taxation to one percent but Swayne ruled the restriction could not be used by the city to avoid a legal order that the city repay its bond debt. In *Rees v. Watertown*, Swayne found himself in the minority, dissenting in favor of a plan to seize public and private land in Watertown and sell it to pay off railroad bonds. The Court refused to such drastic steps but Swayne argued the contract rights of bondholders took precedence over personal property rights.[6]

Swayne took the lead upholding slave contract enforcement even after slavery had been abolished. In *Osborn v. Nicholson* he upheld enforcement of an 1861 slave contract, forcing the buyer to pay the seller even after the slave had been freed. Swayne wrote for eight justices in striking a provision in the Arkansas constitution that cancelled slave contracts. Swayne found that the cancelling of contracts violated the Contract Clause, a startling decision from a Republican Court six years after slavery was abolished.[7]

Swayne's Contract Clause decisions exemplified his dedication to property rights. His dissent in the Slaughterhouse Cases and acceptance of the liberty to contract placed him in the economic rights bloc led by Justice Field. Swayne's dissent bordered on the overwrought as he declared "a more flagrant and indefensible invasion of the rights of many for the benefit of a few has not occurred in the legislative history of the country." Four years later Swayne joined the Munn decision upholding the regulation of grain storage a repudiation of his Slaughterhouse dissent.[8]

Amidst his defense of economic rights, Swayne exerted considerable energy in seeking promotion to chief justice. After Chief Justice Taney's death in 1864, Swayne had his influential Ohio supporters lobby Lincoln for the position, which went to Salmon Chase. With Chase's death in 1873, Swayne again lobbied for the center chair and was displeased to be passed over by the bumbling Ulysses Grant as the president his selections rejected by the Senate, finally picking the obscure Morrison Waite for chief. Swayne's candidacy was harmed by the perception he was intellectually weak and as age and infirmities limited his work, his chances of replacing Chase dwindled. His lobbying was noted by his colleagues with Justice Miller drily noting Swayne and his supporters were "beslobbering the president."[9]

As Swayne's mental decline hastened during the 1870s, his influence marked by opinion writing dwindled, his colleagues forced to work harder as Swayne proved incapable of finishing his tasks. By 1880 illness had struck Justices Clifford and Hunt, preventing them from active participation and with Swayne's decline, the Court limped through its docket, falling behind each term. Justice Strong, tired of performing the work of two justices, resigned hoping to set an example for his colleagues. Only Swayne would follow, resigning at the end of Rutherford Hayes' administration. But during this period, he composed *Springer v. United States*, which would stir controversy over the next two decades.[10] Springer challenged the first federal income tax passed to finance the Civil War. He claimed the income tax was a direct tax forbidden by the constitution unless it was equally apportioned among the states. Swayne rejected the arguments in a unanimous opinion and found the income tax was not a direct tax. The Springer decision was ignored when the Court struck down a second federal income tax in 1895. Springer would be one of his last decisions, Swayne eventually convinced to retire in January 1881, provoking a bitter Senate battle to appoint his successor.

## Samuel Miller

As the only medical doctor to serve on the Supreme Court, Justice Samuel Miller composed some of the most consequential opinions of the era including the first interpretation of the Fourteenth Amendment. A judicial moderate, he clashed with colleagues, including Justice Stephen Field and Justice Swayne, who argued an economic rights doctrine using the newly ratified Fourteenth Amendment. It was in the Slaughterhouse cases that Miller struck the first blow against Field's liberty to contract.[11]

The cases challenged a Louisiana law creating a single state slaughterhouse to limit the environmental damaged caused by animal remains being dumped into the Mississippi River. Butchers claimed their right to pursue the occupation of their choice had been violated under the Fourteenth Amendment's Due Process Clause.

Miller swept aside the butchers' arguments and with it any hope the Fourteenth Amendment would enforce equality in the south. Miller eviscerated the Privileges and Immunities Clause, denying it applied federal rights to states and rejected a liberty to contract under the due process clause. The Slaughterhouse Cases temporarily averted the rise of economic due process but also set back the civil rights movement. A century would pass before the Court applied some federal rights to the states through the Fourteenth Amendment. Miller's distrust of an economic rights agenda stretched back to his earlier dissents in the railroad bond cases.

Having lived along the Mississippi river Miller witnessed the desperation of prairie towns in Iowa, Illinois and Missouri as they struggled to finance railroads using municipal bonds. As the 1857 Depression ruined railroad companies, many towns were left with outstanding debts they could not pay.

Unlike Justice Swayne, Miller believed bondholder demands for repayment had deepened the depression and in disputes pitting bondholders against local governments, Miller consistently supported local governments.[12]

As the bond cases piled up Miller suspected a conspiracy among his colleagues, including the belief Justices Field and Swayne had been bribed by bondholders to rule in their favor.[13] Miller's conspiracy theories caused him to reject the Republicans and interpret ordinary actions including presidential vetoes and the passage of currency laws as examples of malfeasance.[14]

While condemning the corruption of the Grant Administration and congressional Republicans, Miller supported James Blaine, a party leader tainted by the activities criticized by the justices. A former House speaker and perennial presidential candidate, Blaine sought and lost the nomination in 1876, the same year that Miller provided a key vote in the electoral commission that made Rutherford Hayes president.

Even as the economic tide turned against him, Miller remained a relevant force on the Court. In *U.S. v. Stevens* Miller upheld two federal laws recognizing trademarks. Miller broadly interpreted the Congress' copyright and patent powers found in Article One Section Eight and ruled trademark protections were included in that authority.[15]

In 1880 Miller weakened the congressional power of contempt. When investigating the collapse of the Jay Gould trading company, a House committee subpoenaed Gould's associates and demanded answers. Those who refused to appear were cited for contempt. Several of those cited appealed, the decision assigned to Miller. Miller quoted a range of British legal opinions and compared congressional and British parliamentary contempt powers before ruling Congress enjoyed limited contempt powers in seeking testimony from private citizens. Miller complained the congressional investigation of Gould was an invasion of judicial authority and suggested the federal government use the Courts rather than a congressional investigation to recoup money owed it.[16]

In one of his last opinions, Miller displayed judiciousness in ruling for his old rival, Stephen Field. After Field's life was threatened by an angry litigant the justice was assigned a marshal for protection. When Marshal Neagle shot and killed what he thought was a potential assassin, he was jailed by California authorities on murder charges. Miller granted Neagle a writ of Habeas Corpus, ruling the president had the inherent executive authority to assign a federal marshal to protect Field during his circuit riding duties and the state could not interfere with federal authority by jailing Neagle for enforcing federal law. A short time after writing Neagle Miller died, his accomplishments enhancing Lincoln's judicial legacy.[17]

## Judge and Justice Davis

Lincoln's rise from backwoods politician to war president was propelled by his campaign manager, the ungainly Judge David Davis. The judge achieved national attention by running Lincoln's nomination campaign and outmaneuvering the sophisticated eastern politicians to earn the Illinoisan the nomination. Once president, Lincoln rewarded Davis by making him his third Court appointment.[18] Davis was a loyal Lincoln justice, voting with the majority in the Prize Cases to uphold the naval blockade of the south. Davis' dedication to the Republican Party waned with his old friend's assassination and in Ex Parte Milligan, he overruled Lincoln's war policy of trying civilians in military courts.[19]

Milligan was tried in a military court in that state and sentenced to death. In a five to four opinion, Davis struck the use of military courts against civilians where regular courts continued to function. The justice was in the unusual position of joining the Democrats to strike a Republican president's war policies. Davis also found himself in agreement with former Chief Justice Taney, whose Ex Parte Merryman order to release of a civilian from military detention was ignored by Lincoln. Milligan was Davis' sole deviation from Lincoln's war policy as he voted for the test oath for former confederates and the legal tender act.

As Reconstruction policy advanced, Davis dissatisfaction with the Republican Party deepened. A split in the party in 1872 created a political opportunity for Davis, who sought the presidential nomination from the Liberal Republican faction. The rump faction chose newspaper publisher Horace Greeley as a nominee but Davis was offered the nomination of the Labor Reform Party but Davis refused and declared as a political independent, a political stand that would place him in the midst of a constitutional and political crisis.[20]

The 1876 election threatened to cast the country into a second civil war. Faced with conflicting claims over electoral votes, Congress turned to the time honored and politically safe solution, a bipartisan commission certain to divide along party lines. The commission was composed of an equal number of Democrats and Republicans from Congress and the Supreme Court with Davis the independent providing the deciding vote for either Hayes or Tilden.

As the commission's vote approached, Illinois Democrats intervened by electing Davis as United States Senate. Davis immediately resigned from the Court, leaving the commission shorthanded. A Republican justice, Joseph Bradley, took Davis' seat on the commission and provided the deciding vote in favor of Hayes.[21]

Having dodged the political bullet aimed at his reputation, Davis served an eventful single term in the Senate. He supported Democrat Winfield Scott Hancock for president in 1880 and after Hancock was defeated by the Republican James Garfield, the evenly divided Senate left Davis holding the key vote in deciding which party controlled the chamber. After the Garfield assassination, Davis was elected president Pro Tem by Republicans and a few Democrats, making him next in line if the new president, Chester Arthur, died in office. Davis served a single term in the Senate, exhausted by the experience and having angered the very Illinois Democrats who had put him in office. [22] Davis died in 1886, his legal and political career placing him in the midst of the turmoil of the period and leaving a limited mark on the law.

## Stephen Field

As the tenth justice, Stephen Field broke convention during much of his thirty four year career. One of the early California pioneers, Field honed his legal skills settling land disputes, his abilities earning him a seat on the state supreme court. A frontier judge, Field excelled at legal fights, defeating disbarment proceedings and earning a reputation for stubbornness that would follow him to Washington. A strong pro war Democrat, Field bolstered Lincoln's political standing when chosen to fill the new California circuit district and become the tenth justice.[23]

Supporting the battle against the Confederacy as the war raged, Field returned to his Democrat roots during the Reconstruction era. He led a narrow majority in striking oaths for former confederate lawyers and religious leaders. In *Cummings v. Missouri*[24] and *Ex Parte Garland*,[25] Field struck down state and federal test oath laws that required lawyers and reverends to swear they had not supported the Confederacy during the war. Field dredged up the ban on a Bill of Attainder and Ex Post Facto laws, ruling the oaths punished a specified group of people without benefit of trial and made past acts illegal. The justice cobbled together the remaining Democrats on the Court including two members of the Dred Scott majority while four Lincoln appointees were in dissent. Field's support for former confederates may have been influenced by Cummings lawyer, David Dudley Field, the justice's eldest brother. The presence of a brother as counsel would cause modern justices to recuse from the case but Field remained, providing the key vote in the last case his brother would argue before the Court.

The justice also joined David Davis' opinion in Ex Parte McCardle which struck down military commissions used during the war to prosecute anti war Democrats and southern sympathizers. Both McCardle and the test oath cases exemplified Field's independence from his fellow Lincoln appointees. This would extend to Reconstruction policies which he rejected in a series of cases in the 1870s and 1880s

The justice silently agreed with *Cruikshank* and *Reese,* which protected state governments from federal enforcement acts. He dissented in *Strauder v. West Virginia* as the justices struck a state law that banned blacks from serving on juries, and dissented in *Ex Parte Virginia* as his colleagues ruled against a state judge who excluded all black citizens from jury service. He also dissented in *Neal v. Delaware*, which found that the lack of black jurors was a sign of discrimination. Field was quick to accept the state explanation that blacks were denied jury service because they did not meet the state requirement of being sober and judicious.[26] Only in cases from his native California did Field display any concern for civil rights, occasionally ruling for Chinese immigrants.

Sitting as a circuit judge, Field struck down a San Francisco ordinance requiring all jail prisoners to wear hair of a certain length, a policy directed at Chinese men who wore their hair in an extended "queue" down their back. Field ruled the ordinance was applied in a racially discriminatory manner, violating equal protection. His decision would lose him support in California, which sought to limit Chinese immigration to the state.

A decade later, though, Field upheld the national Chinese Exclusion Act. The law banned the entry of new Chinese immigrants and barred reentry of documented aliens who had lived in the United States but left before the law was passed. Field upheld the ban, recognizing plenary authority for Congress in immigration and dismissing claims the law violated American immigration treaties with China.[27]

Field's conservative reputation would be earned during his battle to recognize a liberty to contract under the Fourteenth Amendment. The Slaughterhouse cases presented Field his first opportunity to enforce a Laissez Faire constitutional doctrine. His arguments against state economic regulation, though, convinced only three of his colleagues and Justice Miller's decision rejected Field's broad interpretation of citizens' privileges and immunities under the amendment.

Field dissented, declaring the amendment's due process clause included a liberty to practice one's occupation without government interference. He noted a parade of horribles produced by the slaughterhouse law, warning a twenty five year monopoly could be extended to a century then expanded from cattle to ranching or farming, the storage of grain and all others forms of commerce.[28]

Using the Thirteenth Amendment, Field offered a broad definition of involuntary servitude banned under the amendment. According to Field "a person allowed to pursue only one trade or calling, and in only one locality of the country . . . would be in a condition of servitude.[29] He compared the Louisiana monopoly to that of the French *Ancien* Regime under Louis XVI, noting Louisiana butchers were forced to go to a particular slaughterhouse and pay "tribute" in order to perform their occupation. This was compared unfavorably to French peasants forbidden from hunting, fishing, cooking, grinding meal or selling their commodities all under the direction of a tyrannical monarch.[30] Field's arguments would be repeated through the remainder of his career, eventually becoming accepted doctrine in 1897, the year of his retirement. [31] His final success would not come without a share of failures, his greatest being Munn v. Illinois, which opened the floodgates for state economic regulation and bedeviled the justice throughout his career. [32]

After the Civil War the Democrat Party was in disarray, the southern wing tainted by secession and many northern party leaders seen as disloyal to the union cause. The Democrats struggled to find candidates choosing two governors of New York, a war hero and a Republican newspaper editor to represent them from 1868 through 1880. Having earned the reputation as a Union Democrat, Field was untainted by the war and his first foray into presidential politics came during the 1876 electoral commission. As one of the justices chosen to serve, Field watched in anger as the three Republican justices assigned the disputed electoral votes to Rutherford Hayes. He turned on his colleagues, pushing Democrats to publish a report on the commission and accused Justice Bradley of being improperly influenced by Republican leaders. Field further refused to attend the new president's inauguration as a protest against the election results.[33] Almost immediately after Hayes declared "So help me God," Field began preparations for a presidential run. He composed a campaign biography, highlighting his hardscrabble life during the early days of California statehood. Presenting himself as a pioneer and individualist, he wisely ended the biography just before he reached the Supreme Court, refusing to reopen wounds.[34]

But of all the Democrat candidates in 1880, Field was the one who had a written record he could not escape. He had been a consistent dissenter against federal civil rights laws, expressing the belief that southern state governments would protect the lives and rights of the freedman.[35] His dissents earned him some support in the south but his striking of economic regulations infuriated the Democrat's growing populist wing. While earning the praise of national Democrats, Field failed to convince California delegates of his presidential bonafides. Without controlling a base of support he proved unable to wield those votes in favor of his candidacy, forcing the justice to rely on his one advantage, many wealthy donors and supporters.[36]

The 1880 Cincinnati convention was dominated by a Field for president advertising campaign. The justice's media centered campaign failed to hide his lack of grassroots support and the Democrats, desperate after twenty years in the presidential wilderness, fell back on a familiar strategy of choosing a war hero, Winfield Scott Hancock. During the delegate counts Field never broke the sixty five delegate barrier.[37] An attempt by the justice to win the 1884 nomination was prematurely ended at the California Democrat convention as his state party again refused to endorse him for president.[38]

After Grover Cleveland brought the Democrats back to the White House in 1884, Field reached out to him, seeking influence over California patronage. Cleveland feared Field's unpopularity might transfer to him and ceded patronage control to Field's political opponents, earning the president a powerful enemy. The split between the two highest ranking Democrats in Washington grew in 1888 when Cleveland refused to promote Field to chief justice. The justice saw it as deliberate snub and he refused to resign from the Court during Cleveland's second term so as to deny the president another Court nomination.

As he aged, Field's direct influence waned even as his ideas were adopted by his colleagues, including his nephew, Justice David Brewer. Even as his opinions became less frequent and influential, Field proved he could advance constitutional law and set precedent without composing a single sentence.

One of Field's colleagues on the California Supreme Court, David Terry, had been a fearsome man with a murderous temper and a long memory of past slights. When Field went to Washington in 1863, Terry was fighting for the Confederacy. As Field's reputation grew, Terry became a prominent lawyer in his home state. He soon became embroiled in the sordid affair involving former Nevada Senator William Sharon and his young wife. Acting as circuit judge, Field ruled on behalf of his old friend Sharon's estate and against his common law wife, Sarah. David Terry, her lawyer and soon to be husband, was dragged from the courtroom threatening Field's life. [39]

In response to the threats, President Harrison assigned a federal marshal to guard Field during circuit riding. Returning to California, Field and his marshal, Neagle, stopped in a railroad restaurant where Terry was present. Terry approached the justice, made a threatening move toward him leading Neagle to shoot and kill Terry. Neagle was arrested for murder and sought Habeas Corpus protection, claiming he acted as a federal law enforcement official and could not be charged by the state. The case was appealed to the Supreme Court

With Field on the sidelines, five justices ruled for Neagle, agreeing he was acting under presidential orders and could not be prosecuted by the state.[40] The Neagle decision expanded executive powers and prompted the quote that Field could make constitutional law even while acting as a civilian.

Entering his dotage, Field became ever more fearful the country was under socialistic attack. In *Pollock v. Farmers Home Loan and Trust* five justices struck down the 1894 federal income tax, finding it violated the direct tax provision of the constitution.[41] Field concurred and in a rambling opinion in the form of a stemwinding revivalist speech warned that "the present assault against capital is just beginning," and that if the income tax had been upheld that "our political contests will become a war of the poor against the rich, a war constantly growing in intensity and bitterness."[42] Pollock represented Field's last warning of the dangers of progressivism, again recording his fervent his opposition to government regulation and redistributionist policies.

Never one to surrender his legal positions, Field proved just as obstinate when faced with surrendering his seat. The year 1893 marked Field's thirtieth year as a justice, a milestone reached by only five of his predecessors.[43] By his thirtieth year Field had begun to fail physically and mentally with Chief Justice Fuller steering important opinions away from him. But Field became more determined to break the Court's longevity record. Likely embarrassed by Field's growing hysteria, Chief Justice Fuller and Justice Brewer, Field's nephew, convinced the old justice to resign on December 1, 1897, his departure coinciding with the success of his constitutional views. [44]

Stephen Field proved to be one of Lincoln's and the Court's most influential justices. Thirty years after the president's assassination, Field remained an influence on the law, expressing views that would dominate the Court until the Franklin Roosevelt administration.

## Salmon Chase

Salmon Chase could never be accused of unthinking consistency in his politics. Originally an Ohio Chase switched to the Republican Party over the slavery issue. As governor he became a national figure within the free soil movement and during the 1860 Republican convention, was among the second tier candidates that included Abraham Lincoln. During the convention it was rumored Chase had traded his delegates to Lincoln, receiving a cabinet post in return when Lincoln was elected. [45]

Lincoln appointed Chase as treasury secretary, delegating considerable authority over monetary policy to him. In return Chase worked against Lincoln, even challenging him for the 1864 Republican nomination. Lincoln successfully manipulated Chase, keeping him within the cabinet even when the secretary offered his resignation on several occasions. Once his renomination was safely in hand, Lincoln dismissed Chase but kept him as an ally by suggesting he would be appointed chief justice upon the death of Roger Taney. Chase supported Lincoln's reelection and in return was selected as chief justice in fall 1864. [46]

Lincoln's death and the subsequent battle between Congress and President Andrew Johnson marred much of Chase's career and undermined his legacy. As Congress and the president battled for control over southern reconstruction the Court was trapped. When Congress limited Johnson's appointment power by reducing the Court from ten members to eight, the justices accepted a greater workload. Chase even allowed Congress to recoupe the salaries of the departed justices rather than divide the additional money among his colleagues. [47]

Chase had begun his tenure touring the south and observing early reconstruction efforts. He returned to Washington supporting congressional rather than presidential reconstruction policy.[48] As tensions heightened between the president and Congress Chase aided Republicans in drafting portions of the 1867 Reconstruction Acts then bowed to the congressional decision to remove the Court's jurisdiction over the acts. In *Ex Parte McCardle*, he upheld Congress' decision to remove reconstruction from the Court's appellate jurisdiction even with a case pending before the justices.[49]

The next year Chase wriggled free from the McCardle decision in upholding the Habeas Corpus right in *Ex Parte Yerger*. Chase ruled that the Court could hear Habeas appeals as part of its appellate jurisdiction established under Article III and the 1789 Judiciary Act. Yerger marked the end of strict congressional reconstruction intended to punish southerners by removing their rights as U.S. citizens and placing them under military control.[50]

Chase's reconstruction era opinions included one of the first interpretations of the Thirteenth Amendment. The amendment banned involuntary servitude, a vague phrase challenged in In re Turner. After outlawing slavery, Maryland passed black codes making the freedmen indentured servants to their former masters. Acting as circuit judge, Chase upheld a challenge to the Maryland law, ruling it violated the Thirteenth Amendment and the recently passed 1866 Civil Rights Act.[51]

Chase also upheld congressional reconstruction as a propert exercise of congressional power. Mississippi sought a federal injunction preventing President Andrew Johnson from enforcing the newly passed reconstruction laws. Chase rejected the petition, ruling courts could order an executive official to perform a ministerial act, such as paying a bill, but not halt execution of a law. He noted separation of powers concerns and the pragmatic concern that the federal judiciary lacked means of enforcement against a president who violated an injunction.[52]

In other reconstruction cases Chase dissented in the test oath cases, *Cummings v. Missouri* and *Ex Parte Garland*, when the Court struck down test oaths for former Confederate officials who sought to be lawyers or clergymen. In *Ex Parte Milligan*, he composed a concurring opinion that resembled a dissent, narrowly agreeing with Justice Davis on Milligan's release from military control. Chase emphasized Congress had not authorized military commissions in Indiana, therefore Milligan could not be tried by the commissions but rather would have to be turned over to civilian courts. Chase rejected Davis' contention that Congress could not establish military commissions where civilian courts still functioned, warning that civil authorities could not always be trusted in times of rebellion. Davis' opinion in McCardle is frequently quoted but Chase's concurrence in more balanced in tackling the question of military commissions.[53]

Chase used a Texas bond case to slam the door on the doctrine of secession and lay to rest the political debates over the Civil War. After settling a boundary dispute, Texas received compensation in the form of federal government securities, a portion of which were sold prior to the Civil War. The Texas confederate government sold the remaining bonds to fund the war effort. Once the war ended, the newly reconstructed Texas government sought to retrieve the bonds, leading to *Texas v. White*.[54]

Chase faced a conundrum at the new government of Texas sought control of the bonds. Ruling for the Texas government created by Andrew Johnson would place Chase squarely against congressional reconstruction. Rejecting the claim could be seen as an acceptance of secession. Chase wiggled free by declaring the Texas confederate government was illegitimate and that the end of the war placed Congress in full authority of Texas state affairs, thus cancelling Texas' lawsuit. His opinion provoked three dissents. Justice Grier rejected secession and the new state government while Justices Miller and Swayne rejected the new Texas government in favor of a congressionally reconstructed state government.

Chase further rejected ante bellum law, dissenting in *Osborn v. Nicholson*, as Justice Swayne upheld an Arkansas slave contract. Chase declared such contracts violated "sound morals and natural justice," and the Fourteenth Amendment forbade compensation for emancipated slaves.[55]

As reconstruction cases dwindled, economic regulation cases reached the Court. Chase joined the economic rights bloc, supporting the liberty to contract and rejecting a policy he had enforced as treasury secretary. Chase authored *Hepburn v. Griswold* striking down the Legal Tender Act he had helped write and had enforced during the Civil War.[56] He maneuvered the befuddled Justice Grier into striking down the act then worked hard to prevent the case from being reheard after Grier retired. Chase's best efforts failed as Hepburn was overturned a year later in *Knox v. Lee.*[57]

The chief justice was also the lead dissenter in the Slaughterhouse Cases, actively promoting the Fourteenth Amendment as protecting economic rights. His dissent would be one of his final opinions as he was struck down by a second stroke and died in May 1873.

Chase's legacy as a justice has been marred by his political activities, one of his choosing, the other a constitutional duty for which he set precedent. Always mentioned as a presidential candidate, Chase did not halt his drive to the White House upon reaching the Supreme Court. As Andrew Johnson's administration disintegrated, Chase saw an opportunity to fill a political vacuum by challenging for the 1868 Democrat presidential nomination. Andrew Johnson's impeachment trial offered him the forum to earn Democrat favor.

Chase had a strained relationship with President Andrew Johnson, made worse with the president's reconstruction policy and his refusal to listen to the chief justice's warning against firing Secretary of War Edwin Stanton. The Stanton dismissal provoked Congress into impeachment and made Chase the first justice to preside over a presidential impeachment trial. Chase seized the reins, ruling on which witnesses could testify before the Senate and setting aside some of the chamber's long practiced rules.[58]

Fearing Chase was a loose cannon unwilling to preside over Johnson's removal, Senate Republicans sought to intimidate him.[59] Republicans tried to limit Chase's authority and accused him of improperly influencing senators to vote for acquittal.[60] Chase's dislike of Johnson was tempered by the fear the president's removal would lead to his old Ohio enemy, president pro tem Senator Benjamin Wade, assuming the presidency. Once Johnson was acquitted Chase became the toast of the town among some Democrats provoking a presidential boomlet. His candidacy was boosted by his politically connected daughter, Kate Sprague, and the New York politician and 1876 Democrat nominee, Samuel Tilden.[61] Unfortunately for the chief his abolitionist past was not forgotten by Democrats, who scotched his drive to the nomination.[62] The 1868 convention would be Chase's best chance for the brass ring as by 1872 his health had declined, undermined by the unending disputes on the Court and his daughter's marital problems. In August of that year he suffered a stroke, the chief barely able to function and struggling to attend the inauguration and swear in Ulysses Grant for a second term, one of his last official acts before his death.

## The Lincoln Court

In his five Court appointments Abraham Lincoln sought men who were true to the Union cause and generally supported the Republican – Hamiltonian view of an active federal government building an industrial state. Modern Court observers dismiss much of the post Civil War justices as business oriented and obsessed with economic liberties yet the judicial philosophy of men such as Salmon Chase, Noah Swayne and Stephen Field unleashed economic growth and investment while protecting property rights against real threats.

The Lincoln justice's records on civil rights were more mixed though they may have reflected the president's legacy more than the Republican congresses that followed him. The Chase Court initially retreated from the field of Reconstruction as an angry Congress threatened judicial independence then the subsequent Court proved unwilling to enforce much less expand on the rights created under federal law. But the less contentious reconstruction seemingly favored by the justices may well have represented Lincoln's policy of "Malice toward none, charity toward all," that was rejected by the radical congress. At the same time, the Lincoln justices missed the best opportunity in the century to provide real civil rights protection and equality that would not be achieved until the Warren Court took up the banner.

## Theodore Roosevelt

A man of emotion and action, Theodore Roosevelt appointed three men of considerably different temperaments. Oliver Wendell Holmes, Rufus Day and William Moody were more cautious than their president with only Holmes enjoying a celebrated career. Day is nearly forgotten, only his Dagenhart opinion dusted off and flayed as an example of judicial overreaching. William Moody's career disappeared down the memory hole, one of those unsmiling faces staring back in Court portraits used mainly to show how Holmes aged during his thirty year career.

Justice Horace Grays's retirement in 1902 opened a vacancy for Holmes, Chief Justice of the Massachusetts Supreme Court. Holmes was a Civil War veteran whose namesake, Oliver Wendell Holmes' Sr. was a doctor, writer and literary critic known for his writings that included *The Autocrat of the Breakfast Table.*

Holmes Jr. gained notice in the legal community in 1881 with his book The Common Law, a dissection of the law that placed him among the top judicial minds of the period. Fortunately for Holmes his legal writings were seen as a sign of intellect and ability, much different than the political uproar they would have caused in modern times. Holmes reached the Court at age sixty, one of the oldest men to be appointed justice and seemed likely to serve a minimum decade before retiring. Yet Holmes rejected conventional wisdom and the infirmities of age which struck down his younger colleagues. He served three decades and is placed with John Marshall and Joseph Story as the greatest justices to serve.

Holmes is best remembered for three opinions, his dissent in Lochner and his Court opinions in Schenck and Buck. Three years into his career, Holmes dissented in Lochner, disputing the Court's decision to strike a New York law regulating hours and wages of bakery employees. Holmes accused his colleagues of writing Herbert Spencer's social Darwinist theories into the constitution.[63]

Holmes' most quoted opinion came in 1919 in *Schenck v. United States.*[64] Defending the Espionage Act against the claim it restricted free speech, Holmes reminded readers the First Amendment did not protect all speech highlighting his example of falsely crying fire in a crowded theater and creating a panic. Under Schenck Government could prosecute speech if it represented a clear and present danger of creating disorder. The Clear and Present Danger test would become a hallmark of First Amendment speech law for the next half century, its variations sometimes deviating from Holmes' intent.

Less celebrated was Holmes' snarling epigram written in *Buck v. Bell.* A proponent of eugenics, Holmes could find nothing wrong with a Virginia law mandating sterilization of "mental defectives" in an effort to eliminate continuation of a damaged genetic line. Agreeing that Carrie Buck could be sterilized, Holmes uttered a toss away line that "three generations of imbeciles is enough."[65]

Pithy phrases aside, Holmes' main contribution to the Court included his arguments for judicial restraint. Joining a conservative activist Court which was trained at state and federal economic regulations, in the midst of a rush of conservative activism Holmes' was reduced to dissenting in the most consequential opinions of the period. In addition to Lochner, Holmes also dissented in the two child labor cases and in the liberty to contract cases of the 1920s. His dissents occasionally placed him on the wrong side of history as he voted against Justice Hughes' Bailey decision which banned peonage laws as involuntary servitude. He also dissented when Justice McReynolds struck down a Nebraska ban on the teaching of German. He concurred in *Berea College v. Kentucky* as the Court upheld a state law banning private, integrated schools, thus placing him as a supporter of the Plessy doctrine of separate but equal.[66]

Holmes' restrained vision of the courts continued in *Giles v. Harris* as he refused to apply the Fifteenth Amendment in a voting rights case, asserting that voting qualifications represented a political question beyond the Court's jurisdiction.[67] Giles drew dissents from the usually conservative Justices Brewer and Brown and the reliably liberal Justice Harlan.

Even into his eighties, Holmes summoned a majority for innovative decisions including recognition of regulatory takings under the Fifth and Fourteenth Amendment. When the Pennsylvania Coal Company sued Pennsylvania over a law prohibiting undermining of residential areas, Holmes wrote the opinion recognizing regulatory takings. [68] The company claimed the ban on mining made mineral rights worthless and demanded compensation from the state. Holmes found that regulations were covered under the Fifth Amendment's Takings Clause and required the state to pay landowners when the regulation "went too far."[69]

The Pennsylvania Coal company decision drew a dissent from Holmes' usual ally, Justice Brandeis. When Brandeis joined the Court in 1916, the two men were joined in a relationship that would make both legends in their time. Holmes and Brandeis earned their fame in the sedition and espionage trials of World War One. Under Woodrow Wilson's Espionage Act, anti war newspapers were suppressed and dissidents jailed including Socialist Party leader Eugene Debs who was forced to run for president in 1920 from a jail cell.[70] Those caught up in the Wilson speech dragnet appealed their cases to the Supreme Court.

Holmes and Brandeis agreed on six of seven cases dealing with the Espionage Act after World War One. Holmes' opinion in Schenck was joined by Brandeis as was his opinion in *Debs v. United States.*[71] In Debs, Holmes let stand Debs' conviction and ten year prison sentence for making a speech critical of the war.

Holmes silently agreed when the Court upheld a Minnesota law prohibiting speeches critical of the war.[72] He could not find that the Federal Espionage Act precluded the state act or that the Minnesota law violated the First Amendment. Holmes also upheld the prosecution of a German language newspaper charged with violating the Espionage Act by giving aid and comfort to the enemy when it published stories opposing the American war effort.[73] In Gilbert and Frohwerk Brandeis split from Holmes, dissenting on First Amendment grounds.

In *Abrams v. United States*[74] Holmes and Brandeis criticized Justice Clarke's opinion expanding what constituted clear and present danger. They also dissented when the Court upheld a postal denial of a favorable postage rate to a German language newspaper accused of sedition by the Postmaster General.[75] They dissented in *Pierce v. United States*, taking issue with Justice Pitney's upholding prosecution of the publishers of an antiwar pamphlet. The majority and dissenting opinions became a duel of competing pamphlets as the justices reprinted the anti war messages contained in the Price We Pay, Pierce's feeble attempt to undermine the draft. Pitney found grave danger in the words while Holmes and Brandeis were more sanguine in their analysis. [76]

Holmes and Brandeis were in agreement in two seminal speech cases of the Taft Court. In Justice Sanford's Gitlow opinion, he recognized speech as a right protected under the Due Process Clause then upheld Gitlow's sedition conviction. In his dissent Holmes' added to his memorable phrasemaking noting that "Every idea is an incitement," a concise expression of his belief in a robust First Amendment. [77]

In *Whitney v. California* Sanford upheld a state sedition conviction for Charlotte Whitney for teaching communist doctrine. Brandeis concurred with

Holmes, finding that a conspiracy to commit violent acts existed in Whitney and constituted a clear and present danger.[78]

During the Taft Court of the 1920s, Brandeis became the dominant partner as Holmes approached his ninetieth birthday. As the elder justice passed the two decade mark and approached three decades he gave no sign of resigning even as he stated on multiple occasions he wished to retire in his seventies. Holmes believed his colleagues had remained on the Court even when enfeebled having witnessed younger men including William Moody and Mahlon Pitney ruined by illness and others such as Joseph McKenna hold onto his seat after losing his mental acuity.

Holmes would serve with twenty seven justices including four chiefs during six presidencies, becoming a fixture in the popular mind while gathering young lawyers around him including Felix Frankfurter and Alger Hiss. By 1932, though, Holmes had begun to slow and his colleagues considered how to approach their senior member on the subject. The scene has become part of Court lore as the ninety year old justice was approached by Chief Justice Hughes, who gently suggested retirement to the old justice. Holmes promptly and without dissent composed his retirement letter to President Hoover. His final act came as he left his entire estate to the federal government, which used it to compose a history of the United States Supreme Court.

## William Day

William Day was a conventional Republican in a conventionally Republican state, Ohio. A native of Canton, Day was a successful lawyer who developed a close friendship with William McKinley. After McKinley was elected president, Day was chosen for the State Department, running the department while the sitting Secretary of State, John Sherman, whiled away the months. After Sherman's retirement, Day was promoted, serving a brief time during the diplomatically tumultuous Spanish and American War and resigning in 1899 to become a federal appeals judge. From there he was plucked by McKinley's successor, Theodore Roosevelt, to replace the retiring Justice George Shiras. Consistent with his flair for the dramatic, Roosevelt announced his Supreme Court appointment during a Canton, Ohio speech celebrating William McKinley's life. As the president introduced honored guests he slipped in "Justice William Day," revealing Shiras' replacement without allowing Day to protest the selection.[79]

In his nineteen years as a justice from 1903 to1922, Day straddled the major issues of the era. On civil rights he represented the old Republican tradition of racial equality in *Buchanan v. Warley*.[80] Day struck down a Louisville, Kentucky ordinance mandating housing segregation and ruled segregation affecting property rights exceeded state authority. Day dissented in the Berea decision, arguing against the Kentucky school segregation law and joined Justice Hughes' Bailey decision striking the Alabama peonage law.

His most influential opinion came in *Weeks v. United States* as he built upon the Court's decision in Boyd and created an Exclusionary Rule for illegal searches by federal law enforcement. Weeks would be broadened in 1961 to include state law enforcement.

On economic issues Day tended to favor state economic regulations, dissenting in two major liberty to contract cases, Lochner and Coppage, which struck state laws. Day criticized the majority for striking a proper exercise of state police power to protect citizens' health, safety and welfare. He was less trusting of federal regulation though he authored *Hoke v. United States*[81] upholding the federal Mann Act and its ban on the transportation of women across state lines for the purpose of prostitution. Day recognized Congress' power to prohibit certain forms of interstate commerce because of their inherent evil.

The Hoke decision suggested Day would uphold other federal regulations but in considering the federal ban on child labor, Day composed his most cited and criticized opinion, *Hammer v. Dagenhart*.[82]

A flurry of legislation marked Woodrow Wilson's first two years in office, his New Freedom a smaller version of Franklin Roosevelt's New Deal and Lyndon Johnson's Great Society. Among the new laws was a ban on the interstate shipment of product made using child labor. In Hammer, Day rejected the interstate commerce argument for Keating Child Labor Act, ruling the ban on child labor struck at the states' authority to regulate labor. Because products made from child labor were not inherently dangerous, Congress had not authority to ban them in interstate commerce. Day reinvigorated the doctrine of dual federalism under which states had exclusive power over labor relations. Day maintained the high wall of separation between federal and state powers. Hammer was a startling reversal of course by a Court packed with political progressives from three progressive presidents.[83] Later Day joined the Drexel Furniture decision which struck down the federal Child Labor Tax, an attempt to evade his Hammer decision.

Hammer obscures all of Day's other work, placing him among the justices criticized by Franklin Roosevelt for "horse and buggy" legal reasoning. Day would serve a quiet career, resigning in November 1922, ill health and a hectoring Chief Justice Taft driving him from the Court.[84]

## Moody

Roosevelt's third and final Court appointment may have been his most disappointing. After the death of Justice Henry Brown, swing vote and author of *Plessy v. Ferguson*, Roosevelt was torn between choosing Horace Lurton, a federal appeals judge, and Attorney General William Moody. Lurton was a Democrat, a fact that drew fire Senator Henry Cabot Lodge, who advised Roosevelt to pick a Republican, which he did when selecting Moody. The attorney general rose to prominence with his aggressive pursuit of antitrust prosecution of the meat and oil trusts.[85]

Unfortunately Moody's promise as a progressive went unfulfilled during his four year tenure. Though adding a vote to the Court's progressive wing, Moody was restricted to two years of cognizant service which produced a pair of opinions, one upholding a federal law on workplace injuries, the other adding to the Court's incorporation doctrine.

Better known as the Liability Cases, *Howard v. Illinois Central Railroad Co.* challenged federal law making railroads liable for death or injury to their employees. Justice White and four justices ruled injury or death of employees was considered part of intrastate commerce or the old master servant distinction dating back to the common law, removing it from federal interstate regulation. Moody disagreed, arguing for an expanded interstate commerce clause which overrode the master servant distinction. He also noted railroads were engaged in interstate commerce and covered under Congress' regulatory authority.[86]

While the Liability cases were of immediate importance with little long term influence, Moody's opinion and reasoning in *Twining v. New Jersey* became the focus of the incorporation debate. Twining had been convicted of bank fraud after a trial in which he did not testify. Under New Jersey law the judge noted Twining's refusal to testify, allowing jurors to infer guilt from his remaining silent. Upon his conviction Twining appealed, stating his freedom from self incrimination had been violated by the judge. If his silence was used against him then he would be forced to testify, surrendering that right.[87]

Justice Moody wrote that the Fifth Amendment applied only to the federal government and that the due process clause of the Fourteenth Amendment did not include a right from self incrimination.

Moody enjoyed some influence during the Court's conference over the much debated Insular Cases. The justices were wrestling with the question of extending constitutional protections to newly annexed territories such as Hawaii and the Philippines. According to legend Moody scribbled a cartoon showing twelve tribesmen discarding their spears as they entered a courtroom in preparation for sitting on a jury. His work supposedly convinced his colleagues to limit the constitutional rights granted the native population. Shortly thereafter Moody was struck with arthritis, unable to continue as a functioning justice and forced to retire in 1910.[88]

## The Reagan (Judicial) Revolution

In the history of the American presidency many occupations have been represented including generals, lawyers, businessmen and professional politicians. In 1981 the first actor president was inaugurated as Ronald Reagan brought his big screen skills to the world stage. After making a successful speech for Barry Goldwater's doomed presidential campaign, Reagan served two terms as California governor then unsuccessfully challenged President Gerald Ford for the 1976 Republican nomination. In 1980 he ignored conventional wisdom that he was too old to run for president and defeated the unpopular Jimmy Carter.[89]

Reagan introduced a populist conservatism attacking big government intrusions into people's lives. Reagan's sought to reduce domestic government while defeating communism and removing the threat of nuclear war. His counterintuitive approach to nuclear weapons had the United States building more weapons as part of a strategy to bankrupt the Soviet empire.[90] Destroying communism while reviving the American economy would be Reagan's legacy along with a reinvigorated conservative movement.[91]

During his two terms Reagan utilized his Justice Department to remake the federal judiciary. An intense ideological vetting of judicial nominees ensured selection of movement conservatives and the creation of a reliable "junior varsity" for to future Republican presidents.[92] But Reagan enjoyed less success in choosing Supreme Court justices. Of his four appointments only two, William Rehnquist and Antonin Scalia, proved consistently conservative while Justices Sandra Day O'Connor and Anthony Kennedy disappointed conservatives in key opinions. , proved less consistently conservative. Reagan's nominees also suffered under a Torquemada like confirmation process as Senate hearings saw nominees' reputations and lives destroyed with innuendo and political smears.[93]

## Mrs. Justice O'Connor

Reagan's first Court appointment was foreordained during the 1980 general campaign. During a low point in his candidacy, Reagan promised to choose the first female justice. Justice Potter Stewart's sudden resignation in 1981 sent the administration scrambling to fulfill the president's promise and Reagan struggled to find federal court judges who were both conservatives and women, Reagan settled on an Arizona State Supreme Court justice, Sandra Day O'Connor. A classmate of William Rehnquist at Stanford Law School her career path took a different course. While Rehnquist earned a clerkship with Justice Robert Jackson, O'Connor was reduced into becoming a legal secretary at a small firm.[94] Later elected to the state legislature, she served as the state senate majority leader. As the first female nominee, O'Connor was handled with kid gloves by Democrats and unanimously confirmed. [95]

O'Connor sought a middle ground in abortion, affirmative action and religious issues. Unlike her fellow Reagan appointees, O'Connor trimmed at rather than overruled precedent, preferring to limit the more extreme parts of social policy created during the Warren and Burger Courts. Her moderate image made her a swing vote, much like Justice Stewart and her constitutional agenda proved remarkably pliable and driven more by politics than a core ideology.[96]

Two opinions on the Takings Clause exemplify O'Connor's approach. In *Hawaii Housing Authority v. Midkiff*,[97] O'Connor upheld a state seizure of private property against a claim that redistribution of private property did not constitute public use under the Takings Clause.[98] In Midkiff O'Connor upheld the seizure of private land and its distribution as serving a public purpose, therefore granting government discretion in choosing how to dispose of private property.[99]

Twenty one years later O'Connor dissented when local government seized property for a redevelopment project. In Kelo O'Connor distinguished the seizure of private property for private redevelopment from the Midkiff policy of distributing property to effect a redistribution of property. Yet the justice's distinctions proved hollow suggesting O'Connor was trying to hide the fact she had changed her mind on the issue. [100]

During the Burger Court, O'Connor was a consistent vote against abortion and affirmative action while supporting government in criminal justices cases. Yet for many conservatives, her opinions were off key, as she followed a cautious view of judging that protected the Court's political standing. Her incremental approach to changing the law by rejecting bright lines and absolutist decisions irritated Justice Scalia, who clashed with O'Connor in their approach to judging. [101]

As the Rehnquist Court progressed, O'Connor established her role as a cautious conservative, an approach apparent in her Croson opinion striking down a Richmond affirmative action policy as overly broad.[102] Justice Scalia concurred in Croson, arguing for a complete rejection of all affirmative action policies, an approach O'Connor rejected. In *Employment Division v. Smith*, O'Connor was in the opposite position, concurring with Justice Scalia in a Free Exercise case. Scalia rewrote the Free Exercise doctrine, creating a general applicability standard that O'Connor rejected. O'Connor preferred to maintain the strict scrutiny standard which she used to also reject Smith's claim of a Free Exercise violation. [103]

In Establishment Clause cases O'Connor steered a course between the status quo, in the form of the Lemon test, and the accommodationist policies favored by Justice Scalia. Her major contribution to these changes came in *Agostini v. Felton*, which overruled the Aguilar case. O'Connor reinterpreted the Lemon test by deemphasizing the excessive entanglement portion of the test and ruling that remedial classes taught by public school teachers in parochial schools did not advance religion, the second part of the Lemon test. [104]

Yet O'Connor refused to abandon the Lemon test in total. She concurred in *Mitchell v. Helms*, when Justice Thomas sought to eliminate the advancement of religion portion of the test. [105] O'Connor rejected Thomas' approach, preferring to reinterpret the test to allow greater church state accommodation rather than creating a new test. She also concurred in *Zelman v. Harris Simmons*, as the Court upheld a Cleveland school voucher plan, providing public funds for students to attend religious schools.[106] O'Connor focused on the practical aspects of the program, relying on statistical evidence and financial claims, noting that the decision adhered to past Establishment opinions.

As the first female justice O'Connor was expected to bring a different perspective to sex discrimination, abortion and personal privacy issues. In the early 1980s O'Connor carved out a niche on the abortion issue. In a 1983 dissent

O'Connor opposed the striking of an Akron, Ohio ordinance requiring abortions be performed in hospitals and odering the "humane" disposal of an aborted baby. In her dissent O'Connor laid out her undue burden test which would eventually replace the three trimester test developed in Roe.[107]

Her doctrine was revived in *Webster v. Reproductive Services* as O'Connor joined Chief Justice Rehnquist's opinion upholding notification and waiting period requirements in a Missouri law. In a concurring opinion O'Connor added that the Missouri regulations did not unconstitutionally burden abortion.[108] *Planned Parenthood v. Casey* would make the undue burden test the law even as it made no appreciable difference in the abortion right.[109]

After Casey the justices avoided the abortion issue until *Stenberg v. Carhart.*[110] In Stenberg the Court split over state laws prohibiting the gruesome procedure known as partial birth abortion. O'Connor adhered to her undue burden test and provided the deciding vote in striking the law. O'Connor's pivotal role on partial birth abortion was made more stark in 2007 as a new five member majority upheld a federal ban on partial birth abortion. O'Connor's replacement, Justice Alito, provided the decisive vote in favor of the federal law.[111]

The first female justice was also expected to bring a different perspective on gender discrimination. Suspicious of affirmative action policies involving race, O'Connor proved more supportive of gender policies. In *Johnson v. Transportation Agency,* O'Connor joined the majority in upholding an affirmative action program hiring and promoting women in state transportation jobs. In a separate opinion she expressed little faith in the statistical arguments used to prove discrimination in the past – forcing companies to meet statistical quotas – but noted that the transportation agency being sued had no female employees working at certain jobs. For O'Connor, this bare statistic was enough to prove discrimination. [112]

If O'Connor's approach on social issues curbed rather than overruled excesses from the past, O'Connor proved a hard liner on criminal defense issues and federalism. Having served as a state judge, O'Connor had a decided bias against federal interference in state trials. She led the charge to limit challenges to state court verdicts in federal court and in *Teague v. Lane*, limited the number of appeals filed by convicted criminals and speeding the process of hearing and deciding appeals. [113] In *Coleman v. Thompson* she rejected a death row inmate's federal appeal because he had not filed his state appeal within the time limit set by the state. O'Connor characterized the case as an issue of federalism, drawing hoots from within the Court.[114]

O'Connor's hard line approach to criminal case came to the fore in *Herrera v. Collins*, as the justices considered whether a deathbed confession was sufficient evidence to halt an execution. Justice O'Connor concurred with Justice Rehnquist's opinion that the confession was insufficient to warrant a new trial then adopted the tone of a trial attorney in closing arguments, declaring "the conclusion seems inescapable: the petitioner is guilty."[115]

O'Connor was consistent in supporting states and vibrant federalism. O'Connor voted to strike a federal requirement that states raise their drinking age in order to receive federal highway funds,[116] composed the opinion striking down a federal requirement that states handle nuclear waste within their borders,[117] concurred in an opinion upholding mandatory retirement ages for state judges[118] and voted with the majority applying the Eleventh Amendment to protect states from lawsuits in federal court.[119]

O'Connor's role as a swing justice derived from disagreements with her fellow Reagan appointee, Antonin Scalia. Determined to rewrite Warren and Burger Court precedent, Scalia was driven to distraction by O'Connor's restraint. In a series of separate opinions Scalia rebuked O'Connor for her fuzzy thinking and pedantic writing. A narrative developed among Court observers that Scalia's panegyrics offended the only female justice, driving a wedge between the Reagan justices and weakening the Court.

While insulted by Scalia O'Connor was supposedly influenced by William Brennan in the Johnson affirmative action case and others. The opposite proved true as O'Connor despised Brennan, offended by his intense lobbying that included touching his colleagues. She refused to attend a ceremony honoring Brennan and also did not attend his funeral.[120]

## Rehnquist, Scalia and Kennedy

In 1981 Justice Stewart was provoked into retirement by a high school student's letter. Five years later, Chief Justice Burger left the Court also under unusual circumstances, resigning to promote the Constitution's bicentennial. For a chief known for an obsession with ceremony and the prerogatives of office, it was a fitting end to Burger's tenure. [121]

Reagan seized the opportunity, making a double appointment. He promoted Justice William Rehnquist to chief justice and selected D.C. circuit judge Antonin Scalia to replace Rehnquist as an associate. Scalia was shielded from Senate Democrat criticism which focused on Rehnquist. Both men survived the confirmation process and were mainstays on the Court's right flank.[122]

In 1987 Justice Powell resigned, removing a key vote on social issues including abortion and affirmative action. The 1986 midterm elections had produced a Democrat Senate, complicating the appointment process. When Reagan nominated D.C. circuit judge Robert Bork, Democrat senators tripped over each other to denounce Bork as favoring a return to back alley abortions, segregated lunch counters and slavery![123] The Senate hearings resembled a show trial and Bork received most negative votes of any Court nominee, fifty eight, and added a new word into the crowded Washington lexicon, Borked.

Reagan responded by choosing a more conservative and younger nominee, Douglas Ginsburg, who would tripped up by his penchant for enjoying a marijuana toke with his Yale law students. After Ginsburg pulled out of the process, Reagan sought a nominee who lacked a record or history of sixties' style flashbacks. In early 1988, an exhausted Senate approved Anthony Kennedy, a judge from the Ninth Circuit Court of Appeals.

## Chief Justice Rehnquist

Reagan's promotion of William Rehnquist to chief justice was a reward to the man once dubbed the Lone Ranger for his solitary dissents against what he considered liberal excess. Rehnquist immediately changed the tenor of the Court, his genial personality and quick intelligence making him a favorite of conservative and liberal justices alike. Having suffered under Warren Burger's chaotic tenure, Rehnquist brought order to the Court, tightly controlling debate during the weekly conference while limiting the justices' workload and the number of separate opinions read in open Court.[124] Journalistic accounts of the Burger Court had portrayed an institution beset by conflict and chaos. The sole insider account of the Rehnquist Court revealed a level of collegiality among the justices and adolescent behavior among their clerks.[125]

While improving morale and efficiency, Rehnquist suffered from some of the same impediments as his predecessor in moving the Court significantly right. Success came in the 1988 and 1989 terms as the Court reinterpreted affirmative action and employment law. The justices also redefined Free Exercise Clause doctrine and the most controversial case of the period, Rehnquist cut back on the abortion right in *Webster v. Planned Parenthood.*[126]

Rehnquist's legal success did not transfer into the political arena. Many of the Court's more controversial opinions from 1988 to 1991 were overturned in the 1991 Civil Rights Act. Public and congressional criticism of the decisions made his colleagues more circumspect in their decisions. The end of the 1991 term saw three usually dependable conservatives refused to overturn *Roe v. Wade* and in doing so slowing Rehnquist's momentum.

The 1994 Republican midterm sweep provided the Court with political cover for far reaching opinions. Rehnquist's opinion in *United States v. Lopez*[127] reinstated the clause as a limit on federal power. Lopez challenged the 1990 Gun Free School Zone Act which made it a federal crime to have guns on school property. Speaking for five members, Rehnquist was not convinced by the convoluted explanation given by the government to show how the gun ban was a commerce regulation.[128] Instead Rehnquist ruled that banning guns at high schools was a general criminal law outside congressional power. Lopez would have to be prosecuted under Texas law, the proper venue for criminal cases. With the Lopez case Congress was put on notice that the Court would look closely at the connection between a law and its supposed regulation of commerce.

A short time later the Court undid a 1990 precedent and ruled that federal affirmative action laws would be treated like any other legislation that used race to assign contracts, making it more difficult for the Federal Government to make race a determining factor in who received public monies.[129] The Court also overturned a Boston gay rights law requiring the city's St. Patrick's Day parade to include gays,[130] extended the right to religious speech in two cases,[131] allowed schools to mandate drug testing for high school athletes[132] and reined in federal judges in desegregation cases.[133] The latter case was written by Rehnquist, who criticized federal judges operating school districts. The Kansas City School District had been under federal judicial control for nearly twenty years and during that time the federal courts had ordered tax increases and mandated spending on everything from athletic fields to higher teacher salaries. By 1995 many local residents had enough of sky high taxes without representation and Rehnquist agreed, limiting judicial authority in integration cases.[134]

As an associate justice, Rehnquist failed to revive the Tenth Amendment. As chief justice he rekindled federalism through the obscure Eleventh Amendment. Ratified in 1798, amendment banned citizens from suing their state governments in federal courts. In *Seminole Tribe v. Florida*[135] Rehnquist led five justices in striking a federal law allowing the tribe to sue Florida over a law concerning casinos in Indian reservations. According to Rehnquist, the Eleventh Amendment blocked such suits unless the state waived its sovereign immunity. After the Seminole decision, the Eleventh Amendment became the hot topic among constitutional lawyers and for the next several years the Rehnquist Court expanded immunity in criminal cases,[136] age discrimination cases,[137] disability cases[138] and lawsuits filed by Indian tribes.[139]

During Bill Clinton's second term, the Rehnquist Court was swept up in scandal politics. When Paula Jones sued President Bill Clinton for sexual harassment, Clinton claimed immunity from the lawsuit until he left office. The Court rejected his arguments, finding that executive immunity did not extend to official or personal behavior and allowed the suit to continue. [140] In allowing Jones' lawsuit to continue during Clinton's presidency, the Supreme Court set into motion events ending in a presidential impeachment trial, which would be presided over by William Rehnquist.

The 1999 impeachment trial of President Bill Clinton was only the second in American history but proved less climactic than that of President Andrew Johnson. At no time was Clinton in danger of being removed from office and Rehnquist's role was limited to silently presiding then playing poker in a back room while senators worked out a face saving compromise.[141]

The Rehnquist's Court most famous dispute came *in Bush v. Gore* as the justices set aside state court rulings for Gore in the 2000 disputed presidential election.[142] In doing so the justices halted another in a series of vote recounts, ending the election and making George W. Bush president. The Court was criticized for playing partisan politics but the decision likely prevented a constitutional crisis. In 2004 Rehnquist was diagnosed with thyroid cancers, missing much of the 2004 term even as he made a dramatic entrance into George Bush's second inauguration and remained long enough to swear in the president. Rehnquist would later die in August, 2005.

## Antonin Scalia

Reagan's ranking among the top tier of presidents in the Supreme Court survey is partly based on his appointing legal technicians such as Sandra Day O'Connor and social leaders such as William Rehnquist and the most doctrinaire conservative justice since the 1930s, Antonin Scalia. Unlike many of his Republican colleagues, Scalia was not one to agonize over his decisions or swing with public opinion or conventional wisdom. He rejected balancing tests in constitutional cases preferring bright line rules that were supposed to remove the political element to judging, with mixed results.

Outside the Court Scalia made public statements attracting the type of public attention most justices avoid. Speaking to conservative groups, he bemoaned the treatment of religious beliefs in the public square, criticized the Court's recent opinions on rights of terrorists held in Guantanamo Bay, stated his own views on the meaning of torture and blasted attempts to have the Pledge of Allegiance struck down as unconstitutional. The latter forced him into a recusal, leaving an eight member Court to produce an unsatisfactory opinion in *Elkgrove School District v. Newdow.*[143]

Scalia's scathing dissents targeted his colleagues' sloppy analyses, as he saw it, with Justice O'Connor bearing the brunt of his tart tongue. Her painfully precise, and at times, pedantic opinions drove Scalia to distraction. Scalia berated her concurrence in *Webster v. Reproductive Services*, arguing her reasoning "could not be taken seriously" by anyone "who could read or count."[144] Such comments were the equivalent of fighting words in the Supreme Court and O'Connor would later ridicule Scalia's absolutist approach.[145] In *Casey v. Planned Parenthood* he tore at O'Connor's compromise opinion, declaring it little more than "a collection of adjectives that simply decorate a value judgment and conceal political choices." He quoted Justice Curtis' dissent in Dred Scott, equating that decision with abortion rights while declaring the Casey decision "was more than one should have to bear."[146]

Even with his over the top rhetoric, Scalia offered his own vision of the constitution, one relying on tradition. He dismissed claims of a living constitution, relying instead on traditional interpretation and consensus about constitutional rights. His reliance on tradition is exemplified in two First Amendment cases involving election campaigning and nude dancing.

*Burson v. Freeman* challenged a Tennessee law prohibiting electioneering within one hundred feet of a polling place. Freeman was fined when she attempted to pass out campaign material within the restricted area. In a typically long winded and complicated opinion, Justice Blackmun found the state had a compelling interest in restricting speech. Concurring, Scalia wrote that the Tennessee's law dated back nearly a century and was similar to laws passed in nearly all of the states to prevent voter intimidation. Because the laws were accepted tradition and never considered a violation of free speech rights, no modern court could suddenly discover the laws were unconstitutional. For Scalia, tradition trumped modern constitutional doctrine.[147]

In *Barnes v. Glen Theatre* Scalia agreed with Rehnquist's opinion upholding a ban on nude dancing. He rejected the complex four part text using by Rehnquist, instead focusing on the tradition of public nudity laws. He relied on a rational basis test and found the ban was rationally related to maintaining public order.[148]

Scalia's bow to tradition did not inhibit him from overruling precedent. In *Employment Division v. Smith* Scalia upheld the decision by Oregon to deny Smith unemployment benefits because of his drug use. In the opinion he swept away the strict scrutiny standard used in previous free exercise cases and replaced it with a bright line rule. Under the rule generally applicable laws could limit religious exercise as long as the laws did not explicitly target religious practices.[149]

His crusade for bright lines rather than balancing tests in speech cases included religious speech disputes. After concurring in opinions that used the vague and flexible Lemon test for Establishment Clause cases, Scalia used his opinion in *Capitol Square Review Board v. Pinette* to push for a clearer standard. When Pinette was denied permission to place a cross in the Ohio Capitol square because of its religious connotation – and Pinette's Klan affiliation – Scalia seized the opportunity to expand on the religious speech doctrine. According to Scalia private religious speech could never be banned in a public forum, such as the capitol square because the Establishment Clause only forbade government endorsed religious speech.[150]

Scalia's most fervid opinions coincided with his desire to overturn *Roe v. Wade*. At times the justice seemed driven to distraction by his colleagues' tinkering with abortion rights but faced with a majority unwilling to follow his lead, the justice sought to undermine pro abortion groups and prop up anti abortion groups. One of his greatest abortion victories occurred in *Bray v. Alexandria*. In Bray, abortion supporters sought to use the federal antiracketeering statute known as RICO, to have anti abortion protesters charged under federal law as if they were members of the mafia. Under RICO, attempts to undermine legitimate business with threats or use of force could garner the guilty party jail time and hefty fines. Scalia rejected the claim, ruling the right to an abortion was protected from government interference rather than private interference and thus there could be no conspiracy against that public right.[151]

Scalia also pushed hard to remove a judicial weapon used against anti abortion protesters, the federal court injunction. In *Madsen v. Women's Clinic*, Chief Justice Rehnquist upheld several restrictions placed on abortion protesters by a federal judge. Scalia dissented in those instances, writing a sweeping argument that would have weakened federal injunction powers. The justice wanted all injunctions covered under the heightened scrutiny standard usually reserved for laws governing speech or other fundamental rights. Scalia charged that injunctions used to squelch protests should be treated the same as laws doing the same and could be upheld only if the judge could show a compelling interest and that the injunction was narrowly tailored so as not to limit too much speech. Using Scalia's reasoning the Madsen injunction would have been struck down on those grounds as would other federal injunctions against abortion protests. [152] Scalia's Madsen dissent recalled the progressive era battles over federal injunctions against unions and labor protests.[153] But as with the justices of that era, Scalia was unable to attract a majority, speaking for only three justices in dissent and the injunction remained in force.

Scalia's influence extended into the twenty first century as he took pruning shears to what he considered the overreaching of the Warren and Burger Courts. In *Vieth v. Jubelirer* he tackled two issues, legislative gerrymandering and the political question doctrine. Since the 1960s the Court had become entangled in the political thicket of legislative redistricting, creating a set of standards legislatures should follow in drawing district boundaries. In Vieth Scalia attempted to push aside those using the political question doctrine. Joined by three justices, he found that the drawing of district boundaries was nonjusticiable and beyond the Court's expertise. Scalia wanted to overrule Justice Whites Bandemer decision that had cast doubt on the constitutionality of gerrymandering and return to Justice Frankfurter's Colgrove standard. [154]

Scalia regained some influence as the Rehnquist Court passed to the Roberts Court. A challenge to a District of Columbia handgun ban offered him the opportunity to revive the Second Amendment. After Heller was rejected for a handgun permit by the district he challenged its ban on handgun possession. His arguments focused on the Second Amendment and a claim that it protected an individual right to keep and bear arms. Writing for a five member majority, Scalia analyzed the amendment's meaning, focusing on key phrases such as "bearing arms," "the right of the people" and "a well regulated militia." His historical emphasis was a shift from the usual balancing test argument used by the Court in defining individual rights.[155] While Scalia struck down the gun ban and identified an individual right to keep and bear arms he left open questions of whether the Second Amendment applied to state and local gun laws and the degree of gun regulation allowed under the amendment. Yet Heller represented a victory for Scalia in striking at gun control laws. Closing in on a quarter century of service, Scalia remained the intellectual leader of the conservative bloc, neither age nor experience toning down his criticism of his predecessors or colleagues or his perception of their misguided analysis.

## Anthony Kennedy

By far the least predictable of the Reagan appointees, Kennedy began his tenure as the swing vote in a five member majority rewriting civil rights laws, free exercise law, abortion and discrimination law. Kennedy appeared to have embraced Justice Scalia's views and rhetoric as he accused liberal justices of antagonism toward religion in striking down a Christmas nativity display.[156] The conservative successes during the 1989 term provoked a congressional reaction as the Democrat controlled Congress used its political muscle to snap back the justices, passing the 1991 Civil Rights Act to overturn some of the decisions.

Congressional irritation halted Kennedy's slide to the right and in 1992 Kennedy penned *Lee v. Weisman*, an oddly reasoned opinion that redefined religious coercion to include hurt feelings.[157] Possibly hoping to silence criticism from the left for joining the likes of Chief Justice Rehnquist and Justice Scalia, he found himself hit by a barrage from the right for consorting with the wrong element including Justices Blackmun and Stevens.[158]

Kennedy tacked right during the 1994 term as the Court revived the Commerce Clause, struck at federal affirmative action and took another stab at defining the Establishment Clause. [159] Kennedy proved to be the fifth and deciding vote in each of the cases. His only deviation occurred in *U.S. Term Limits Inc. v. Thornton*[160] striking down congressional term limits passed by the Arkansas state legislature.[161] Besides Thornton, though, Kennedy proved a loyal soldier in igniting a conservative legal doctrine, contributing opinions in the obscure subject of state sovereign immunity.

Using historical analysis in *Alden v. Maine*, Kennedy overturned part of the 1938 Fair Labor Standards Act allowing individuals to sue in state courts. [162] In *Idaho v. Coeur d'Alene*, Kennedy extended a Scalia opinion granting states immunity from lawsuits filed by Indian tribes.[163] By tackling an issue that was off the political radar screen, Kennedy escaped the scathing criticism from his early years on the Court. His reintroduction to the conservative bloc continued in *Stenberg v. Carhart* where five justices struck down a state ban on partial birth abortions. Kennedy agreed with the dissenters in approving a total ban on a form of abortion and seemed to step from back from his pro abortion ruling in Casey.[164]

Kennedy's flirtation with the conservatives ended abruptly in 2003 with *Lawrence v. Texas* as Kennedy overturned Bowers v. Hardwick, which had upheld state sodomy laws. According to Kennedy, the amendment targeted a minority based on sexual orientation. He found that the state's belief homosexual conduct was immoral was insufficient reason for banning the conduct. [165]

Kennedy also delivered a blow to one of the conservative's favorite obscure constitutional provision, the Twenty First Amendment. In *Granholm v. Heald*, Michigan's regulation of out of state wineries was challenged as a regulation of interstate commerce, a power reserved for Congress. Under the interstate commerce clause, only Congress could regulate products shipped across state lines, but the Twenty First Amendment granted states absolute authority over alcohol within their borders.[166]

In Heald, Kennedy wrote for a five member majority that found the commerce clause prohibited states from favoring in state wineries at the expense of out of state wineries. According to Kennedy, the Twenty First Amendment was not intended to allow for commercial discrimination but only gave the states the power to prohibit alcohol within the state.[167]

In Kennedy's twentieth year on the Court he remains an enigma. Accused of being easily manipulated by his clerks and too easily swayed by political opinion, Kennedy has proved influential in the mode of a Potter Stewart or Lewis Powell rather than an Antonin Scalia or William Brennan. Kennedy slowed rather than halted the Court's move to the right, composing conservative opinions then retreating when the Court appeared politically threatened. The departure of Justice O'Connor in 2006 and her replacement by the conservative Justice Alito may have heightened Kennedy's importance as a swing justice.

President Reagan's four Supreme Court appointments shifted the institution to the right even as it disappointed some in the conservative movement who sought a wholesale repudiation of the Warren and Burger Courts. The Rehnquist Court was nearly wholly a Reagan creation, his successor and vice president appointing two more justices, the Reagan-Bush half dozen dominating the instution until Rehnquist's death in 2005. During that time Reagan's justices reinvigorated federalism and a more restrained view of the judiciary exemplified by the rapid decrease in the number of decisions handed down by the Court. Finally by appointing younger justices, Reagan extended his influence far beyond his presidency, including settling an electoral dispute and extending Republican dominance of the executive for another eight years.

## Notes

1. Possibly the most egregious of these came in Kansas City, Missouri as a federal judge seized power over the city's school district and implemented a policy of higher taxes, more spending and expensive programs all in the name of advancing educational opportunity. The result was a bloated school system with a higher dropout rate and a bureaucracy that was answerable to no one.
See *Missouri v. Jenkins* 495 U.S. 133 (1990)

2. Silver, David, *Lincoln's Supreme Court* (Champaign IL: University of Illinois Press, 1998), 48-49. Miller was ranked among the top of fifteen near Greats, Blaustein and Mersky, 46.

3. Labbie, Ronald and Jonathan Lurie, *The Slaughterhouse Cases* (Lawrence KS: University of Kansas Press, 2003), 170-171.

4. 68 U.S. 175, 204 (1864)

5. Ross, Michael, *Justice of Shattered Dreams* (Baton Rouge LA: Louisiana State University Press, 2003), 90-91.

6. 75 U.S. 575 (1869),86 U.S. 107 (1873)

7. 80 U.S. 654, 656 (1871)

8. 83 U.S. 36, 129 (1873)

9. Fairman, Charles, *Mr. Justice Miller and the Supreme Court* (Cambridge MA: Harvard University Press, 1937), 100.

10. 102 U.S. 586 (1881)
11. 83 U.S. 36 (1873)
12. Ross, 168-169
13. Ross, 222
14. Ross, 224-225
15. 100 U.S. 82 (1879)
16. *Kilbourne v. Thompson* 103 U.S. 168, 190, 194-195 (1880)
17. *Cunningham v. Neagle* 135 U.S. 1,59-60 (1890)
18. King, Willard, *Lincoln's Manager* (Cambridge: Harvard University Press 1960), 136-137; Donald 248-249.
19. 71 U.S. 2 (1866)
20. King, 279-281
21. Rehnquist, 141
22. King, 299- 300
23. Kens, Paul, *Stephen Field* (Lawrence, KS: University of Kansas Press, 1997), 59.
24. 71 U.S. 277 (1867)
25. 71 U.S. 333 (1867)
26. 103 U.S. 370, 402
27. *Chinese Exclusion Cases*130 U.S. 581 (1889)
28. 83 U.S. 36, 90
29. 83 U.S. 36, 91
30. 83 U.S. 36, 93-94
31. 83 U.S. 36, 84 (1873)
32. 94 U.S. 113, 143-144(1877)
33. Swisher, Carl Brent, *Justice Stephen J. Field* (Chicago:University of Chicago Press, 1967), 278-280.
34. Field, Stephen, *Personal Reminiscences of Early Days in California* (Cambridge MA.: De Capo Press, 1968).
35. Swisher, 288-289
36. Swisher, 289-290
37. Swisher, 297
38. Swisher, 307
39. Kens, 275-278
40. *In re Neagle* 135 U.S. 1(1890)
41. 157 U.S. 429 (1895)
42. 157 U.S. 429, 608
43. Bushrod Washington 1798-1829, John Marshall 1801-1835, Joseph Story 1811-1845, William Johnson 1804-1834 and John McLean 1829-1861.
44. King, Willard, *Melville Weston Fuller* (Chicago: University of Chicago Press, 1950), 225-227.
45. Donald, David Herbert, *Lincoln* ( New York:Simon and Schuster, 1996), 249.

46. Donald, 508

47. Part of that punishment was a prospective reduction in the size of the Supreme Court as Congress expected Justice Grier to retire creating a vacancy thatwould not be filled. Niven, 410.Congress annually appropriated money forten justices since 1863 but as the number of justices dwindled, the appropriations remained thesame.Chase allowed Congress to take thesalaries of the vacant seats andspend it elsewhere rather than dividing it among his colleagues and providingthem with a pay raise.

48. Niven, John, *Salmon P. Chase* (London: Oxford University Press, 1995), 395.

49. Nevin, 417

50. *Ex Parte Yerger* 75 U.S. 85 (1868)

51. Hyman, Harold, *The Reconstruction Justice of Salmon Chase* (University Press of Kansas, 1997), 124-125.

52. *Mississippi v. Johnson* 71 U.S. 475 499, 501-502 (1867)

53. 71 U.S. 2, 141-142 (1866)

54. 74 U.S. 700(1869)

55. 80 U.S. 654, 663-664 (1871)

56. 75 U.S. 603 (1870)

57. Nevin, 440-441

58. Nevin, 418- 420

59. Nevin, 423

60. Nevin, 421

61. Sprague and Tilden headed up the Committee of One Hundred which were delegates pledged to Chase before the convention began.Franklin, John Hope, "The Election of 1868" in *History of American Elections* eds. Schlesinger, Arthur Jr. and Fred Israel, (New York: Chelsea House Publishers, 1971), 1256.

62. Franklin,1254

63. 198 U.S. 45, 76 (1905)

64. 249 U.S. 393 (1919)

65. 274 U.S. 200, 208. (1927)Holmes went further in his call for eugenics, warning that without such sterilization policies the country was faced with being "swamped with incompetence" and that society would face the unpleasant choice of either "executing (Buck's) degenerate offspring for crime," or "let(ting) them starve for the imbecility." Novick, Sheldon, *Honorable Justice* (New York: Little Brown and Co, 1989), 351-352.

66. 211 U.S. 45 (1908)

67. 189 U.S. 475 (1903)

68. *Pennsylvania Coal v. Mahon* 260 U.S. 393 (1922).

69. 260 U.S. 393, 416

70. In a startling turnabout of ideology, Wilson the progressive jailed Debs while the supposedly arch conservative Warren Harding pardoned Debs upon

entering office.

71. 249 U.S. 211 (1919)

72. *Gilbert v. Minnesota* 254 U.S. 325 (1920)

73. *Frohwerk v. United States* 249 U.S. 204 (1919)

74. 250 U.S. 616 (1919)

75. *Milwaukee Social Democrat Publishing Co. v. Burleson* 255 U.S. 407 (1921)

76. 250 U.S. 239 (1920)

77. *Gitlow v. New York*268 U.S. 652,674 (1925)

78. 274 U.S. 357 (1927)

79. Bickel and Schmidt, 73

80. 245 U.S. 60 (1917)

81. 227 U.S. 308 (1913)

82. 247 U.S. 620 (1918)

83. 247 U.S. 251 (1918)

84. The decision advanced passage of a federal constitutional amendment banning child labor.The advent of the New Deal and a shift in the Court made the amendment a redundancy and it remains unratified to this day.

85. Lurton would be appointed to the Supreme Court four years later by President William Howard Taft.

86. 207 U.S. 463 (1908)

87. 211 U.S. 78 (1908)

88. Highsaw, 186

89. Hayward, Steven, *The Age of Reagan* (New York: Primus Life, 2001), 483- 484.

90. Schweizer, Peter, *Reagan's War* (New York: Anchor Books, 2003), 141.

91. Reeves, Richard, *President Reagan* (New York: Simon and Schuster 2006), 477.

92. Schwartz, Herman, *Right Wing Justice* (New York: Nation Books, 2004), 62- 63.

93. Comiskey, Michael, *Seeking Justices* (Lawrence KS: University of Kansas Press, 2004), 505.

94. Maveety, Nancy, *Justice Sandra Day O'Connor* (New York: Rowman Littlefield, 2002), 15-16.

95. Maveety, 18

96. One biographer deemed her approach as jurisprudential accomodationist, academic speak for a conservative fact based approach to the law and an aversion to overturning precedent. Maveety, 30.

97. 467 U.S. 229 (1984)

98. The state scheme was part of a redistributionist policy that sought to divide land more equally as land ownership on the islands was limited to a small percentage of citizens.

99. In a few short paragraphs O'Connor dismissed the argument that public use did not include private ownership of land but instead required government to show some public purpose in their seizure of private property.

100. *Kelo v. New London Connecticut* (2005). The city of New London seized private property to sell it to the Pfizer Corporation for the hope that the land would be redeveloped and provide more economic growth and tax revenues than the current property.

101. A prime example came near the end of O'Connor's tenure. In *Lawrence v. Texas*, O'Connor concurred as the Court struck a Texas anti-sodomy law while distinguishing it from the law she voted to uphold in *Bowers v. Hardwick*. In a tedious opinion, she found the Texas law banned only homosexual sodomy, a clear attack on a disfavored group, while the Georgia law banned all forms of sodomy, an attack on a disfavored activity. According to O'Connor the Texas law violated liberty while the Georgia law did not. Lawrence exemplified how O'Connor remained a moderate force while upholding a precedent she helped create.

102. *Richmond v. Croson* 488 U.S. 469 (1989). The Richmond affirmative action plan prohibited discrimination against Aleuts and other minority groups not generally found in Virginia, a point of emphasis for O'Connor.

103. 494 U.S. 872 (1990)

104. 521 U.S. 203 (1997)

105. 500 U.S. 793 (2000)

106. 536 U.S. 639 (2002)

107. *Akron v. Akron Center* 462 U.S. 416, 454 (1983). Justices Rehnquist and White, the original dissenters in Roe v. Wade, may have been surprised that they were signing onto an opinion that would be used nine years later to uphold the very abortion right they wanted overturned.

108. *Webster v. Reproductive Health Services* 492 U.S. 490, 522 (1989)

109. *Planned Parenthood v. Casey* 505 U.S. 833 (1992)

110. 530 U.S. 914 (2000)

111. *Gonzales v. Carhart* 505 U.S. 124 (2007)

112. 480 U.S. 616, 657 (1987)

113. 489 U.S. 288 (1989) O'Connor tried to preserve her reputation as a moderate conservative by linking her opinion to Justice Harlan's concurrence in *Mackey v. U.S.* 401 U.S. 667 (1971). Harlan established rules for when retroactive application of a Court ruling, a key part of the Teague opinion. Harlan was seen by his colleagues and Courtobservers as a "true judge" who was moderate and non ideological in his rulings, the role O'Connoryearned to assume in the Rehnquist Court.O'Connor also took the unusual step of overruling a Warren Court precedent, *Fay v. Noia* 372 U.S. 391 (1963), the creation of her old adversary, William Brennan.

114. 501 U.S. 722 (1991) "This is a case about federalism," began her opinion, a broad hint that Coleman's appeal was not going to win, 501 U.S. 722,

727. The hoots came from some of the clerks opposing capital punishment, Lazarus, 498.

115. 506 U.S. 390, 425 (1993)

116. *South Dakota v. Dole* 483 U.S. 203 (1987). O'Connor dissented, claiming the Twenty First Amendment gave states complete power over alcohol regulations, including setting a driving age, and that the federal government could not place restrictions on state power, 483 U.S. 203, 212. Oddly enough, O'Connor was joined by Justice Brennan, the one member of the Court with whom she always had a strained relationship.

117. *New York v. United States* 505 U.S. 144 (1992). New York was forced to either dispose of nuclear waste at its own cost or pay a hefty fine to the federal government to complete the task.O'Connor found the two bad alternatives eliminated the state's police powers under the Tenth Amendment, representing the first time since the 1930sthat the Court used the Tenth Amendment to limit federal power.

118. *Gregory v. Ashcroft* 501 U.S. 452 (1991). O'Connor revived the old argument whether federal anti discrimination laws applied to state employees and found that they did not when it came to mandatory retirement ages for judges.O'Connor narrowly read federal law, ruling state judges were policymakers exempt from federal agediscrimination laws.

119. *Seminole Tribe v. Florida* 517 U.S. 44 (1996)

120. Maveety, 74

121. Savage, David, *Turning Right* (New York: John Wiley and Sons, 1993), 5.

122. Savage, 8-9,24-25

123. Bork, Robert, *The Tempting of America* (New York:The Free Press, 1990), 268.

124. Rehnquist, William, *The Supreme Court* (New York: Alfred Knopf, 2004), 150.

125. Lazarus, Edward, *Closed Chambers* (New York: Penguin, 2005), 266-268.

126. 492 U.S. 490 (1989)

127. 514 U.S. 549 (1995)

128. According to the solicitor general, the presence of guns at schools prevented learning, which prevented students from achieving high academic standards, injuring their opportunity for entering college and limited their job opportunities, lowering their lifetime income and thus reducing the amount of interstate commerce in which they participated.

129. *Adarand v. Pena* 515 U.S. 200 (1995)

130. *Hurley v. Irish Americans* 515 U.S. 557 (1995)

131. *Capitol Square Board v. Pinette* 515 U.S. 753 (1995) and *Rosenberger v. University of Virginia* 515 U.S. 819 (1995)

132. *Veronia v. Acton* 515 U.S. 646 (1995)

133. *Missouri v. Jenkins* 515 U.S. 70 (1995)
134. 515 U.S. 70, 101-102
135. 517 U.S. 44 (1996)
136. *McMillian v. Monroe County* 520 U.S. 781 (1997)
137. *Kimel v. Florida Board of Regents* 528 U.S. 62 (2000)
138. *University of Alabama v. Garrett* 531 U.S. 356 (2001)
139. *Idaho v. Coeur d' Alene* 521 U.S. 261(1997)
140. *Clinton v. Jones* 520 U.S. 681 (1997)
141. When the Senate's sergeant at arms discovered the chief justice and others playing poker for money, he warned the chief justice gambling was illegal in the Senate and could lead to arrest.After leaving, the sergeant at arms returned several minutes later to find the money out of sight, thus preventing political if pettyscandal.
142. 531 U.S. 98 (2000)
143. 542 U.S. 1 (2004)
144. 492 U.S. 490, 535-536 (1989)
145. *Rosenberger v. University of Virginia* (1995) O'Connor mocked Scalia's "categorical platitudes" and lectured him on "the hard task of judging" that required justices to draw lines based on the facts, 847.
146. 505 U.S. 833, 985-986 (1992)
147. 504 U.S. 191, 217 (1992)
148. 501 U.S. 560, 573, 575 (1991)
149. 485 U.S. 660 (1988)
150. 515 U.S. 753, 766 (1995)
151. 506 U.S. 263, 278-279 (1998)
152. 512 U.S. 753, 800 (1994)
153. *In Re Debs* 158 U.S. 564 (1895)
154. *Vieth v. Jubelirer*541 U.S. 267 (2004),*Davis v. Bandemer* 478 U.S. 109 (1986).
155. *District of Columbia v. Heller* 128 S.Ct. 2783 (2008)
156. *Allegheny County v. ACLU* 492 U.S. 573, 657 (1989)
157. Kennedy used the coercion test to strike down a high school graduation prayer in Lee describing the graduation prayer in terms of the "embarrassmentand intrusion" produced in listeners. 505 U.S. 577, 595 (1992).
158. Simon, James, *The Center Holds* (New York: Simon and Schuster, 1995), 189. Kennedy was portrayed slowing the Court's lurch to the right.
159. These changes in philosophy have been attributed to Kennedy's choices for clerks.A former clerk – eager to show his own influence – wrote that Kennedy's clerks scrambled to get him to choose their favorites for the next year with liberals and conservatives battling for the justice's soul – and vote – and pushing their conservative or liberal candidates, Lazarus, 332
160. 514 U.S. 779 (1995)

161. In a concurring opinion, Kennedy swept aside the historical analysis in Justice Stevens' and Justice Thomas'opinions and argued insteadthat term limits violated federal sovereignty but allowing states to set terms for members of Congress.

162. 527 U.S. 706 1999

163. 521 U.S. 261 (1997) During his first term, Kennedy may have begun the Eleventh Amendment revolution with his decision in *Dellmuth v. Muth* 491 U.S. 223 (1989). In Dellmuth Kennedy found that the Education of theHandicapped Act did not explicitly overrule state sovereign immunity, thus preventing parents from suing states under the law.

164. 530 U.S. 914 (2000)

165. 539 U.S. 558 (2003)

166. 544 U.S. 460 (2005)

167. 544 U.S. 460, 478

# Chapter 4

# Woodrow Wilson (9) Dwight Eisenhower (3)

Woodrow Wilson and Dwight Eisenhower were leaders in their respective fields before reaching the White House. The two presidents ran very different administrations, Wilson an activist, Eisenhower more restrained. When they left office both men were seen as failures though as the decades passed their successes overcame their troubles. Of their eight Supreme Court appointments, three are generally recognized as greats, placing the two presidents in the near great category for those selections.

Professional politicians have dominated the presidency. During the nineteenth century pols clawed through the party machinery, earning the nomination through a combination of guile, ruthlessness and vote trading. During the twentieth century media savvy became the route of advancement as glib and photogenic candidates worked their way into the White House. But two twentieth century presidents followed a different path, moving from the heights of their chosen profession into the presidency. Both Woodrow Wilson and Dwight Eisenhower garnered high honors in the field of academia and the military respectively and presided over successful two term administrations.[1]

Wilson was one of the nation's first political scientists, earning prominence in his field with publication of his 1886 work, *Congressional Government*, where he criticized congressional dominance of government during the bland days of the first Grover Cleveland Administration. Wilson's work was the blueprint for what the professor would do if elected to high office. Once in the White House Wilson became a Hamiltonian president, full of vigor and making demands on Congress. His first two years in office saw more legislation passed than any time up to that point and second only to the hundred days of Franklin Roosevelt. He grasped the foreign policy reins during the Great War and made his office the center of international affairs.[2]

Eisenhower was one of only a handful of five star generals.[3] Recognized as the savior of Western Europe, he used his military fame as a stepping stone to the White House. Unlike Wilson he lacked the time to make deep analysis of the office but was guided by the belief that his predecessors had created a bloated presidency. A low key administration was his goal as exhibited in the title of the best analysis of his presidency.[4] Eisenhower's two terms would emphasize management of crises rather than setting an expansive agenda. The president's rock hard realism and behind the scenes manipulation differed considerably from Wilson's idealism and rhetorical thrusts.

Though differing in their approach to the office, Wilson and Eisenhower shared similar post presidential rankings and experienced an ebb and flow in their approval. Wilson left office in near disgrace, health broken, ideals rejected by the electorate. Eisenhower's suffered, his administration criticized as representing the status quo, his low key approach rejected in favor of the inflated rhetoric of the 1960s. Yet both presidents saw their standing rise as their successors proved less able and by the turn of the twentieth century both men were listed among the top tier of presidents.

There were also similarities in their Supreme Court choices. Wilson filled three vacancies while Eisenhower appointed five justices including a chief justice. Both men made choices from both sides of the political spectrum as Wilson chose the arch conservative James McReynolds and the liberal Louis Brandeis while Eisenhower selected the arch liberals Earl Warren and William Brennan and the more conservative John Harlan II. Both men were displeased with some of their choices, though Eisenhower expressed that displeasure as only a military man could.[5]

Both Wilson and Eisenhower were rated high for their Court choices though Wilson's ranking is based on his selection of Brandeis, who shared his economic and political philosophy, while Eisenhower's high rankings can be attributed to his selection of Earl Warren and William Brennan, neither of whom shared Eisenhower's philosophy.

## Woodrow Wilson

The relative obscurity of most Supreme Court justices shields them from popular affection or hatred. Even most Court observers lack strong personal feelings about past or current justices. Yet Woodrow Wilson's first appointee has earned a consensus negative rating from nearly all those familiar with his twenty seven year career.[6] James Clark McReynolds was one of the most fearsome and loathed characters to ever don the black robe. His judicial career, marked by ground breaking opinions and bitter dissents, included a tenacious loyalty to a constitutional doctrine rejected by much of the country during the Great Depression.[7]

His first important position in Washington was as a member of the Taft Justice Department. As a prosecutor in antitrust cases McReynolds came to dislike monopolies, a view inherited from a Jacksonian suspicion of corporations and centralized power. McReynolds' antitrust views meshed with Wilson, who promoted him to attorney general. Yet McReynolds' misanthropy led to clashes with Wilson's closest advisors including Colonel Edward House. McReynolds' pettiness was on full display during a conversation with House as the attorney general rejected several judicial candidates for such sins as lacking a chin, being overweight or having a misplaced mole on their ear.[8]

McReynolds' handling of a potential political scandal involving the son of a prominent California democrat ended his tenure as attorney general. Drew Caminetti, was accused of violating the Mann Act by transporting prostitutes to Reno for immoral activities.[9] McReynolds delayed the prosecution, angering Wilson, who was unwilling to fire his attorney general, instead promoting him to the Court and forcing the institution to deal with McReynolds for the next quarter century.[10]

Appointed under a progressive administration, McReynolds joined the Court's conservative bloc and became the target of progressives who felt betrayed by his rejecting their philosophy. McReynolds' opposition to the New Deal sharpened the criticism of his career, though many of his strongest critics continued to quote from two of McReynolds' best known opinions, *Meyer v. Nebraska*[11] and *Pierce v. Society of Sisters.*[12]

Meyer challenged a Nebraska statute banning the teaching of German to students prior to the eighth grade. The law was part of the anti German reaction fostered by American entry into World War I. Meyer, a teacher, was charged with violating the law for teaching a ten year old student the German language. In his opinion, McReynolds tackled the issue of the authority of states to regulate private and public school curriculum. The justice outlined a series of rights protected as liberty by the constitution including the right of parents to educate their offspring. Quoting Plato and delving into the educational practices of ancient Greece, McReynolds attacked the idea of excessive government control over education.[13] Though Meyer was an isolated case, McReynolds' sweeping language was later expanded to create a right to procreation in *Williamson v. Oklahoma* and in *Griswold v. Connecticut.*

In Pierce an Oregon law required all students to attend public schools. The Catholic Church challenged the law on Free Exercise grounds and McReynolds composed the opinion striking the law. Extended his Meyer decision, McReynolds ruled that parental rights under the constitution included choosing to send their children to a private religious school.[14] McReynolds also authored opinions striking a similar law in Iowa and overturning a federal law in Hawaii targeting Japanese schools.[15]

Even with Pierce and Meyer in his judicial scrapbook, McReynolds would not have risen beyond obscurity had he not led judicial opposition to the New Deal. The justice threw down the gauntlet against the New Deal in a dramatic Court session as the justices rejecting bondholders' challenge to the president's decision to take the country off the gold standard.[16] McReynolds' dissented, his anger spilling over into an explosive extemporaneous declaration that the constitution was gone, comparing Roosevelt's decision to the tyranny of Nero and crying that "shame and humiliation are upon us." The media buzzed at this rare breaking of Court decorum and it made McReynolds public enemy number one for those who believed the Court was giving the New Deal a raw deal.[17]

By 1935 it became clear Roosevelt's plans were unacceptable to the Court. The justices struck the National Industrial Recovery Act as an improper delegation of power to the executive. They also struck down the Agricultural Adjustment Act and the Guffey Coal Act as exceeding the taxing and commerce regulating powers respectively. McReynolds joined the majority in each, his tendentious writing style and outspoken views unlikely to garner a majority of his colleagues.

After Roosevelt's reelection in 1936, McReynolds and Court conservatives found themselves under siege, the justices openly worrying about the president's plans and making arrangements to move his assets to Canada to prevent federal seizure. The justice became the public face of the Court's opposition to the New Deal as he received scores of postcards and letters calling for his resignation or worse.[18] As the pressure heightened McReynolds participated in discussions of which of the four horsemen would resign, serving as the sacrificial lamb to appease the angry Roosevelt before he destroyed the Court.[19]

The break came in spring 1937 as the Court performed an about face and began upholding federal labor laws including a minimum wage and the right to unionize and collectively bargain. In *Laughlin v. NLRB*, Chief Justice Hughes upheld the Wagner Act allowing union organization under federal protection. Dissenting, McReynolds verged on apoplexy, warning the Court's decision expanded the definition of commerce to allow the national government to regulate nearly all economic behavior.[20]

## "Justice Pussywillow"

Serving as a member of the conservative majority that sandbagged many progressive reforms, McReynolds was a target of historical criticism for his opinions and votes. But it was his personal behavior that earned him the title of the most hated of the four horsemen. The justice's anti Semitism were hidden from public sight though familiar to his brethren. The Court's 1924 term photograph session was cancelled as McReynolds refused to stand beside Justice Brandeis, the Court's sole Jewish justice.[21] He treated Justice Clarke with disdain and held low opinions of many of his colleagues. Yet the details of McReynolds' personal life told the story of a bon vivant who enjoyed hunting, donated much of his estate to charity and adopted a score of British children made orphans by World War II. [22]

Justice McReynolds' personal life may be the most scrutinized of all the justices. His clerk for the Court's all important 1936 term was John Knox, who composed an autobiography that placed the dour McReynolds in a different light. A bachelor, McReynolds had many lady friends, some of whom became attached to Knox. A humorous scene unfolded during the term as Knox was being entertained by one of the lady friends and the justice arrived unexpectedly, forcing the clerk to scramble and escape unseen. The scene resembled one of the comedy sketches that preceded many of the motion picture features of the period.[23] Yet McReynolds would not inspire loyalty from his acquaintances or employees as he died in 1948 in the hospital without the benefit of family or friends present.

The justice's relationship with his black servants was also a sign of the times. As a southern Democrat, McReynolds was not known as a progressive on racial issues and was mainly contemptuous of his cook and butler, who responded in kind. Eager to gossip about McReynolds and his lady friends, the servants gave the justice the name "pussywillow," allowing them to openly speak of him without the justice being the wiser. [24]

After the 1937 switch, McReynolds spent his last four years as a lonely dissenter. Justice Van Devanter retired in 1937 and was followed by Justice Sutherland in 1938 with Justice Butler dying in 1939. McReynolds watched as the legal world around him began to crumble, leaving him to dissent in some of the major decisions of 1937 to 1941.[25]

Seemingly holding onto his seat in the hope of allowing Roosevelt's successor to fill his vacancy, McReynolds was displeased by the third term movement and the president's reelection in 1940. During that time he composed few memorable opinions beyond a 1939 case that earned him additional enemies, gun owners. In *United States v. Miller* McReynolds upheld a federal ban on "sawed off shotguns" against a Second Amendment claim. [26] Writing for a unanimous majority, McReynolds narrowly read the amendment, tying it to the need for militias and ruling sawed off shotguns were not standard equipment used by militiamen. Miller is quoted extensively by those favoring state and national gun control laws, though McReynolds never found that ownership of guns could be prohibited.

McReynolds' resignation was greeted with glee by the Roosevelt Administration, which had made him judicial enemy number one. His reputation suffered because of his anti Semitism and his having served on the wrong side of legal history. McReynolds joined his colleagues Justice Butler and Justice Van Devanter as judicial failures.[27]

## John Clarke

Two years after elevating McReynolds from Attorney General, Wilson faced two court vacancies in the midst of a presidential election. In his choices, the president selected one of the most prominent justices to serve, Louis Brandeis, and one of the most obscure, John Clarke.

Clarke proved to be the least effective of Wilson's appointees. The justice was destined to be a liberal voice, along with Brandeis, who would change the Court's direction but his brief six year tenure was stained by a predisposition to abandon his ideals in the midst of a fight. During an equally brief political career, Clarke had run for the Senate but dropped out of the primary, complaining about the difficulties of a political campaign and instead accepted the position as federal judge.[28] He did earn respect of Ohio Democrats by challenging Mark Hanna in 1903 though he was defeated in the state legislature.[29]

Clarke opposed the Court's conservative decisions but his voice was drowned out by allies and opponents alike including Holmes, Brandeis and McReynolds. Except for the occasional memorable opinion, Clarke was reduced to authoring now forgotten concurrences and dissents. Unable to adjust to the Court's routine, Clarke was exhausted by the demands of the job particularly the weekly conferences. A hypochondriac, his fear of illness was exacerbated by the sudden death of his two sisters. Reflecting on his own mortality, Clarke chose retirement at the relatively young age of sixty five.[30]

Clarke was also affected by the shoddy treatment dealt him by Justice McReynolds. Known for his boorish and bigoted personality, McReynolds was not reticent in expressing his many dislikes and Clarke proved to be one of them.[31] After six years the sensitive Clarke fled, another notch on McReynolds' belt as he sought to purge the Court of undesirables.[32] Clarke's decision to resign was also driven by his dedication to Wilsonian internationalism.

Clarke's soaring idealism was marked by excess energy and a blind spot about disagreements. The Court's work blocked his vision of sweeping vistas and Clarke became bored with the technical issues and minutiae plaguing the justices. Part of that vision was preventing another world war, a mission that Clarke sought to fulfill after his retirement.[33]

As the League of Nations and world order collapsed, Clarke worked to create a new institution, the United Nations, which held its inaugural meeting six months after Clarke's death.[34]

Clarke's internationalist impulses overshadowed a lackluster Court career that included few important opinions. Clarke was a regular vote to uphold state and federal economic regulations including railroad rate commissions and a federal law banning child labor. His economic liberal views did not extend to civil liberties as Clarke approved of Wilson's draconian laws against dissenters during World War I,

Wilson's dreamy internationalism became domestic authoritarianism with passage of the Espionage Acts. Dissenters were arrested for challenging the war and when their appeals reached the Supreme Court, Clarke fell in line and upheld limits on political criticism. Clarke joined *Schenck v. United States*, upholding a twenty year sentence for Schenck for distributing pamphlets against the military draft. The stiff sentence was upheld even though the war had ended and any threat posed by Schenck had passed.

Following hard on the heels of Schenck, Clarke's opinion in Abrams v. United States is widely quoted and his most illiberal.[35] Abrams was part of a group of bumbling anarchists who, true to their political dogma, suffered poor organizational skills. They struggled to distribute their pamphlets attacking the war, eventually settling on tossing them from the window of a New York high rise. Guilty more of littering than sedition, Abrams was nonetheless arrested and convicted of violating the Espionage Act. His appeal to the Supreme Court fared better than Schenck's, garnering him two votes but not enough to have the conviction overturned. Instead Justice Clarke reinterpreted Holmes' Clear and Present Danger Test and found that Abrams' comical efforts to criticize the draft represented a threat to the war effort and thus could be prosecuted under the First Amendment.[36] Clarke's effort was unsatisfying as he misinterpreted the Clear and Present Danger and drew a dissent from its creator, Justice Holmes.

That same year Clarke authored a cranky dissent attacking the Eighteenth Amendment in the Prohibition Cases.[37] The Court had struggled for a century with the issue of alcohol, their decisions angering either brewery interests or prohibitionists. The justices were likely pleased to have the burden lifted from them as Congress and the states took the issue from their docket with passage of the Eighteenth Amendment granting the federal government the authority to regulate alcohol. In the Prohibition Cases the Court upheld the Volstead Act and the Eighteenth Amendment in granting power to the federal government. Clarke disagreed, interpreting the amendment as continuing rather than settling the debate over alcohol regulation.

Serving only six short, unproductive years, Clarke was a disappointment to Wilson and progressives who wanted him to provide a liberal/progressive vote on the Supreme Court. But if Wilson failed with Clarke, Louis Brandeis exceeded the president's expectations.

## Louis Brandeis

Louis Brandeis achieved several firsts upon reaching the Supreme Court in 1916. Not only was he the first Jewish justice he was also the first justice to have established a legal practice focusing on public interest law. During the last decades of the nineteenth century, presidents packed the Court with lawyers who argued on behalf of railroads and against state and federal regulations. Once on the bench the judges continued their dedication to corporate rights, ruling in favor of business over government. Brandeis' arrival was the first step in reversing the trend. Brandeis built a career on arguing in favor of workers and states regulating business. In addition to practicing public interest law, he also changed the method of arguing before the Court. Utilizing statistics and empirical evidence, the Brandeis Brief became a tool for supporting economic regulations. In *Muller v. Oregon*, Brandeis successfully argued with statistics that women and minors deserved greater workers' rights because of the physical and psychological damage caused by long working hours and low pay. Brandeis convinced all nine justices that the liberty to contract should be waived in favor of setting wages and working hours for these "weaker" groups.[38]

Having earned plaudits from progressives, it was not unexpected that Brandeis was nominated for the Supreme Court by the chief progressive of the time, Woodrow Wilson. But the appointment of the "people's lawyer" produced a backlash from many who saw Brandeis' vision as socialistic.[39] Among his opponents was former president William Howard Taft. Taft pined for a seat on the Supreme Court and used his contacts to try and influence Wilson to appoint him to one of the two open seats. Wilson chose Brandeis, angering Taft who mounted a campaign to defeat him. The effort proved to be more wind than fury and Brandeis was easily confirmed. [40]

Justice Brandeis became a fixture on the ideological left of the Court along with his fellow Wilson appointees, John Clarke, and Oliver Wendell Holmes. It would be the relationship between Holmes and Brandeis that would swell the reputations of both men as their dissents became the rallying cry for progressives.

Initially Brandeis followed the experienced Holmes in his opinions. Later as Holmes' career wound down, Brandeis became the leader. In 1919, Brandeis joined Holmes' creation of the Clear and Present Danger test.[41] Brandeis would join Holmes' dissents during the 1920s as the test was stretched to limit speech Holmes supported.[42]

But it was not First Amendment cases but rather the battle to uphold state and federal economic regulation earned Brandeis his liberal credentials. He joined Holmes' dissent in the child labor cases and was one of three regular dissenters in the 1930s cases attacking New Deal laws and provoking the Court crisis of 1937.

In *New State Ice v. Liebmann* Brandeis' dissent included one of his more quotable phrases criticizing the Court as it struck an Oklahoma law regulating the ice business. [43] Brandeis argued the states were "laboratories" for testing economic regulations during the Great Depression.[44] The laboratories for experiment phrase would be the rallying cry for progressives pushing minimum wage and forty hour week laws. Brandeis coined another phrase in Olmstead v. United States.[45] In Olmstead Chief Justice Taft upheld warrantless wiretaps of phones. Brandeis dissent, opining the Fourth Amendment included a "right to privacy" that required government to receive judicial approval before listening to private conversations. [46]

Brandeis made a brief appearance in the Court Packing crisis of the 1930s. Faced with Franklin Roosevelt's contention that the justices were falling behind in their workload, Chief Justice Hughes sprung into action, composing a letter noting that the justices had completed work on all of their cases and did not need

the help of additional justices. Hughes had Justice Van Devanter and Justice Brandeis, representing both sides of the political spectrum, sign the letter in a sign of institutional opposition to the Roosevelt plan. It would be Brandeis' only public comment on the political battle but provided cover for Chief Justice Hughes in his battle to rescue the Court from the Roosevelt attack.

During the debate over the Court's direction, Brandeis managed to interpret the newly ratified Twenty First Amendment. In *State Board v. Young's Market*, Brandeis ruled the Twenty First Amendment granted states absolute authority over production, sale and importation of alcohol within state boundaries. [47] It was the importing of alcohol that raised questions about the amendment and whether states could regulate interstate commerce. But Brandeis swept away those concerns, ruling the amendment granted states plenary power over alcohol.[48]

Brandeis would not become part of a consistent and comfortable majority until the final years of his career. In Erie v. Tompkins, Brandeis overruled a decision written by Justice Story allowing federal judges to create a federal common law in diversity of citizenship cases. [49] The Erie decision closed the door on forum shopping by corporations challenging state economic regulation. Prior to Erie businesses incorporated in different states, creating a diversity claim and moving the dispute from state to federal court. After Erie federal courts enforced state law, eliminating many of the challenges to state economic regulations.[50]

Erie would prove to be his last seminal decision as Justice Brandeis suffered declining health, his final year as a justice spent considering his replacements. Brandeis approved of Roosevelt's selection of William Douglas, who would become the most liberal justice of his era.

## Wilson's legacy

For Woodrow Wilson, the celebrated Brandeis, the forgotten Clarke and the reviled McReynolds presented a mixed record of Supreme Court appointments. The most progressive Democrat president since Andrew Jackson proved unable to enforce his will against the federal judiciary, watching the courts strike two child labor laws and weaken protection of labor organizations. Justice Clarke's sudden resignation and Brandeis relegation to the role of dissenter during the Taft Court was the coda to the early progressive attempts to reform the Supreme Court. It would not be until another member of the Wilson Administration, Franklin Roosevelt, became president that Wilson's plans would bear fruit.

## Ike and his "Damned Fool Mistakes"

Dwight Eisenhower's rise to the presidency was not without controversy. His handling of subordinates during the North African, Italian and Normandy campaigns earned him plaudits and criticism as he worked with allies such as British General Bernard Montgomery while keeping rein on such figures as General George Patton.[51] His decision not to attack toward Berlin or occupy Czechoslovakia during the last weeks of the war signaled Eisenhower had little stomach for fighting communism in central Europe. Simultaneously "Ike" proved able to make the transition from wartime leader to peacetime officer, obeying political authorities and keeping his opinions to himself while other generals, including Patton, saw their military careers come to an abrupt end when they clashed with Washington.

A brief tour as president of Columbia University and commander of NATO forces included frenetic recruiting from both political parties for him to run as president. In 1952 Eisenhower entered the Republican campaign, relying on political pros such as Richard Nixon to collect the necessary delegates for the nomination.[52] His 1952 election victory returned Republicans to the White House and control of Congress, representing the height of the party's popularity as Eisenhower operated a presidency separate from the Republican party.

During his eight years the former general enjoyed close working relationship with Democrats in Congress including Lyndon Johnson in the Senate and Sam Rayburn in the House. Focusing on foreign policy, Eisenhower managed situations rather than implementing broad changes in policy, fighting off calls for attacking China or rolling back communism in Eastern Europe. His domestic policy saw him battle against greater government spending. Eisenhower left office a popular president but with a short list of accomplishments and a weakened Republican Party split between its conservative and liberal wings. Eisenhower's standing among historians rose in comparison to his successors, whose involvement in the Vietnam War destroyed their presidencies. His choices for the Supreme Court reflected favorably on his legacy, though not without Eisenhower's mixed feelings on the subject.

## Earl Warren

During his two terms, Dwight Eisenhower faced five vacancies on the Supreme Court and the opportunity to remake the institution. Entering office he faced a Court with seven Democrat justices, one independent and a sole Republican. By the time of his retirement in 1961, the Court was an Eisenhower shaped institution with four Republicans, including the chief justice. Yet for his opportunities to effect change, Eisenhower sometimes bemoaned his choices, expressing dissatisfaction with their decisions.[53] He was particularly upset with his choice of chief justice as the Warren Court became synonymous with liberal activism.

Earl Warren began his political career as a California prosecutor then state attorney general who oversaw the Japanese internment program.[54] While reviving the state Republican Party during his three terms as governor, Warren maintained his distance from other statewide Republican candidates, including William Knowland and Richard Nixon, who were competitors for the presidency.[55] Chosen as the party's vice presidential candidate in 1948, Warren did not earn the respect of his running mate, Thomas Dewey, who described him as that "big dumb Swede."[56] Yet Dewey's political acumen was suspect and Warren proved his political mettle, holding together a fractious Republican Party in a state known for its bizarre politics.

In 1952 Warren battled for the Republican presidential nomination, using the California delegation to buoy his bid for the top spot on the ticket. The governor was outmaneuvered by Richard Nixon, who used his influence with the delegates to undermine Warren's campaign.[57] For his efforts Nixon received the vice presidential nomination while the governor received a conditional promise of a seat on the Supreme Court.[58]

Within months of Eisenhower's inauguration the center chair became available after Chief Justice Vinson's sudden death and Warren received a recess nomination in the fall of 1953.[59] The president wanted a chief who could unify a divided court, much like Warren had unified California Republicans.

## Brown

A rich vein of judicial research has been the freshman effect, studies of the opinion output of new justices during their first year on the Court.[60] It has been suggested that justices require several terms before they can adjust to the demands of their position. Warren disproved that thesis in his first year, breaking a deadlock on segregation that plagued the Court since the time of Chief Justice Stone. By 1953 the justices was in the midst of dismantling southern segregation, striking down the white primary[61] then overturning segregation of graduate and law schools.[62] The justices then struck restrictive covenants and in Chief Justice Vinson's last term heard arguments on secondary and primary school segregation. The justices were divided, rescheduling the cases for argument during the 1953 term.[63]

Brown was argued in December 1953 just as Warren settled into his job. During the justices' conference on the case, the new chief was unequivocal in his demand that segregation be overturned. Warren took the opinion for himself and drew the votes of two undecided justices, Tom Clark and Felix Frankfurter.[64] Justice Jackson planned a concurring opinion but was struck down by a heart attack and agreed to join Warren's opinion.[65] This left Justice Reed, who promised a dissent. Warren applied friendly pressure, isolating Reed and eventually pulling him into the unanimous majority.[66]

Warren's efforts were made even more delicate by the fact he was a recess appointment and lacked the protection of life tenure. If Warren's efforts to overturn segregation had become public, southern senators would have likely filibustered the appointment.[67] Instead Warren enjoyed the most successful first term for a chief justice since John Marshall. Brown v. Board of Education jump-started the civil rights movement and pressured Washington leaders.

Yet Brown failed to address the difficulties of implementing desegregation. Only in 1955 would a second Brown decision transform federal judges into trustees of public education with authority to implemented integration policies and beyond.[68] Southern resentment was directed at the federal district and appeals courts and made once obscure federal appointees high profile leaders in the integration battle.[69]

Brown highlighted Earl Warren as a political leader. His greatest gift as chief justice was not his intellect or writing ability but his social skills, as Warren tended to decide cases based on his intuition and relied on his colleagues, particularly Justice Brennan, to provide legal reasoning.[70] The two justices would meet before the Court's weekly conferences, working out their strategies and voting arrangements to ensure a smooth, working conference.

In addition to Brown, Warren and his Court became synonymous with opinions liberalizing criminal justice procedures and changing the method of apportioning state legislative districts. During the 1950s, the chief justice's agenda was slowed by Justice Frankfurter, who regularly mustered majorities against Warren. Congress also took aim at the Court. When Warren constrained the scope of congressional investigations into domestic communism, his opinion in *United States v. Yates* provoked furious congressional criticism and considerable nervousness among his colleagues. The next year Warren would be in the minority as Yates was all but overruled in the Barenblatt decision. Justice Brennan's opinion in *Jencks v. United States* allowed for greater use of classified material in a federal trial and generated the federal "Jencks" Act which overruled part of that decision. [71]

But opposition within the Court began to break down after Frankfurter suffered a stroke in 1962. His retirement coupled with Justice Whittaker's nervous breakdown created two vacancies for a Democrat president. With two new arrivals, the 1962 term represented the start of the Warren Revolution.

Warren's revived influence came in the legislative redistricting cases such as *Reynolds v. Sims*.[72] In 1962 the justices had agreed questions of state redistricting were not political questions.

In Reynolds the Alabama's legislative redistricting efforts were challenged under the Equal Protection clause. Alabama operated a bicameral legislature with one house based on population, not unlike the U.S. House of Representatives, and another chamber based on equal representation usually for each county, not unlike the U.S. Senate. The arrangement gave rural areas greater representation in one chamber.

In Reynolds, Warren mandated one man one vote for all state legislative chambers, reaching the result by noting the House and Senate were the result of a checks and balances that prevented rapid lawmaking. Another interpretation has the Senate created to protect numerical minorities from the House. Suddenly redistricting and the drawing of boundaries for all state and local offices became a legal issue, adding to the Court's workload.[73]

In *Miranda v. Arizona* Warren sought to ensure confessions were not acquired using police coercion, violence or trickery.[74] The first section of Miranda was a polemic denouncing coercive interrogation tactics and was followed by the mandate that suspects taken into custody be told of their right to remain silent and their right to counsel. Any confession, information or evidence obtained without these warnings would be excluded from trial.

Known for his liberal opinions, Warren also shifted to the right in a visceral reaction to certain issues. In *United States v. O'Brien* he recognized symbolic speech under the First Amendment. Warren upheld O'Brien's conviction for burning a draft card, a form of symbolic speech, refusing to place the Court on the side of Vietnam War protesters.[75] In *Terry v. Ohio* Warren backed away from the Mapp decision, ruling police could conduct public pat down searches of suspects during questioning.[76] In 1961 Warren fought the tide of separation of church and state, upholding Sunday blue laws against an Establishment Clause challenge.[77] Warren found that the Sunday closing laws had a secular purpose of providing a day of rest for workers.

The chief favored obscenity laws and granting prosecutors discretion in making obscenity convictions.[78] Warren dissented in *Street v. New York,* voting to overturn Street's conviction for flag desecration.[79] Warren argued government could ban flag desecration under the First Amendment. It would be one his last opinions, an unusual end to his career.

More controversial was Warren's chairing the commission investigating the Kennedy assassination.[80] The Warren Commission was a hodgepodge of political leaders and Washington insiders[81] enjoying more political than investigatory skills. Years after the Commission reported Oswald was the lone assassin, conspiracy theorists continued spinning stories of multiple gunmen and government involvement. A decade later a congressional committee questioned the commission's findings, further fueling the conspiracy theorists. The distrust of the Warren Commission was a failure in public relations, unable to convince Americans a thorough investigation had been conducted. [82]

Watching political events unfold in early 1968, Warren decided to resign while a friendly president was in office. But Lyndon Johnson's political instincts abandoned him and he promoted Associate Justice Abe Fortas to the center chair. Opposition was fierce from southern Democrats and Republicans, a filibuster forcing Johnson to pull the nomination in summer 1968. It would be Warren's old political enemy, Richard Nixon, who would select his replacement.

## John Marshall Harlan

Two more disparate personalities could not be found than Justice John Marshall Harlan (1877 to 1911) and his grandson, John Marshall Harlan (1954 to 1971). The senior Harlan was a massive man of ferocious opinions expressed with the force of a wild bull. His grandson was quiet, solicitous of others and preferred quiet persuasion over brute legal force. The second Harlan was the typical corporate lawyer, a traditional conservative suspicious of judicial power.[83] Harlan's studied neutrality was reflected in one simple act, his refusal to vote in national elections so as not to have a personal interest in any case before the Court. [84]

The second Harlan arrived at the Court only months after *Brownn*, an ironic twist of fate as his grandfather had been the sole dissenter in *Plessy v. Ferguson*, which was overturned in Brown. Harlan replaced Robert Jackson, a Frankfurter ally and soon assumed the same role. Harlan supported "all deliberate speed" in integrating public schools, favoring Frankfurter's slower approach.[85]

Justice Harlan reflected the careful, status quo conservatism of the Eisenhower Administration. Concerned with judges assuming a political role, he urged restraint throughout his career and backed the Court away from its more controversial opinions, including Watkins v. United States, which limited congressional authority to investigate. In *Barenblatt v. United States* Harlan offered a careful opinion allowing broader investigatory powers while differentiating between Barenblatt and Watkins. For all his efforts, though, Harlan could not conceal the fact the Court was retreating from a year old precedent in the face of congressional opposition. [86]

Although known as the Warren Court's primary dissenter, challenging the Court's liberal tilt, Harlan occasionally broke the mold. His dissent in *Poe v. Ullman*[87] challenged his ally Justice Frankfurter on the issue of justiciability. Poe challenged a Connecticut law banning the distribution of contraceptives, though the law had not been enforced against Poe. Frankfurter seized that fact and ruled the doctor had not suffered an injury that would allow him to sue. Harlan disagreed, arguing procreation rights were part of the ordered liberty protected under the due process clause, a doctrine championed by Frankfurter,[88] finding that the doctors and patients had suffered an injury and could sue. He also argued the contraception law violated the basic tenets of liberty under the Fourteenth Amendment.[89] Three years later with Frankfurter gone, Harlan joined the majority in *Griswold v. Connecticut* which challenged the same law. Harlan rejected Justice Douglas' hodgepodge explanation of penumbras and emanations creating a right to use contraception, preferring his earlier approach of procreation as a traditional right.[90] [91]

Barenblatt and Poe reflected the different faces of Harlan, sometimes the defender of government prerogatives against individual rights, other times the libertarian on social issues.[92] On criminal justice matters, though, Harlan favored government, dissenting in Mapp and Miranda. In Mapp he warned against imposing a single standard for federal and state law enforcement.[93] In Miranda he took issue with the warnings mandated by the Court but also its attack on "coerced" confessions, warning that Miranda would enforce "voluntariness with a vengeance" and exclude most confessions even if they were voluntary.[94] But Harlan concurred in Gideon v. Wainwright granting counsel to defendants in felony cases.[95] The justice lamented the passing of Betts v. Brady, which denied right to counsel, wishing the precedent had been granted a more "respectful burial."[96] His criticism of Justice Black's Gideon decision focused on the tone and Black's tendency to view past decisions as examples of injustice. Harlan's final dissent came in *United States v. New York Times,* popularly known as the Pentagon Papers Case. For the final time Harlan battled with Justice Black, arguing the Alabaman's absolute ban on prior restraints was excessive and that the Court had acted with undue haste in deciding the case in a few weeks. A few weeks later Harlan would be forced to resign, stricken with cancer, and dying at the end of 1971. His efforts were recognized by an unusual source, Justice Brennan, who said Harlan was the one true judge in the Warren Court.[97]

## William Brennan

In the midst of his reelection campaign, Dwight Eisenhower faced a Court vacancy after Justice Minton's sudden retirement. Deluged by the demands of the campaign and twin international crises in the Suez and Hungary, Eisenhower selected William Brennan who represented a winning political trio, Democrat, Catholic and Irish.[98] A justice on the New Jersey Supreme Court, Brennan would be one of the last justices with only state court experience.[99]

Brennan had an immediate impact, joining the chief justice's bloc in most constitutional cases and in his first term developing a new doctrine on obscenity in *Roth v. United States.*[100] It would be the first of several constitutional doctrines created by Brennan.

Roth was also one of the few major decisions Justice Brennan and Dwight Eisenhower agreed upon as the new justice joined Chief Justice Warren and Justices Black and Douglas throughout the 1960s.[101] Where Black and Douglas provided some of the intellectual heft for decisions, Warren and Brennan were responsible for rounding up the needed votes. Brennan proved to be particularly adept at vote counting as he composed decisions that papered over important differences with other justices and used broad language to appeal to the liberal side of his colleagues. Brennan would be in the mix throughout much of his thirty four year career, initially writing critical decisions that modified the law then fighting a rearguard action against a growing number of conservative justices.

Throughout the 1960s Brennan and his colleagues struggled with a national obscenity definition. Brennan recast obscenity in a series of cases including his Memoirs decision where he ruled any work lacking socially redeeming value could be considered obscene.[102] Memoirs, Redrup and Jacobellis muddied the obscenity issue, forcing the justices to consider the content of movies and books on a case by case basis. During the late 1960s the Court had "movie days" where the justices watched pornographic material to determine if it was obscene. By the 1970s frustration was boiling and in 1973 Brennan's national standard was tossed aside for a local standard approach, virtually eliminating obscenity cases from the docket.[103]

Brennan was more successful in rewriting the doctrine of libel. In *New York Times v. Sullivan,* Brennan all but eliminated the ability of public officials to sue the press for libel. Under Brennan's actual malice standard a public official suing for libel would have to prove that the newspaper or other media outlet had deliberately published a falsehood.[104] Brennan later attempted to extend the actual malice standard to public figures such as celebrities and to ordinary citizens, with less success, though the actual malice standard earned Brennan media adulation throughout his career.[105]

Another Brennan doctrinal change redefined the political question doctrine. Redistricting had been dismissed as a political question in *Colgrove v. Green*, but in *Baker v. Carr* Brennan overturned Colgrove, ruling courts were suited to decide whether a redistricting plan violated the Equal Protection Clause by diluting votes. Brennan identified several factors under his political question doctrine to determine whether a case was justiciable.[106]

The advent of the Burger Court weakened Brennan's influence and much of the remainder of his career was consumed protecting doctrines. Brennan achieved early success, the 1971 and 1972 terms fondly recalled by Brennan partisans as he drove the Court to strike the death penalty and create an abortion right.

Unlike the civil rights movement of the 1960s, the women's rights movement saw no dramatic shift in the treatment of women in society. While gender discrimination was prohibited in hiring and promotion, full equality was never achieved through congressional action, the judiciary becoming involved starting in 1973. In *Frontiero v. Richardson*, Brennan tried to make women a discrete and insular minority with special constitutional rights. But lacking the votes, Brennan cobbled together only a plurality which approved of his sweeping opinion.[107] Later he would modify his approach, skirting Frontiero in favor of weaker protections against gender discrimination.[108]

The justice was more successful in creating abortion rights. Though he did not personally author the opinion, Brennan has received credit for guiding Justice Blackmun in composing the broadest opinion possible and creating a near absolute right to an abortion.[109] Thirty years later, *Roe v. Wade* remained mostly unchanged, the thirty million plus legal abortions a major part of his legacy along with the rekindling of the conservative movement and the strategy of Republican presidents stacking the courts with anti abortion judges.

Brennan also struck a blow against the practice of patronage hiring at the state and local level. In *Elrod v. Burns*, Brennan wrote that the hiring or firing of government employees based on their party membership violated their right to free association. Under Elrod government agencies would no longer be emptied of appointees once control of government changed political parties. Instead government employees were protected from firing even if they were hired because of their party connections.[110]

After the Court's muddled decision on affirmative action in the Bakke case, Brennan grasped the opportunity to place his own imprint on the issue. After Justice Douglas' forced retirement in late 1975, Brennan became the senior associate justice with the power to assign opinions when he was opposed by the chief justice. During this time he earned the reputation of hogging the best opinions for himself.[111] *USW v. Weber* was one of those opinions. Weber claimed an affirmative action policy hired black workers ahead of white workers, violating the 1964 Civil Rights Act which prohibited hiring discrimination based on race. Brennan rejected the claim, noting the union may have violated the letter of the law but that the spirit of the law supported using race based policies to favor black employees over white employees. [112]

Weber legalized race based hiring policies favoring minorities, a dramatic shift from the civil rights era. As with Roe, the Weber decision produced a political movement that sought to undo legalized discrimination.

As Ronald Reagan began appointing conservatives to the Court, Brennan struggled to sway votes, instead forcing him to rely on a core bloc of four liberals, the modern edition of the Four Horsemen of the Roosevelt era, which fought hard to protect Brennan's doctrines. He managed a few victories including *Texas v. Johnson,*[113] granting First Amendment protection to flag burning and *FCC v. Metro Broadcasting*, upholding federal affirmative action policies. [114] He also cobbled together a majority in a critical Eleventh Amendment case and several Establishment Clause cases, though his writings there proved to be more transitory, being overruled within a decade after he left the Court. [115]

As his influence waned, Brennan became dogmatic and sarcastic in his opinions, dissenting death penalty cases and decrying capital punishment as cruel and unusual. By 1990 Brennan was unable to perform his work and resigned rather than force the Court to work with a disabled justice, as it had during Justice Douglas' illness.

Brennan's legacy is mixed depending upon one's partisan point of view. Liberals tend to celebrate him as a guarantor of rights and as an innovative justice who changed American law for the better. Conservatives are more likely to criticize than praise his results oriented opinions which favored certain groups over others. Certainly the man who appointed him, Dwight Eisenhower, expressed his disapproval with Brennan, placing him with Warren as one of the two greatest disappointments of his presidency.

## Charles Whittaker

The volume of cases heard and decided by the Supreme Court each term forces the justices to apply their reasoning, make a decision and move onto the next dispute. Justices who agonize over opinions tend to have short and unproductive careers, Eisenhower's fourth Court appointment, Charles Whittaker, exemplifying the danger in spending too much time making decisions.

After Stanley Reed's resignation in 1957, Eisenhower selected a Kansas City lawyer recommended by his brother. Charles Whittaker was an Ike appointee to the Eighth Circuit Court of Appeals and was the first judge to serve at all three levels of the federal judiciary, though his experience proved more a hindrance once reaching the Supreme Court. [116] Observing his colleague, Justice Potter Stewart remarked Whittaker lacked "the power of decision."[117]

Intimidated by his colleagues and lacking a clear constitutional philosophy, Whittaker was besieged from the right and left as he struggled to master the facts in scores of cases. In an early opinion, *Perez v. United States*, Whittaker was unable to compose a decision.[118] Justice Douglas discovered Whittaker nearly in tears over his struggles, Douglas tried to calm Whittaker by offering to write the Court's opinion then compose his own dissent.[119] While Douglas was known for telling story of doubtful truthfulness, his anecdote about Whittaker held a nugget of truth, the justice paralyzed with indecision and exerting little influence among his colleagues.[120]

In *Bartkus v. Illinois*, a double jeopardy case, Whittaker was besieged on all sides for his vote.[121] During the conference discussion of the case, Whittaker voted to strike Bartkus' conviction but after a lobbying campaign from Frankfurter, he voted to uphold the conviction. Then Justice Black pushed Whittaker to stick with his initial decision but the justice refused to switch his vote, the pressure adding to his emotional stress.[122]

The battle over legislative redistricting shattered Whittaker's fragile stability. Besieged by the chief justice and the always forceful Justice Frankfurter, Whittaker's resolve crumbled. The psychological break came in an antitrust suit, *Brown Shoe v. U.S.* as Whittaker struggled with the complex antitrust laws while trying to keep in his focus in the legislative redistricting cases.[123] Already a heavy user of psychiatric drugs, Whittaker cracked and Chief Justice Warren made a push for his retirement.[124] A series of medical tests found Whittaker's mental and physical condition had so deteriorated he could not continue on the Court without endangering his health and sanity. Whittaker's departure was followed closely by Justice Frankfurter's resignation, eliminating two conservative votes and ushering in the height of the Warren Court.

## Potter Stewart

Few justices serve on the Court without earning enemies either among their colleagues or among those closest to the institution. Dwight Eisenhower's fifth and final Court appointee was one of those rare breed who was liked and respected by his colleagues. Justice Potter Stewart defied easy ideological categories, instead spending is career as the quintessential swing votes in closely divided cases. His lack of a clear ideology also explains the lack of a formal biography, the only Eisenhower appointee to be so ignored.[125] When asked if he were a liberal or conservative, Stewart responded that he was a lawyer. His sudden departure in 1981 was prompted by a high school girl's letter inquiring about his long service on the Court, some twenty three years, and the wisdom of allowing new blood to serve.[126]

Stewart's opinions tended to be more personal than political. He dissented on many of the Warren Court's criminal rights cases but approved of the majority's opinions in press, speech and civil rights cases. Of all his writing, Stewart's most memorable line came from a Warren Court obscenity case. In a concurring opinion commenting on the Court's struggle with defining obscenity, Stewart stated that he knew it when he saw it.[127] Unfortunately pithy phrases make bad law and Stewart's comment did little more than highlight the futility of establishing a national standard. When the Court reached a consensus on the subject in *Miller v. California*, Stewart dissented, possibly not recognizing the solution even when it was before his eyes.

Stewart also dissented in some of the major Warren Court criminal rights decisions including Escobedo and Miranda though he joined Mapp and Gideon. [128] Stewart also doubted the wisdom of selective incorporation, joining Justice Harlan's dissents in several cases.[129]

The justice refused to accept the two major religion cases, concurring narrowly in *Sherbert v. Verner*,[130] where he argued denying Sherbert unemployment benefits because she was fired on religious grounds violated the Free Exercise Clause then providing benefits rewarded the practice of religion and violated the Establishment Clause.[131] Stewart's arguments would become the basis for the rewriting of the Free Exercise Clause in *Smith v. Employment Division.*

Stewart dissented alone in *Abington v. Schempp* as the justices struck a state policy allowing students to read bible verses over the public address system at the start of school. [132] The Court ruled the policy was state involvement in religious practice, aided religion and violated the Establishment Clause. Stewart disagreed, raising the argument that the Free Exercise and Establishment clauses were in conflict and denying the reading of verses might be a Free Exercise violation.[133]

Usually not known for his broad opinions or sweeping generalizations, Stewart was responsible for reviving the work of the post Civil War Republican Congress in two cases, *Jones v. Mayer*[134] and *Runyon v. McCrary*.[135] Unlike the Fourteenth Amendment, which had ignited a flurry of constitutional challenges to state law, the Thirteenth Amendment was rarely litigated. Ratified in 1865 it abolished slavery and prohibited involuntary servitude, neither of which was widely violated. Acting on the amendment, Congress passed the 1866 Civil Rights Act, which banned discrimination in a variety of private activities including contracts and the buying, selling and ownership of property. In Jones Stewart would give teeth to the amendment and 1866 law, finding that discrimination in the sale of housing was covered under the law and that the Thirteenth Amendment banned not only slavery but the badges and incidents of slavery which placed the freedman in a legally inferior position.[136]

Stewart extended the reach of the law in Runyon. The case challenged a private Virginia school which practiced racial discrimination. The Runyons sued under the 1866 act, claiming their right to make a contract had been violated by the private school. Stewart and six other justices agreed, though his Runyon opinion was written in a clearly defensive manner and was contradictory in its reasoning. Stewart ruled that parents had the right to send children to schools that taught racial segregation but that the law prohibited racial segregation within the schools.[137] Runyon would serve as the zenith of the Thirteenth

Amendment and the badges of slavery argument with future courts limiting its reach.[138]

## Lightning Striking

Warren's departure in 1969 and the resignation of Justice Fortas for improper dealings opened a hole in the liberal majority. By 1971 the addition of four Nixon appointees split the Court between liberals and conservatives. The Burger Court (1969-1985) was supposedly controlled by the much discussed but rarely photographed "swing" justice. These justices are rumored to hold the key to decisions, deciding whether the Court moves to the left or right. Stewart, along with Justice White, earned the title, starting with *Furman v. Georgia.*[139] As strong law and order justices, Stewart and White were surprising joiners in the decision to overturn capital punishment. The gaggle of opinions in Furman supporting the ruling proved to be more confusing than enlightening but Stewart's pithy phrasing held a kernel of truth and a suggestion on how the states could reinstate the death penalty.

In his concurring opinion Stewart complained that many death penalty laws were too inconsistent in applying capital punishment. The justice argued death sentences were imposed freakishly and compared the process to being struck by lightning with some defendants sentenced to death while others were spared without any logic.[140] With his colorful phrasing, Stewart suggested the states compose systematic capital punishment procedures to make the death penalty constitutional. In 1976, Stewart joined a plurality of three justices examining new capital punishment laws.[141] With his Furman concurrence and his opinions in Gregg, Justice Stewart deserved the title of founder of the modern death penalty.[142]

Stewart proved to be less influential in other areas of the law, dragging down his legacy. As a "swing" justice at times it seemed Stewart was more concerned with splitting the difference between competing sides than writing a consistent opinion. This was true in his opinions on the rights of criminal defendants including two self incrimination opinions at the end of his career that had similar facts but diametrically opposed results.

In *Brewer v. Williams*, Williams was convicted of murder of a small girl after confessing to the crime and revealing the location of the body. After being arrested for the murder hundreds of miles from where it was committed, Williams consulted an attorney who ordered him not to speak. During the drive to jail, one of the police officers commented on the need of the little girl's parents to provide her with a proper Christian burial. After this comment Williams revealed where he had buried the body, with his confession and the body used to convict him.[143]

Williams appealed, arguing that he had been interrogated without benefit of counsel. The Court agreed with Justice Stewart ruling the police had interrogated Williams during the drive because their comments were intended to elicit a confession.[144] Williams had been denied counsel and the evidence, including the body and his confession, could not be used in his next trial. The opinion was challenged by four angry dissenters who accused Stewart of expanding the right to counsel and protection against self incrimination to an extreme.

The dissents may have shaken Stewart as he cast off much of his Brewer decision only two years later in *Rhode Island v. Innis.*[145] Innis was arrested for murder and while being driven to the police station one of the police officers mentioned the possibility of neighborhood children finding Innis' gun and injuring themselves. Innis led the police to the weapon which was used to convict him of murder. In appealing his conviction, Innis used Brewer to argue that the comment was interrogation intended to get him to confess without benefit of counsel. When the case reached the Court it appeared that Innis had a strong argument but two justices, White and Stewart, changed their mind. In a tour de force of ignoring the past, Stewart wrote that Innis and Brewer were entirely different decisions. The police had not intended to elicit a confession from Innis in mentioning the possibility of injured children but had only made a random comment. Innis had voluntarily waived his right to counsel and to remain silent when he told the police about the weapon.[146]

Somehow during the reading of his opinion in Innis Stewart maintained a straight face as he denied the Court had changed its mind about the right to counsel but in comparing the result in Brewer with the result in Innis it is apparent that Stewart bent to public opinion or to his colleagues and switched his vote.

The addition of five Republican appointees may have moved Stewart toward the Court's conservative wing. The Gregg opinion was a renunciation of a past position, his opposition to the death penalty melting away under the heat of public opinion. His broad reading of the Thirteenth Amendment and its badges of slavery was also diluted as affirmative action policies reached the Court. Stewart became a reliable vote against race based policies, joining Chief Justice Burger and Justices Rehnquist and Stevens in the Bakke case then dissenting in the Weber and Fullilove decisions that upheld private and federal affirmative action respectively.

His departure in 1981 had the effect of further moving the Court to the right as his replacement Justice O'Connor voted with Justice Rehnquist on a regular basis.

## Notes

1. Both Wilson and Eisenhower have earned places among the near great presidents in recent surveys.In the CSPAN poll Wilson placed seventh and in the Wall Street Journal poll he placed eleventh.Eisenhower placed ninth in the CSPAN and Wall Street Journal surveys.

2. Heckscher, August, *Woodrow Wilson* (Newtown CT: American Political Biography Press, 1999) For an alternative view of Wilson's foreign policy see Fleming, Thomas,*The Illusion of Victory* (New York:Basic Books, 2003)

3. These included George Washington, Ulysses Grant, George Marshall and Douglas MacArthur.

4. Greenstein, Fred, *The Hidden Hand Presidency* (Baltimore: John Hopkins University Press, 1994).

5. Eisenhower described two of his choices, Earl Warren and William Brennan, as damned fool mistakes and when asked what mistakes he had made the former president replied "two and they are both on the Supreme Court."

6. Blaustein Albert and Roy Mersky,The *First One Hundred Justices* (Hamden CT: Archon Books, 1978)

7. Bickel, Alexander and Benno Schmidt, *The Judiciary and Responsible Government* (New York: Cambridge University Press, 2007), 343.

8. Bickel and Schmidt,352

9. Bickel and Schmidt, 425

10. McReynolds recused himself when the Caminetti case reached the Supreme Court. *Caminetti v. U.S.* 242 U.S. 470 (1917)

11. 262 U.S. 390 (1923)

12. 268 U.S. 510 (1925)

13. 262 U.S. 390, 402-403

14. 268 U.S. 510, 535-536

15. *Bartels v. Iowa* 262 U.S. 404 (1923) and *Farrington v. Tokushige* 273 U.S. 284 (1927) In Farrington federal law established a complex regulatory system for private "foreign" schools which allowed inspectors to force registration and to conduct inspections of the schools' curricula and classrooms

16. Norman v. Baltimore and Ohio Railroad 294 U.S. 240; Nortz v. United States 294 U.S. 330; Perry v. United States 294 U.S. 330 (1935)

17. McKenna, Marian, *Franklin Roosevelt and the Great Constitutional War* (New York: Fordham University Press, 2002), 244.

18. Knox, 173-174

19. Knox, John and Dennis Hutchinson and David Garrow ed,*The Forgotten Memoir of John Knox.*(Chicago:University of Chicago Press,2004), 170.

20. 301 U.S. 1 (1937) In *Wickard v. Filburn* (1942), the Court upheld federal regulation of intrastate commerce if it was substantially related to interstate commerce.

21. Pringle, Henry F, *William Howard Taft* (Newton, CT: American Political Biography Press, 1998)

22. McReynolds donated tens of thousands to charity after his retirement including money used to care for British children then bequeathed much of his fortune to charity after his death.

23. Knox, 220-221

24. Knox, 35

25. McReynolds dissented in *Steward Machine v. Davis* 301 U.S. 548 (1937) where the Court upheld the Social Security Act.He also dissented in *Herndon v. Lowry* 301 U.S. 242 (1937), which was one of the early free speech cases where the Court struck down a sedition law on free speech grounds.*Erie v. Tompkins* 304 U.S. 64 (1938) where the Court rewrote the procedure for diversity of citizenship cases and *U.S. v. Carolene Products* 304 U.S. 144 (1938) where a famous footnote recognized insular and discrete minorities along with fundamental rights as specially protected also saw McReynolds dissent.The justice dissented in *Mulford v. Smith* 307 U.S. 38 (1939) upholding the second Agricultural Adjustment Act and overruling *U.S. v. Butler* 297 U.S. 1 (1936).Oddly enough both Butler and Mulford were written by Justice Roberts.He was also the only dissenter when the Court overturned an Alabama loitering law in Thornhill.Overall McReynolds held onto his ideology, unlike Justice Robertsand Chief Justice Hughes who accepted the new world of the RooseveltCourt.

26. 307 U.S. 174 (1939)

27. Blaustein and Mersky, 48

28. Warner, Hoyt Landon. *The Life of Mr. Justice Clarke* (Cleveland: Western Reserve University Press, 1959), 56-57.

29. Bickel and Schmidt,409

30. Clarke lived for another twenty years, prompting speculation about his resignation.Warner, 112-113

31. Warner, 75

32. McReynolds refused to sign the standard letter of regret to Clarke from the justices.Warner, 115

33. Bickel and Schmidt, 413

34. Warner, 138-139

35. 250 U.S. 616 (1919)

36. Clarke warned that Abrams and his cohorts were seeking to "incite disaffection, sedition, riots, and ... revolution," with their pamphlets during the national emergency 250 U.S. 616, 624-625

37. *Rhode Island v. Palmer* 253 U.S. 360, 411 (1920)

38. In his opinion, Justice David Brewer remarked upon the inherent weakness of women and how legislation could be used to protect females and ensure they could carry out their God given right of bearing and caring for children.208 U.S. 412, 422-423 (1908)

39. The newspaper of record, the New York Times, denounced Brandeis for his emphasis on social justice and accused him of introducing radicalism into a conservative institution, Bickel and Schmidt, 376.

40. Brandeis also had his supporters including Wisconsin Senator Robert LaFollette and curiously enough the virulent racist Senator "Pitchfork" Benjamin Tillman of South Carolina, Bickel and Schmidt, 378

41. The case was *Schenck v. United States* and included another felicitous phrase that of yelling fire in a crowded theater.

42. *Abrams v. United States* 250 U.S. 616, 625 (1919)
43. 285 U.S. 262 (1932)
44. 285 U.S. 262, 312
45. 277 U.S. 438 (1928)
46. 277 U.S. 438, 474
47. 299 U.S. 59 (1936)
48. This decision would be partly overturned in 2006 in *Heald v. Michigan* as fivejustices found the Twenty First Amendment did not give states authority to discriminate between out of state and in state alcohol and that the dormant commerce clause prohibited that discrimination.
49. 304 U.S. 64 (1938)
50. Purcell, Edward, *Brandeis and the Progressive Constitution* (New Haven CT: Yale University Press,2000), 114-115
51. D'Este, Carlos, *Eisenhower* (New York: Henry Holt and Co, 2002), 693-695.
52. Morris, Roger, *Richard Milhous Nixon* (New York: Henry Holt and Co, 1990), 707-709, 711-712.
53. Newton, Jim, *Justice For All* (New York: Riverhead, 2006), 354-355 Eisenhower expressed dismay at his appointees decisions during the "Red Monday" cases involving domestic communism.
54. Schwartz, Bernard, *Super Chief* (New York: New York University Press, 1983), 15-16.
55. As part of the unusual California primary system of the period, Warren ran in the Democrat and Republican primaries in 1950, winning both and facing no significant competition in the general election.Warren was seen as the perfect bipartisan candidate, appealing to all sides, not unlike Eisenhower. Shwartz 18-19
56. Smith, Richard Norton, *Thomas Dewey and his Times* (New York: Simon and Schuster, 1984), 608.
57. Ambrose, Stephen *Nixon The Education of a Politician 1913-1962* (New York: Simon and Schuster, 1987) ,258-259.
58. Schwartz, 3
59. Abraham, 201-202; Schwartz, 4-5
60. For example,Thea Rubin and Albert Melone"Justice Antonin Scalia: A First Year Freshman Effect"72 *Judicature* 98 (1988), Robert Dudley "The Freshman Effect and Voting Alignments" 21 *American Political Quarterly* 360 1993, Christopher Smith, Joyce Baugh, Thomas Hensley and Scott PatrickJohnson" The First Term Performance of Justice Ruth Bader Ginsburg" 78 *Judicature* 74 1994,Thomas Hensley, Joyce Baugh and Christopher Smith "The First Term Appointment of Chief Justice John Roberts" 43 *Idaho LawReview* 625 2007
61. *Smith v. Allwright* 321 U.S. 649 (1944)

62. *Sweatt v. Painter* 339 U.S. 629 (1950)*McLaurin v. Board of Regents* 339 U.S. 637 (1950)

63. Kluger, Richard, *Simple Justice* (New York: Vintage, 2004), 778-779.

64. Kluger,866-868

65. Gerhardt, 97

66. Kluger, 882

67. Kluger 868-869

68. *Brown v. Board of Education II*394 U.S. 294 (1955)

69. These would include Judge Minor Wisdom and J Waties Waring, both of the fifth circuit court of appeals and Judge Frank Johnson in Alabama.Peltason, J.W, *Fifty Eight Lonely Men* (Champaign IL: University of Illinois Press, 1971).

70. Schwartz, 205-206, Powe, Lucas, *The Warren Court and American Politics* (Cambridge MA: Belknap Press, 2002), 303.

71. 353 U.S. 657 (1957)

72. 377 U.S. 533 (1964)

73. The Court became entangled in state constitutional amendments regulating representation in *General Assembly of Colorado v. Lucas* 377 U.S. 713 (1964); cases involving state reapportionment, *Swann v. Adams* 383 U.S. 210 (1966), *Burns v. Richardson* 384 U.S. 73 (1966), *Kilgarlin v. Hill* 386 U.S. 120 (1967); and for county races, *Avery v. Midland County* 390 U.S. 474 (1968), school boards, *Sailors v. County of Kent* 387 U.S. 105 (1967) and city council elections, *Dusch v. Davis* 387 U.S. 112 (1967)

74. 384 U.S. 436 (1966)

75. 391 U.S. 367(1968) In O'Brien Warren created the complicated four part test that would be used in future symbolic speech cases.

76. 392 U.S. 1 (1968)

77. *McGowan v. Maryland* 366 U.S. 420 (1961)

78. See *Roth v. United States*354 U.S. 476 (1957) joining majority establishing a national obscenity standard; *Jacobellis v. Ohio* 378 U.S. 184 (1964) dissenting when Court struck down obscenity prosecution; *Ginzburg v. U.S.* 383 U.S. 463 (1966), joining majority; *Mishkin v. New York* 383 U.S. 502 (1966), joining majority in upholding obscenity convictions.

79. 394 U.S. 576 (1969)

80. Schwartz, 497-501

81. They included Gerald Ford, Richard Russell, Allen Dulles, John Sherman Cooper, John McCloy and Hale Boggs.

82. Newton, 446-447

83. Yarbrough, Tinsley, *John Marshall Harlan: Great Dissenter of the Warren Court* (New York: Oxford University Press, 2001),341-343.

84. Woodward and Armstrong, 127n.

85. Yarbrough, 235

86. 360 U.S. 109 (1959)

87. 367 U.S. 497 (1961)

88. 367 U.S. 497, 536

89. 367 U.S. 497, 539

90. 381 U.S. 479, 484, 490-491

91. 381 U.S. 479, 500

92. One of his later opinions was the notorious *Cohen v. California* in which Harlan ruled that a jacket containing the words "Fuck the Draft" was protected under the First Amendment.403 U.S. 15 (1971).Oddly enough Justice Black the First Amendment absolutist dissented and argued in favor of government to criminalizing obscenities.

93. 367 U.S. 643, 680

94. 384 U.S. 436, 506 (1966)

95. 372 U.S. 335 (1963)

96. 372 U.S. 335, 349

97. Woodward and Armstrong, 224.

98. Abraham, 208

99. Justice Sandra O'Connor, appointed in 1981, was the last justice lacking federal court experience.

100. 354 U.S. 476(1957)

101. Brennan was the "moderate" liberal, disagreeing with the absolutist positions of Black and Douglas while agreeing with the chief justice, Newton 348-349.

102. *Memoirs v. Massachusetts*383 U.S. 413 (1966)

103. *Hamling v. U.S.* 418 U.S. 87 (1974), *New York v. Ferber* 458 U.S. 747 (1982), Massachusetts v. Oakes 491 U.S. 576 (1989), *Osborne v. Ohio* (1990). The next set of obscenity cases began with federal internet regulation, the first attempt in a quarter century to create that elusive national obscenity standard.

104. 376 U.S. 254, 279-280 (1964)

105. *Associated Press v. Walker*388 U.S. 130 (1967), actual malice applied to public figures, in this case an army general.*Rosenbloom v. Metromedia* 403 U.S. 29 (1971) applying actual malice to ordinary citizens.This would be overruled in *Gertz v. Welch* 418 U.S. 323 (1974). One of his eulogizers in the volume of the Harvard Law Review celebrating his career at the time of his death was Nina Totenberg, National Public Radio correspondent for the Supreme Court, who tossed away her studied neutrality for a few moments to write glowingly of the man she had been assigned to report on. Totenberg, Nina"Justice Brennan" 104 *Harvard Law Review* 133-40.

106. 369 U.S. 186 (1962)

107. 411 U.S. 677 (1973)

108. *Craig v. Boren* 429 U.S. 190 (1976).Brennan switched to an intermediate level of scrutiny for gender cases, tossing aside his earlier preference for strict scrutiny.

109. Woodward and Armstrong, 239

110. 427 U.S. 347 (1976)
111. Woodward and Armstrong,
112. 443 U.S. 193 (1979)
113. 491 U.S. 397(1989)
114. 497 U.S. 547 (1990)
115. *Pennsylvania v. Union Gas*491 U.S. 1 (1989)
116. Miller, Richard Lawrence. *Justice Whittaker* Westport, CT.:Greenwood Press 2002
117. Vestal, 273.
118. 356 U.S. 44 (1958)
119. Miller, 72-73
120. Miller, 61
121. 359 U.S 121 (1959)
122. Lawrence, 125-126.
123. 370 U.S. 294 (1962)
124. Lawrence, 150-151.
125. Vestal, 273-274
126. "Surprise from the Swing Man" *Time* June 29, 198148.The letter came from a St. Cloud Minnesota high school student who asked the rhetorical question on why Stewart had remained on the Court for so long.
127. *Jacobellis v. Ohio*378 U.S. 184, 197 (1964)
128. This contrasted with Stewart's opinion in *Massiah v. U.S.* 377 U.S. 201 (1964), expanding the prohibition against self incrimination.
129. The cases included *Malloy v. Hogan* 378 U.S. 1 (1964), *Duncan v. Louisiana* 391 U.S. 145 (1968) and *Benton v. Maryland* 395 U.S. 784 (1969).
130. 374 U.S. 398(1963)
131. 374 U.S. 398, 416
132. 374 U.S. 203 (1963)
133. 374 U.S. 203, 309
134. 392 U.S. 409 (1968)
135. 427 U.S. 160 (1976)
136. 392 U.S. 409, 423.
137. 427 U.S. 160, 176.This would have created the unusual case where racial segregation was preached within an integrated school.
138. *Patterson v. McLean Credit Union* 491 U.S. 164 (1989). In Patterson, the Court refused to extend Stewart's arguments about denying the right to contract to instances of sexual or racial harassment on the job.
139. 408 U.S. 238 (1972)
140. 408 U.S. 238, 309
141. *Gregg v. Georgia* 428 U.S. 153 (1976)
142. 428 U.S. 153, 192-193.
143. 430 U.S. 387 (1977)
144. 430 U.S. 387, 399-401

145. 446 U.S. 291 (1980)
146. 446 U.S. 291, 302-303

## Section 2

# Successful Failures: Great Presidents who failed at their judicial nominations

Administrations deemed successful rarely suffer from the in depth examination of policies reserved for less successful presidents. Four presidents ranked among the greats fell to the category of average or below average for their Supreme Court appointments.

## Chapter 5

# Andrew Jackson (17) Harry Truman (26)

Known for their obstinacy and determination, Andrew Jackson and Harry Truman rose to the ranks of great presidents partly on the success of biographies about their presidents. Yet their nine total Court appointments flopped, Jackson's blamed for sparking the Civil War with the Dred Scott decision and Truman's lacking intellectual depth and mostly overshadowed by their colleagues.

Harry Truman and Andrew Jackson are the populist vision of American presidents, stubborn, independent, honest men whose plain speaking frequently created controversies. Both excited political passions in their era and are generally regarded as near great presidents. Yet their Supreme Court appointments tarnished their legacies, Jackson's justices with the Dred Scott decision and Truman's with a general fecklessness.

## Andrew Jackson

Few presidents of the nineteenth century excited as much anger and fear in his opponents than did Andrew Jackson. Portrayed as a barely literate backwoodsman bent on creating a military dictatorship, Jackson was a stubborn man who rarely forgot a slur and always found a way to get even with his opponents. Seemingly swindled in the 1824 presidential election, Jackson spent four years denouncing his opponent, John Quincy Adams, and working for his defeat. Once in the White House Jackson did not forget the financial disaster brought down on him by the Bank of the United States and spent two terms trying to destroy it. Opponents such as Henry Clay and John Calhoun experienced Jackson's wrath, with the president threatening to hang his former vice president if South Carolina carried out its secessionist threat. But lacking an attention to detail, Jackson leaned on his subordinates, including Roger Taney and Martin van Buren, to implement his agenda. They were successful in guiding his policies through Congress, earning Jackson a ranking among the greatest of presidents.

But neither Jackson nor his advisors proved adept at filling the five slots opened on the Supreme Court during his administration. Instead Jackson displayed remarkable ineptness in his choices, placing political loyalty above merit, while making almost random appointments based on political expediency. The appointment of John McLean to the Court exemplified this approach.

## John McLean

Having a loose sense of loyalty and a pliable ideology is considered an advantage in the hothouse political environment of Washington D.C. Jackson's first Court appointment, John McLean, took this strategy to the extreme. A native of Ohio, McLean served in all three branches of government as a legislator, as a judge on the Ohio Supreme Court and as a member of James Monroe's and John Quincy Adams' cabinet.[1] In 1824 he had been an Adams supporter against Jackson, going so far as to lobby his own brother, an Ohio congressman, to vote for Adams. McLean was rewarded, allowed to keep his position as postmaster general, an office bulging with patronage positions that could be used to collect political debts.[2]

Adams' struggle in office caused McLean to jump ship and become a Jackson supporter during the 1828 election, earning Jackson's favor but also exciting suspicions of McLean's presidential aspirations. Removing that threat became an early concern for Jackson, who took advantage of a vacancy held over from the Adams administration.[3]

The sudden death of Justice Robert Trimble afforded Adams a final appointment opportunity in the dying days of his presidency. His choice, John Crittenden, was defeated in the Senate and Jackson arrived at the White House with a Court vacancy to fill.[4] Jackson offered the position to William Barry but with the McLean political threat looming a complex agreement was worked out. Barry assumed McLean's position as postmaster general and McLean accepted the seat on the Court. Jackson and his advisors must have sighed with relief that a political rival was locked away in the Court where he could not run for president. McLean would prove them wrong.

## McLean for President

From the beginning of his Court career, Justice McLean was unable to resist the urge to place his name in the arena and seek the office at every opportunity. In 1832 the Democrat Party was controlled by Andrew Jackson and challenging the popular president would be a political suicide mission. McLean also could not challenge the leader of the opposition Whig Party, Henry Clay, who was certain to win the party nomination. The justice then turned to a third party, the Anti Masons, which was born of suspicion of Jackson's and other leader's membership in the Masonic organization. The party offered McLean the nomination, eager to attract a prominent official to their cause but the justice's political instincts were awakened as he realized the party was doomed to disaster.[5]

His hopes dashed in 1836, McLean mounted candidacies for the Whig and Republican nominations. The justice's closest call came in 1848 when he was the early frontrunner for the Whig nomination. But the Mexican War intervened and McLean was tossed aside for a general, the popular Zachary Taylor, who won the nomination and the presidency.[6] The breakup of the Whig party in 1854 saw McLean jump ship onto the new Republican party. He ran a distant second in 1856 to the nominee, John Fremont. Undeterred, the nearly eighty year old McLean sought the 1860 nomination but it was not to be. Only his death in April, 1861 ended his quest for office.

McLean used his seat as political forum, opinions campaign documents used to influence political opinions rather than an expression of law. Yet even with his every spare moment consumed with the White House, McLean managed to author opinions of import and a dissent against one of the institution's worst decisions, *Dred Scott v. Sandford.*

Serving in the last years of the Marshall Court, McLean hastened disintegration of the chief justice's influence over his colleagues. Previous to McLean's arrival Marshall and his colleagues had stayed together in a boarding house, creating a camaraderie that melded seven very different men into an institution that spoke with a single voice. But McLean refused to join this informal organization, choosing his own living space and bringing his wife to stay with him.[7]

McLean's opinions reflected an independence of thought. At times it appeared McLean favored the most unusual answer to a problem rather than the one attracting a majority. These unusual tendencies were evident in the Charles River Bridge Case.[8] As one of the first constitutional opinions issued by the Taney Court, the chief justice used the case to reinterpret the Contract Clause. Taney ruled the Contract Clause did not restrict states in the use of their sovereign police powers. The decision drew a dissent from Marshall's close friend and colleague, Justice Story, who saw the decision as a retreat from the former chief justice's views. McLean's political leanings might have compelled him to join Story's dissent while his status as a Jacksonian might drive him to line up beside Taney. Instead he composed a soon forgotten opinion claiming the Court lacked jurisdiction.[9]

The death of Chief Justice John Marshall not only changed the occupant of the Court's center chair but also the direction of the institution. The new chief, Roger Taney of Maryland, was Jacksonian in his outlook, suspicious of national power and supportive of slave owners and their arguments. McLean, on the other hand, may have been the last Federalist to serve in high political office. His dedication to nationalism, as defined by Marshall, became more fervid with Taney's arrival. As the Court tilted toward states' rights and a pro slavery agenda, McLean became a lonely voice in pushing for total federal power over commerce among the states. The commerce issue divided the Court more than slavery, though the two would become mixed during McLean's thirty two years on the Court.

One of the commerce disputes dating from the Marshall Court focused on whether people could be considered articles of commerce to be regulated by the federal government. The split on the question coincided with the split over slavery. McLean consistently ruled people were commerce while his southern colleagues denied such a connection. Though the question may appear archaic and technical to a 21st century reader it was critical to the era. If people could be regulated as commerce, Congress could use its authority to limit or even abolish slavery as a commercial activity. The suggestion that Congress could regulate slavery produced an outcry among southern politicians and McLean stoked the controversy by offering the argument in the *Passenger Cases*[10] and *Cooley v. Port Board of Wardens*.[11]

The Passenger cases involved immigration and the imposition of taxes on ships carrying immigrants into New York. The taxes funded a marine hospital to care for immigrants but were challenged as a state regulation of commerce. The Court agreed the state had overstepped its bounds. McLean concurred with the decision arguing the transportation of people could be considered commerce and could not be regulated by the states.[12] With his abolitionist leanings, McLean implied federal regulation of slavery was plausible but the author of the Court opinion, Justice Wayne, calmed southern fears by rejecting McLean's reasoning.

McLean dissented in another critical commerce case of the period, the Cooley decision. He disagreed with the Court when it allowed city authorities to regulate commerce activities by taxing ships if they did not use local captains to steer into ports.[13] For McLean federal control of commerce was complete and no other government could regulate it.[14]

Yet McLean's dedication to federal power proved less complete when combined with the slavery issue. *Groves v. Slaughter* mixed the issues of slavery and commerce with a challenge to the Mississippi constitutional ban on the transport and sale of slaves from other states.[15] The Court dodged the slavery issue by ruling on a technical point but McLean took the opportunity to approve the Mississippi ban, declaring slavery and the slave trade a local issue that could be prohibited by states.[16] This was a far cry from his arguments that movement of people across state lines was interstate commerce under the control of Congress.

## The Dissent

McLean's presidential ambitions distorted his opinions but saved him from the ignominy suffered by his fellow Jackson appointees. McLean was the only one of four Jackson justices to reject the reasoning in Dred Scott, though his dissent smacked more of politics rather than legal reasoning.

Disappointed at being defeated for the 1856 Republican nomination, McLean geared up for the next contest. Planning his next campaign, he composed a dissent in Dred Scott polemical in style and directed at the northern electorate rather than a legal audience.[17] McLean's dissent was overshadowed by Justice Curtis' dissent, which is generally quoted as the definitive critique of Dred Scott and composed in the precise legal language expected of a Supreme Court opinion.[18]

Yet McLean is given credit, or blame, for triggering the full Dred Scott opinion. McLean's dissent to the first opinion tackled the question of slavery in the territories. By raising the issue the justice is blamed for provoking his southern brethren into widening the Dred Scott ruling.[19] Yet blaming McLean for this exercise in institutional suicide ignored the fact the southern justices including Justice Catron and his correspondent, James Buchanan, sought a final settling of the slavery question.

Dred Scott marked the end of the Supreme Court's political relevance for another decade but McLean proved more resilient. Hailed as only one of two dissenters from the notorious opinion, he rode the wave into the 1860 Republican convention but once again was passed over for the nomination. His last great political act came during the 1861 secession crisis. While enjoying a dinner with President James Buchanan, McLean listened as the issue of Fort Sumter was raised. Hearing the president consider recalling Major Anderson, the commander of Fort Sumter, McLean exclaimed "You dare not do it sire, you dare not do it," trying to insert steel into the spineless politician dithering over secession.[20] McLean would die in April 1861 as the secessionist crisis reached a tipping point.

## Henry Baldwin

Justice Henry Baldwin's selection to the Supreme Court marked one of the rare occasions when Andrew Jackson was praised for his moderation and good sense. Unfortunately the good feeling generated by Baldwin's appointment ended almost the moment he reached the Court.

In 1830 the death of Bushrod Washington presented Jackson with another Court vacancy. The president struggled with the choice of a man who could be John Marshall's equal. John McLean had offered little resistance, seemingly obsessed with his quest for the presidency and Jackson was criticized for not appointing a justice who could oppose John Marshall and his allies. In replacing Justice Washington, Jackson considered John Gibson of the Pennsylvania Supreme Court, a judge who would be lost to history except for his opinion in *Eakin v. Raub*.[21] In Eakin, Gibson argued against judicial review, favoring elections over judges to check legislators. Gibson's opinion has become a regular feature in constitutional texts when discussing the opponents of judicial review. Gibson's notoriety as a Marshall Court critic who denied courts the power of judicial review sank his nomination.[22]

With Gibson out Jackson selected Henry Baldwin. A former congressman from Pennsylvania, Baldwin was an early Jackson supporter, having defended the general during the debate over whether to censure him over his actions in Florida, then backing his 1824 and 1828 runs for the presidency. Baldwin was mentioned as a possible cabinet appointment but in 1830 received the more prestigious Court appointment.[23]

Baldwin's mercurial personality wreaked havoc on what had been a collegial Court. The justice clashed with his colleagues, composing opinions where he snarled at their rulings.[24] During his first term in 1831 he composed seven dissents, the most by any justice during any term up to that time.[25] The justice resented Court reporter Richard Peters for his veiled criticism of Baldwin's opinion. Baldwin threatened to resign after his first term, but his anger subsided and Baldwin returned to the Court.

Baldwin struggled to maintain his sanity. In 1833 he missed most of the Court's term resting in a hospital, likely receiving treatment for his mental problems.[26] With bankruptcy staring him in the face, Baldwin became convinced the general public was eager to read the constitutional philosophy of a Supreme Court justice. He composed commentaries of his own Court opinions and made them available for sale. But his efforts came to naught and his finances remained a muddle, forcing him to sell personal items, including his prized library, to raise money.[27]

A man comfortable writing on his own behalf, Baldwin proved a proficient dissenter. The chief justice was driven to distraction by Baldwin's behavior as the justice's contribution to the institution tended to be mainly negative, his opinions confusing the issue or irritating his colleagues while temper tantrums split the justices.[28] Composing few Court opinions during his tenure, his legacy is one of a distressed man whose physical and mental deterioration burdened the institution.

## James Wayne

Four of Jackson's Court appointments served more than a quarter of a century as a justice. As the longest serving Jackson justice, thirty two years, Justice James Wayne presented a mixed record as a southern nationalist who opposed secession while voting against Dred Scott's freedom.

Wayne was the quintessential southern nationalist, torn between national and sectional loyalty. A Georgia slave owner whose son fought for the Confederacy, Wayne remained a unionist throughout his career. Elected to Congress just as Andrew Jackson was entering the presidency, Wayne proved a loyalist to the Jacksonian cause. He was one of the rare southern congressmen supporting the president during the South Carolina secession crisis. He voted for the Force Bill, providing the president authority to use military force to enforce federal law in South Carolina.[29] Wayne also approved of the removal of federal deposits from the Bank of the United States, angering many of his constituents.[30] More attuned to Georgians was his support of removing the Cherokees from the state, another Jackson policy where Wayne proved his loyalty. For his efforts the congressman was rewarded with a seat on the Supreme Court, replacing William Johnson in 1835.[31]

Serving most of his tenure with Roger Taney, Wayne was a close friend of the chief and other southern justices including Philip Barbour and John Catron. But on issues of national power Wayne split from his colleagues, who favored state rather than federal control over commerce. Wayne was closest in his views to Justice McLean, and voted with him in the Passenger Cases and in the Cooley decision. In both Wayne and McLean argued for an exclusive congressional power to regulate interstate commerce. He was also a key vote in the License cases.

Wayne's nationalism included expanding presidential power. In Ex Parte Wells, Wayne ruled presidential pardoning power included the power to commute a sentence. [32] He upheld President Fillmore's decision to commute Wells' death sentence to one of life in prison, writing that the pardoning power was not limited to the full and complete pardon listed in Article II. As was his tendency, Justice McLean dissented with the argument Wells had not been pardoned, instead his condition of death had been changed from dying on the scaffold to dying in prison of old age.[33]

Wayne also offered one of the early opinions, *Barber v. Barber*, recognizing rights of women to sue in Court. Barber was a divorce case that challenged the right of a woman to sue her husband in court.[34] Under common law women could not sue their husbands without aid of a "best friend" filing the suit for them. Wayne recognized that women could sue their husbands to enforce a divorce settlement in another state. Mrs. Barber's divorce in New York courts could be enforced in Wisconsin using federal jurisdiction. The Barber decision also added to the Court's Full Faith and Credit interpretation and what legal documents could be enforced in different states. Wayne the nationalist tied together the states in a national legal community, earning a dissent from the Court's states' rights bloc, including Chief Justice Taney.

Drawing on his Jacksonian nationalism, Wayne joined Justice McLean, another nationalist, in dissenting in the Court's commerce cases. The most prominent of these was *Cooley v. Port Board of Wardens.* In Cooley Justice Curtis strengthened the dormant commerce clause first created in *Gibbons v. Ogden.* Curtis ruled states could regulate elements of interstate commerce that were purely local in nature, such as the piloting of boats in a harbor. McLean and Wayne dissented, arguing for plenary federal authority in regulating interstate commerce.

If Wayne's nationalist beliefs were dominant in the commerce cases, they became secondary when faced with the slavery issue. Wayne's acquiescence in Dred Scot tainted his legacy. Chief Justice Taney denied Congress authority to regulate slavery in the territories, making the issue a purely state issue. Dred Scott was a victory for the extreme states' rights bloc, those who sought to expand slavery through the western territories under the protection of the constitution and federal law. Wayne had rejected such views as a congressman in 1833 and as a justice in the commerce cases but the slavery issue and loyalty to his section placed him among the Court radicals.

Wayne participated in the conference maneuvering as he rejected Justice Nelson's opinion denying Dred Scott's petition for freedom. Nelson had avoided the explosive issue of Congressional regulation of slavery, simply one in a series of pro slavery opinions by the Taney Court. Dissatisfied, Wayne suggested during a February 1857 conference the opinion be broadened to strike at congressional authority to ban slavery in the territories.[35] Wayne convinced his colleagues and Chief Justice Taney's opinion included many of Wayne's arguments, the Georgian joining it after offering a brief concurrence.[36]

Just as suddenly as Wayne offered solitude for the states' rights extremists, he rejected their secessionist strategy. Returning to his Jacksonian nationalist roots, Wayne rejected the confederacy, refusing to join his home state in leaving the union and having his property seized for the crime of remaining a United States citizen.[37] His son joined the Confederate army and Wayne likely spent many a restless night wondering if his son was part of the casualty list from the battles fought a hundred miles to the south.

Even with his family split along sectional lines, Wayne supported the war effort. In 1861 Wayne upheld Lincoln's order for volunteers during the dangerous early months of the war. Wayne ruled Lincoln was exercising the inherent power to protect the constitution and the government, even it if meant making war against the South.[38]

In 1863 Wayne turned back a challenge to the Legal Tender Act, the law used by the Lincoln Administration to fund the war. Wayne ruled the judiciary lacked authority to hear the case, striking a back door challenge to the war's constitutionality.[39] That same year Wayne provided a fifth vote upholding the federal policy of blockading the southern ports. The Prize Cases upheld Lincoln's ordering of the blockade, an act of war, without congressional approval.

Wayne's dedication to the union could only be stretched so far and reconstruction efforts drew him back to his southern roots. The justice was offended by the state and federal requirement that all former confederates take an oath before being allowed to serve in a government position, to practice law or as a clergyman. Wayne provided the key vote in the Cummings and Garland cases striking down those loyalty oaths.[40] The Georgian sought conciliation with the South but his 1867 death silenced his voice just as the Court was cast into the reconstruction maelstrom.

## Chief Justice Taney

For two decades, Chief Justice Roger Taney developed the reputation as an honorable and competent successor to John Marshall, guiding the Supreme Court through the constitutional shoals of Antebellum America. Even his critics would admit he did not resemble the radical Jacksonian senators feared during his two confirmation battles in 1835 and 1836.[41] But his twenty years of work was destroyed by a single unforgivable misstep, his authoring of the Dred Scott decision.

A loyal Jacksonian, Taney suffered and benefitted from his loyalty to the president. Appointed attorney general in 1831 where he drafted Jackson's bank veto message, Taney was appointed treasury secretary and removed federal deposits from the Bank of the United States.[42] An angry Congress responded with a censure resolution against Jackson, with little effect, then turned on Taney, rejecting his nomination as Treasury Secretary on the very day it was sent to the Senate, a record for the usually slow moving chambe.[43]

A Senate rejection usually marks the end of a political career, but Jackson did not forget Taney's loyalty. With Justice Duvall's resignation opening a vacancy on the Court, Jackson nominated Taney as his replacement, a deliberate slap at the Senate. Jackson nominated Taney during Congress' 1834 lame duck session even as those year's midterm elections promised a Jackson majority in the chamber for the next session.[44] Senators refused to consider Taney's nomination then voting to eliminate Duvall's seat on the Court.[45]

Taney was again jobless but not forgotten and when John Marshall died in 1835 Jackson nominated him for the Court's center chair. Facing a Democrat friendly Senate, Taney's nomination was bundled with Philip Barbour's nomination to replace Duval, both men sliding through the Senate.[46]

Taney inherited a court responsible for creating a powerful and respected federal judiciary that exercised the power of judicial review. John Marshall wielded his power against the politically weaker states while remaining a comfortable distance from the more powerful Congress. Marshall's success was not complete as he left unanswered questions on the extent of congressional commerce power and demarcation between federal and state power. His cautious application of judicial review was recognition of the judiciary's tenuous political position. Much of this legacy would be destroyed by Taney with his misstep in Dred Scot as the chief justice became synonymous with the case that helped spark the Civil War.

Another Marshall legacy was the tight rein he maintained on his colleagues and the consensus opinions that presented the justices as a united front against any challenge to the institution. Taney loosened those controls, the justices seizing the opportunity to write separate opinions and at times returning the Court to his seriatim past.[47]

Early in his tenure, Taney redirected the Court toward a Jacksonian agenda favoring economic growth over contract rights and state power over congressional authority. His success came in three cases during his first term, the new chief composing the seminal decision in the Charles River Bridge Case.[48]

Taney considered whether the Charles Bridge company's exclusive contract to operate a bridge across the Charles River was violated when the Warren Bridge Co. was allowed to build a nearby competing bridge. Marshall had decided similar cases in favor of the original contract but Taney set a new course. The chief wrote that the state could not surrender its police powers to provide for the health, safety and welfare of its citizens. Because building a bridge was considered part of the police powers, Massachusetts could commission a second bridge without violating the original contract.[49]

In two other cases, *Briscoe v. Commonwealth of Kentucky*[50] and *New York v. Miln*,[51] the Taney Court loosened the Federalist constraints on states' rights. In Briscoe, Justice McLean upheld the use of certain forms of bank notes that expanded the money supply but were not considered state bills of credit which would constitute a currency. Allowing state banks to issue these notes allowed for an expanded money supply just as the country was pitching into the depths of the 1837 depression. In Miln, the Court ruled in favor of a New York regulation of immigrants, a power usually reserved to the federal government.

The promised "Jacksonian Revolution" though did not occur as Taney and his colleagues struggled to undo parts of the Marshall legacy. Lacking Marshall's personality or power of argument, Taney saw the Court splinter in two important commerce cases of the 1840s, the License Cases[52] and the Passenger Cases.[53] The License cases were unanimous but featured six opinions, including five concurrences that confused rather than enlightened the issues. The Passenger cases saw no majority opinion with eight separate opinions and Taney dissenting against a nationalist majority that included Justices McLean and Wayne. The return to seratiam opinions in the two cases, offered the image of an institution adrift.

In 1849 Taney defined the political question doctrine within American law. A Rhode Island rebellion resulted in the Supreme Court case of *Luther v. Borden*.[54] The obscure Dorr Rebellion pitted a group of farmers against the Rhode Island government formed under a colonial era state constitution. When the dispute reached the justices, Taney avoided the controversy, instead ruling the issue was a political question. Taney ruled the entire question was covered under Article IV and the Republican government clause which granted Congress rather than the judiciary authority to determine if a state was a republic and to act accordingly. Judicial involvement would violate the separation of powers.[55] Taney's doctrine would be used by his successors to avoid issues such as legislative apportionment and the Senate rules for removing an impeached federal judge.

Taney's struggles were unexpected as the 1837 Judiciary Act had created a southern dominated Court. The Act expanded the Court to nine members and reorganized the circuits to include five southern circuits, guaranteeing a Court dominated by the slave holding region. By 1857, there were seven justices with southern roots or who favored southern policies all leading to Dred Scott.[56]

Dred Scott was a Missouri slave who claimed his freedom after his owner, an Army doctor, took him to Minnesota territory which was free under the federal Northwest Ordinance passed prior to adoption of the constitution. If Dred Scott was a free man in Minnesota it would follow he would be a free man once he returned to Missouri and he brought this argument to the Supreme Court.

After taking the assignment to compose a broader opinion, Taney was swept away by the furor of his declaration that Congress could not regulate slavery in the territories. Taney failed to recognize the gap between abolitionist and pro slavery zealots, believing that a middle ground existed that would be filled by the Court opinion. The chief justice was swept in the slavery arguments of the period which had shredded the political middle, creating a huge divide.[57] The chief declared that Dred Scott could not sue because he was not considered a citizen and could never become a citizen because under both the Declaration of Independence and the constitution free blacks were not considered citizens with the right to sue.

Taney's argument misread Article I Section 8 and the Territories Clause, ruling it did not empower Congress to ban slavery in the territories, as it had with the Missouri Compromise.[58] Acting on this strained interpretation, Taney struck down the compromise, only the second federal law overturned by the Court. While the ruling had little practical effect as the 1820 had been overridden by the 1850 Compromise, Taney's tortured reading of the territories clause angered even northern supporters of slavery. The decision went further in protecting slave owner property rights under the Fifth Amendment, finding that federal regulation of slavery in territories violated those property rights, thus opening the possibility of expansion of slavery into northern territories.[59]

Northern fury was used by the Republican Party to win majorities in Congress and elect Abraham Lincoln. For the first time since the Jefferson Administration, the justices faced an aroused Congress. During the Civil War, Taney was an impotent force, his ruling in *Ex Parte Merryman* ignored by the executive and the military.[60]

During a Confederate inspired revolt in Maryland in spring 1861, John Merryman was imprisoned in nearby Fort McHenry. Merryman sought his release, his request eventually reaching Chief Justice Taney who ordered the military to produce Merryman for a Habeas Corpus hearing. When his order was ignored, the chief composed an opinion denouncing Lincoln for suspending Habeas Corpus without congressional approval, implying the chief feared the country was on the brink of a military dictatorship.[61]

The Merryman opinion was a political document intended to be used by Lincoln's critics to attack his war policies. The chief wrote the opinion in a week then leaked it to newspapers and personally financed pamphlets to be distributed to the public. Supporters of the Merryman decision were limited to secessionists, confederate newspapers heaped praise on the "truth" and "logic" of the chief, compliments that were certain to inflame northern opinion against him.[62] It was at that time the chief expressed the personal preference for a peaceful division of the country over the possibility of war.[63]

President Lincoln handled Taney by ignoring him and the Court. He allowed three Court vacancies to linger, reducing the number of filled seats to six, a bare quorum. Illnesses prevented a majority of justices from meeting, rendering the Court inoperable for several months. Beset by illness, dogged by political attacks from Congress, Taney spent his last years on the fringes of power, spending idle days doodling opinions striking down Republican policies that had not yet been challenged.[64] He was voluble in declaring the secessionists resembled the revolutionaries who had overthrown the British crown.[65]

Taney died in October 1864; his death mourned by Democrats but greeted with some relief by Republicans who feared the chief might outlive the Republican administration before it could replace him. These sentiments were expressed best by Senator Benjamin Wade who had said in 1860 he prayed hard every night that Taney remain alive long enough for Lincoln to replace him. But as the chief lingered, the senator feared he had prayed too well.[66]

## Philip Barbour

When Jackson faced two vacancies in 1835, he utilized a tandem nomination to take the political pressure from Roger Taney. His choice of Philip Barbour exemplified his strategy of choosing men based on ideology and personal loyalty. A native Virginian, Barbour spent much of his adult life battling for states rights in Congress, before the Supreme Court and in his home state.

Elected to Congress in 1814, Barbour defended General Andrew Jackson against a censure resolution and defended the South during the furious debates over the Missouri Compromise. A practice lawyer, Barbour argued *Cohens v. Virginia* before the Marshall Court, losing in his argument that the Supreme Court lacked authority to hear appeals of state Supreme Court decisions.[67] Barbour used his position as House speaker to support Jackson for president in 1828 and rewarded with a Supreme Court seat.[68]

The new justice was an ardent state's rights advocate, his views exemplified in *New York v. Miln.* Barbour upheld a New York City immigration regulation, finding it did not impose on Congress' commerce power or its authority to regulate immigration. Miln undermined the Marshall position on the Commerce clause and sharpened fears of Taney's critics that a new states rights agenda was on the march.[69]

But Barbour's contribution to the Taney Court was limited to four years, his sudden death in 1841 removing states rights' stalwart from a Court already filled with such men.

## John Catron

Jackson's final appointment, John Catron, was not confirmed until Jackson left office. John Catron was the most political of Andrew Jackson's Court nominees. The Tennessean Catron enjoyed close relationships with Jackson, House Speaker and future president James Knox Polk and another future president, James Buchanan. Catron was the principal author of the 1837 Judiciary Act which created two new circuits including one in Tennessee from which he was nominated. Chosen in early 1837 he was not confirmed until Martin van Buren was in the White House but quickly earned the reputation as a savvy insider. In his twenty seven year career, Catron offered few opinions of note, comfortably settling into the Taney Court's states' rights and pro slavery majority. Enjoying influence with his colleagues, he was able to manipulate the institution's internal workings and legal opinions.[70]

The Court's clerk, Richard Peters, was a Marshall Court holdover, kindling Catron's suspicions of his reliability. The justice organized a putsch at the start of the 1843 term, scheduling the vote to remove Peters when two of the clerk's supporters were unavailable.[71] Catron removed Peters but his success angered his colleagues, who began to suspect his loyalty to their institution.

Catron is best remembered for his behind the scenes lobbying during the Dred Scott case. Argued in the interregnum between James Buchanan's election in November 1856 and his inauguration in March, 1857, Dred Scott was discussed in the Catron's letters to president-elect James Buchanan. Buchanan wanted the Court to make a definitive ruling on the slavery issue to remove a controversy before he entered office, and was concerned when Catron's letters revealed the Court's divisions.[72]

In February the justices made the fateful decision to expand the Dred Scott decision to address the slavery issue. Chief Justice Taney's opinion initially garnered only five votes. Catron leapt into action, writing Buchanan and asking him to lobby Justice Grier, another old friend and fellow Pennsylvanian, who had yet to join Taney's opinion. At the same time Grier wrote Buchanan asking his old friend to lobby Catron for his vote. Eventually Catron and Grier would join Taney's opinion. [73]

In a concurring opinion Catron offered his own interpretation of a technical issue in Dred Scott, the scope of treaties under the constitution. Catron claimed the regulation of slavery was limited by treaties, with the Louisiana Purchase treaty explicitly protecting slave owner rights. Under Article VI, treaties were given the same authority as constitutional amendments thus Congress could not outlaw slavery in territories acquired under the purchase.[74] Catron's views on the scope of treaties was rejected by his successors but became part of constitutional law after a 1920 decision from Justice Oliver Wendell Holmes.[75]

When Tennessee seceded from the union, Catron traveled to Nashville to hold circuit court in defiance of much of the state. His presence unwelcome, Catron was threatened with physical force and he promptly traveled to St. Louis where he denounced treason and threatened Missourians who attempted to secede. The justice's swift and certain action helped keep the state out of the Confederacy.[76]

Catron kept a low profile in Washington, partly blamed for sparking the Civil War though he voted with Taney in the *Prize cases* and *Ex Parte Val-*

*landigham.* Catron died in 1865 after several years of ill health, the Republican Congress responding by eliminating his seat, thus preventing President Andrew Johnson from choosing his successor.

## Dred Scott and the Taney Court

Rarely does a Supreme Court decision ravage a justice's much less an entire Court's reputation. The Court that approved racial segregation in *Plessy v. Ferguson* is long forgotten with Plessy's author, Henry Brown, consigned to the footnotes of history. The "Four Horsemen" may be considered the villains of the Roosevelt era but still retain a modicum of respect. Justice Blackmun's foray into abortion politics may have earned him criticism but did little to raise or lower his status as a mediocrity.

Roger Taney and his brethren in Dred Scott cannot escape their legacy of a blatant political decision colored with racism. Taney, denounced as a southern sympathizer and precipitator of the Civil War, is tied to his political patron, Andrew Jackson, whose legacy of Court appointments places him among mediocrities, a long fall from his near great status for his administration. Jackson's propensity for appointing political friends links him closely to Harry Truman, ranked among the lowest of twentieth century presidents based on the four men he appointed as justices.

## Harry Truman

In 1933 Franklin Roosevelt inherited a conservative Supreme Court determined to halt his New Deal agenda. Part of his legacy was a refurbished liberal Court with nine appointments including the promotion of a liberal Republican to be chief justice. His successor, Harry Truman, was expected to continue the liberal tradition, though during his seven years in office the Court underwent a profound change nearly as great as the one presided over by Roosevelt.

Chosen for vice president in 1944 with the single qualification that he was not Henry Wallace the sitting vice president, Truman was held at arm's length by Franklin Roosevelt, who had opposed Truman's 1940 reelection to the Senate.[77] Truman was excluded from foreign policy decisions including development of the atomic bomb, leaving the man from Missouri with a host of difficult decisions and little information after Roosevelt's death. Faced with a new world order with the United States leading a bloc of democratic states, Truman could not be blamed for expending less effort on replacing justices from a comfortably liberal court. But Truman's missteps in his four selections placed him among the worst twentieth century presidents for his Court appointments. These failures are partly traceable to his experiences with the Pendergast machine, which emphasized loyalty over competence. Truman's four Court selections would be the most political, based on personal friendships and dedication to the Democrat Party rather than competence or a judicial philosophy

The end of the war brought its own challenges as Truman struggled to build a new coalition and the American economy struggled to adjust from wartime to peacetime economy. Runaway inflation was followed by labor strife in the 1940s as the Roosevelt coalition of southerners and northern urbanites cracked, never to be fully reconstituted. Truman's 1948 reelection was a harbinger of the end of the solid south and the splitting off of the far left. The Korean War, with its stated goal of limited success would be repeated in Vietnam while corruption plagued the highest reaches of the administration with attorney general J. Howard McGrath forced to resign in 1952 because of scandals in the tax collection service.

Amidst this Truman filled four Court vacancies selecting two former Senate colleagues and two high level cabinet secretaries, all with limited if any judicial experience. Three of the four justices have earned ratings among the worst to have served, joining three of the Four Horsemen from the Court Packing era. Chief Justice Fred Vinson is the only chief to suffer the indignity of being rated a failure while Justice Tom Clark rose above his three colleagues to the comfortable ranking of mediocrity.[78] Rated just above George H.W. Bush for twentieth century presidents based on their nominees, Truman joined Jackson as presidents ranked as near greats for their administrations while tumbling to lower rankings for their Court selections.[79]

The resignation of Justice Roberts in 1945 and sudden death of Chief Justice Stone in 1946 were followed by the appointments of Senator Harold Burton and Treasury Secretary Fred Vinson. Two more deaths were followed by the appointments of Sherman Minton and Tom Clark.

## Burton and Vinson

When Justice Roberts resigned in a huff after bitter disputes with Justice Black, Truman sought to calm the justices' nerves with an old Senate colleague, Ohio Senator Harold Burton. A first term senator, Burton served on Truman's committee investigating waste in the defense industry, refusing to turn committee hearings onto partisan attacks on the White House, earning Truman's respect.[80] Burton's political skills were needed on a sharply divided Court and his political moderation produced little ideological change on the Court. Burton was unanimously approved by the Senate in a bow to senatorial courtesy as Truman received a side benefit from the nomination when Ohio's Democrat governor appointed a Democrat to serve out the Republican Burton's term. Burton's easy confirmation may have been the height of his success as a lackluster judicial career ranked him among eight failures.[81]

Chief Justice Stone's death in 1946 was followed by maneuvering for his position, leading Justice Jackson to remark that, "Washington loves a funeral, particularly if it creates a vacancy."[82] Jackson, absent from Washington while serving as the chief prosecutor for the United States in the Nuremberg trials, believed he had been promised the chief justice position by Franklin Roosevelt in 1941. But by 1946 Roosevelt was dead, Truman was president and Jackson was thousands of miles from the center of power.

Jackson's enemies moved to scotch his promotion. A series of leaks to friendly columnists produced articles warning Justice Black had threatened to resign if Jackson was promoted.[83] Jackson supporters denounced the attacks, accusing Black and others of leaking internal information to the press but the stories had the intended effect as Truman rejected Jackson's promotion for fear of further recriminations. The president chose another consensus builder, Treasury Secretary Fred Vinson, who proved even less able than Stone in reining in his colleagues. The seven year Vinson Court (1946-1953) was marked by recriminations and drift.

## Clark and Minton

Death is an occasional and not entirely unexpected visitor to the Supreme Court. Many justices serve well into their seventies, leaving their office only after a debilitating illness or death. The summer of 1949 proved pivotal to Court liberals as two of their brethren, Wiley Rutledge and Frank Murphy, died. With the glow of his upset victory dimming and postwar problems starting to dominate his presidency, Truman tried to regain his political footing, appointing a Senate crony, Sherman Minton and his attorney general, Tom Clark. Elected to the Senate in 1934, Minton was an eager New Dealer who had leapt onto Roosevelt's coattails. This strategy was less effective in Republican oriented Indiana and Minton was defeated for reelection in 1940. Roosevelt, though, did not forget Minton's unwavering support and appointed him to the Seventh Circuit Court of Appeals.[84]

Neither outstanding nor controversial during his time on the court, Minton would have spent the rest of his career in the obscurity of the federal appeals system except for Truman who remembered his old friend and promoted him to serve as one of the more obscure Supreme Court justices. During his seven year career Minton preferred a restrained vision for the Court while supporting government in attacking domestic communism. Minton proved a Truman loyalist in the most important presidential power decision of the period, the president's 1952 seizure of steel mills and frequently joined Chief Justice Vinson in supporting the Truman Administration.[85]

After Justice Wiley Rutledge's death in September, 1949 Truman replaced him with Attorney General Tom Clark, a loyal but controversial figure who had initiated Truman's loyalty program and pushed civil rights. Clark had earned his Justice Department slot to his work with Truman's committee investigating War Department spending. Clark's cooperation infuriated the Roosevelt Administration but earned Truman's respect and gratitude.

As a justice Clark was an outspoken anti-communist, enforcing loyalty oaths to remove communists from the executive branch. Clark's prosecution of Alger Hiss earned him the enmity of the Democrat left, including New Dealers.[86] During his confirmation hearings, Clark was attacked from the left for being too hard on communists and savaged on the right for being too accommodating to communists.[87] The center held and Clark was confirmed with his subsequent career serving as the one bright spot on Harry Truman's Supreme Court legacy.

## Fred Vinson

Chief justices are considered *primus inter pares*, first among equals and are expected to maintain at least the façade of harmony among their bickering brethren, calming tempers and smoothing over differences to allow the institution to function as the third branch of government. Chiefs are also expected to provide some form of intellectual leadership, guiding the justices as best they can to an intellectually consistent result. Unfortunately for Harry Truman, the man he chose as Chief Justice failed in both areas.[88]

Vinson's colleagues viewed the chief justice with contempt. Justice Douglas accused Truman of suffering from an inferiority complex that forced him to appoint Vinson to heighten his sense of intellectual superiority.[89] Justice Frankfurter, never one to mince words about the perceived intellectual deficiencies of his colleague, described Vinson as "confident and easy going and sure and shallow."[90] With his colleagues sniping at his back, Vinson struggled to assert his authority as he was ignored by the de facto leaders, Justices Black and Frankfurter.

Few would have mistaken Vinson for a constitutional scholar but Harry Truman sought a social leader, one who could calm the disputes over his decision to replace Harlan Stone, but Vinson was not up to the task.[91] Vinson's seven years were the eye of the storm, located between the bitter years of Chief Justice Stone and the revolutionary times of Earl Warren. The angry divisions continued but at a subdued volume as Vinson smoothed over differences rather than exacerbating them.[92] Vinson preferred consensus, but the political and personal divisions on the Court prevented compromise. The chief lost control of his colleagues during the Rosenberg spy case as Justice Douglas pushed hard for the Court to hear the case. When his colleagues refused, Douglas published a dissent criticizing the decision. To settle the dispute Vinson met with Attorney General Herbert Brownell and the two men decided to end the controversy with a special Court hearing followed by a predetermined rejection of the Rosenberg's appeals and an execution order.[93] Forced to lean on the attorney general to save him from his colleagues, Vinson lost what little influence he had retained with the justices. Ineffective as a social leader, Vinson proved even less successful as an intellectual leader. His major opinions were poorly reasoned, muddying the law rather than enlightening issues.

His most quoted opinion also proved to be his most controversial. In Dennis v. United States[94] leaders of the American communist party appealed their convictions under the Smith Act, with banned supporting overthrow of the American government. Leaning heavily on his interpretation of the Clear and Present Danger Test, Vinson upheld the convictions and ruled that teaching communist doctrine represented a clear and present danger to government. Vinson's reasoning drew scorn from several of his colleagues with the Dennis case used as evidence of anti-communist hysteria.[95]

As civil rights grew as an issue, the justices struggled with the South's segregation policies, attacking the problem at the margins and building precedent against Jim Crow laws. The NAACP's full-fledged attack on segregation received a favorable hearing in the Vinson Court as the organization challenged separate schools and discriminatory housing laws. Vinson opinions in *Sweatt v. Painter*[96] and *Shelley v. Kraemer*[97] began the process. In Sweatt Vinson struck down a segregated law school under the theory that separate law facilities failed to provide a learning environment for a proper legal education. While not striking down the separate but equal regime, Vinson chipped away at its underpinnings.

In Shelley Vinson vastly expanded the reach of federal courts when he struck down restrictive covenants that prohibited the sale of houses to certain racial minorities. Because the sales and covenants were private actions not covered under the Fourteenth Amendment, Vinson manipulated the definition of state action to strike the covenants. The chief ruled that because the covenants were enforced in state court, the enforcement was a form of state action forbidden under the Fourteenth Amendment.

Vinson's reasoning was scrutinized for expanding the definition of state action to include private contracts. If all contracts were considered part of the public domain, then Congress could regulate the most private of actions, deepening doubts about the chief's intellectual capabilities. The chief's limitations were on display in *Breard v. City of Alexandria.*[98] In Breard Justice Reed upheld a city ordinance banning house to house solicitation, ruling the ban did not violate the First Amendment. Vinson dissented, choosing to interpret the law as an interstate commerce regulation beyond the reach of local government. Vinson's confusion of speech and interstate commerce produced an irrelevant argument that was not joined by his colleagues.

In a trio of cases, Vinson was able to balance the right and left wings of the Court in speech cases. In *Niemotko v. Maryland* [99] the chief struck the convictions of Jehovah's witnesses charged with trespassing after they conducted religious meetings at a park after being turned down for a permit. Vinson found that the city's refusal was based solely on the local government's dislike of the group's message. The opinion drew on the usually knee jerk concurrence from Justice Frankfurter who needed to express his own interpretation in writing.

Vinson also struck the conviction of an itinerant preacher, Carl Kunz, after he conducted a religious service on a city sidewalk without a permit.[100] Vinson dismissed the government's claim that Kunz's reputation for provoking disorder with his inflammatory speeches was sufficient grounds for denying him the permit. The opinion drew a dramatic dissent from Justice Jackson which was three times longer than Vinson's Court opinion. The more controversial of the three decisions was *Feiner v. New York*[101] as Vinson struggled to differentiate his decision with the year old Terminiello case.[102] Feiner was arrested for agitating a crowd while he spoke on a sidewalk and Vinson upheld the conviction for disturbing the peace. While the facts for Terminiello and Feiner were similar, Vinson chose to ignore the similarities, not mentioning the earlier case and instead praising police for preventing a potential riot.[103]

During Vinson's final term, his lack of leadership all but paralyzed the Court. In 1952 a group of cases were filed that would later become Brown v. Board of Education. The NAACP led the charge, challenging segregation of elementary and secondary schools. The first Brown arguments were heard in December, 1952, producing mixed results during the Court's conference on the case. The Chief Justice and Justice Reed appeared to support upholding Plessy while Justices Black and Douglas were the strongest votes for immediately overturning separate but equal. The vote in the conference was confused as either five justices voted to strike Plessy or five justices voted to uphold separate but equal with the end result being delay.[104]

Justices Frankfurter and Jackson were uncertain of their positions, seeking reargument to reconsider the issues including how to enforce an integration decree. This view was strengthened by Justice Black's warning that overturning Plessy could lead to violence triggered by southern Democrat politicians and demagogues using the Court's decision to maintain political power.[105] The final decision was to hold the case for reargument in October 1953, though Vinson would not be leading the Court, felled in September 1953 by a fatal heart attack.[106]

## Tom Clark

With his trademark bow tie, toothy grin and earthy manner, Tom Clark was easy to mistake for a merchant living in the dusty Texas town of his childhood. Overshadowed by his more illustrious colleagues, Clark composed seminal opinions of the Warren Court while casting aside his reputation as a conservative anti-communist.

Fourteen of Clark's eighteen years as a justice were served on the Warren Court where he was a consistent conservative vote on law and order, speech and anti communist cases. During the 1950s he performed as his critics predicted, composing few opinions of note and relying mainly on separate opinions to offer his views.[107] Among these were decisions limiting Congressional investigations into communism. Clark's dissent in *Watkins v. United States*[108] accused the majority of micromanaging congressional powers and protecting communism. The dissent resonated with members of Congress and his colleagues and in *Baren-*

*blatt v. U.S.*[109] the Court backed away from Watkins and transformed much of Clark's dissent into law.

Another Clark dissent prodded Congress into action. In *Jencks v. United States*,[110] the justices ruled that defense attorneys could have access to secret intelligence material in national security cases. As a former attorney general Clark reacted vehemently against the decision. In his dissent he warned that the ruling would open up American intelligence files to all lawyers, harming national security. Congress agreed, swiftly passing legislation to overrule Jencks.[111]

## Every Liberal's Favorite Conservative

The 1960's were the most active years of the Warren Court revolution and of Clark's career as he composed his most memorable and controversial opinions. From 1961 to 1967 Clark authored four opinions that continued to exert influence into the next century.

The Exclusionary Rule remains a point of contention in the political fight over rights of criminal defendants as it excludes illegally seized evidence from trial as a deterrent to police misconduct. The rule was first enforced by the Court in *Weeks v. United States*[112] but applied only to federal trials until *Mapp v. Ohio*.[113] Mapp began as an obscenity case as police searched Mapp's house for incriminating evidence but found only obscene magazines. What had been an obscenity case became a seminal Fourth Amendment decision when Clark was convinced by his colleagues during an elevator ride to apply the Exclusionary Rule to state cases.[114] The justice with the strongest law and order background was roundly criticized by police and the public for creating a rule that allowed the guilty to be freed. Clark's ruling would be weakened by a series of exceptions created during the Burger and Rehnquist courts, allowing more warrantless searches under exigent circumstance yet Mapp remains one of Clark's most quoted opinions.

If excluding evidence and freeing guilty defendants was not controversial enough, two years later Clark authored the opinion striking down bible reading in public schools. Students in the Abington School District read bible verses at the start of each school day, a policy challenged under the Establishment Clause.[115] In Abington Clark began the process of building an Establishment Clause doctrine, finding that bible readings advanced religion. Clark ruled government must remove itself from promoting any religious views, including sponsoring school sponsored bible readings.[116] The justice's "advancing religion" standard continues to be used in the twenty first century while Abington and its progeny is a source of irritation to those favoring greater religious freedom within the public sphere.[117] If Clark's decision angered his conservative supporters, two years later the justice would anger his fellow Texans who supported segregation.

Having spent his youth in the segregated South, Tom Clark was an unlikely leader in the fight for racial integration. As attorney general he followed Harry Truman's lead, pushing for integration in the public and private spheres. As a justice he had not been an early proponent of integrating schools but joined Brown v. Board of Education without comment. In 1959 he authored an opinion striking down a segregated coffee shop at a Wilmington city parking garage.[118] But the piecemeal legal fight against segregation ended in 1964 with passage of the massive Civil Rights Act. The law forbade discrimination in hiring and public accommodations on the basis of race, ethnicity, gender or religion. Segregationists in the South immediately challenged the act and the Court expedited the appeals into Heart of Atlanta Motel v. United States.[119] The Court unanimously upheld the federal law with Clark assigned the task of finding the proper grounds in the constitution. Clark hit upon the Commerce Clause, finding that segregation limited the ability of people to travel thus harming interstate commerce and providing Congress the authority to act.[120] Clark's expansive view of the Commerce Clause opened new avenues for legislation, allowing the federal government to regulate behavior once considered the sole province of state and local government. Heart of Atlanta earned Clark plaudits from former critics for shutting the door on state sponsored segregation. Some of this praise would turn to criticism as he considered the issue of televised trials.

Clark was the first justice to tackle the constitutional tension between press coverage of a trial and the right of a defendant to receive a fair trial. *In Estes v. Texas*[121] Clark faced constitutional issues and political pressures as he considered the corruption conviction of Billy Sol Estes, one of Lyndon Johnson's oldest Texas cronies. Estes had been convicted after a change of venue forced by national and local media coverage of his indictment and trial. After his conviction Estes appealed, claiming the media attention had biased the jury against him. Clark agreed, composing a list of deleterious effects television coverage on trials including how coverage negatively affected the judge, the lawyers, the witnesses, the defendant and the jurors.[122] A year after the Estes case he would rule on another prominent case, the details of which spawned a popular television show and widespread media coverage.

The murder trial and conviction of Dr. Sam Sheppard in the late 1950s continues to be a source of controversy and investigation nearly fifty years later. Shepherd was convicted of murdering his wife in a Cleveland suburb. The facts of the crime and Sheppard's prominence had attracted the focus of the news media during the trial. The trial judge allowed television cameras in the courtroom to record the proceedings and to show tape during later broadcasts. The trial quickly turned into a mob scene and Shepherd based his appeal on the bias created by the media coverage.[123]

Clark, the law and order justice, agreed. In granting Sheppard a new trial Clark warned that television turned solemn legal proceeding into Roman circuses with spectators condemning the accused while lawyers, witnesses and even judges mugged for the cameras.[124] While Clark's negative views of the media earned him few friends in the world of journalism, his description of the effect of television on a trial became reality nearly three decades later during the OJ Simpson trial and verdict.

During the last years of his Court tenure, Clark witnessed one of his colleagues, Arthur Goldberg, be wheedled off the Court by President Lyndon Johnson, who exposed the justice to his infamous "Johnson treatment." Though fellow Texans, Clark had a distant relationship with Johnson and less easily influenced by him. Johnson applied indirect pressure, seizing on the resignation of Attorney General Nicholas Katzenbach to promote Clark's son, Ramsey, to the position. This placed the justice in the difficult position of having a conflict of interest when the United States government argued a case before the Court. A man of strict ethics Clark immediately resigned, opening a vacancy for Johnson to fill.[125] Whether the president knew or simply guessed that Clark would leave is unknown though his appointment of Ramsey Clark proved to be one of the most ill advised choices in American history.[126]

After leaving the Court Clark became the first director the Federal Judicial Center, an innovative creation providing resources to individual judges while streamlining the organization of the federal courts. He also served as a "pinch hitting" judge, hearing cases when a Court became backlogged, his judicial career extended until his death in 1977.

Clark's eighteen years as a justice have been largely forgotten. Lacking a full scale biography, Clark's contribution to the Warren Court is forgotten in comparison to the larger than life careers of Hugo Black, William Douglas and Earl Warren. Yet Clark was the best among the Truman justices, composing historic opinions and placing his own imprint on the law. Clark rose above the caricature of his talents and overcame the segregationist tradition of the south, achieving more than ever expected. [127]

## Burton and Minton

It is not difficult to search the U.S. reports and discover an important opinion written by Fred Vinson or Tom Clark. The same could not be said for Harold Burton and Sherman Minton. Neither man is remembered for a prescient dissent or groundbreaking decision. Rather Burton and Minton labored in obscurity, their tenures long forgotten even as they dragged down Truman's legacy.

As a Republican senator from the comfortably Republican Ohio, Burton was expected to be out of place in the more liberal Roosevelt Court. Appointed for his close relationship with the president, Burton exhibited independence both from his roots and from Harry Truman. Burton was one of the three justices who voted to hear the appeal of the convicted spies the Rosenbergs[128] and joined an opinion striking a contempt citation for a newspaper for criticizing a judge.[129] He adhered more closely to traditional Republican beliefs as one of the early supporters of striking down school segregation.[130] He also dissented in *Pennsylvania v. Nelson,*[131] which struck down a state sedition law because it conflicted with a similar federal law. At times he was swayed by argument, initially voting to overturn a criminal libel law[132] then providing the fifth vote to uphold the same law.[133]

Harold Burton's main contribution to the Court may have been his detailed notes of the justices' weekly conferences. Many of his colleagues' records were destroyed upon their death to maintain the confidentiality of conferences,[134] but Burton's records were used to analyze the Vinson and Warren courts including voting alignment patterns for cases such as Brown v. Board of Education.[135] Burton's thirteen year career ended in 1958 as illness forced him to resign.

Sherman Minton's tenure was as unspectacular as Justice Burton's. Minton was affected by his New Deal experiences, including the courts' hostility toward much of Roosevelt's agenda. As a senator Minton watched New Deal programs be struck by the Supreme Court and became convinced the judiciary was an obstacle to progress. Fearful of judicial activism he moved to the opposite extreme, believing judges should rarely if ever overturn a law passed by the people's elected representatives.[136] Minton followed his philosophy in economic cases, making him popular among the Roosevelt justices, but also in civil liberties cases, earning him criticism from those same justices. His economic views were most apparent in his dissent in the Sawyer case. Minton agreed with Chief Justice Vinson that the Truman seizure of the steel mills were part of his inherent executive powers and the authority granted under federal law.[137]

## Truman Legacy

The publication of David McCullough's Pulitzer Prize winning biography of Harry Truman contributed to the renaissance in Truman's reputation. Yet even as his administration rose in esteem in polls, he could not shake the legacy of failed Supreme Court appointments. Oddly enough Truman's choices were more likely to be favored by Republicans and conservatives who had savaged his administration while liberals were more disappointed. Truman's low rankings based on his Court selections place him within that rare category of great administrations and near failed Court appointments. He is joined in that group by another president who seemed unable to reproduce success in his Supreme Court appointments.

## Notes

1. Swisher, Carl Brent, *The Taney Court* (New York: MacMillan Publishing, 1974), 46-47.

2. Weisenburger, Francis, *The Life of John McLean* (Columbus:Ohio State University Press, 1937), 48-50.

3. Weisenburger, 66-67
4. Abraham,75
5. Holt, Michael, *The Rise and Fall of the American Whig Party* (New York: Oxford University Press, 1999),15
6. Holt, 263-265
7. Smith, Jean Edward, *John Marshall* (NewYork: Henry Holt, 1996), 507
8. Swisher, 21
9. Swisher, 86-87.
10. 7 How. 283 (1849)
11. 53 U.S. 299 182
12. Swisher, 388-389.
13. Swisher, 405-406.
14. McLean's views on the Commerce Clause would have eliminated the tangled and confusing doctrine known as the dormant commerce clause which continues to bedevil justices and governments into modern time.
15. 40 U.S. 449 184
16. Swisher, 368-369
17. Fehrenbacher, 414
18. In Fehrenbacher's seminal work on Dred Scott, he quote extensively from the Curtis opinion and limits mention of McLean's opinion to those questions where the two dissenters were in agreement, Fehrenbacher, passim 404-14.
19. Fehrenbacher, 309-310
20. Swisher, 727
21. Friedman and Israel,575
22. Abraham, 79
23. Swisher, 49.
24. Swisher, 50-51 One of his targets was Joseph Story, a justice of undeniable talent, who was verbally attacked by Baldwin for some imagined slight.
25. Monroe, Elizabeth,"Henry Baldwin" in *The Supreme Court Justices* Melvin Urofsky, ed. (New York: Garland Press, 1994), 1.
26. Friedman and Israel,576
27. Swisher, 51-52.
28. Friedman and Israel, 580
29. Lawrence, Alexander, *James Moore Wayne Southern Unionist* (Westport CT: Greenwood Press, 1970),58-60.
30.Lawrence 72-73
31. Lawrence79
32. 18 Howard 307(1858)
33. 18 Howard 307, 317-318
34. 62 U.S. 582 (1859)
35. Fehrenbacher, 311
36. Fehrenbacher, 389-390
37. Lawrence, 189

38. Lawrence, 186-187
39. Lawrence, 188
40. Lawrence, 203
41. Abraham, 80-81
42. Remini, 105
43. Remini, 172
44. Lewis, Walker, *Without Fear or Favor* (New York: Houghton Mifflin, 1965), 239.
45. Remini, 260
46. Abraham, 81-82
47. The variety of opinions offered in the Passenger and License cases exemplified the division of the justices on critical issues and Taney's inability to rein in his colleagues.
48. 36 U.S. 420 (1837)
49. Schwartz, Bernard, *A History of the Supreme Court* (New York: Oxford University Press, 1993), 75-76.
50. 36 U.S. 257 (1837)
51. 36 U.S. 102 (1837)
52. 46 U.S. 504 (1847)
53. 48 U.S. 283 (1849)
54. 48 U.S. 1 (1849)
55. Lewis, 334-335
56. 60 U.S 393 (1857)
57. Fehrenbacher, 560
58. Fehrenbacher, 351-352
59. Fehrenbacher, 381
60. 17 Fed. Cas. 144
61. Swisher, 850
62. Swisher, 851
63. Swisher, 850
64. Fehrenbacher, 556
65. Fehrenbacher, 556-557.
66. Swisher, 969-970
67. Smith,458
68. Abraham, 81
69. Schwartz, 78-79 One of those critics was former president but now Congressman John Quincy Adams, who characterized Barbour as "a shallow pated wildcat" who had designs on destroying the constitution.
70. Swisher, 62.
71. Swisher, 304
72. Fehrenbacher, 307
73. Fehrenbacher, 311-312
74. Fehrenbacher, 402-403

75. *Missouri v. Holland* 252 U.S. 416 (1920)

76. Swisher, 859

77. McCullough, David, *Truman* (New York: Simon and Schuster, 1992), 236-238.

78. Blaustein, Albert and Roy Mersky, *The First One Hundred Justices* (Hamden CT:Archon Books, 1978), 49.

79. Truman was ranked twenty sixth, just below Benjamin Harrison, based on his four Court appointees.

80. Berry, Mary Frances, *Stability, Security and Continuity: Mr. Justice Burton and Decision Making in the Supreme Court* (Westport Ct.:Greenwood Press, 1978).

81. According to Blaustein and Mersky, Burton was among the eight failures to serve on the Court.

82. Gerhart, Eugene, *America's Advocate: Robert Jackson* (New York: Bobbs Merrill, 1958).

83. Gerhart, 144

84. Gugin, Linda and James St. Clair, *Sherman Minton* (Bloomington IN: Indiana University Press, 1997),146-157.

85. Rudko, Frances, *The Truman Court* (Westport CT: Greenwood Press, 1988).

86. Tanenhaus, Sam, *Whittaker Chambers* (New York:Modern Library, 1998).

87. Beeman, Mary, *New Deal Justices Tom Clark and the Warren Court* (University Microfilms, University of Texas dissertation, 1993).

88. Steamer, Robert, *Chief Justice* (Columbia S.C.University of South Carolina Press, 1986), 274-275.

89. St. Clair, James and Linda Gugin, *Chief Justice Fred Vinson of Kentucky* (Lexington: University Press of Kentucky, 2002), 174. Douglas had his own issues with Truman, believing the Missourian was chosen over him for the 1944 vice presidential nomination.

90. St Clair and Gugin, 174

91. Steamer,276

92. St. Clair and Gugin163

93. St. Clair and Gugin 248-252

94. 341 U.S. 494 (1951)

95. Powers, Richard Gid, *Not Without Honor* (New Haven CT: Yale University Press, 1996), 226-227.

96. 339 U.S. 629 (1950)

97. 334 U.S. 1(1948)

98. 341 U.S. 622(1951)

99. 340 U.S. 268 (1951)

100. *Kunz v. New York* 340 U.S. 290 (1951)

101. 340 U.S. 315 (1951)

102. *Terminiello v. Chicago* 337 U.S. 1 (1949)

103. Gugin and St. Clair 273

104. Wiecek,697

105. Wiecek, 697-698

106. Showing his contempt for the chief justice, Felix Frankfurter remarked that Vinson's death was the first sign that there was a God.Kluger, 829

107. Clark's majority opinions during this time included *Joseph Burstyn v. Wilson* 343 U.S. 495 (1952) saw Clark overturn a 1915 case and apply the First Amendment to motion pictures; *Dean Milk v. Wisconsin* 340 U.S. 349 (1951) striking a state statute regulating milk containers on the Commerce Clause grounds; *Radovich v. NFL* 352 U.S. 445 (1957) in which he refused to extend antitrust exemption to professional football.

108. 354 U.S. 178 (1957)

109. 360 U.S. 109 (1959)

110. 353 U.S. 657(1957)

111. Beeman 324-325

112. 232 U.S. 383 (1914)

113. 367 U.S. 643 (1961)

114. Schwartz, Bernard, *Super Chief* (New York: New York University Press, 1983), 393.

115. *Abington v. Schempp* 374 U.S. 203 (1963) Chief Justice Warren may have chosen Clark because of his close ties to organized religion, his regular church attendance and his reputation as a conservative.Beeman 250-251

116. 374 U.S. 203, 226

117. The advancing religion test became one of three requirements in the Court's Lemon test devised in 1971.The test requires the government to show all laws have a secular purpose, do not advance or inhibit religion and do not create an excessive entanglement with religion.

118. *Burton v. Wilmington Parking Authority* 365 U.S. 715 (1961)

119. 379 U.S. 241 (1964)

120. Having served during the Roosevelt Administration when it was battling a conservative Supreme Court, Clark was a typical New Dealer when it came to deferring to Congress and in broadly interpreting the Commerce Clause. In Atlanta Motel, he proved to be more of a New Deal Democrat than a southern Democrat.Beeman, 137-138

121. 381 U.S. 532 (1965)

122. 381 U.S. 532, 545-550

123. *Sheppard v. Maxwell* 384 U.S. 333 (1966)

124. Clark's Sheppard opinion would be modified fifteen years later in *Chandler v. Florida* 449 U.S. 560 (1981), which allowed television cameras to operate in a state trial court.Clark's warnings of a media circus were taken more seriously by federal courts, which continue to ban cameras in the courtroom.

125. Woods, Randall,*LBJ Architect of American Ambition*(Cambridge MA.: Harvard University Press,2006), 788-789. Hoping to crown his reputation as a civil rights president, Johnson favored appointing the first black justice.

126. A similar situation occurred when Charles Evans Hughes was appointed to be Chief Justice in 1930.His son was solicitor general at the time and responsible for arguing cases before the Court.With his father sitting on the Court there was no way to avoid a conflict of interest except for the son toresign his position, which he did, thus furthering his father's political career while ending his own.

127. Most of the works on Clark on limited to brief biographies, dissertations and fleeting descriptions of the justice in works on the Warren Court and its justices.

128. Berry,118-119

129. *Craig v. Harney*331 U.S. 367 (1947)

130. St. Clair320

131. 350 U.S. 497 (1956)

132. *Beauharnais v. Illinois*343 U.S. 250 (1952)

133. Berry, 99

134. The only major biography of Burton came from an unusual source, Mary Frances Berry, a lifelong Democrat and member of the Civil Rights Commission, she spent much of her tenure embroiled in controversy and authored a scathing report of the 2000 Florida recount, accusing Republicansofvoter intimidation while finding little evidence of it.

135. His records were used by judicial scholars such as S. Sidney Ulmer and Doris Marie Provine in their examination of judicial behavior.

136. Gugin and St. Clair,145

137. 343 U.S. 579, 668

## Chapter 6

# James Polk (29) William McKinley (33)

James Polk and William McKinley were the most successful one term presidents, both men adding to American territory during brief and popular wars and ranked among above average presidents. Neither man though is celebrated for those achievements. There three Supreme Court nominees are also obscure, composing few opinions of note and placing both presidents at the bottom half of the ratings.

The presidencies of James Polk and William McKinley have been relegated to obscurity even as their achievements rank them among the top half of chief executives. Both men presided over brief but successful wars and added territory to the United States while reviving their office after a period of stagnation and weakness. Both men also died within a few months of the end of their first term, Polk of cholera after leaving office and McKinley by an assassin's bullet.

Both men have been treated kindly in presidential rankings. Though mostly a footnote or stray paragraph in history books, Polk and McKinley have risen from modern obscurity to rank in the top half of presidential rankings, with Polk occasionally rising to the near great category.[1]

Yet both men's rankings plunge when their Court appointments are considered. Polk drops to the bottom tier, thirty first out of thirty-nine presidents while McKinley falls even further to thirty-six of the thirty nine, between the twin failures James Garfield and Franklin Pierce. Polk ranked one place above Martin van Buren, the lowest ranked president among those making at least two Court appointments. The disparity between the two sets of rankings can be attributed to the obstacles faced by Polk and McKinley in choosing the best candidate and the resulting failures of their justices unprepared for prime time.

## The Dark Horse

Of all the men who have served their country in the White House only a few cast a shadow over their successors. One of these, Andrew Jackson, proved influential long after he left the White House in 1837 as his ideas dominated the period known as the Jacksonian era. One of his successors was able to recapture the spirit of Jackson's two terms, James Knox Polk.[2]

A fellow Tennessean, Polk served as Speaker of the House during the last two years of Jackson's administration, helping guide the president's agenda through Congress. Polk returned home to be elected governor but then lost reelection and a third election to regain the office. His career in a downward spiral, Polk made one last attempt at national prominence by attending the 1844 Democratic presidential convention in Baltimore as a vice presidential candidate. When the convention deadlocked desperate delegates turned to him as a dark horse candidate. [3]

Having won the nomination almost as a fluke, Polk looked certain to lose at the hands of the Whig presidential nominee, Senator Henry Clay. Instead Polk won the presidency even as he lost Tennessee, the only candidate to lose his home state but win the presidency.[4]

Polk entered office weighed down with foreign policy crises remaining from the Tyler Administration. Running on a platform of seizing the Pacific coastal area under the slogan "fifty four forty or fight," Polk ignored the campaign rhetoric upon becoming president and negotiated with the British, agreeing to a compromise that was well below the promised boundary. His handling of the Mexican War was seen as a conspiracy to extend slavery but the conflict settled most of the southern boundary and stabilized the southwest.

Polk's foreign policy successes did not extend to his domestic program. Polk faced a Congress revitalized after destroying the presidency of John Tyler. As the first vice president to succeed into the top office after the death of the president, Tyler spent much of his four years asserting his power and fighting a Congress that opposed him at every step. Tyler's difficulties were most apparent in his choices for the Supreme Court. Tyler nominated six candidates to fill two vacancies.[5] Five of his nominees were rejected by the Senate, the sixth being approved during the last days in office.

Tyler's difficulties presented Polk with an opportunity and a potential trap. A successful appointment would reassert executive authority over the appointment process while a rejected nominee would embolden Congress to oppose the new president. Polk sought a safe choice, offering the position to James Buchanan, his secretary of state and former Pennsylvania senator. As was his tendency Buchanan tarried, making Polk wait for months before rejecting the offer and leaving the president with the same difficult decision.[6]

The unexpected death of the renowned Joseph Story further complicated Polk's decision. Story was the last of the traditional Federalist justices, a man not in tune with the Taney Court's states' rights agenda. To fill Story's seat,

Polk chose Levi Woodbury, his service as a New Hampshire senator earning him a form of senatorial courtesy as he was swiftly confirmed. With one vacancy filled, the president continued to face the open seat remaining from the Tyler Administration.

To fill the seat Polk chose George Woodward, a state judge from Pennsylvania but the nomination drew opposition from Pennsylvania politicians, Senator Simon Cameron and James Buchanan. Their battle for control of the state's patronage jobs doomed Woodward's nomination and it was rejected by the Senate.[7] The desperate Polk then returned to his first choice, Buchanan, and offered him the job. Buchanan vacillated, weighing whether his ambition for the presidency would be harmed or helped by joining the Court and decided the prospect of the White House was more attractive than a drafty courtroom in the basement of the capitol. Buchanan's refusal meant Polk faced the unfilled vacancy eighteen months into his presidency. Polk's fourth choice was Robert Grier, a close acquaintance of Buchanan who excited little opposition and allowed Polk to return his focus to more important foreign policy issues.

Levi Woodbury and Robert Grier served nondescript careers, agreeing with the prevailing legal orthodoxy. Neither Woodbury nor Grier displayed the temperament to challenge the status quo, damaging Polk's legacy.

## Levi Woodbury

Woodbury enjoyed political success before joining the Court. A veteran of the political battles of the Jacksonian era, Woodbury served as Jackson's Navy and Treasury Secretary, a post he occupied during the Van Buren Administration. After Van Buren was defeated for reelection, Woodbury returned to the Senate where he allied himself with the "doughface Democrats" supporting the South contrary to their constituents.[8] Yet his easy Senate confirmation did not ensure fitness or greatness in office as Woodbury's five years on the Court proved unexceptionable.

During his tenure the justices tackled the unresolved issue of the Commerce Clause and new controversies involving the rights of slave owners. Woodbury fit in with the pro slavery ideology of the Court and his decision in *Jones v. Van Zandt* he cast his lot with the southern majority. [9]

Van Zandt, an Ohio farmer, had taken in nine runaways and was caught by two bounty hunters who returned the slaves to their Kentucky owner for a price. Van Zandt was charged with harboring the runaways—a version of receiving stolen property—and brought to trial under the 1793 federal fugitive slave law. He was found guilty and the verdict was appealed to the Supreme Court. With Woodbury writing the justices upheld the power of the federal government to prosecute anyone who did not report runaway slaves and aided their flight.[10]

In *United States v. Libby* Woodbury, serving as a circuit judge, weakened the constraints on the hated slave trade. When the United States charged the captain of the ship *Porpoise* with slave trading, Woodbury presided at the trial and declaring he was unconvinced the ship was engaged in the slave trade.[11] In his opinion Woodbury displayed a propensity for supporting slave power and favoring the testimony of slave traders over evidence provided by federal officials.

Because of his short time on the Court and a lack of any other significant opinions, Woodbury's decisions in the Van Zandt and Libby cases cast him as a slavery supporter. His acquiescence in other pro slavery opinions also placed Woodbury's career in a negative light. In a collection of decisions known as the *Passenger Cases*,[12] Woodbury offered a separate opinion that granted the states the power to exclude free blacks from the state, casting doubt on the constitution's Privileges and Immunities Clause which was believed to protect free travel through the states for all American citizens. After slavery was abolished, Woodbury's opinions were lumped together with the Antebellum court and its favoritism toward the peculiar institution. Neither these opinions nor his subsequent efforts to win the presidency enhanced his or Polk's legacy.

By 1848 the Democratic Party was in turmoil as Polk held to his one term promise and the men who had challenged him for the 1844 nomination appeared headed toward another deadlock. James Buchanan, having twice turned down Court nominations for his chance at the presidency, was a candidate along with Michigan senator Lewis Cass. Cass' and Buchanan's weaknesses during the 1844 convention raised the likelihood of another deadlock. One alternative to the front runners was Justice Woodbury, whose Jacksonian credentials were not in doubt. Others favored Woodbury as a possible vice presidential candidate for John Calhoun, who was considering a final campaign.[13] Unfortunately for Woodbury the Democrat convention went for Cass, the justice a distant third in delegates.[14] His death in 1851 ended his quest for the presidency.

Levi Woodbury was one of a series of justices who served during the 1840s and 1850s and left a faint imprint on the era.[15] Committed to the legal orthodoxy of the period, Woodbury authored no groundbreaking opinions during his five years. While a longer tenure on the Court might have produced a display of unexpected brilliance or originality, it is more likely the justice would not have veered from the course set by the Taney Court as it careened toward the Dred Scott decision and disaster.

## Robert Grier

If Justice Woodbury's reputation suffered based on his short tenure, then Robert Grier's may have suffered from his twenty-four years as a justice. Grier is another forgotten face on the Antebellum Court, only his role in the writing of Dred Scott and the confusion of his last days earning him any historical distinction.

Few Supreme Court decisions produce a consensus on the wisdom of a particular decision. Dred Scott has been universally panned by Court scholars and laymen as a prime example of judicial overreaching.[16] The seven justices in the majority were forever tarred with having denied rights to citizens based on their race and poured fuel on the fire that would eventually erupt into the Civil War. Dred Scott produced enough outrage on its own but the backroom maneuvering of the justices and the president-elect James Buchanan lent credence to the dark rumors of a slave holding conspiracy. Amidst the turmoil created by the decision stood Justice Grier, a pivotal figure in the content of the decision and the justices who joined it.

The Dred Scott case reached the United States Supreme Court just as the 1856 presidential election was ending. Justice Grier's Pennsylvania friend, President-elect James Buchanan, feared the Court's decision would dampen enthusiasm for his new administration and sought early knowledge of the result.[17]

Buchanan leaned on two sources, writing first to Justice Catron then to Justice Grier. Both men revealed that the Court was ruling against the Missouri Compromise and the authority of the federal government to regulate slavery in the territories. Justice Catron warned that only five members had joined Taney's opinion on the subject of slavery in the territories and the majority was composed entirely of justices from the south. Such a regional decision might be unacceptable to the nation and Catron sought Buchanan's help in convincing Grier to join the opinion. Before the president-elect could contact Grier, he received a letter from the justice expressing concern that Justice Catron might not be on board for the full decision.[18] Considering the two men worked side by side, hearing cases and discussing them in conference, their ignorance of the views of the other sounds more like a badly plotted situation comedy than a discussion of a pivotal Supreme Court decision. Buchanan was able to guide both justices into joining the Dred Scott opinion, giving it a six-member majority with a single northern justice, Robert Grier. [19]

While Grier wrote only a short opinion in the case, he was remembered as the sole northern justice to agree the constitution denied citizenship based on race and that Dred Scott could never become a citizen whether free or slave. His participation in the Dred Scott majority cast doubt on his loyalty to the Union cause, but with the Civil War raging, Grier authored the *Prize Cases*, a decision upholding presidential war power.[20] With the attack on Fort Sumter, President Lincoln used his powers as commander in chief of the military to mobilize troops for an army and impose a naval blockade of southern ports. The captured ships would then be transported north and sold for prize.[21]

Unfortunately for Lincoln Article I of the constitution reserved for Congress the authority to blockade ports as part of its authority declare war. Owners of several of the seized ships sued for the return of their property, noting that the wrong branch of government had exercised the war power and claiming that the Union ships were engaged in unauthorized military action. With six justices from the Dred Scott majority remaining on the Court, many Republicans feared that the Court would strike down the original blockade and hand the president a stinging defeat. Congress reacted with a not so subtle piece of legislation expanding the Court to ten members, a warning to the justices that more seats would be opened to dilute the votes of those members seen as supporting the Confederate cause.[22] With a tenth justice on the verge of being appointed by Lincoln, the Court rendered its decision.

Grier upheld the executive's inherent power to protect the nation from military attack. Grier noted presidential authority to defeat rebellions by using powers not listed in the constitution. According to Grier the president could raise an army to protect the nation and enact war measures such as naval blockades.[23] Grier upheld all of Lincoln's measures, refusing to grant the ship owners any money yet the opinion did little to rehabilitate his reputation.

The prize cases represented the zenith of Grier's career as old age took its toll on his physical and mental faculties.[24] By the mid 1860s Grier was slipping, drawing criticism from his colleagues including Justice Miller who expressed impatience with Grier's refusal to resign.[25]

Grier, though, would not leave according to Miller's schedule. During his last five years on the Court, Grier struggled with his workload, leaked information about opinions in his rambling and frequently changed his mind. When confronting the constitutionality of the Legal Tender Act, Grier stumbled, voting to uphold the law even as his vote contradicted one of his earlier positions on the issue. [26] Wanting to strike down the law, Chief Justice Salmon Chase was able to convince the befuddled Grier to change his vote and to support a new majority in favor of striking the law.[27] The uproar among the justices convinced Grier to retire but only after passage of a law allowing him to collect his salary until his death. Grier would die a few months later.

James Polk's administration was marked by a series of accomplishments that placed him within the upper tier of American presidents. His choices for the Supreme Court, though, would not be included in the list of those accomplishments. Polk was challenged by a Senate spoiling for a fight after it had defeated five of John Tyler's appointees. In response he chose nominees thought to be acceptable to the Senate. His two appointees, Levi Woodbury and Robert Grier, did little to enhance the Court's or the president's reputation.

Both justices were part of the pro slavery consensus on the Court, ruling in favor of slave owners and exacerbating rather than calming the roiled political waters of the era. The gray, predictable Grier and Woodbury wrote few decisions of lasting import and nothing that challenged the legal consensus. Serving only five years, Woodbury was spared the ignominy suffered by Grier at having joined Dred Scott. Instead he is largely forgotten. Grier's place in history was marred by Dred Scott and the taint of being on the wrong side of the central moral issue of the nineteenth century.

## William McKinley

The 1896 presidential election was dominated by the currency question and a debate over how the country would enter its second century. The contest between the middle aged and stolid William McKinley and the young, active William Jennings Bryan was a battle not only between two parties but between two different approaches to government. Bryan sought dramatic changes in policy with an active national government redistributing resources and a regulating business. McKinley reflected traditional Republican Party policies tempered by a more active government than was favored by his predecessors.[28] McKinley's convincing win made the Republican Party dominant once again and provided the new president with opportunities that past presidents did not enjoy.

McKinley's administration was dominated by foreign policy. A crisis had developed in nearby Cuba as a rotting Spanish empire faced collapse. American rhetoric favored Cuban independence and after a mysterious explosion on the Battleship Maine in a Cuban harbor, Americans demanded retaliation. The president investigated and discovered evidence of Spanish involvement which led to the short-lived Spanish-American War.

The conflict required only a few months of battle as the decrepit Spanish military crumbled in defeat. The result was the first colonies for the United States in the Caribbean and the Pacific. McKinley's reputation swelled with each military victory and his presidency became associated with what Secretary of State John Hay called the "Splendid Little War."[29]

McKinley, much like Polk, enjoyed foreign policy success that did not always translate to domestic policy. The economic expansion that followed his inauguration may have been by luck or design. The same explanation could be given to McKinley's uncanny ability to include great men in his administration. His was the only presidency that had three future Nobel Prize laureates serving, Charles Dawes, Elihu Root and Theodore Roosevelt but his sole choice for the Supreme Court would prove less successful. In 1897 the resignation of Justice Stephen Field offered an opportunity for the president but McKinley's sound judgment in his appointments was exhausted when he chose Joseph McKenna for the Supreme Court.

## Joseph McKenna

Justice Stephen Field was not a man to be intimidated by his colleagues. By the inauguration of William McKinley on March 4, 1897, Field was approaching his thirty fourth year as a Supreme Court justice. He was also approaching Chief Justice John Marshall's record of service on the Court. Field had ignored the subtle hints and not so gentle suggestions from his colleagues that it was time to retire. He had complained about the lack of opinions assigned to him by the chief justice and ignored the plaintive cries of Democrats asking him to leave the Court while Democrat Grover Cleveland controlled the White House. Field hated Cleveland, having battled the president over patronage appointments in the justice's home state of California, and had stated publicly he would not retire while the Democrat was in office.[30]

But when Cleveland was succeeded by Republican William McKinley, Field's colleagues thought the spring of 1897 presented a prime opportunity to make another run at convincing the old justice to leave. Leading the effort was Field's nephew, Justice David Brewer, who carefully avoided the topic of retirement but suggested possible replacements that would please Field. After a few months of prodding the old justice relented with two conditions. The first was a post-dated retirement letter setting December 1 1897 for his departure, a date that allowed him to surpass John Marshall's record. Field also extracted a promise from McKinley to appoint Joseph McKenna, McKinley's attorney general and a friend of Field's patron, Leland Stanford. The arrangement provided Field with unprecedented influence in choosing his successor while marring McKinley's record of appointment excellence.

The McKenna selection excited considerable opposition from federal judges on the west coast and from an unlikely source, Chief Justice Melville Fuller, who told the president he opposed his choice.[31] Much of the criticism of McKenna focused on his ties to the controversial Leland Stanford as Progressive politicians complained the new justice was another in a long line of railroad lawyers on the Court.

But for all of the fire and brimstone among the federal judiciary, there was little opposition in the Senate. Populist Party senator William Allen expended energy in trying to defeat the appointment during the Senate's executive session but on January 21 1898, the chamber approved McKenna without a formal vote. The *New York Times*, which had composed a scathing editorial opposing McKenna as incompetent, characterized the debate on his nomination as a "proceeding devoid of general interest" among the senators.[32] McKenna's nomination was approved along with a long list of consuls and postmaster as if a seat on the Supreme Court was of the same importance as the Augusta Georgia postmaster.

McKenna was replacing a legendary justice and reaching the Court in the midst of a political crisis. The Court's decision striking down the federal income tax had ignited progressive opposition and demands for checking or eliminating the power of judicial review. Other decisions allowing federal injunctions against strikers and greater judicial oversight of state and federal regulatory agencies heightened the political pressure on the justices. With several decisions made on a five to four vote with Field in the majority, McKenna was cast as a possible swing vote able to turn the Court from its conservative course. Yet the new justice proved indecisive, changing his votes as the majority changed. During the next twenty-seven years, McKenna proved maddeningly inconsistent even as he showed a preference for federal power over state control.

## Lochner v. New York

Early in his career, McKenna played a key role in the most notorious decisions of the era, *Lochner v. New York*.[33] Lochner challenged a state law setting working conditions for bakers and was a classic dispute between state police power used to protect citizens' health, safety and welfare and the doctrine of liberty to contract.

During the initial conference discussion of the case five members supported the New York statute as constitutional but later McKenna recounted that his father had operated a bakery and he did not consider baking a dangerous profession requiring special legislation. This coincided with the charge that the law was special interest legislation passed to protect one group of workers from competition. When the Lochner decision was announced, five justices had voted to strike down the law.[34]

Lochner was the height of the liberty to contract doctrine, the case serving as viable precedent for only three years. The subsequent case of *Muller v. Oregon* is generally seen as a sub silentio overruling of Lochner. McKenna joined the unanimous majority in upholding a minimum wage for women and minors.

Though at times suspicious of state economic regulation, McKenna proved more flexible in upholding federal economic regulation under the commerce clause. In *Hoke v. United States* McKenna upheld the federal Mann Act making it illegal to transport women across state lines for the purpose of prostitution. The justice gave the commerce clause a generous reading, finding that transport of people was interstate commerce and the federal law was attempting to prevent an evil under the guise of commerce.[35] In *Hipolite Egg v. United States* McKenna upheld a section of the Pure Food and Drug Act empowering the federal government to seize and dispose of contaminated food.[36] Four years after Hipolite, McKenna wrote *Bunting v. Oregon* upholding another Oregon minimum wage law, this time for men, and built on the reasoning used in Muller while making Lochner even more irrelevant.[37]

Though an occasional force for moderation on the Court, McKenna's opinions were quickly forgotten, his pedestrian writing style overshadowed by the rhetorical flourishes of his more illustrious colleagues including Oliver Wendell Holmes. Justice Holmes is recognized by most scholars as one of the greatest justices to serve on the bench. McKenna was a skeptic, his harshest dissents in reaction to Holmes' opinions. From 1910-1925, over one third of the justice's dissents and concurring opinions were to Holmes' opinions and his criticism of Holmes ran in the face of popular and elite support for the old justice, only injuring his judicial legacy.[38]

Beyond economic cases, McKenna authored precedents in Eighth Amendment and free speech and press cases. *Weems v. United States* originated in the Philippines when the islands' antiquated Spanish legal system was confronted by the American judiciary. Weems was convicted of embezzlement and under Spanish law was sentenced to fifteen years of hard labor, in chains. The restraints on Weems would be continuous throughout his sentence, constraining his movement while eating, sleeping and working. Weems appealed, arguing the penalty was cruel and unusual punishment mostly because it was disproportionate to the crime.

McKenna wrote for a unanimous Court overturning Weems' sentence and appending the disproportionate punishment doctrine onto the Eight Amendment.

Weems sentence was deemed disproportionate because his crime, embezzlement, was not as serious as other crimes that received much less severe punishment.[39] McKenna's opinion became a point of contention in Eighth Amendment jurisprudence starting in the 1980s as the states and federal government began imposing tougher sentences for drug crimes.[40]

The newest mass medium to hit the United States, the motion picture industry, would challenge the Court and its reading of the First Amendment much like the internet did at the turn of the twentieth century. In *Mutual Films v. Industrial Commission of Ohio* McKenna wrote for a unanimous Court that motion pictures represented neither speech nor press and thus were not covered by the First Amendment. An Ohio commission was granted authority to ban movies, prompting a challenge from the movie industry that the censorship violated both the Interstate Commerce Clause and the First Amendment. In dismissing both claims, McKenna allowed states and localities to establish censorship boards.[41]

McKenna also joined in the anti German hysteria that continued after World War One. In *Schaeffer v. United States* he upheld a charge against two Pennsylvania German newspapers which were convicted of undermining the war effort, giving aid to the enemy and interfering with the draft.[42] McKenna approved of the use of the Espionage Act and expanded the scope of Holmes' Clear and Present Danger test. The creator of that test, Holmes, would dissent, further exacerbating the tension between the two.

## The Cubist Justice

Having taken the seat of the doddering Justice Field, McKenna was aware of the difficulties presented to the Court by a mentally disabled justice. During the 1920s, as McKenna's mental faculties declined, he refused to resign. Chief Justice Taft was forced to work around his incapacitated colleague, complaining that McKenna decided cases based on an "impressionistic principle" and that he was a "cubist on the bench and cubists [were] not safe on the bench."[43] Taft was forced to take cases originally assigned to McKenna because the justice would not write the decision as the justices had voted.

Not one to allow "his" Court to be undermined by a disabled justice, Taft maneuvered to convince McKenna to leave. The chief justice pushed his colleagues to pay the elderly justice a visit and implore him to leave, but they refused. Justice Holmes, approaching ninety, worried about setting a precedent that could be used against him. Taft then paid a visit to McKenna's physician, convincing the doctor to declare that the justice was incompetent and could not continue on the Court. Taft made another attempt on his colleagues, using the professional medical opinion as evidence that McKenna had to leave. He was able to convince all of the justices, except for McKenna, who exhibited the obstinate temper of a sickly, old man who would not accept his disability. Finally Taft produced a united front of all eight justices and McKenna was convinced to leave at the end of the 1924 term.[44] The justices attempted to calm the elderly justice's fear that he would be forgotten once gone by throwing a retirement party. McKenna left, dying shortly thereafter, mostly forgotten.

McKenna's ragged record on the Court did not speak well for McKinley's only choice for the high court. Yet the justice's voting record did reflect McKinley's philosophy favoring federal commerce power and continued anti-trust prosecutions. But the justice's odd opinions, his belligerent attitude at the end of his tenure and his serving with outsized personalities that made him shrink in comparison, relegated the justice to the lower end of judicial rankings. For the most part McKenna is a forgotten justice, wrote no opinions with ringing phrases to inspire future generations or his successors. Unfortunately for McKinley he survived only long enough for one appointment. If the president had lived through his second term he would have had two further vacancies to fill and establish a record. His vice president, Theodore Roosevelt, took advantage of his first term—McKinley's second if he had survived—to choose Oliver Wendell Holmes. But as was true for the presidents at the lower end of the spectrum, a single appointment placing them among the lowest ranked presidents.

## Notes

1. According to the CSPAN ranking, McKinley was the fifteenth highest ranked president and Polk the twelfth highest ranked president.

2. Bergeron, Paul, *The Presidency of James K Polk* (Lawrence KS: University Press of Kansas, 1987), 16.

3. Bergeron, 19

4. DeGregorio, William, *The Complete Book of the U.S. Presidents* (New York: Gramercy Books, 2002),772 Polk easily won the electoral vote by sixty-five and the popular vote by some thirty eight thousand votes.Albert Gore won the popular vote by nearly half a million but came up short on the electoral vote. Both men lost their home votes by less than one percent.

5. Abraham, Henry, *Justices, Presidents and Senators* (New York: Rowman Littlefield, 2008), 85.

6. Bergeron, 163-164

7. Swisher, Carl, *The Taney Period* (New York: MacMillan, 1974), 226.

8. Swisher, 235

9. 46 U.S. 215 (1847)

10. Swisher,552

11. Swisher, 694

12. 48 U.S. 283 (1849)

13. Peterson, Merrill, *The Great Triumvirate*(New York: Oxford University Press, 1987), 342

14. Degregorio,180

15. These included John McKinley (1837-1852) and Philip Barbour (1837-1841)

16. Fehrenbacher, Don, *The Dred Scott Case* (New York: Oxford University Press, 1978), 286-287.

17. Fehrenbacher, 311-312

18. Fehrenbacher, 312

19. Fehrenbacher, 314

20. 67 U.S. 635 (1863)

21. Swisher,878

22. Swisher,889-890

23. Swisher, 890

24. Fairman, Charles, *Reconstruction and Reunion* (New York: Macmillan Publishing, 1971), 83-84. During this time Grier asked the clerk of the Court ifhe could stay in the capitol so as to avoid climbing the steps to the Supreme Court. The clerk feared the damp capitol would harm Grier's health, refused.

25. Fairman, Charles, *Mr. Justice Miller and the Supreme Court* (New York: Russell and Russell, 1966),164-165.

26. *Hepburn v. Griswold* 75 U.S. 603 (1870)

27. Fairman, 713-715

28. Gould, Lewis,*The Presidency of William McKinley*(Lawrence, KS: University of Kansas Press, 1980), 161-165.

29. Traxel, David, *1898 (*New York, Alfred Knopf, 1998), 285

30. Kens, Paul Justice, *Stephen J. Field* (Lawrence, KS: University of Kansas Press, 1997), 344.

31. King, Willard, *Melville Weston Fuller* (New York: MacMillan, 1950), 229-230.

32. *New York Times*February 22, 1898Pg 4

33. 198 U.S. 45 (1905)

34. Kens, Paul, *Lochner v. New York* (Lawrence KS: University of Kansas Press, 1998), 148.

35. 227 U.S. 308 (1913)

36. 220 U.S. 45 (1911)

37. 243 U.S. 426 (1917)

38. Novick,256

39. 217 U.S. 349 , 381

40. See *Harmelin v. Michigan* 501 U.S. 957 (1991) where Justice Scalia cast doubt on the constitutional viability of the disproportionate punishment doctrine, though his views earned only two votes.

41. 236 U.S. 230 (1915)

42. 251 U.S. 466 (1920)

43. Pringle, Henry,*William Howard Taft* (Newtown CT: American Political Biography Press, 1967), 968.

44. Pringle, 967

# Chapter 7

## Thomas Jefferson (24) John Kennedy (22)

Thomas Jefferson and John Kennedy are known for their youthful achievements and stirring rhetoric. Ranked among the top fifteen presidents, both men suffer from a lack of substantive achievement. Their Supreme Court appointments exhibit this weakness, their five choices mainly forgotten and adding little to the legacies of the presidents who appointed them.

Thomas Jefferson and John Kennedy are linked in American history by youthful achievements and stirring rhetoric. As a leader of the American Revolution Jefferson attained greatness prior to his fortieth birthday. Articulate, intelligent and charismatic, Jefferson was a leader in the first cabinet, pushing George Washington to resist the natural inclination toward the Federalists and Alexander Hamilton. Creator of what would become known as the Democrat party, Jefferson introduced party discipline into government.[1] Jefferson's social liberalism pulses through the veins of every major Democrat political leader. Jefferson's vision of an expanded America was fulfilled in the Louisiana Purchase while the conquering of a new frontier was John Kennedy's passion.

Kennedy's connection to Jefferson can be summed up by a story dating from his brief White House tenure. Meeting with a group of Nobel laureates, Kennedy remarked that the White House was witnessing its greatest collection of minds since Thomas Jefferson dined alone.[2] Kennedy also brought some of the culture to the White House that reflected Jefferson's life. A bon vivant who introduced grace and style to the White House after the ragged Eisenhower years, Kennedy replaced a tired administration with an active and vital one. The same could be said for Jefferson after he replaced the cranky John Adams. Jefferson was credited with composing the Declaration of Independence while Kennedy claimed credit for the Pulitzer Prize Winning Profiles in Courage.[3]

Both men's presidencies were marked by missed opportunities rather than dazzling achievements. Jefferson recognized that the heights of his career came well before his presidency, refusing to include the eight years in the White House on his tombstone. Kennedy's success proved illusory, his record sparse when compared to the soaring rhetoric of his campaign or the accolades following his death.

Jefferson and Kennedy benefited from the public relations efforts mounted on their behalf. While ranked among the top tier of administrations, there remain questions about their placement. In one poll, Kennedy was recognized as the most overrated president by the very people who ranked his administration as tenth among forty two presidents.[4] Based on their Supreme Court appointments, both men's rankings plummet.

## Jefferson

When Thomas Jefferson arrived in Washington City his legacy was secure and his two terms added little to his legacy. His presidency began under a cloud, the 1800 election a hard fought partisan battle finally settled in the cloakrooms of the House of Representatives. Jefferson claimed his prize though at some cost to his reputation.

Jefferson's presidential achievements included securing the country's western border with the Louisiana Purchase which also hastened the movement westward producing challenges for his successors. His foreign policy initiatives proved problematic as a destructive embargo against Britain and France nearly destroyed the American economy. But it would be Jefferson's war with the judiciary that caused him the most grief.

Jefferson's disdain for the federal courts began during the waning days of the John Adams' administration as the lame duck packed the judiciary with Federalist judges. Infuriated by Adams' court packing and the 1801 Judiciary Act, Jefferson confronted the judges. With his Senate ally John Breckinridge, Jefferson moved swiftly to repeal the 1801 Judiciary Act, maintaining the Supreme Court at six members. Congress canceled the Court's 1802 term to prevent Federalist justices from reinstating the act and sending the message Congress would react to any judicial provocation.[5]

Jefferson also moved against Adams' midnight appointments, ordering James Madison not to deliver judicial commissions to the new judges under the assumption they could not serve without the commissions. Judge William Marbury, appointed as justice of the peace for Washington City, challenged Jefferson's decision and *Marbury v. Madison* placed the Court and Jefferson in direct conflict.

In Marbury, Chief Justice Marshall outmaneuvered the president by asserting the right to judicial review but refusing to grant the judicial commission on technical grounds the Court lacked jurisdiction to hear Marbury's suit. Marshall gave both sides a victory, Marbury the political victory that Madison should have delivered his commission and Jefferson the legal victory that the Court could not order the administration to deliver it.[6]

Jefferson then moved his efforts back to Congress, as the House voted impeachment charges against Judge John Pickering in March 1803 and the Senate removed him in March 1804. In 1805 the House filed impeachment charges against Justice Samuel Chase for his enforcement of the Alien and Sedition Acts. Chase defended his position and the independence of the judiciary, his acquittal ending Jefferson's war against the judiciary.

With Marshall and the Federalists' firmly ensconced in the judiciary, Jefferson turned to his appointment power, selecting Republican judges he believed would challenge the Federalists. But the strategy proved a failure, Marshall's guile and personality allowing the chief to co opt Jefferson's judges. The president's efforts were undermined by the radical states' rights arguments of some of his political allies and enemies, including Spencer Roane and his Richmond Junta. Their radical states rights arguments bound Marshall and his colleagues in upholding federal judicial power from states rights challenges. Marshall offered a powerful argument for centralizing power in the national government while his opponents placed state loyalty above national identity.

## William Johnson

In eight years Jefferson replaced two Federalist justices and filled a new seat created by the 1807 Judiciary Act. The death of the colorless Alfred Moore in 1803 provided the first vacancy. Jefferson reached deep into the hive of states' rights politicians and plucked William Johnson from the South Carolina State Supreme Court. Only thirty two in an era where youth had built the new republic, Johnson was considered a feisty and independent thinker pliable enough to accept Jefferson's direction.

Johnson's nomination and confirmation exhibits the evolution of the process. Johnson received notice of his nomination only after it was approved by the Senate, though he had not been informed he was being nominated.[7] Even with the president and Congress locked in a battle against a Federalist judiciary, there was little discussion of Johnson's qualifications. His acceptance of the new post was not guaranteed and after agreeing to serve he delayed his arrival on the Court for a year in order to complete his state Supreme Court term.[8]

As Jefferson's first Court appointee, Johnson faced the twin obstacles of high expectations and little authority to meet those expectations. As the junior among six justices, Johnson was the sole Republican voice on a Federalist

Court. With Jefferson challenging judicial authority and the institution, his appointee might have been expected to challenge Marshall.[9]

Instead the attacks produced the opposite effect, binding all the justices to the institution. Johnson's opinions differed from Jefferson's expectations, even as he assumed the role of the Court's first great dissenter. Johnson acquiesced in the Marshall's pro Federalist decisions, his rare dissents producing a limited impact. Unexpectedly Johnson's reputation for independence led him to reject Jefferson's rather than Marshall's views.

Jefferson expressed discontent with Johnson and the Court in a series of letters. The former president complained of Marshall's dominance and Johnson cast blame on his colleagues for being too ready to follow Marshall's lead. He denounced Justice Cushing as incompetent, Justice Chase as unable to write or think and Justice Washington and the chief justice as "one judge" a commentary on their tendency to vote together.[10]

Jefferson critiqued the decisions in *Gibbons v. Ogden* and *McCulloch v. Maryland* as examples of dangerous centralization of power. Implied in his criticisms was disgust at Johnson for silently agreeing in the McCulloch opinion and his arguing for plenary congressional power over commerce in Gibbons. [11] Jefferson's long held suspicions of federal courts led him to challenge the decision in *Cohens v. Virginia* which established federal dominance over state courts.[12]

Yet Johnson was more active in his opinion writing than Jefferson portrayed in his letters. From 1805-1835, Johnson composed half of the separate opinions issued by the justices.[13] But his silence in major constitutional cases angered Jefferson who expected Johnson to directly challenge Marshall. [14]

Johnson struggled with personal relationships on the Court, disliking both of Marshall's closest friends, Bushrod Washington and Joseph Story. He also criticized the Court reporter, Henry Wheaton for misquoting an argument made before the justices.[15]

The Marshall consensus fragmented as Johnson's career wound down. New justices challenged the chief, less intimidated by Marshall as his influence dipped precipitously. In *Ogden v. Saunders* Johnson joined Justice Washington in a bankruptcy case, forming a majority with the two newest justices Smith Thompson and Robert Trimble while the chief was forced into dissent.[16] Johnson would die shortly before Marshall in 1834, another in a long line of men who built the Supreme Court into a formidable political and legal institution.

## Livingston and Todd

Beside William Johnson, Jefferson appointed two justices, neither of whom met his expectations. Brockholst Livingston and Thomas Todd left little mark on the institution and failed to slow Marshall's Federalist agenda.

Chosen to replace Justice Patterson, Livingston had thrived in a political career best described as opportunistic. A New Yorker, Livingston's high political aspirations were blocked by Governor John Jay who did not support

Livingston's political plans. His rise though the Federalist Party stymied, Livingston performed a political pirouette and joined Jefferson's Democrat-Republican party. When the party seized control of New York government, Livingston was rewarded with a seat on the state high court. Though his decisions received mixed reviews they attracted Jefferson's attention and Livingston was appointed to the Court in 1806.

Safely in office Livingston performed another political switch, joining the Federalist Marshall. Livingston authored few opinions of note, his expertise in admiralty and prize law aided the justices in untangling disputes caused by the Jeffersonian embargo.[17] Livingston favored private property rights over the federal embargo, weakening Jefferson's foreign policy.[18]

In addition to his political switch, Livingston transformed his personality. Known for his temper—he had fought and won a duel eight years prior to joining the Court—Livingston became the Court's raconteur, calming tempers with a joke or story.[19] His death in 1823 broke a string of eleven consecutive terms of the Court working with the same members and was taken hard by Chief Justice Marshall who praised the obscure justice's contribution to the Court.[20]

Todd may be best known for marrying the younger sister of Dolley Madison – who was also Bushrod Washington's former sister-in-law.[21] On the Court Todd was frequently ill, missing nearly a third of the nineteen terms in which he served. His output was small, eleven Court opinions and a single dissent, though some of his colleagues managed less.[22] Todd's significance was linked to his impeccable Jeffersonian credentials, reducing criticism of opinions by calming his supporters' ire. While riding circuit, Todd displayed his expertise in land claims and when he fell ill in 1823, several land cases were deferred until his return.[23] His stock ownership in the Second Bank of the United States engendered dark conspiracy theories about the Bank's influence in the national government and partly fed the Jacksonian movement.[24]

As a Kentuckian he had firsthand knowledge of the frontier and was the first justice added to the seven- member Supreme Court in order to ride circuit in the growing west.[25] His death in 1826 sped the disintegration of the Marshall consensus.

## The 1000 Days

John Kennedy's administration may be one of the most analyzed thirty four months in American history. His shortened terms has been romanticized by historians who pondered what could have been and film makers who occasionally portrayed him as an American savior surrounded by Judases bent on his destruction.[26] Yet his brief presidency was marked by substantive failure—the Bay of Pigs—missteps – the Cuban Missile Crisis—and a lack of leadership—the Civil Rights Movement. Personal scandal was hidden from public view by a compliant and dazzled media but has since been revealed and tarnished the Camelot myth.

The machinations of his father Joseph Kennedy and John Kennedy's tendency to follow in his father's footsteps when it came to personal scandal further tarnished the era.[27] Kennedy's half- hearted push for civil rights was successful after his death and myths notwithstanding the Vietnam War began in earnest during the Kennedy Administration.[28] Yet the youngest elected president has maintained high rankings among recent historians. Kennedy's failures were forgotten after his assassination as the Harvard educated president was compared favorably with his rough hewn successor who managed only a teachers' college degree.

John Kennedy enjoyed a less tumultuous relationship with the Supreme Court than Jefferson. The Warren Court of the early 1960's was moving toward a liberal consensus and Kennedy's two Court appointments completed the transformation. In 1962 Justices Whittaker and Frankfurter resigned, knocking out the props of the conservative bloc.

## Arthur Goldberg

Kennedy struggled with Whittaker's replacement after Chief Justice Warren denounced his first choice, William Hastie as too conservative even as Hastie would have been the first black justice. The same complaint was filed against Kennedy's second choice, Paul Freund, forcing him to appoint deputy attorney general Byron White.[29]

For Frankfurter's vacancy Kennedy selected his labor secretary, Arthur Goldberg, who negotiated the AFL and CIO mergers and lobbied Congress against anti labor legislation before becoming Labor Secretary.[30]

"A walking constitutional convention" was the less than appealing description given to Justice Goldberg by his predecessor, Felix Frankfurter.[31] Lacking judicial experience, Goldberg disdained precedent and Court tradition and became a regular vote with Justices Black and Douglas, who supported an absolutist approach to rights, in *New York Times v. Sullivan*[32] and *Griswold v. Connecticut.*[33]

In Sullivan, Justice Brennan required public officials prove the press acted with actual malice – deliberately printing a falsehood – before the official could win a libel suit.[34] Brennan's extensive opinion proved to be insufficient for Goldberg who joined Justices Black and Douglas who favored absolute protection for the press from libel suits, granting the press immunity in criticizing government officials without regard to whether the criticism was factually correct.[35]

In Griswold, the Court struck down a Connecticut law banning the sale or use of contraception. Justice Douglas ruled that the First, Fourth and Fifth Amendments facilitated a general right to privacy.[36] The muddled opinion was dotted with penumbras and emanations, weakening its constitutional grounding.[37] Goldberg concurred, agreeing to a right to privacy but basing his argument on the amorphous Ninth Amendment, from where he discerned a privacy right.[38]

When the 1964 Civil Rights Act was challenged there was little doubt the Court would uphold the law. The one uncertainty was the decision's constitutional grounding. In the *Heart of Atlanta Motel* decision Justice Clark upheld the law as a regulation of interstate commerce.[39]

Concurring with the decision, Justice Black rejected the Commerce Clause as a grounding for the opinion, preferring the Fourteenth Amendment as the source of congressional power. Goldberg joined Black in seeking to overturn the Civil Rights Cases, which limited Congress' power to prohibit discrimination using the Fourteenth Amendment. Goldberg's preferred approach would have broadened Congress' civil rights role, allowing it to attack discrimination without connecting it to commerce.[40]

Goldberg's opinion in *Escobedo v. Illinois* launched the Court toward expanding the right from self incrimination. Escobedo confessed to his brother–in–law's murder after several hours of questions and after being refused access to a lawyer. In his opinion, Goldberg expanded the self incrimination right to extend from the courtroom to the interrogation room. Interrogation could occur only with the aid of counsel, limiting the possibility the police would wring a confession from a suspect. Escobedo was controversial but forgotten during the public furor over Miranda, which expanded Goldberg's reasoning to require police to warn suspects of their rights.[41]

Goldberg served three terms on the Court, being stricken with a dangerous case of the "Johnson treatment." Throughout his brief tenure Goldberg was uncomfortable in an institution isolated from rough and tumble politics and was frustrated by his colleagues' cautious approach to legal questions.[42] Knowing of Goldberg's discontent Lyndon Johnson dropped hints the justice could exercise his diplomatic skills in the international arena. The death of Adlai Stevenson in 1965 opened the position of United Nations' ambassador and Goldberg became fixated on negotiating an end to the rapidly expanding Vietnam War.[43]

With Goldberg pining for a new position, Johnson seized the opportunity to replace him. The frequently repeated story, likely apocryphal, had the president telling the justice he was announcing the justice's resignation and his appointment to the United Nations. Whether Goldberg left voluntarily or was lured from the Court by Johnson, the president took credit for the sudden resignation.[44] A more likely explanation had Goldberg resigning with Johnson agreeing to appoint him U.N. ambassador after promising Goldberg carte blanche in ending the war.[45]

Goldberg's tenure was the second shortest of any twentieth century justice, and combined with a limited written record did little to aid Kennedy's legacy in his Court appointments.[46] After his ambassadorial career ended, Goldberg returned to law and politics, offering a confused argument as counsel in the pivotal case of *Flood v. Kuhn.*[47] Goldberg mistakenly overstated the length of Curt Flood's career while a long winded recitation of his career statistics including batting average, fielding percentage and awards wasted over half of his allotted 30 minutes.[48] A return to politics included a 1970 run for New York governor and a crushing defeat by Nelson Rockefeller, though Goldberg was successful in organizing conservatives to support the much distrusted Republican.

## Whizzer White

Justice Goldberg's three terms on the Court limited his opportunities to write groundbreaking opinions. John Kennedy's second appointee, Byron White, served thirty one terms, ample time to create a written record. Yet for all his experience, White remains an enigma, his opinions reflecting his personality rather than a legal philosophy.[49]

Byron White was a believer in federal power, a hardliner on crime and a traditionalist on social issues. Serving under three different chief justices, Earl Warren, Warren Burger and William Rehnquist, each with different agendas, White assumed a different role in each. During the Warren Court, White dissented in Escobedo and Miranda,[50] dissented in *Mallov v. Hogan*,[51] which applied the right from self incrimination to the state but authored *Duncan v. Louisiana*, applying the right to a jury trial to certain misdemeanor cases.[52]

White was more accommodating on civil rights and the integration issue. As assistant attorney general he witnessed violence during the civil rights movement and became convinced the federal government had the authority to protect individuals from state governments.[53] He joined the Court's opinion striking down the conviction of civil rights demonstrators in South Carolina though he upheld similar convictions in a Florida case.[54] One of his strongest civil rights opinions came in *Reitman v. Mulkey*, which struck a California referendum overturning a state housing discrimination law.[55] Yet during the 1970s and 1980s he dissented when the Court sought to expand civil rights using the Thirteenth Amendment.[56]

In social policy White became progressively more conservative. He joined Douglas' opinion in Griswold, creating a right to privacy but refused to expand those rights to include abortion or gay rights. White also had a mixed record on speech and press cases, voting with the majority in the Sullivan case but later expressing concern and arguing that libel be redefined.[57]

## White and the Burger Court

Earl Warren's retirement and the appointment of four conservative Nixon appointees changed the Court's dynamics and White's role in it. White became a swing vote, the fifth and deciding justice for any opinion overruling or weakening a Warren decision. In *Miller v. California* he provided the fifth vote allowing local and state governments authority to define obscenity. The previous year White provided the fifth vote in Furman v. Georgia, striking the death penalty as cruel and unusual punishment. White ruled the death penalty was applied inconsistently and suggested creating a new method for applying the death penalty.[58]

The 1972 term witnessed another White flip flop as he eschewed his concurrence in Griswold and dissented in *Roe v. Wade* as the right to privacy was extended to include abortion. In the early abortion cases, During the 1980s White joined Chief Justice Burger and Justices Rehnquist and O'Connor in voting to uphold abortion restrictions but never comprised a majority. Only in *Webster v. Reproductive Services* would White join a majority in a major abortion opinion, but he would never see the Roe decision overturned. [59]

Byron White's early athletic career may have contributed to his antipathy toward the media. Fixed with the unfortunate nickname "Whizzer White" the justice distrusted the news media and regularly voted against the press. White joined Brennan's opinion in *New York Times v. Sullivan* but later questioned whether protections against libel claims were overly broad. After 1964 White began trimming the Sullivan decision.

In *Branzburg v. Hayes,* White ruled a grand jury investigating drug abuse could subpoena a reporter responsible for a report on drug sales and force that reporter to testify as to his sources.[60] According to White journalists enjoyed no First Amendment right to refuse to testify and failure to cooperate with a grand jury investigation could lead to imprisonment until sources were revealed. Branzburg was used by prosecutors for the next thirty years to squeeze information from reporters, occasionally jailing a reporter who did not cooperate.[61]

Four years later White struck another blow at the press. In *Zurcher v. Stanford Daily*, he upheld a police search warrant used to seize material from newspaper offices. The newspaper argued only a subpoena was necessary but White allowed police to obtain a warrant and conduct wide ranging searches of newspaper offices.[62] The Zurcher decision produced the predictable outcry from the media and pushed Congress to overturn the ruling, making it more difficult to use search warrants against newspapers, unlike ordinary citizens.[63]

White ruled in *Herbert v. Lando* that newspaper employees could be deposed in libel suits, allowing lawyers to question the paper's editorial process. The employees could be forced to answer questions about whether the paper had knowingly printed falsehoods and failure to testify would lead to contempt of court charges. Building on Branzburg, White ruled there was no First Amendment right to refuse to testify.[64] The justice's rulings drew scorn from the professional journalists who portrayed White as a crotchety justice whose anti press bias dated back to his locker room days. This was in contrast to the glowing reviews given to Justice Brennan, who generally supported press privileges.[65]

White assumed leadership in the conservative revolution during the Rehnquist years. During the 1988 and 1989 terms White was responsible for a constitutional revolution overturning precedent on discriminatory intent and the right to sue states.

In *Wards Cove v. Atonio* workers sued an Alaska canning plant claiming discrimination in the promotions process. They relied on statistics showing the number of minority managers was significantly lower than the percentage of minorities in the entire workforce. Under previous Court decisions such statistics were considered proof of racial discrimination under federal law. Wards

Cove changed the burden of proof by forcing plaintiffs to prove discrimination while making it more difficult to use statistics as proof of discrimination. The Wards Cove case drew a hostile response from Congress, the 1991 Civil Rights Act overturned Atonio, reinstating the burden of proof struck by White.[66]

If Wards Cove proved revolutionary, White's decision in *Will v. Michigan State Police* opened new avenues for the protection of states' rights. Will sued the Michigan State Police claiming he was denied a promotion. Under Section 1983 of the 1871 Civil Rights Act, Will charged police officials with violating his civil rights under the color of law. Yet Section 1983 bumped against the Eleventh Amendment ban on individuals suing states in federal courts. The Court had created the legal fiction that suing a state official was not suing the state, allowing Will's charges to be heard. In Michigan State police, White ruled the Eleventh Amendment prohibited such suits against the states, demolishing the legal fiction, and if taken to its logical end, would have prevented suits against state officials in federal courts.[67]

White's move to the political right did not prevent him from clashing with one of his conservative brethren, Justice Antonin Scalia. White's pragmatism clashed with Scalia's absolute philosophy and produced some of the most memorable opinions of the era.

A lighthearted exchange came in *Barnes v. Glen Theatre* as the Chief Justice upheld an Indiana law banning nude dancing at public bars. Scalia agreed with the result but disdained Rehnquist's complex symbolic speech test. Scalia focused on the history of public indecency laws then utilized an example of a voluntary gathering of seventy thousand nude Indianans in the Hoosier Dome. Scalia argued those in the stadium could be found guilty of public indecency even if all were consenting adults.[68]

White responded to Scalia's unusual hypothetical with one of his own as people gathered in private homes, "cavorting naked" without violating public indecency laws. The debate over nude Hoosiers amused more than one reader accustomed to dry opinions and White showed a rare deft touch in parrying Scalia.[69]

The two justices also tangled in an Establishment Clause case, *Lamb's Chapel v. Center Moriches*. The case used the confusing Lemon test, which was another judicial creation ridiculed by Justice Scalia as unworkable. Scalia noted that the test had undergone so many changes that it had come to resemble a late night horror movie monster that continuously shuffled around looking for victims no matter how many times it was killed.[70] White responded by snickering at Scalia's "cinematic diversion" while defending the Lemon Test even under its many interpretations.[71] The friendly barbs between the two justices did not prevent them from agreeing on most issues decisions but White refused to back down from Scalia, one of the few justices to take on the justice without fear of his barbed responses.

Bill Clinton's 1992 election as president cleared the way for the Democrat White to retire and allow a Democrat president to appoint his successor. His 1993 retirement announcement was conducted in the same terse manner as many of his opinions. White would later come to regret his early departure while he remained in good health, a feeling he passed onto his old friend William Rehnquist, who chose to remain in office even while terminally ill.

Unable to forge greatness in their careers, Jefferson's and Kennedy's justices brought down the inflated rankings of their presidencies. Both men would be rated among the mediocre presidents in light of the five men they chose for the Supreme Court.

## The Jefferson/Kennedy Legacy

Though frequently mentioned among great presidents, neither Thomas Jefferson nor John Kennedy enjoyed success in their Court appointments. Thomas Todd, Brockholt Livingston and Arthur Goldberg served either limited terms or composed few opinions of note. Todd and Livingston suffered the same disabilities as their colleagues of the era, being overshadowed by John Marshall. Goldberg was marginalized by his brief tenure and a tendency to place himself outside the mainstream of an activist, liberal court. Yet each president had a single justice of note.

William Johnson earned the title of the first dissenter but the Marshallian consensus of the period meant he wrote fewer separate opinions in three decades than modern justices compose in a single term. His major achievement was not creating chaos or dissension in a still weak institution but rather following the chief justice's lead in building a strong federal government with plenary powers.

While much of Johnson's thirty year career coincided with Jefferson's retirement years allowing the former president to view his appointee's handiwork, John Kennedy would not be granted that opportunity. Killed a little over a year after Byron White's arrival on the Supreme Court, Kennedy would not witness the justice's remarkable transformation. Always suspicious of the activism favored by his fellow Kennedy appointee, Justice Goldberg, White became a critic of the Warren Court and its successor the Burger-Brennan Court. Though maintaining a belief in a powerful federal government, he was less inclined toward liberal social policies including abortion, affirmative action and gay rights. White would prove a disappointment to the very people who idolized Kennedy and who expected a liberal judge in the mold of a Hugo Black. White's dislike for complex philosophies or rigid formulas made his opinions less quotable and memorable though his decisions would have a lasting impact on the law.

## Notes

1. Jefferson initiated the congressional caucus system of choosing party nominees for president.

2. Reeves, Richard, *President Kennedy* (New York: Simon and Schuster, 1991), 59.

3. Strong suspicions abound that Profiles in Courage was written by speechwriter Ted Sorenson and that Joseph Kennedy used his influence to convince the Pulitzer Committee to award John Kennedy the prize. Reeves, Thomas, *A Question of Character* (New York: Free Press, 1991), 142.

4. The CSPAN rankings listed Kennedy as the most overrated. CSPAN.org

5. Ellis, Richard, *The Jeffersonian Crisis* (New York: Oxford University Press, 1971), 50-51.

6. Nelson, William, *Marbury v. Madison* (Lawrence:University of Kansas Press, 2000), 63.

7. Morgan, Donald, *Justice William Johnson* (Columbia: University of South Carolina Press, 1954), 50-51.

8. Morgan, 51

9. Morgan, 182

10. Morgan, 182

11. Morgan, 158-162

12. Morgan, 160

13. Morgan, 178. During the period 1805-1833 Marshall wrote 465 opinions, Story 181 opinions and Johnson 172 opinions including thirty four dissents and twenty one concurrences.

14. Morgan, 182-183

15. White, Edward, *The Marshall Court and Cultural Change* (New York: Oxford University Press, 1991) 335-336.

16. Morgan 187

17. I n sixteen years Livingstone wrote thirty eight Court opinions and only eight dissents, Smith 350

18. Smith, Jean Edward, *John Marshall* (New York: Henry Holt, 1996), 417.

19. Smith 350

20. Smith, 469

21. Smith,409

22. Morgan, 189

23. White, 320

24. White, 320, Morgan, 189

25. Smith, 351

26. The Oliver Stone picture JFK offered as fact the paranoid delusions of a New Orleans district attorney who ranted through much of the film about the military industrial complex and a secret government cabal bent on fighting a war in Vietnam and eliminating all opposition, including the president of the United States.

27. Reeves, Thomas, 240-243 Reeves documents the rumors about Kennedy's numerous extramarital affairs both in and outside the White House.

28. Reeves, Richard 636-640

29. Hutchinson,Dennis, *The Man who was once Whizzer White* (New York: Free Press, 1998), 313-314.

30. Stebenne, David, *Arthur Goldberg* (New York: Oxford University Press, 1996), 120, 217.

31. Schwartz,

32. 376 U.S. 254 (1964)

33. 381 U.S. 479 (1965)

34. 376 U.S. 254, 280-281

35. 376 U.S. 254, 298

36. 381 U.S. 479, 485

37. Glancy, Dorothy "Douglas' Right to Privacy: a response to his critics"155 in Wasby, Stephen ed. *He Shall Not Pass this Way Again* (Pittsburgh PA: University of Pittsburgh Press, 1990).

38. 381 U.S. 479, 495-496

39. *Heart of Atlanta Motel v. United States* 379 U.S 241 (1964)

40. 379 U.S. 241, 246

41. 378 U.S. 478,493 (1964)

42. Stebenne, 346

43. Stebenne, 347-349

44. Abraham, 222

45. Stebenne, 347-348

46. Justice James Byrnes served a single term, 1941-1942.

47. 407 U.S. 258 (1972). Though he won the case on behalf of Flood, the decision may have been one of the oddest ever composed by a justice with the first section dedicated to listing the names of great baseball players of the past.

48. Snyder, Brad, *A Well Paid Slave* (New York: Viking Press, 2006), 268-274.

49. The only biography of the justice uses just one hundred and twenty pages to discuss his Court career and over three hundred thirty pages describing his life before reaching the pinnacle of his career.Much of the discussion of his legal opinions are limited to three terms, 1971, 1981, and 1991.

50. One of his first major dissents came in *Massiah v. United States* 377 U.S. 201 (1964) when he questioned the wisdom of the exclusionary rule and expressed the dismay of many Americans and their "dissatisfaction at preventive

programs aimed at eliminating crime," at 208 and warned against "additional barriers to the pursuit of the truth," at 209.

51. 378 U.S. 1 (1964)

52. 391 U.S. 145 (1968)

53. Hutchinson, 264-266

54. *Edwards v. South Carolina* 372 U.S. 229 (1963); *Adderley v. Florida* 385 U.S. 39 (1966)

55. 387 U.S. 369 (1967)

56. See *Jones v. Alfred Mayer Co.*392 U.S. 409 (1968) in which the Court revived Section 1982 banning certain types of private discrimination as a badge of slavery.See also *Runyon v. McCrary* 427 U.S. 160 (1976) when federal anti discrimination law was expanded to include private schools.

57. See *Herbert v. Lando* 441 U.S. 153 (1979) and *Masson v. New Yorker* 501 U.S. 496, 525 (1991).

58. 408 U.S. 238, 313-314 (1972)

59. 492 U.S. 490 (1989)

60. 408 U.S. 665 (1972)

61. During the 2005 investigation of Scooter Libby, Vice President Cheney's chief of staff, the federal prosecutor jailed reporter Judith Miller from the New York Times and threatened reporter Matthew Cooper of *Time* Magazine for refusing to reveal who had provided the name of a cover CIA agent.The courts rejected any First Amendment claim of privilege, the same privilege rejected by White in Branzburg.

62. 436 U.S. 547 (1978)

63. The 1980 Privacy Protection Act forbade the use of search warrants to search newspaper offices unless a member of the press was believed to have committed a crime.

64. 441 U.S. 153 (1979)

65. Hutchinson, 382-383

66. 490 U.S. 642 , 659 (1989)

67. 491 U.S. 58, 72(1989)

68. 501 U.S. 560, 576 (1991)

69. 501 U.S. 560, 596

70. 508 U.S. 384, 396 (1993)

71. 508 U.S. 384, 399

## Section 3

# Failed Successes: Failed presidents choose great justices

Failed administrations are characterized by scandal, economic collapse or poor crisis management. Presidents consigned to the bottom of presidential rankings are rarely remembered for their successes yet a select few presidents appointed justices of uncommon ability even in the midst of an unsuccessful presidency.

## Chapter 8

# John Adams (2) James Madison (7)

As founders of the American republic, John Adams and James Madison exercised the levers of power in the very institutions they helped create. Their ideas about government, politics and human behavior, though, did not translate into presidential success with each ranked among the average presidents. Each man, though, chose one of the first two great justices to serve on the Supreme Court with Adams ranked second based on his appointment of John Marshall.

John Adams and James Madison belong to the rare breed of politicians whose presidencies were the low point of their political career. Adams' contribution to the American Revolution placed him among the most influential founders. After two terms as vice president Adams succeeded George Washington, a compliment that doomed his presidency as he was compared unfavorably to the founding father.

James Madison's contribution to the republic came after the revolution. His efforts in the constitutional convention formed the basis of the American ideology, with power divided between national and local governments and among the three branches. His efforts on behalf of the completed constitution aided in its ratification and provided commentary on constitutional clauses and their meanings.[1] His shift from the Federalist ideology favoring a Hamiltonian government to a states' rights approach was part of a general political shift as the Federalists fell out of favor and the Jeffersonians became dominant. His two term presidency should have been the culmination of his career however it destroyed his political legacy as catastrophe befell his administration.[2]

Foreign crises dominated both presidencies. Adams was beset by domestic pressures as the Federalists sought war with France and the opposition wanted war with the British.[3] A foundering economy and Adam's reliance on the Alien and Sedition Acts to curb political dissent led to his defeat in 1800.[4]

Madison inherited a chaotic foreign policy as Jefferson's embargo brought much of the country's economy to its knees. Madison proved no more effective than his predecessors at balancing the demands for war and when it came, the British humiliated the administration by burning the capital.

Politically inept, both presidents were categorized as mediocre chief executives, memorable neither for greatness nor failure.[5] Yet looking beyond their administrations to their Supreme Court choices, both men achieved a remarkable turnaround, rising to the category of great and near great. Though the men chose five justices, both earned their high rankings for a single appointment to the Court, John Marshall for Adams and Joseph Story for Madison.

## Adams and the Supreme Court

The Supreme Court of the 1790s was a body of limited power and even less visibility. During his administration, Adams appointed Federalist justices, following Washington's lead. Of his three appointments, only one, John Marshall, achieved greatness while Alfred Moore was long forgotten. Bushrod Washington, Adams first choice, would not live up to his famous name though his efforts on behalf of his uncle magnified the former president's role in creating the republic.

Bushrod Washington, George Washington's nephew, was the son of George's older brother, Augustine. Washington was a prodigy, graduating from law school while still a teen, voracious study habits led to blindness in one eye.[6] Bushrod enjoyed a close relationship with John Marshall, serving with him in the Virginia ratifying convention. In 1798 the former president called both men to Mount Vernon and tried to convince them to run for Congress. Marshall ran and won but Bushrod enjoyed only a brief political career. [7]

The death of James Wilson left John Adams with a dilemma few presidents faced, two qualified candidates for a Court seat. Adams preferred Marshall to fill the vacancy but the future chief recommended Washington for the seat.[8] In picking Washington, Adams chose a loyal Federalist who tied his administration to that of the popular president while augmenting Federalist influence over the federal judiciary.

Bushrod Washington also served as the curator of Mount Vernon after the death of Martha Washington. He left the plantation open for visitors until discovering many of these early nineteenth century tourists were taking souvenirs later found in auctions sold as genuine Washington memorabilia. After closing public access to Mount Vernon, Washington commissioned his friend John Marshall to compose the former president's authorized biography.[9]

Beyond preserving the first president's legacy, Justice Washington joined in the nascent abolitionist movement, becoming a member of the American Colonization Society planning to deport freed slaves to the West African nation of Liberia. Washington was criticized when he paid off debts by selling the plantation's slaves south, his refusal to emancipate undermining efforts at solving the slavery issue.[10]

Washington's one legal opinion on slavery, though, strengthened the abolitionist movement. When South Carolina senator Pierce Butler came to Philadelphia to serve in Congress he brought his household slaves. When Butler left office, one of his servants, Ben, refused to return to South Carolina. Abolitionists seized upon the issue, taking *Hopper v. Butler* to circuit court, Washington ruled for Ben and Pennsylvania law. Washington found that once in a free state, slaves had the legal rights of citizens and could sue and refuse to return to their bondage. [11]

Another of Washington's circuit court cases, *Corfield v. Coryell*, became the basis for the Fourteenth Amendment. Corfield challenged a New Jersey case banning out of state oyster dredging. Washington upheld the law but then proceeded to define the privileges and immunities protected as part of every citizens' natural liberty including working in one's chosen occupation.[12]

Corfield elicited little comment when decided but during debate over the 1866 Civil Rights Act, its main sponsor, Illinois Senator Lyman Trumbull quoted Coryell in describing the bill's scope. Washington's definition of liberty was copied by Justices Rufus Peckham, James McReynolds and William Douglas who included a variety of rights protected as a privilege and immunity enjoyed by all citizens.[13]

Washington's circuit opinions expressed his natural law views of judging. Chief Justice Marshall dominated the Court limiting Washington opinion writing opportunities. The two justices agreed on most issues with Washington disagreeing with Marshall on three opinions in thirty years, earning him Justice William Johnson's characterization as Marshall's puppet and a cipher that blindly followed the chief.[14] The sole constitutional split between the two involved bankruptcy law with Marshall changing his mind from an earlier decision.

Granted power over bankruptcy, Congress's inaction on the issue forced states to act after the 1819 depression. A pair of state bankruptcy cases, *Sturgis v. Crowninshield*[15] and *Ogden v. Sanders*[16] produced the rare split. In Sturgis, Marshall built a unanimous majority around his opinion that states could enact bankruptcy laws when the federal government failed to act. In this he created a type of dormant Bankruptcy Clause in much the way he created a dormant commerce clause in *Gibbons v. Ogden*. Marshall declared the New York bankruptcy law violated the Contract Clause by wiping out debts acquired before the law was passed. At the same time he left allowed for state bankruptcy laws forgiving debts made after the law was passed.[17]

Justice Washington agreed to Sturgis but eight years later led a revolt in the Ogden case challenging the Sturgis loophole. The decision produced a rare Marshall dissent with Washington upholding the bankruptcy law and allowing states to pass similar laws when Congress refused to act. Marshall dissented, ignoring his Sturgis opinion and granting Congress exclusive powers over bankruptcy legislation. Ogden was one of the early indicators that Marshall was losing control of his institution with the deciding vote cast by the newest justice, Robert Trimble.[18]

Washington enjoyed a professional relationship with Justice Joseph Story, exchanging letters on cases.[19] Washington stepped in for Story when the younger justice struggled with his opinion in *Biddle v. Green*.[20] After achieving statehood, Kentucky struggled with property deeds issued by Virginia. Under a compact between the two states, Virginia law was to determine ownership of disputed property but when Kentucky passed a new law sweeping away that Virginia law, property holders sued, claiming Kentucky impaired obligation of the original contracts.[21] Justice Story agreed, striking the Kentucky law and infuriating Kentucky politicians. The politicians proposed a constitutional amendment removing the Court's jurisdiction over state laws under the constitution.[22]

The Court backtracked, Washington composing a second opinion that retained much of Story's reasoning but softened the language to settle Kentuckians' anger. He ruled the compact was a contract that could not be overturned by Kentucky law.[23]

Bushrod Washington died in 1829, one of the last of the original Federalist judges and Marshall's closest friend and ally in the Court. Though forgotten his efforts in the political and judicial arenas, by continuing the Washington family's political legacy he is one of our most underappreciated public officials.

## Alfred Moore

The shortest and lightest man ever to serve on the Supreme Court, Alfred Moore stood under five feet tall and tipped the scales at ninety pounds. His diminutive size may well have led to the medical problems that made him a justice in name only. Appointed in 1799, Moore missed more terms on the Court than he served, resigning in 1804 due to illness.[24] Composing no opinions, his judicial record is limited to his circuit duties which included South Carolina and Georgia. The distances traveled may have played havoc with his health.[25] Known for his sense of humor, Moore played no role in the Marshall Court, his departure giving Thomas Jefferson his first choice for justice, providing the chief with another vote in favor of his nationalist policies.

## John Marshall

Few justices overshadow the president who appointed them but John Marshall proved to be a justice of uncommon abilities and rugged determination. Marshall had an illustrious career in the Revolutionary War and then returned home to become a prosperous Virginia lawyer. He briefly served as a member of the House of Representatives then earned public acclaim as one of the three ambassadors who were part of the XYZ affair. Impressed by Marshall's forbearance, John Adams appointed him Secretary of State and the two men guided the country between British and French supporters, both of whom sought war with the other country.

John Adams struggled to replace Chief Justice Ellsworth, offering the job to John Jay, who refused, then selecting Marshall. As the nation's fourth chief justice Marshall earn the reputation as a great American founder, defining the position of chief justice much as Washington defined the position of chief executive. Marshall also excelled at the three tasks usually connected to the position: intellectual leader, social leader and administrator.[26]

As social leader, Marshall relied upon his charm and intellect to influence his colleagues. Marshall led discussions and bargaining during group meals and evenings at the justices' boarding house. Marshall discouraged separate opinion and his skillful writing molded the justices' disparate views into a single Court opinion.[27]

The chief also excelled at intellectual leadership, shouldering much of the opinion writing burden while his colleagues struggled to handle their circuit riding duties. Marshall placed his imprint on the constitution and the powers of the presidency, Congress and judiciary.

As administrative leader, Marshall's learning curve was fraught with danger. The 1800 presidential election made the Democratic- Republicans the governing party and kicked off a determined effort to undermine the federal judiciary. In his final day John Adams packed the courts with Federalists, infuriating the opposition, which responded by repealing the 1801 Judiciary Act and cancelling the Court's 1802 term. Jefferson refused to grant Adams' judges their commissions, leading to Marshall's greatest victory.[28]

*Marbury v. Madison* has been analyzed and criticized and quoted more than any judicial opinion. The dispute began when William Marbury, one of Adams' midnight judges, was refused his commission as justice of the peace. He sued Secretary of State James Madison in the Supreme Court which had been given jurisdiction over such issues. In deciding Marbury, Marshall balanced his personal desire to tweak the Jeffersonians with his knowledge that Congress would attack the Court if it issued a partisan decision.

Marshall castigated Madison for refusing to provide Marbury's judicial commission but instead of ordering Jefferson to deliver the commission, the chief ruled Marbury had sued in the wrong court. Reading Article III the chief justice ruled the Court's original jurisdiction was fixed and when Congress expanded that jurisdiction in 1789 it had violated the Article. With federal law in conflict with the constitution it was the Court's responsibility to strike the law. Marshall's assertion of the power of judicial review allowed him to dismiss Marbury's case, strengthen the federal judiciary and avoid a political crisis if Jefferson refused to deliver the commission. Marshall used Marbury to score political points without provoking the president, but the decision would not be the last time the two men would clash.[29]

Aaron Burr was one of those politicians who gave politicians a bad name. A New Yorker, he was chosen by Jefferson as a vice presidential candidate for the 1800 presidential contest. The election produced an electoral tie between the two men and when Burr refused to step aside for Jefferson, the decision was handed to the House of Representatives, where Jefferson was chosen as the lesser of two evils. In response to the constitutional crisis Congress passed the Twelfth Amendment creating the current Electoral College system.[30] Tossed from the 1804 ticket by a still seething Jefferson, Burr became a soldier of fortune and during his travels to the southwest became entangled in international intrigue and hardball domestic politics.

Barraged with reports that Burr was undermining the United States, Jefferson concluded his former vice president was engaged in treason and ordered Burr arrested. The trial, held in Marshall's Richmond circuit court, captured the capital's attention through the late summer of 1806 as Jefferson turned the screws to destroy his political rival.[31] No friend of Burr, Marshall has been credited with the vice president's acquittal as Burr's defense attacked the federal government and made Jefferson the issue by subpoenaing documents from the executive. Having railed against executive power during his campaign against John Adams, Jefferson was tempted to claim privilege but when Marshall ordered the president to comply, Jefferson did so but with a remarkable lack of grace.[32]

The trial then became bogged down in the debate over the meaning of treason rather than Burr's guilt. Jefferson sought a broad definition but Marshall recognized the danger in using the treason weapon against political enemies.[33] After the government presented its case, Marshall narrowly defined treason and guided the jury toward an acquittal.[34] Burr was acquitted and treason became a rarely used weapon in the federal arsenal. Jefferson responded by sending trial transcripts to Congress, imploring its members to impeach the chief but the majority of Democrat- Republicans had tired of the president's war on the judiciary and declined to act. [35]

As a federalist Marshall favored the centralizing force of the national government. He believed that only an activist federal authority could create a national market and assumed the duty of strengthening the three national branches. His decisions on the commerce clause, the necessary and proper clause and Article III established the supremacy of Congress and the federal judiciary against the state. One of his most important opinions on this subject came in *Gibbons v. Ogden*.[36]

Gibbons was a dispute over the newest technology of the period, the steamship. Travel between the states of New Jersey and New York became more efficient with formation of a steamship company granted a New York monopoly. Congress granted Gibbons a federal monopoly under its authority to regulate interstate commerce, creating the unusual condition of two mutually exclusive monopolies for the same business.

Eventually the two steamship companies took their dispute to the Supreme Court. Marshall faced the quandary of centralizing all commercial regulations in the federal government or allowing states to create commercial barriers to trade. In Ogden the chief justice split the difference by ruling that federal authority over commerce took precedence and overturned the state monopoly. He then granted states the authority to regulate some interstate commerce in the absence of federal law.[37]

Marshall expanded his commerce definition in *Brown v. Maryland*.[38] The state taxed importers of goods into the state and Brown, an importer by trade, challenged the law as an unconstitutional state regulation of interstate commerce. Maryland defended its law as a proper sales tax but the chief justice focused on when goods became intrastate commerce after being shipped across state lines. Marshall reached a nineteenth century solution that would not last beyond the industrial revolution. According to the chief, goods became part of intrastate trade once they were removed from their original package for sale to consumers.[39]

Land speculation fed by corruption in some of the branches of the second bank of the United States led to financial panic and the 1819 Depression. As the economy crumbled, the state of Maryland began taxing the BUS' state branch in an effort to chase it from its borders. The tax was challenged in *McCulloch v. Maryland* and Marshall expanded national power at the expense of the states.[40]

In McCulloch, Marshall interpreted the necessary and proper clause of Article One Section Eight as granting Congress plenary powers. He ruled the clause extended congressional authority, countering the strict constructionist argument that a national bank was unconstitutional because it was not mentioned among Congress' enumerated powers. The bank was a necessary instrument for enforcing Congress' power to tax, spend, borrow and regulate currency. The question remained whether the state could tax a federal entity with Marshall ruling they could not, noting "the power to tax is the power to destroy" and that under the constitution federal law was supreme to state law and a federal institution could not be destroyed by any state.

Using the obscure Contract Clause, Marshall struck harder at state power. The clause was one of those last minute additions to the constitution, added only as the framers prepared to publish the document.[41] The clause forbade states from abrogating contracts, usually in the form of debt moratoriums, thus protecting property from majority rule. Seen as a redundancy to the ban on ex post facto laws, the Contract Clause was used by Marshall to protect vested rights from state legislators.

The movement west from the thirteen Atlantic colonies created a thirst for land. Speculators sought to buy up unsettled territories for low prices by convincing states legislatures to sell the land. A group of speculators hit upon a traditional method of success, bribing Georgia legislators to sell lands along the Yazoo River for pennies on the dollar. The speculators then sold the same land to hapless northerners who saw the southwest as a profit making opportunity.

When Georgians learned of their legislators' perfidy they tossed them out of office in the next election and the new legislature promptly overturned land sales to the speculators, leaving many innocent landowners facing the possibility of losing their titles. In *Fletcher v. Peck* the Supreme Court considered the constitutionality of land grant repeal.[42]

Marshall faced the conundrum of upholding the fraud by honoring the contracts with the crooked speculators or allowing the legislators to seize land from innocent owners at the loss of thousands of dollars. Marshall found the Georgia legislature was attempting to abrogate the contracts between the speculators and landowners even though the contracts to sell the land had been purchased with bribes. The decision forced Georgia to honor the contracts.

Marshall expanded the clause in *Dartmouth College v. Woodward*, protected the governing charters of public universities and other organizations from state intrusion. New Hampshire had sought to change the governing board of Dartmouth College set down by the British government prior to the revolution. When the state sought greater control over the board it triggered a debate over public power and private rights. The chief justice ruled New Hampshire colony signed a contract with the college and while the form of government had changed the agreement had to be honored.[43]

Fletcher and Dartmouth saw the Court flex its muscles at the expense of the states. Fearful of allowing federal encroachments on their power, state judiciaries challenged the ability of the Court to rule on state disputes.

Virginia banned lottery sales within the state. The Cohens brothers were charged with selling national lottery tickets in the state. After their appeal was denied by the Virginia Supreme Court the justices ruled state high court decisions could not be appealed to federal courts. The state judges relied on the Eleventh Amendment, which banned citizens from suing states in federal court. The Virginia Supreme Court went so far as to strike down Section 25 of the 1789 Judiciary Act which provided for appeals to the United States Supreme Court.[44]

Marshall swept aside the Virginia court's rulings, finding that state sovereign immunity applied only to original jurisdiction not appellate and that federal courts were the proper venue for hearing appeals of constitutional cases. The chief asserted federal predominance over interpreting federal law and constitution. Marshall upheld Congress' authority to operate national lotteries in states but dismissed the appeal on the technical issue that the national lottery law limited sales to the District of Columbia.[45]

Marshall's successes came during his first two decades as chief but in the last decade he struggled with an increasingly restive Court. Marshall benefitted from a stable Court membership from 1801 to 1829, with only seven new justices in nearly three decades. The consensus began to crumble with Justice Robert Trimble's appointment in 1826 but it was Andrew Jackson who offered Marshall his most dangerous opponent.

Jackson entered office believing each branch interpreted the constitution according to its beliefs. His first two Court appointees, John McLean and Henry Baldwin, revolted against the chief's control with Baldwin's mental illness unnerving his colleagues and heightening tensions.

Marshall and Jackson clashed during the 1830s with their most famous imbroglio occurring in *Worcester v. Georgia*.[46] In a treaty with the Cherokee tribe, the government granted the Indians control over significant lands in northern

Georgia. When the state of Georgia sought to extend state laws within those lands, it challenged federal supremacy in the region and triggered a potential constitutional crisis. Marshall ruled the Cherokee were covered under federal law made by treaty and implied the federal government was responsible for protecting the Indians, prodding the Jackson Administration to act. Andrew Jackson was to have responded that "John Marshall issued his decision, let John Marshall enforce it."[47]

But Worcester would one of Marshall's few successes during the Jackson Administration. Beset by a hostile president and justices who were unwilling to follow his lead, Marshall backed away from his usual nationalism, moving with the political winds. In *Willson v. Blackbird Creek* Marshall recognized state police powers to regulate health and safety of citizens.[48] In *Barron v. Baltimore* Marshall agreed that the Bill of Rights applied only to the federal government. When the city of Baltimore diverted river water from Barron's wharf turning it into a dry dock, Barron argued the city had taken his property without just compensation. The chief justice dismissed Barron's claim that the Fifth Amendment applied to state governments, noting the American Revolution was based on a fear of national not local power and that state citizens should rely on their state constitutions to protect their rights.[49]

Marshall's death in 1835 ended an era but began a legacy of an independent and vibrant federal judiciary. After Marshall, the Supreme Court was recognized as one of the most powerful courts in the world.

## James Madison

Few men have entered the presidency with such hope, experience and ability and served so poorly in office. Celebrated as one of the most important framers of the constitution and as the father of the Bill of Rights, James Madison underwent one of the most dramatic political conversions in American history. As a contributor to the Federalist Papers arguing in favor of ratification of the new constitution, Madison allied with Alexander Hamilton and other Federalists favoring a strong central government.

As his political career flourished, Madison moved to the left, toward the Jeffersonian and states' rights arguments. Composing the Virginia and Kentucky resolutions, Madison laid the groundwork for what would later become interposition and secession of states from the union.[50] By 1801 he was firmly within the Jeffersonian camp, serving as his secretary of state and provoking the political crisis that would become Marbury v. Madison. His loyalty earned him the nod as Jefferson's successor.

Madison's presidency proved a disaster. The international conflict bequeathed him deteriorated as the British scattered the American government during the War of 1812 before burning the capital. The Democrat- Republicans dominated government yet Madison's administration was torn by factionalism as hard driving congressional leaders such as Henry Clay sought to propel the legislative branch into the forefront.

## Gabriel Duvall

Madison's two selections to the Supreme Court present a case study on how not to choose justices. When the last two Washington justices, William Cushing and Samuel Chase, died Federalist influence waned. Madison hoped to replace two Federalists with two Jeffersonians and weaken Chief Justice Marshall's hold on the judiciary.

Madison required four appointments to replace Cushing. The first was former attorney general Levi Lincoln, who was easily confirmed but refused the appointment for health reasons. Madison then chose the partisan route, appointing Alexander Wolcott, a strong Jeffersonian, who received the fewest votes, nine, of any Court nominee. Madison then picked the American ambassador to Russia, John Quincy Adams, who also turned down the nomination. Finally Madison made his fourth and best pick, Joseph Story.[51]

Replacing the irascible and controversial Samuel Chase proved much easier as Madison's first choice, Gabriel Duvall, was easily confirmed. Duvall's career was one of missed opportunities. He declined appointment as delegate to the constitutional convention from the state of Maryland, instead remaining as chief justice of the state. Not a strong writer, he either joined most of the Court's opinions or dissented without opinion, as he did in the Dartmouth College Case and managed to compose only fifteen opinions in his twenty three year career.[52] He proved a burden to his colleagues, spending nearly a decade in blissful deafness that made it impossible for him to follow oral arguments. Duvall was convinced to leave only when Andrew Jackson promised to appoint a fellow Marylander, Roger Taney, to replace him.[53]

## Joseph Story

Joseph Story was one of the few intellectuals and legal philosophers to serve. His *Commentaries on the Constitution* were a clause by clause explanation of the document. Such interpretations today would earn the justice catcalls from legal commentators and possibly a subpoena from one of Congress' judiciary committees but during the Marshall era such legal acumen was recognized as a benefit rather than a liability for a Supreme Court justice.

Story was the sole member of the Marshall Court to escape obscurity and attain prominence in his own right. The youngest justice to serve – only thirty two when appointed – Story used his thirty four year career to place his own mark on American law. Story became a force almost immediately as he composed the opinion in *Martin v. Hunter's Lessee*, one of the few constitutional opinions of the era not authored by Marshall.[54]

The Martin case dredged up the controversial Jay Treaty and the decision by the state of Virginia to seize land owned by Lord Fairfax, a British loyalist. The treaty set the terms for settling land disputes but when Virginia refused to compensate British owners of seized lands, the Supreme Court ordered the land be returned to its original owners.

At that moment the Virginia state judiciary transformed a simple land dispute into a constitutional crisis. Jealous of state prerogatives and suspicious of federal judicial tyranny, the Virginia high court ruled the national Supreme Court lacked the power to overturn a state court decision. To emphasize their point, the Virginia judges struck down part of the federal Judiciary Act of 1789 which allowed the federal judiciary to hear appeals from state courts.

The gauntlet had been tossed, Virginia judges daring their federal colleagues to accept the challenge to national power. The Supreme Court, speaking through Story, did not back away and in Martin ruled the constitution and federal law properly granted the Supreme Court authority to hear appeals of state court opinions. Story found the Virginia state courts overstepped boundaries in striking federal law and refusing to accept a Supreme Court decision.

Story's opinion favoring federal over state judicial power was noth extraordinary but Story's youth made him an unusual author of such an important decision. In his mid thirties and in the midst of his third full term as a justice, Story was chosen by his colleagues to face down a rebellious state court and the states' rights movement. The justices' trust and belief in the young justice's abilities was a sign of the esteem in which they held him and this acclaim would deepen during the next three decades.

John Marshall's death marked an end of an era and the beginning of the end for Justice Story. The arrival of the Jacksonian justices marked a shift in the direction of the Court as Marshall's property rights and nationalistic decisions were replaced by states' rights oriented opinions. The change began in 1837 as Story dissented in a trio of cases marking the start of the Taney Court.[55] As Taney and his colleagues trimmed around Marshall Era opinions, Story saw his influence decline even as he fought to maintain the federalist ideal. In his last five years as a justice, Story created a doctrine that would last nearly a century and twice commented on the slavery controversy.

In the 1840s, Story had two bites at the slavery issue. The *Amistad* case, made famous by a 1999 motion picture, was a denunciation of the Spanish slave trade. [56] The Amistad was a Spanish slaver that was seized by slaves and sailed into New York Harbor. When the Spanish claimed the slaves were merchandise that should be returned to the ship's owners, the Supreme Court balked. Story found that while slaves might be considered property, the men who seized the Amistad had been kidnapped from Africa as part of the slave trade and because the trade had been outlawed by the British and the United States, the Amistad slaves could not be returned to the Spanish. Amistad was one of the first instances in which the Court recognized that slaves had rights. While Amistad was a narrow decision affecting only a small group of slaves, Story's opinion in *Prigg v. Pennsylvania*,[57] had more far reaching consequences.

Prigg was a bondsman who hunted down fugitive slaves who escaped into free states. In Pennsylvania he discovered a fugitive and returned him to Maryland. Prigg was charged with kidnapping under Pennsylvania law but challenged the charge as he was simply enforcing the 1793 federal fugitive slave law allowing bondsmen to return slaves to their owners.

Justice Story agreed with Prigg, dismissing the kidnapping charges and ruling that Prigg and other bondsmen had the legal right to hunt fugitive slaves, even in free states, and forcibly return them to the south, thereby forcing fugitives to flee to Canada to escape slavery. At the same time Prigg and others were granted immunity from state laws against kidnapping or the use of force in subduing fugitives.[58] While allowing bondsmen to operate in free states, Story also ruled that free states were not required to enforce the federal fugitive slave law, forcing slave owners to track down their property. This portion of the ruling exacerbated the slavery debate as southerners sought government aid in hunting down fugitives and led to the 1850 fugitive slave law that all but forced free states to capture and return fugitive slaves.

More obscure but no less important was Story's opinion in *Swift v. Tyson*.[59] Under the constitution, federal courts settled disputes between citizens of two different states. Federal judges were required to interpret and enforce state laws, much to the chagrin of state judges who were suspicious of any federal intrusion into state power. In Swift, Story tried to untangle the growing confusion as a routine dispute became one of the most far reaching opinions handed down. Story's solution was to allow federal judges to create their own common law, drawing upon British common law and the laws of states. Story allowed the federal judiciary to ignore state court rulings in favor of their own, a vast expansion of judicial power, especially originating from the states' rights oriented Taney Court. Story was determined to make the Court's 1845 term his last but his sudden death cheated him of retirement and the accolades that would have accompanied his departure.

## Story, Duvall and Madison

James Madison's rise into the rank of great presidents is based purely on his belated choice of Joseph Story as a justice. Story's opinions during and after the Marshall era placed him among the judicial greats. His ruminations on the meaning of the constitution provided an early interpretation of the document and served as a resource for a generation or more of judges and law students

## Notes

1. Leibiger, Stuart, *Founding Friendship* (Charlottesville VA.: University of Virginia Press, 1999), 84-85.

2. The War of 1812 and its stalemated outcome was considered the first war lost by the United States.

3. McCullough, David, *John Adams* (New York: Simon and Schuster, 2002), 496- 497.

4. McCullough, 566-567

5. The average ranking of the CSPAN and Wall Street Journal polls placed Adams in the mediocre category as fifteenth among forty one presidents ranked while Madison was rated three places lower.

6. White, Edward G, *The Marshall Court and Cultural Change* (New York: Oxford University Press, 1991),347.

7. Smith, Jean Edward *John Marshall* New York: Henry Holt, 1996), 240.

8. White, 345.

9. Marshall, John, *George Washington* (Indianapolis:T he Liberty Fund, 2000).

10. Staudenraus, P.J, *The African Colonization Movement* (New York: Octagon Books, 1980), 15-17.

11. Bell, Malcolm, *Major Butler's Legacy* (Athens GA: University of Georgia Press, 1987), 141-142. Stoner, James "Heir Apparent Bushrod Washington" in *Seriatim* Scott Douglas Gerber ed. (New York: New York University Press, 1998), 343.

12. 6 F Cas 546; Berger, Raoul,*Government by Judiciary* (Cambridge: Harvard University Press, 1977)

13. Berger, 31; Peckham's opinion in *Allgeyer v. Louisiana* 165 U.S. 578 (1897) defined liberty as a right to practice one's vocation and make economic decisions without government interference, 590. In *Meyer v. Nebraska* 262 U.S. 390 (1923), these rights were expanded to include educating one's children (400) while in *Doe v. Bolton* 410 U.S. 179 (1973), a companion to Roe, Justice-Douglas expanded it further to include activities such as strolling and loafing, 214.

14. Morgan, Donald, *Justice William Johnson* (Columbia: University of South Carolina Press, 1954), 182.

15. 17 U.S. 122 (1819)

16. 25 U.S. 213 (1827)

17. Smith, 439-440

18. Smith 498-499. The Ogden case involved two separate suits with Justice Marshall joining Justice Johnson's opinion striking down one of the state laws on narrower grounds.

19. White, 348-349

20. 21 U.S. 1 (1823)

21. White, 641-642

22. White, 642-643

23. White, 646

24. Smith,341

25. Smith,290

26. Steamer, Robert, *Chief Justice* (Columbia S.C.: University of South Carolina Press, 1986), 9-3. Steamer identifies the three main roles of the Chief justice and identifies chiefs most capable at each,.

27. Smith, 402-404

28. Smith 322-323

29. Nelson, William, *Marbury v. Madison* (Lawrence KS: University Press of Kansas, 2000),61-63.

30. Larson, Edward,*A Magnificent Catastrophe* (New York: Free Press, 2007), 267-269.

31. Smith, 358

32. Smith, 365

33. Much like many men of his time Marshall would have been familiar with Seutonius' writings on the rule of Tiberius and the treason trials held after the execution of Sejanus) in which senators were convicted of treason for such innocuous actions as carrying into the lavatorya coin with the picture of Tiberius stamped on it. *The Twelve Caesars* (London: Penguin Books,1979), 142.

34. The debate was between proponents of the broad definition of treason known as constructive treason which included any contact or connection with those engaged in treasonous activities including meetings, conversations, letters or business dealings.Marshall favored the government having to prove an overt act under its treason prosecutions.

35. Wheelan, Joseph, *Jefferson's Vendetta: The Pursuit of Aaron Burr and the Judiciary* (New York: Carroll and Graf, 2005), 78.

36. 22 U.S. 1 (1824)

37. Marshall's opening for state commerce laws created the dormant commerce doctrine.It also drew a separate opinion from Justice William Johnson who argued for total congressional control over interstate commerce.

38. 25 U.S. 419 (1827)

39. Smith 497-498

40. 17 U.S. 316 (1819)

41. Rossiter, Clinton,1787 *The Grand Convention* (New York:Macmillan, 1966), 230.

42. 10 U.S. 87 (1810)

43. 17 U.S. 518 (1819)

44. Smith, 460-462

45. *Cohens v. Virginia*19 U.S. 204 (1821)

46. 31 U.S. 515 (1832)

47. Remini, Robert, *Andrew Jackson* V2 (Baltimore Md: Johns Hopkins University Press, 1998), 276-277.

48. 27 U.S. 245 (1829)

49. 32 U.S. 243 (1833)

50. Ketchum, Ralph, *James Madison* (CharlottesvilleVA: University of Virginia Press, 1990), 395-396.

51. Abraham, 71-72

52. White, 321

53. White, 326

54. 14 U.S. 304 (1816) Marshall did not participate in the case as he had purchased a parcel of land that was under dispute.

55. *Charles River Bridge Co v.Warren Bridge* 36 U.S. 420 (1837) *Briscoe v. Kentucky* 36 U.S. 257(1837) *New York v. Miln* 36 U.S. 102 (1837)

56. *U.S. v. Amistad* 40 U.S. 518 (1841)

57. 41 U.S. 539 (1842)

58. Fehrenbacher, 44

59. 41 U.S. 1

# Chapter 9

# Rutherford Hayes (13) Calvin Coolidge (11) Herbert Hoover (5)

Single term presidents are usually labeled as failures or below average. Rutherford Hayes, Calvin Coolidge and Herbert Hoover all suffered the ignominy of serving only four years yet in that time each chose Supreme Court justices of exceptionably ability. These choices moved them above the average ranking with Hoover rising to the top five of presidents based on Court nominations.

Single term presidents struggle for recognition of their achievements. Most single term presidents may lose their reelection campaign, are denied their party's nomination or voluntarily leave office after a single term. Three presidents, Rutherford Hayes, Calvin Coolidge and Herbert Hoover, served a single term but reached and departed office under different circumstances.

Hayes was propelled into office under the cloud of a disputed election and the partisan vote of an electoral commission. His presidency split the Republican Party on the patronage issue and Hayes did not seek renomination. Coolidge was elevated into the presidency after President Harding's death. Serving five and a half years, Coolidge was popular but he chose to serve only one elected term. His replacement, Hoover, confronted problems left over from the Coolidge Administration, his presidency destroyed by economic depression.

The three administrations are logged among mediocre or failed presidencies, Coolidge's successful administration blamed for the subsequent depression and rated the lowest of the trio. Yet the three men rose above mediocrity in their Court appointments, Hoover catapulting to the rank of great while Hayes and Coolidge climbed to the top half of all presidents.

## Rutherford Hayes

Known more for his disputed presidential win than his administration, Rutherford Hayes has been ranked among mediocre presidents for his one term. The disputed election was triggered by widespread violence and fraud in southern states and was ended only by the vote of a fifteen member electoral commission voting on party lines to grant Hayes all of the disputed electoral votes. The compromise of 1877 included a presidential promise to end reconstruction in the south, handing the region to the Democrat Party for the next century. It also marked the end of civil rights enforcement, leaving the question to the judiciary. With three Court appointments, Hayes had the opportunity to create a strong civil rights majority but only his first selection, John Marshall Harlan continued the radical Republican tradition of promoting equality.

## The Last Radical

By 1877 public exhaustion with civil rights and the Democrat controlled House of Representatives marked the end of political reconstruction. As the responsibility for enforcement of civil rights laws fell on the federal judiciary, Supreme Court appointments became a critical tool in promoting equal rights. The Lincoln and Grant justices had a mixed record on the subject and Hayes' appointees would continue the turn away from reconstruction policies.

Hayes first selection, Kentuckian John Marshall Harlan had climbed to political prominence through flexible political associations that saw him join the Whig party then favor the 1860 Constitutional Union Party and finally become a Republican. An uncompromising unionist, Harlan fought for his state to remain within the union during the Civil War then after the war supported emancipation even as a former slave owner. A delegate to the 1876 Republican convention, Harlan supported Hayes's candidacy and once elected the president rewarded Harlan with a judicial nomination.[1]

Joining a Republican dominated Court, seven of nine justices were Republicans, eight of nine appointed by Republican presidents, Harlan was thrust into the debate over the civil rights laws passed during the Grant Administration. During the 1879 term, the justices offered a mixed message on civil rights enforcements, upholding some prosecutions, striking down others. Harlan generally joined decisions expanding enforcements of rights while dissenting in decisions narrowly interpreting laws.

In 1883 Harlan published one of his more dramatic dissents, part legal treatise, part reconstruction sermon. In the *Civil Rights Cases*, the court overturned part of the 1875 Civil Rights Act prohibiting private race discrimination. Justice Bradley ruled Congress lacked authority to regulate private behavior. Harlan dissented alone, arguing the Equal Protection Clause prohibited discrimination and the Thirteenth Amendment banned badges of slavery including societal discrimination.[2]

Thirteen years later Harlan would be alone in dissent in another civil rights case, this one examining the constitutionality of segregated railway cars. In *Plessy v. Ferguson* the Court upheld a Louisiana law creating separate railroad cars for black and white passengers. Justice Brown's decision separated political and social equality, finding that the Fourteenth Amendment protected the former but not the latter. Plessy opened the door for separate but equal public accommodations ranging from hotels and restaurants to bathrooms and drinking fountains. [3]

Harlan rejected the decision, returning to his arguments in the Civil Rights cases and declaring the constitution created political and social equality and racial segregation was a badge of slavery prohibited by the Thirteenth Amendment.[4] Harlan's views were dismissed at the time as the last call of Radical reconstruction, but by the 1950s, Harlan had assumed the role of a prophet. When Plessy was overturned in the Brown decision, Harlan's vision of civil rights and racial equality moved from the shadows, his opinions becoming more than the quaint ramblings of a crank justice.

Harlan also mounted a quixotic campaign to apply the Bill of Rights to the states. His single success at incorporation came when the Fifth Amendment's just compensation clause was applied to the states. The Chicago Railroad Company sued the city of Chicago for paving over a railroad line, claiming the city had taken private property and demanded compensation. Harlan ruled the Fifth Amendment's takings clause applied to state and local government as a liberty right protected by the Fourteenth Amendment.[5] It would be nearly thirty years before the Court applied a national right, that of free speech to the states.

Entering the Court as it struggled with civil rights cases, Harlan saw the institution transform into a body focused on economic rights. Harlan's consistency in supporting civil rights did not extend to economic rights. The term before Harlan's arrival Chief Justice Waite upheld an Illinois law setting grain elevator rates, seeming to turn back economic rights claims. Through the 1880's the Court maintained a balance between economic rights and the power of the states to regulate business. But Waite's death in 1888 and his replacement by Melville Fuller shifted the Court's focus. From 1894 to 1897 the Court issued a series of decisions that allowed the use of federal injunctions against labor strikes, limited the antitrust laws to pure interstate commerce, struck down the federal income tax and created the liberty to contract. Harlan dissented in the first three, showing his libertarianism had limits but accepted the liberty to contract. In 1898 he struck at state attempts to regulate railroad shipping rates in *Smyth v. Ames*.[6] The Union Pacific company challenged rates set by a Nebraska commission as too low. Nebraska argued the commission had the expertise to set the rates but Harlan disagreed, ruling the courts could review the rates and determine if they violated due process rights. Future rate regulations would be examined to see if they allowed the railroad a fair rate on their investments, representing the judiciary's first attempt to control the growing regulatory state. [7]

Smyth would be overturned in the 1940s, a forgotten part of Harlan's legacy, but his most famous dissents in the *Income Tax Cases*[8] and *Lochner v. New*

*York*[9] would add to his reputation. When a bank shareholder challenged the income tax enacted during Grover Cleveland's second administration, the question of constitutionality turned on an obscure prohibition against direct taxes. Chief Justice Fuller and four justices struck the income tax in a long winded opinion that convinced few readers. Harlan dissented, words exciting little comment until while reading the dissent, he turned and confronted Justice Field and the Chief Justice, shaking his fist in their direction and condemning their judicial activism.

A decade later, Harlan dissented in a contentious case involving a New York regulation of bakery workers. The Lochner case is usually associated with Justice Oliver Wendell Holmes' dissent and his famous phrase about the enactment of Herbert Spencer's Social Darwinist theories into the constitution. Harlan's dissent was more conventional as he charged his colleagues with the crime of judicial activism and replacing legislative judgment with their own dislike of economic regulation. [10]

Lochner represented a passing of the progressive torch from Harlan to Holmes. Both men shared views on the law while differing in their methods. Holmes believed Harlan overly emotional in his approach while Harlan was unimpressed with Holmes' intellectualism, categorizing him as one of the overly educated northeasterners who looked down on a simple Kentucky country lawyer. During one conference Harlan responded to a Holmes argument with "That won't wash" and Chief Justice Fuller calmed tempers by miming a washboard and saying "But I keep scrubbing away."[11]

But Holmes' arrival and that of three Roosevelt appointees added votes to Harlan's side. In *Atkin v. Kansas*, he struck a blow against the liberty to contract by upholding an eight hour work day law. [12] The next year he upheld an early Roosevelt antitrust prosecution by forming a coalition that included conservative Justice David Brewer while surviving a Holmes' dissent. [13] In one of his last opinions, though, Harlan spoke from dissent in another antitrust case.[14] The American Tobacco case saw Chief Justice White reinterpret the Sherman Antitrust Act, ruling the law forbade only "unreasonable" restraints on interstate trade. Harlan blasted the chief for his blatant legislating from the bench.[15] The American Tobacco dissent would be Harlan's last, the old justice dying a few weeks later though the Harlan family would return to the Court when Dwight Eisenhower appointed John Marshall Harlan II in 1954.

## Woods and Matthews

As his administration wound down, Hayes faced two Court vacancies. Justice Swayne's resignation in January 1881 presented Hayes with a Hobson's choice. The lame duck Senate controlled by Democrats after the 1878 midterms was in no mood to confirm a Republican partisan. Passing along the nomination to president elect James Garfield might weaken the new president as he tried to guide his nominee through an evenly divided Senate. Recognizing the political limitations, Hayes reached to the deep South and federal judge William Woods of Alabama. A former confederate from Georgia, Woods was a sop to the southern states. Rejecting Woods would likely lead to a northern replacement, forcing the Senate to swallow hard and confirm Woods with minimal rancor.[16]

Hayes used Justice Bradley's retirement to reward another 1876 supporter, Stanley Matthews, who argued Hayes' case before the electoral commission and was certain to excite Democrat passions. Infuriated by the selection, Senate Democrats tabled the nomination, leaving it to President Garfield, who allowed the nomination to be reconsidered by the new Congress. After considerable debate Matthews was confirmed by a single vote.[17]

Woods and Matthews added little to Hayes' reputation for Court appointments as neither matched the giant Harlan for years of service or importance. Woods appointment may be the starting point for the Court's turning away from civil rights. As a southerner Woods was suspicious of federal interference in the states and voted to limit the scope of civil rights laws.

In *Presser v. Illinois* Woods earned posthumous scorn from the National Rifle Association as he ruled that the Second Amendment did not apply to the states and firearms could be regulated at the state level.[18] In Presser Woods was unwilling to use the Fourteenth Amendment to apply the Bill of Rights to the states. This reluctance continued as Woods joined the Civil Rights Cases, limiting the Fourteenth Amendment to state action. The same year he went further, hollowing out the rights created under the 1871 Ku Klux Act.

In *United States v. Harris*, Woods ruled the civil war amendments did not empower Congress to punish private discrimination. Intimidation of voters and civil rights activists were state concerns and state criminal laws would be enforced by state officials.[19] Harris saw the Court pull back from civil right enforcement. It would be Woods' one memorable contribution to the era, his six year tenure forgotten even among Court scholars even as it marked the justices' turn toward economic rights.

Stanley Matthews enjoyed a brief but more celebrated career than Woods. When asked to list the great justices who preceded him, Justice Felix Frankfurter included Stanley Matthews among Marshall and Story. His eight year career cut short by tuberculosis Matthews left a broad imprint on the law.

During the 1880s the Equal Protection Clause was transformed from a mandate for racially neutral laws into a weapon used against economic regulation. Matthews bucked that movement in *Yick Wo v. Hopkins*. In a bout of xenophobia directed against Chinese immigrants, California passed a permit requirement for all laundries operating in wooden buildings. Though the law was presented as a health and safety measure, Matthews struck it upon discovering the ordinance was enforced exclusively against Chinese operated laundries. The Hopkins decision was a rare use of equal protection against laws enforced in a discriminatory manner.[20]

After broadly interpreting the Equal Protection Clause, Matthews offered a narrower view of the Due Process Clause. After Hurtado was convicted of murder and sentenced to death, he appealed, claiming he was denied his right to a grand jury indictment. Matthews rejected the claim, ruling a grand jury indictment was not a critical aspect of due process as it only bound the defendant over for trial.[21] Drawing upon an interpretation of due process dating back to the *Magna Carta*, Matthews ruled grand jury indictment was not a traditional due process right, Hurtado remains good law, grand jury indictment not one of the rights applied to the states during the twentieth century. It would remain Matthews most cited opinion, his bright career cut down by tuberculosis in 1889, even as it enhanced Hayes' Court legacy [22]

Rutherford Hayes managed three Court selections in his single term. His choice of John Marshall Harlan proved to be his best as Justices Woods and Matthews were mostly forgotten.

## Calvin Coolidge

In his book *Presidential Anecdotes*, Paul Boller dedicates the most pages to the usual presidents, Washington, Lincoln and Franklin Roosevelt and to an unexpected chief executive, Calvin Coolidge.[23] Known for humorous quips in reaction to a gushing admirer or furious critic, "Silent Cal" was blamed for the 1929 stock market bubble leading to the Great Depression. After leaving office Coolidge disappeared from popular memory until a boomlet of fame during the Reagan Administration when the president hung Coolidge's portrait in the Oval Office after which he again receded into the shadows.

Ranked among the mediocrities or near failures as president, Coolidge jumped into the upper ranks based on his single Court appointment. In 1925 Justice William McKenna was forced from the Court by an impatient Chief Justice Taft. Coolidge promoted Attorney General Harlan Stone, who had grown unpopular among Coolidge's strongest supporters.[24]

Stone joined Justices Holmes and Brandeis to form a liberal bloc, earning Chief Justice Taft's enmity as he labeled Stone the "enemy" for discarding Coolidge's conservative economic views.[25] Stone ignored the critics, spending his first decade mainly in dissent as he supported many New Deal measures, earning the respect of Presidential Roosevelt. The 1937 judicial revolution saw Stone find his voice and change constitutional law in the unlikeliest of cases.

Interpretation of federal laws can be a mundane task focusing on the meaning of a few words and *United States v. Carolene Products* promised to be one of those routine cases until Justice Stone added a provocative footnote. Prior to 1937 Carolene products would have been decided on Commerce Clause grounds but the old constitutional order had been overthrown and Stone opened a new approach to constitutional issues. [26]

Stone's forum was footnote four where he stated the Court would defer to government economic regulation, requiring that such laws must only be rationally related to a proper government power. Stone ruled the justices would impose a higher level of scrutiny if government sought to limit basic rights such as speech, association and religious practice. Greater scrutiny would also be applied to laws targeting "discrete and insular" minorities.[27] Government would be required to show a compelling interest for laws targeting disfavored groups and would become the basis for overturning public school segregation, for broadening the rights of women, for voting rights and for religious exercise rights. The Carolene Products footnote created a constitutional "double standard" with economic rights treated as the proverbial red headed stepchild compared to civil liberties. In addition the rational basis test would become the lowest level of scrutiny used by the courts in examining a law. After Carolene Products, government regulations would be upheld with barely a whimper and the great debate over Congress' economic powers came to an end.

Stone would find himself in dissent in one last major constitutional case in the waning days of the Hughes' Court. He challenged Justice Frankfurter's Gobitis decision upholding a mandatory flag salute. Stone argued free exercise of religion guaranteed Jehovah's Witnesses the right to refuse to salute graven images. Stone would see his dissent become law three years later in Barnett.

Franklin Roosevelt's reelection in 1940 offered Stone his final opportunity for advancement. Chief Justice Hughes retired and with war beckoning Roosevelt sought a bipartisan appointment for the Court's center chair. He chose Stone as chief justice creating the Stone Court packed with Roosevelt justices. Yet Stone's triumph, his rise to chief, would also harm his legacy, the Stone Court marked with dissension and likely driving the chief justice to an early death in 1946.

## Herbert Hoover

The mere mention of Herbert Hoover in a presidential election draws blanched looks from Republicans seeking to avoid comparison to the unpopular president and glee from Democrats who want to tie their opponents to the man blamed for the Great Depression. Starting in 1932 and continuing into 1992—with Democrat barbs about George Herbert Hoover Bush—Democrats cited the former president's administration as a sign of Republican cold heartedness. Hoover's legacy of economic incompetence was a complete turnaround from his earlier portrayal as the great engineer, responsible for overseeing a massive program to feed World War I refugees. In 1920 he was mentioned as a potential Democrat presidential nominee but instead served in two Republican administrations as Secretary of Commerce.[28]

Hoover was distrusted by conservatives who criticized his policies as examples of failed social engineering. Calvin Coolidge complained Hoover had given him nothing but bad advice while serving in his cabinet and derisively referred to the secretary as the "Wonder Boy."[29] Chief Justice William Howard Taft worried aloud that upon his departure his replacement would be among the "Bolsheviki" appointed by Hoover.[30]

The Hoover Administration is ranked among the lower mediocrities but the ranking of his Supreme Court appointments earned Hoover a spot among the great presidents. Two of Hoover's appointees, Charles Evans Hughes and Benjamin Cardozo are ranked among the greatest justices. Cardozo is recognized for his opinions while Hughes earned high rankings for protecting the Court during the 1937 Court packing controversy.[31]

In 1930 Hoover enjoyed a rare opportunity for presidents, two Court vacancies within a two month period. His first decision was replacing Chief Justice William Howard Taft who tightly controlled a bickering Court beset by personal and ideological divisions. Taft's replacement would have to be as forceful in containing the powerful personalities. Before Hoover selected a new chief, Justice Sanford died, offering an opportunity for the president to regain his political footing in the midst of depression..

To replace Taft, Hoover reached into the past choosing Charles Evans Hughes, associate justice from 1910 to 1916 before resigning to accept the 1916 Republican presidential nomination. Hughes had a progressive reputation and was politically closer to Theodore Roosevelt than William Howard Taft.[32] Hughes's nomination was held up by a coalition of Democrats and progressive Republicans who reflexively opposed Republican presidents. Criticism of Hughes focused on his work as a corporate attorney, the bogeyman for Democrats and farm state Republicans. Progressives expressed fears Hughes would move the Court to the right, ignoring that he was replacing the conservative William Howard Taft. Hughes escaped the Senate with twenty six votes against his nomination, the second most for a successful chief justice.[33]

Hoover's choice to replace Sanford was less successful. Judge John Parker was one of those rarest of creatures in 1930, the southern Republican. An appeals court judge from North Carolina, Parker faced the first concerted drive by interest groups to defeat a Supreme Court nomination. Parker was attacked by unions for opposing labor laws while civil rights groups charged him with supporting segregation in the Democrat south.[34] A politically weakened Hoover was unable to help Parker and his nomination went down in flames.[35] Parker's qualifications for high office were not forgotten fifteen years later when President Harry Truman considered Parker to replace Justice Roberts and appointed Parker as a judge to the Nuremberg trials.

Judge Parker's defeat led to confirmation of Owen Roberts, his nomination passing the Senate as interest groups were satiated by the Parker defeat and offered little resistance. The Roberts and Hughes tandem were swing votes on the 1930s Court, both men swept up in the political maelstrom over the New Deal.

In 1932 ninety year old Justice Oliver Wendell Holmes was convinced by his colleagues to leave the Court after thirty years. With the presidential election approaching and his political fortunes depleted by the Great Depression, Hoover sought political consensus on Holmes' replacement. The favored candidate among Democrats and Republicans was Chief Justice of the New York Court of Appeals, Benjamin Cardozo. Among his chief supporters in the Senate was Idaho Republican William Borah, who had voted against Parker's nomination.[36] Within the Court Chief Justice Hughes and Justice Stone told Hoover of their support for Cardozo. Opposition to Cardozo centered in the Supreme Court as

Justices Van Devanter, McReynolds, Sutherland and Butler, composing the Court's conservative wing. But by 1932 conservative influence had waned and the struggling Hoover needed a political victory rather than ideological purity, propelling him to select Cardozo.[37]

Charles Evans Hughes enjoyed one of the more eventful political careers in the first half of the twentieth century. In the two decades before becoming chief justice Hughes served as New York governor, associate justice, presidential nominee, secretary of state and influential Washington attorney. He presided over the 1922 Washington Naval Conference and completed an agreement scrapping many Japanese, British and American warships. His disarmament policies, though, suffered historically with the conference blamed for spurring Japanese militarism.[38]

Leaving national office in 1925, Hughes remained an influential figure in Washington, chosen by Chief Justice Taft as special master in a dispute between the city of Chicago and neighboring states over Chicago's construction of a canal to solve the city's sewage disposal problems. The canal diverted water from Lake Michigan, angering the city's neighbors. Relying on Hughes' report, Taft composed an opinion favoring Chicago.[39]

Returning to the Court fourteen years after resigning, Hughes discovered the political winds had shifted against the Court's economic oriented jurisprudence. Hughes was caught between conservative justices opposed to economic regulations and a president determined to regulate the economy.

Roosevelt's New Deal delegated broad authority to the president, challenging three decades of constitutional doctrine. An inevitable clash between institutions and ideology led to attacks on the Court's independence.[40] Defending his institution Hughes softened the judiciary's rulings on economic regulations by composing *Home Building and Loan Association v. Blaisdell.* Hughes upheld a temporary state moratorium on mortgage foreclosures, recognizing the constitution must be flexible to allow government to handle economic crises.[41]

After Blaisdell the chief upheld Roosevelt's decision to take the country off the gold standard.[42] He provided the key vote in *Nebbia v. New York*, upholding a state law setting a minimum price for milk.[43] Hughes dissented in *Morehead v. Tipaldo* as a narrow majority struck a New York minimum wage law.[44]

Hughes, though, led the Court in striking the National Industrial Recovery Act (NIRA). The act promoted public-private partnerships enforcing industrial codes of practice and production limitations. The National Recovery Administration struggled, its authoritarian approach challenged as an improper delegation of legislative power to the president.

In *Schecter v. United States*[45] and *Panama Refining v. Ryan,*[46] Hughes dealt the NIRA a death blow. In Schecter Hughes ruled Congress granted the president excessive authority to enforce "fair competition." Congress provided insufficient guidance for the president to enforce that competition, allowing the executive to make laws rather than enforcing them. In Panama Refining, Hughes ruled limitation on oil production was executive legislating.

The Schecter and Panama Refining decisions were attacked by the Roosevelt administration as a Supreme Court out of control, economic "royalists" undermining the New Deal. Critics ignored that liberal stalwarts such as Brandeis and Harlan Stone joined both of Hughes' opinions. But the battle was joined as the Court struck down the Agriculture Adjustment Act[47] and the Guffey Coal Act,[48] and increased the political heat on the Court.

Flush with his crushing reelection victory in 1936, Franklin Roosevelt challenged the sole national institution that flaunted his will. The president offered a bill increasing the Court by six members, claiming the enlarged Court would improve efficiency as younger justices aided their elderly colleagues in writing opinions. Most observers recognized the plan as an attempt to dilute the influence of conservative justices. Roosevelt defenders argued past presidents including Jefferson, Jackson and Lincoln had added seats to the Court though those expansions were based on population growth and the addition of new states.[49]

Southern and progressive Democrats attacked the plan, fearing its effect on the judiciary's independence. With massive Democrat majorities in Congress, Roosevelt seemed destined to make the Court bow to his demands.

But Hughes was determined to protect the institution. He produced a letter signed by Justice Van Devanter and Brandeis contradicting Roosevelt's assertions the Court had fallen behind in its work. The letter cast the debate in terms of a battle over the Court's independence rather than a political fight between conservatives and liberals. At the same time, Hughes guided his colleagues along a more moderate path, voting to uphold New Deal laws to lessen the political pressure on the Court. In the infamous switch in time, Hughes garnered Justice Robert's vote to uphold federal labor and state wage laws. In *West Coast Hotel v. Parrish*, Hughes expressed dismay that state minimum wage laws ran afoul of the liberty to contract doctrine. Declaring the constitution included no such right, Hughes swept aside forty years of precedent while surrendering to political reality that liberty to contract was unacceptable to the American public.[50]

In *NLRB v. Jones and Laughlin Steel Co*, Hughes upheld the Wagner Act, a keystone of the New Deal protecting labor organization and mandating collective bargaining. The chief overturned four decades of commerce decisions while recognizing Congressional authority to regulate labor to prevent economic strife. Parrish and Laughlin was a signal the Court would adapt in return for protecting its independence and Hughes became one of the few national politicians to hand Roosevelt a major political defeat.[51]

Though the 1937 switch appeared to weaken Hughes' control over his institution, the appointment of five Roosevelt justices from 1937 to 1941 added to his influence and legacy. In *Dejonge v. Oregon*, Hughes swatted down DeJonge's conviction on an anti syndicalism law, casting doubt on the authority of the states to limit speech they considered seditious and insurrectionary.[52]

In 1938, the chief ordered the University of Missouri law school to admit a black student. Hughes rejected the state's offer to pay Gaines' tuition to law schools in surrounding states, finding the equal protection clause required states to provide education to their citizens and thus allowing Gaines into the state law school.[53]

Hughes also joined the move toward judicial restraint, denying judges authority to strike state rules for constitutional ratification.[54] In one of his final opinions Hughes recognized time, place and manner restrictions imposed on speech. In Cox, Hughes ruled localities could place permit requirements on public demonstrations to ensure ordered liberty. All requirements would be content neutral to prevent discrimination against unpopular groups or ideas. [55]

After Franklin Roosevelt's reelection and third inauguration, Hughes retired, leaving a stable but chastened institution that splintered the moment he left. His abilities were recognized by those who disagreed with his politics as Justice Douglas listed him as the greatest chief justice he served with, even greater than the popular Earl Warren.[56]

## Owen Roberts

Charles Evans Hughes and Benjamin Cardozo may be ranked in the top tier of justices but it was their fellow Hoover appointee who played a central role in the Court packing controversy. Owen Roberts straddled ideologies, seemingly unmoored from a consistent doctrine and with the Court split between conservatives and liberal blocs, Roberts provided the necessary vote for the right bloc. Yet early in his career, Roberts' deviations from conservative doctrine raised hopes among Roosevelt supporters he would vote for New Deal legislation.

As chain stores became a fixture in many states, governments sought to limit their reach through restrictive licensing policies. Roberts struggled with an economic rights doctrine utilizing the Equal Protection Clause to protect corporate rights. In *State Board v. Jackson*, Roberts upheld a state tax on chain stores, ruling the states could treat chain stores differently without violating the Equal Protection Clause. [57] But later Roberts contradicted his Jackson decision, striking similar chain store taxes. In *Liggett v. Lee* he overturned a Florida tax because it increased taxes on both established and new chain stores.[58] He later overturned a federal tax on restaurants in Alabama that served malt liquor beverages. According to Roberts the tax punished local establishments for violating state law.[59] In *Binney v. Long*, he struck down a state estate tax on equal protection grounds because it treated heirs differently.[60] In *Stewart Dry Goods v. Lewis*, Roberts overturned gross sales tax that charged chain stores with a higher percentage of tax than single stores again ruling the tax violated equal protection.[61] In a partial reversal Roberts joined Cardozo's opinion in *Fox v. Standard Oil* upholding a chain store tax on gas stations, further clouding his views on the equal protection clause.[62]

Roberts was no more consistent in liberty to contract decisions. In Nebbia Roberts upheld a New York law setting retail prices for milk, rejecting the liberty to contract claim that setting prices was protected by the Fourteenth Amendment. Two years later in *Morehead v. Tipaldo* Roberts provided the fifth vote for striking a New York minimum wage law as a violation of the same liberty to contract. In the midst of the Court packing crisis Roberts provided the fifth vote in West Coast Hotel discarding the liberty to contract doctrine. Parrish represented the famous switch in time and was thought to have been provoked by political pressure yet Roberts' vote in Parrish occurred months before Roosevelt offered his plan.

Roberts' inconsistency continued on other New Deal legislation. He provided the fifth vote in Blaisdell and joined the Gold Clause cases, both economic regulations opposed by the conservative bloc. Roberts returned to his conservative roots in 1935 and 1936, joining Schechter and Panama Refining in striking the National Industrial Recovery Act. He authored opinions in *Railroad Retirement Board v. Alton Railroad*[63] and *Butler v. United States*,[64] striking New Deal laws regulating railroad pensions and agricultural production. Roberts drew the ire of liberals for his "mechanical" approach to judicial review.

The rise of the Roosevelt Court and the replacement of conservative justices with New Deal liberals changed Roberts' role but did not end his influence on the institution. During the final four years of the Hughes Court, Roberts was a[65] central figure in the Court's new emphasis on civil liberties and its rejection of economic rights doctrines. Shortly after the famous switch, Roberts authored *Herndon v. Lowry* overturning Herndon's conviction for violating a Georgia state insurrection law. A communist party organizer, Herndon was charged with participating in communist meetings that incited disorder and threatened the government. Roberts swept away the state's charge, finding there was no clear and present danger of an insurrection. In his decision, Roberts was again at odds with the four conservatives who dissented.[66]

Roberts also reversed his Butler opinion, upholding the second Agricultural Adjustment Act. Roberts' ruled the sale of tobacco constituted interstate commerce and government marketing plans were within congressional authority. He attempted to differentiate Mulford from Butler but the retreat from his precedent was clear.[67]

In 1940 Roberts contributed to the growing incorporation movement and in *Cantwell v. Connecticut* applied the Free Exercise Clause to state governments.[68] In Cantwell Roberts relied on Justice Cardozo's ordered liberty test, explaining the exercising of religious faith was a tradition of American liberty. His zeal for incorporation was less complete than the Roosevelt justices desire to apply all rights to the states. In *Betts v. Brady* Roberts rejected granting felons the right to counsel, differentiating the case from Justice Sutherland's Powell decision. According to Roberts the Powell defendants were young and ignorant of the law, faced an angry public and were granted only a few days to mount a defense without benefit of counsel. Betts faced none of these obstacles and was found to have defended himself ably in his case. Betts would be overturned some two decades later in Gideon v. Wainwright.[69]

Hughes retirement in 1941 removed Roberts' closest ally and with the rise of the Roosevelt justices, he was marginalized. After 1941, Roberts moved from swing vote to Court scold, challenging the Roosevelt justices for overturning precedent and rewriting constitutional doctrine. At the same time he maintained his relevance by joining the new "conservative" wing of the Court.

Roberts did not pine for the "good old days" of liberty to contract and a limited commerce power, joining Wickard and Darby, which extended congressional commerce power over nearly all economic activities. Roberts was outspoken in the more technical cases including antitrust, agency regulations and labor law as he accused the majority of favoring unions over business, government over business all while weakening the Court as an equal branch of government. Roberts took offense at his colleagues' moralistic tone and their tendency to write condescendingly of dissenters and past doctrines.

Outnumbered, Roberts resorted to dissents in *Barnette* and *Korematsu* the two major civil liberties cases of the era. In Korematsu Roberts castigated Justice Black for upholding the imprisonment of Japanese Americans based purely on their race.[70]

Roberts' disgust with the Roosevelt Court extended to their political maneuvering. One target of his wrath was Justice Douglas' behind the scenes campaign for the 1944 vice presidential nomination. By 1945 Roberts was isolated from his colleagues, refusing to shake hands with Justices Black, Murphy and Douglas at the start of weekly conferences. Lacking influence with the Roosevelt justices, Roberts refused to participate in conference discussions, issuing a terse "uphold" or "overturn" in each case. His disdain for the Court's direction became public in 1944.[71]

In *Smith v. Allwright*, Roberts' produced his most quoted opinion. The Court struck down the Texas white primary banning black voters from the Democrat primary. Smith overruled a Roberts' precedent, provoking him into accusing the majority of treating precedent like "railroad tickets, good for this day and train only." The pithy phrase was a departure from Roberts's usual plodding style.[72]

Roberts' dissents may not have changed the minds of his fellow justices but it infuriated them, his colleagues taking their revenge with Roberts' retirement in 1945. As was tradition, Chief Justice Stone composed a boilerplate letter of regret filled with compliments for Roberts' career. Justice Black protested and refused to sign the letter unless its complimentary tone was diluted. Stone, exhausted and having less than a year to live, allowed Black to rewrite the letter to his preferences before distributing it to the justices. When it was learned Black had rewritten the letter, Justice Frankfurter protested, refusing to sign Black's letter. The debate degenerated into finger pointing forcing Stone to make averbal statement about Roberts in open court, unapproved by anyone.[73]

## "Saint" Benjamin

Sainted is not a term associated with public officials but Hoover's third justice, Benjamin Cardozo, earned the compliment during a brief tenure on the Supreme Court which was overshadowed by a more illustrious career on the New York Court of Appeals.

The judiciary and politics were in Cardozo's blood. His father, Albert, served as a state judge in New York City. As a member of the Tammany political machine, Albert Cardozo earned the distasteful reputation as a party hack who used his Court to protect the corrupt political organization.[74]

His son, Benjamin enjoyed a cleaner reputation as an innovative mind on the New York Court of Appeals. Cardozo's greatest influence came in rewriting liability law in *Palsgraf v. Long Island Railroad* and *McPherson v. Buick.* In Palsgraf, Cardozo ruled a railroad was not liable for the injuries suffered by Palsgraf while she was waiting on a railway platform. In McPherson, Cardozo ruled consumers could sue manufacturers of faulty products, rather than suing the retailer who simply sold rather than manufactured it.[75]

Cardozo systematized his views lecture series on the proper method of judging and the role of the judiciary in the American system. Cardozo criticized the dominant judicial method of formalism, finding it too inflexible in meeting the legal requirements of a changing society. He preferred a methodology based on sociology which allowed judges to change with society and interpret the constitution to meet changing needs.[76] Later Cardozo's lectures would be published in book form.[77]

Cardozo joined the Court under the additional pressure of replacing the legendary Oliver Wendell Holmes. One of his early opinions ended doubt to his ability to answer the call as he ruled against the state of Texas in *Nixon v. Condon.* Seeking to silence the black vote, the Texas Democrat state committee allowed only white voters in primaries. Nixon was denied his vote in the primary and challenged the law under the Equal Protection Clause. Cardozo agreed with Nixon, finding that the Democrat committee was engaged in state action because it operated primary elections, usually considered a state function.[78] Cardozo borrowed from a Holmes opinion that striking a similar law [79]

Though mentioned in the same breath as Justices Holmes and Brandeis, Cardozo authored few opinions of note during his six years. His early opinions challenged the Court's application of the Equal Protection Clause battling with Justice Roberts over the state regulation of chain stores.

The state of Florida imposed hefty licensing fees on chain stores in an attempt to prevent their spread across the state while protecting small, local retailers. Several of the chain stores challenged the law on due process and equal protection grounds, claiming the license fee took property without benefit of due process and unconstitutionally discriminated against large chain stores.[80]

Justice Roberts ruled the state violated the stores' rights, treating them unequally based on their size. Cardozo dissented, arguing the tax was neither arbitrary nor discriminatory as the state had valid reasons for treating chain stores differently than others though he did not inquire into those reasons.[81]

Cardozo joined Justices Brandeis and Stone in supporting most New Deal measures though as the Court struck down federal economic regulations, he was limited to dissents. Cardozo did join the majority in Blaisdell and the Gold

Clause cases. He was also part of the unanimous majority in Schechter striking down parts of the NIRA but composed a solo dissent in Panama Refining, arguing the law was not an improper delegation of legislative power. [82]

After Chief Justice Hughes' opinions in Parrish and Laughlin, the New Deal appeared safe from the Court. Cardozo extended the Roosevelt Administration's winning streak by upholding a central part of the New Deal, the Social Security Act. In *Davis v. Steward Machine*, Cardozo ruled the retirement program and its method of forced payment into a government fund was a proper use of federal taxing power. [83] In a companion case Cardozo penned an opinion upholding the federal unemployment insurance scheme that was also part of the Social Security Act. [84] Cardozo rejected claims the Tenth Amendment to limited congressional taxing authority, overriding Chief Justice Taft's Drexel opinion granting Congress authority to tax for redistribution of wealth.

While any of the liberal or moderate justices could have composed the mundane Davis opinion, Cardozo's analytical abilities were necessary for *Palko v. Connecticut.*[85] After Palko was convicted of murder and sentenced to life in prison, the state of Connecticut appealed the sentence, which was overturned. In a retrial, Palko was again convicted and sentenced to death. Palko appeals, arguing the second trial violated the ban on double jeopardy. The Double Jeopardy Clause of the Fifth Amendment had never been applied to the states and in Palko Cardozo would continue that interpretation.

Cardozo ruled the second trial was the same result Palko would have sought if appealing the verdict. Granting a defendant a new trial after he had been found guilty and sentenced could not be considered double jeopardy, which required an acquittal to be applied to a defendant. .

Cardozo then struggled to make sense of the Court's haphazard incorporation doctrine. Cardozo's new doctrine systematized the incorporation effort as he ruled on those rights "rooted in the traditions and conscience of the people" contributed to the balance between order and liberty. Such rights would be applied to the states on a case by case basis.[86] Cardozo accepted the rights to speech, press, assembly, counsel and just compensation were part of ordered liberty and correctly incorporated to the states. But protection against double jeopardy was not considered part of ordered liberty and would not be applied to the states.[87] Palko's death sentence was upheld, double jeopardy would not be applied to the states for another quarter century and Cardozo's successors would wrestle with his ordered liberty test for the next thirty years.

## Hoover's Court Legacy

Herbert Hoover's four years as president proved to be some of the most disastrous since James Buchanan and would be matched in terms of economic mismanagement only by Jimmy Carter. But unlike Buchanan and Carter, Hoover would choose men for the Supreme Court who would add to his legacy. Charles Evans Hughes' management of the Supreme Court and his defense of an independent judiciary placed him on par with John Marshall in battling a zealous chief executive. Hughes' eleven years as chief justice were the last by any chief operating the Court as an institution rather than a collection of nine law offices. His 1941 resignation unleashed personal disputes that undermined the Roosevelt Court effectiveness.

Hoover's selection of Roberts and Cardozo produced more ordinary than spectacular results. As the prototypical swing vote, Roberts placed the needs of the institution over his personal beliefs rescuing the institution from the abyss and ending over half a century of economic rights doctrines. A moderate in the 1930s, Roberts took up residence on the Roosevelt Court's right wing.

Benjamin Cardozo was one of the few bipartisan consensus selections made to the Supreme Court. Reaching the pinnacle of his career at an advanced age, though, Cardozo had few opportunities for greatness, his judicial achievements limited mainly to his earlier career, though his opposition to the "Four Horseman" placed him on the right side of history as written by New Deal historians.

## Notes

1. Beth, Loren,*John Marshall Harlan*(Lexington KY: University Press of Kentucky,1992),102-105.

2. 109 U.S. 3, 36.In his opinion Harlan described the long history of racial discrimination and slavery and the intent of the framers of the Thirteenth and Fourteenth Amendments to reconstruct American society toward racial equality.

3. 163 U.S. 537 (1896)

4. 163 U.S. 537, 556

5. *Chicago, Burlington and Quincy Railroad Co. v. Chicago*166 U.S. 226 (1897)

6. 169 U.S. 466 (1898)

7. 169 U.S. 466, 527.Harlan granted state legislatures authority to pass rate laws and set rates but found that if the rates were too low they would deny railroads property without the benefit of due process, a constitutional issue that could only be settled by the judiciary.

8. *Pollock v. Farmers Home Loan and Trust*157 U.S. 429 (1895)

9. 198 U.S. 45 (1905)

10. 198 U.S. 45, 66. Harlan related social science data supporting the argument in favor of a limited work day and was peeved that Lochner all but overruled his decision in *Atkin v. Kansas*.

11. King, Willard. *Melville Weston Fuller*, (Chicago: University of Chicago Press, 1967), 290

12. 191 U.S. 207 (1903)

13. *Northern Securities Co. v. United States* 193 U.S. 197 (1904)

14. *United States v. American Tobacco* 221 U.S. 106(1911)

15. 221 U.S. 106, 193. Harlan noted that Congress explicitly refused to add the term "unreasonable" to the Sherman Act but that the chief justice had taken it upon himself to rewrite the law and ignore congressional intent.

16. Abraham, 154

17. Abraham, 154

18. 116 U.S. 252 (1886)

19. 106 U.S. 629 (1883) Harris was a unanimous opinion even as it followed closely on the reasoning of the Civil Rights Cases, which had drawn a sharp dissent from Harlan.The justice acquiesced in Woods' narrow reading of theThirteenth and FourteenthAmendments and his refusal to extend the badge of slavery argument thatHarlan made in the civil rights cases.

20. 118 U.S. 356, 375. (1886). The use of statistics was the first hint toward a realist approach to constitutional interpretation as Matthews dug into the application rather than the text of the law.

21. *Hurtado v. California* 110 U.S. 516 (1884)

22. Matthews' narrow reading of due process and incorporation of rights through the Fourteenth Amendment might have drawn Justice Frankfurter's approval and his listing of the justice among the greats.Hurtado would be one of the precedents Frankfurter would cite when arguing for his approach to incorporating rights through the Due Process Clause.

23. Boller, Paul, *Presidential Anecdotes* (New York: Oxford University Press, 1981), 233-250

24. Abraham, 183.Stone would be the first Court nominee to testify before the Senate Judiciary Committee, setting a precedent that would produce so much discomfort for his successors.

25. Mason, 69-70

26. 304 U.S. 144 (1938)

27. 304 U.S. 144, 153

28. Fausold, Martin, *The Presidency of Herbert Hoover,* (Lawrence KS.: University of Kansas Press, 1985), 9-10

29. Sobel, Robert, *Coolidge: An American Enigma* (Washington D.C.: Regnery Press, 1998), 242

30. Mason, Alpheus Thomas, *The Supreme Court from Taft to Warren* (Baton Rouge: Louisiana State Press 1968), 67,81

31. Both Hughes and Cardozo rank among the greats in a series of polls while Roberts ranked among the mediocrities in the Blaustein and Mersky poll.

32. Yet Roosevelt despised Hughes, complaining he was a "cold fish" and implying he was not the proper heir to Roosevelt's progressive legacy.

33. Fausold, 89.The most negative votes were 33 in 1986 when William Rehnquist was promoted from associate justice to chief justice.

34. Fausold, 91-92.

35. The final vote was 41-39.

36. Kaufman, Andrew,*Cardozo* (Cambridge Mass.: Harvard University Press, 1998), 463-464.

37. Abraham, Henry, *Justices Presidents and Senators* (New York: Rowman and Littlefield, 2008), 159-161.

38. Goldstein, Erik, *The Washington Conference 1921-1922* (London: Routledge, 1994); Glad, Betty, *Charles Evans Hughes and the Illusions of Innocence* (Champaign, Il.: University of Illinois Press, 1966).

39. Pringle,1028-1029;*State of Wisconsin v. Illinois* 278 U.S. 367 (1929)

40. Many Roosevelt allies in the press and academia produced books lambasting the justices for blocking needed reforms. Pearson, Drew and Robert Allen, *The Nine Old Men* (New York: Doubleday, 1937) was a caustic attack belittling the personal and professional lives as only the scurrilous Pearson could.Jackson, Robert, *The Struggle for Judicial Supremacy* (New York: Vintage Books, 1941) was a recounting of the fight between Roosevelt and the Court with Jackson offering a partisan account of how conservatives had undermined the constitution and the New Deal.

41. 290 U.S. 398 (1934)

42. *Norman v. Baltimore and Ohio Railroad Co.*294 U.S. 240 (1935)

43. 291 U.S. 502 (1934)

44. 298 U.S. 587 (1936)

45. 295 U.S. 495 (1935)

46. 293 U.S. 388 (1935)

47. *United States v. Butler* 297 U.S. 1 (1936).Hughes joined Roberts' opinion striking down the law as an unconstitutional use of federal taxing power.

48. *Carter v. Carter Coal Co.*298 U.S. 238 (1936).Hughes joined Sutherland's opinion struck down federal regulation of the coal industry and coal miners.

49. The Court's size was increased as new states were added. The 1807, 1837 and1863 Judiciary Acts were a response to the need for justices to participate in circuit riding.

50. 300 U.S. 379, 392 (1937)

51. 301 U.S. 1 (1937)

52. 299 U.S. 353 (1937)

53. *Ex Rel Gaines v. Canada* 305 U.S. 377 (1938) The decision, though, did not provoke a standoff between school officials andthe courts as would occur in the 1950s and 1960s as Gaines mysteriously disappeared before he could be admitted to the state law school.

54. *Coleman v. Miller* 307 U.S. 433 (1939), *Chandler v. Wise* 307 U.S. 474 (1939)

55. *Cox v. New Hampshire* 312 U.S. 569 (1941)

56. Douglas, William, *The Court Years* (New York: Random House, 1980), 42.

57. 283 U.S. 527 (1931)

58. 288 U.S. 517 (1933)
59. 296 U.S. 286 (1935)
60. 299 U.S. 280 (1936)
61. 294 U.S. 550 (1935)
62. 294 U.S. 87 (1935)
63. 295 U.S. 330 (1935)
64. 297 U.S. 1 (1936)
65. Leuchtenberg, 96
66. 301 U.S. 242 , 260(1937)
67. *Mulford v. Smith*307 U.S. 38 (1939)
68. 310 U.S. 296 (1940)
69. 316 U.S. 455 (1942)
70. 323 U.S. 214, 226 (1944)
71. Simon, James, *The Antagonists* (New York: Touchstone Books, 1989),159.
72. 321 U.S. 649, 670 (1944); Roberts' opinion in *Grovey v. Townsend* 295 U.S. 45 (1935) was overturned in Smith.
73. Simon, 159
74. Klein, Maury, *The Life and Legend of Jay Gould* (Baltimore: Johns Hopkins Press, 1997),, 114.
75. Posner, Richard, *Cardzo: A Study in Reputation* (Chicago: University of Chicago Press, 1993) 16-17.
76. Kaufman 204-206
77. Kaufman 217
78. 286 U.S. 73, 89-90 (1932)
79. *Nixon v. Herndon* 273 U.S. 536 (1927) Cardozo later joined a unanimous Courtin upholding the "white primary" which banned black voters from membership in the Texas Democrat Party, the latest attempt by the Democrats to skirt the Fourteenth and Fifteenth Amendments.*Grovey v. Townsend* 295 U.S. 45 (1935)
80. *Liggett v. Lee*288 U.S. 517 (1933)
81. Cardozo would dissent in other cases involving business taxation.He was on the losing side in *Concordia Fire Insurance v. Illinois* 292 U.S. 535 (1934), *Stewart Dry Goods v. Lewis* 294 U.S. 550 (1935), and *Colgate v. Harvey* 296 U.S. 404 (1935). He did compose the opinion upholding a tax targeting gas stations in *Fox v. Standard Oil Co.* 294 U.S. 87 (1935) and saw his dissents become accepted as law in *Great Atlantic and Pacific Tea Co. v. Grosjean* 301 U.S. 412 (1937).
82. 293 U.S. 388, 434-435 (1935)
83. 301 U.S. 548 (1937)
84. *Helvering v. Davis* 301 U.S. 619 (1937)
85. 302 U.S. 319 (1937)
86. 302 U.S. 319, 326

87. 302 U.S. 319, 329

# Chapter 10

# Ulysses Grant (19) Warren Harding (20)

Neither Ulysses Grant nor Warren Harding are recognized for substantive achievements during their presidencies. Beset by scandal and economic problems, both administrations ranked as failures. Selecting a total of eight justices, Grant and Harding chose men of achievement who enhanced their legacies for Supreme Court appointments.

Economists and politicians speak of a race to the bottom to describe governments competing for business development by lowering wages. A race to the bottom also describes the over half century battle between the Grant and Harding Administrations to be ranked among the lowest of failed presidents. The two presidencies are tarred by scandal and general ineptitude during nearly eleven combined years in office.

Grant and Harding suffered the greatest indignities from their friends as scandals struck at the top of their administrations. Grant saw his first vice president, Schuyler Colfax, forced from office, while his own wife would be investigated for her business relationship with financier Jay Gould.1. His Secretary of War William Belknap was the first and to this moment only cabinet secretary to be impeached while his Secretary of the Interior, Columbus Delano, was forced out of office for allowing members of his department to defraud Indian tribes.2.

Harding entered office with his own "Ohio gang" including his Attorney General, Harry Daugherty, who was prosecuted for lying to Congress. Harding's Secretary of the Interior, Albert Fall, sold oil leases to Harry Sinclair while the head of the Veteran's Bureau was responsible for embezzlement. Harding's reputation was not saved by his sudden death in the middle of his term as his legacy was defined by critics who saw little good in a conservative administration.

Economic problems plagued both administrations. Rapid industrialization and a currency and financial system struggling to handle the growth produced several panics and a depression during Grant's two terms. The so called Gilded Age produced men of immense wealth and a burgeoning industrial class who struggled toward middle class status.

Warren Harding entered office during a post war depression, the worst in a quarter century. The newly minted Federal Reserve System fumbled with interest rates and money supply while government cost cutting and elimination of wartime agencies contributed to economic dislocation.[3] Harding and the Republicans suffered in the 1922 election much as they had benefited in 1920 by blaming the Democrats for hard times. Prosperity began in 1923 but it would be Harding's successor, Calvin Coolidge, who received much of the credit.

Grant and Harding shared another similarity, four Supreme Court nominations during their presidency. Their choices for the vacancies proved to be a bright spot during their tenure, propelling them from a failed ranking to the more respectable average category.[4]

## U.S. Grant

Among American presidents, Ulysses Grant entered the White House with a level of accomplishment rivaling some great presidents. Not since George Washington had a general received the accolades for leading the country through war while his military career placed him on par with Douglas MacArthur, George Patton and William Sherman. Modern interest in Grant includes two major biographies over the past quarter century that produced a Pulitzer Prize and a Pulitzer nomination. Yet for all of his success after 1861, Grant's early adult life cast light on the claim that any man could become president.

A graduate of West Point his civilian life was marked by failure as Grant was reduced to selling firewood in the streets of St. Louis.[5] The Civil War changed his fortunes and was transformed into a military hero demanding unconditional surrender of Fort Donelson. Subsequent victories at Vicksburg and Chattanooga propelled him to the status of presidential contender. Grant swore off presidential aspirations in favor of focusing on defeating the Confederacy. His military victories and the subsequent political chaos of reconstruction revived Grant as a presidential contender and in 1868 easily won the presidency.[6]

The general's successful campaign slogan of "Let us have peace" served him poorly as the Grant Administration buffeted by scandal, controversy over civil rights and economic crises.[7] At times Grant appeared overwhelmed, designating authority to Senate spoils men and to his closest advisors, both groups redefining venality in politics. Public fatigue with reconstruction undermined civil rights enforcement while economic depression led to the revitalization of the Democrat Party in the 1874 midterms.

Grant's problems came later in his two terms but his opportunities were immediately apparent. The battle between Congress and Andrew Johnson lapped over to the Supreme Court as congressional Republicans began eliminating Court vacancies reducing membership from ten in 1865 to eight by 1868.[8]

With Johnson out of the White House, Congress rewarded Grant with a Court seat, increasing membership to nine in the 1869 Judiciary Act. Justice Grier's retirement created a second vacancy but Grant fumbled the opportunity and turned it into a humbling defeat.

Grant's first choice, Attorney General Ebenezer Hoar, was meritorious but a political disaster. As attorney general Hoar challenged the tradition of senatorial courtesy by carefully checking the judges who senators proposed for district court slots. Furious senators responded by handing Hoar and Grant a resounding confirmation defeat. The president's second choice was his former boss, Edwin Stanton, a Democrat beloved by Senate Republicans for his battles with Andrew Johnson. Stanton was easily confirmed but promptly died.[9]

Grant's next choices, William Strong of Pennsylvania and Joseph Bradley of New Jersey, sailed through the Senate, the chamber exhausted from the effort and the two selections representing the best selections Grant would make.[10]

While the battle over the seats filled by Strong and Bradley bruised Grant, filling his third vacancy proved easier. Justice Nelson resigned in 1872 as the votes were being counted in Grant's smashing reelection. Grant chose Ward Hunt from New York. Known as the Conkling judge after the powerful New York senator and close Grant confidant, Hunt served an uneventful nine year tenure marked by loyal support Grant's civil rights policies.

With his presidential hopes dashed, Chief Justice Chase died in late spring 1873. Grant's positive experience with the Ward Hunt nomination was followed by more bumbling as he considered four choices before stumbling upon a mediocrity. He fell into his old habit of favoring party and personal loyalists, his initial choice being Senator Conkling, the flamboyant and controversial leader of the Senate Republicans. Fortunately the monastic setting of the Court proved unappealing to the senator and he declined the nomination.[11]

Grant followed a foolish choice with a surprisingly wise one, offering the slot to Secretary of State Hamilton Fish but the New Yorker declined. Facing another appointment debacle, Grant deepened his misery by nominating Attorney General George Williams. Under suspicion for corruption, Williams faced a difficult confirmation process as opponents focused on his personal extravagance and claims of misused government funds. Grant tightened the party screws on Republican senators but the Judiciary Committee revolted, threatening to take the unheard of step of unanimously rejecting the nomination and forcing the president to withdraw Williams.[12]

Desperation gripped the administration and names were tossed about in search of a confirmable candidate. The rejected Hoar became the frontrunner but Grant shrank from another confirmation defeat and chose a former Pierce Administration official, Caleb Cushing. The former attorney general had switched to the Republicans during the war but his cozy relationship with men such as Jefferson Davis and his advanced age made Cushing a political liability and the nomination was withdrawn after much criticism.[13] With four potential nominees off the books, Grant was reduced to picking random names and arriving at Morrison Waite, an obscure Ohio lawyer, who lacked Washington enemies, a singular achievement at the time, and was easily confirmed.[14]

Waite is unfavorably compared to other chiefs and to his contemporaries, the chief's career overshadowed by Justices Miller, Field, Harlan, Bradley and Matthews. His greatest attribute was hard work, composing opinions in place of disabled colleagues including Justices Clifford and Hunt while struggling to handle the Court's burgeoning workload. Waite failed to keep the Court current, a four year backlog of cases having formed when Waite died in 1888.[15]

The Waite Court was a transitional institution, the Court dogged by civil rights cases during the first decade but refocusing on economic rights cases by the time of the chief's death. During Chief Justice Chase's final term, the Court interpreted the Fourteenth Amendment for the first time in the Slaughterhouse Cases. Justice Miller's opinion rejected arguments to turn the amendment's due process clause into a weapon to use against economic regulation. In *Munn v. Illinois*, Waite built on Miller's opinion as he upheld law setting prices at grain elevators. [16] Relying on Justice Bradley's arguments, Waite rejected the claim that regulation of prices violated the liberty to contract. Instead Waite found that grain elevators were clothed with a public purpose and therefore could be regulated by government. [17] The chief's public purpose doctrine created more questions than it answered and was gradually chipped away at until being overruled in 1927. [18] Munn slowed attempts by some justices, including Stephen Field to overturn state economic regulation and allowed the Waite Court to focus on civil rights.

Waite's civil rights record was mixed. The first six years of the Grant Administration saw passage of the Ku Klux Act, the 1871 Civil Rights Act and the 1875 Civil Rights Act, all reconstruction laws intended to enforce equality for freedmen. As public interest in the issue waned, the federal judiciary became the battleground with Waite enjoying a Republican majority and an opportunity for strict enforcement of civil rights laws.

The early results of the Waite Court were not hopeful. In U.S. v. Cruikshank, the Court considered the notorious Grant Parish Massacre in Louisiana when freedmen were murdered by Klansmen as part of a conspiracy to prevent black voting. 19. Cruikshank and others were prosecuted under the 1870 Ku Klux Act, which made it a federal crime to violate any citizen's civil rights. Waite overturned the convictions, asserted government had not proven the massacre was racially motivated or based on civil rights. He then denied Congressional authority to prosecute murder cases which were under state jurisdiction.

In *U.S. v. Reese*, Waite further limited the scope of the civil rights acts, finding that the Fifteenth Amendment did not create a right to vote that could be enforced under federal law but rather forbade racial discrimination in state voting laws. [20] In a rambling opinion Waite ruled the Act was overly broad in banning voting discrimination because Congress lacked authority under the Fifteenth Amendment to ban such discrimination. Two years later in *Hall v. DeCuir* Waite struck down a Louisiana law banning segregation in steamboats, ruling the boats were engaged in interstate commerce and thus outside the reach of state law. [21] Cruikshank, Reese and Ducuir offered little hope to civil rights supporters and represented a retreat from the reconstruction promise of equality.

The Chief Justice further refused to carve out exceptions for women's rights or religious minority rights in a pair of cases. Waite's view of the Fourteenth Amendment did not include gender based rights as he upheld the Missouri constitutional ban on women voting. [22] The Missouri ban was challenged under the Fourteenth Amendment's Privileges and Immunities Clause with Waite composing a meandering opinion separating citizenship from vote which he considered a privilege not extended to all citizens.[23]

In *Reynolds v. U.S.* Waite coined a phrase that would dominate the Court's Establishment Clause cases in the twentieth century. Reynolds challenged a federal anti polygamy law on free exercise grounds, claiming the law targeted the Mormon religion and its practices in the Utah territory. Waite began his opinion quoting Jefferson's letter to the Danbury Baptist Association where the president used the phrase "wall of separation between church and state." [24]

After arguing for a separation of church and state, Waite upheld the federal ban on polygamy, finding the federal law was based on a traditional ban on polygamy and allowing multiple marriages would "permit every citizen to become a law unto himself."[25] The Reynolds opinion would be cited by both sides in future religion debates. Justice Black, a strict separationist, brought "separation of church and state" into modern Court lexicon in Everson; Justice Scalia used Reynolds in removing free exercise as a fundamental right in his Smith opinion.

The crushing workload and the bickering among his colleague's shortened Waite's time on the Court and his death in 1888 was the first directly attributed to a Court case. The grand invention of the era, Alexander Graham Bell's telephone, produced a bevy of patent lawsuits.[26] Argued in early 1888, the Telephone Patent cases included hundreds of pages of evidence and arguments. Waite sifted them and required a month to compose an opinion favoring Bell's claim. The patents case fills the entire volume 126 of the U.S. report and is followed by the announcement of Waite's death.[27] Exhausted by the cases, the chief had contracted pneumonia, was unable to read his opinion in open court and died a few days later.

## Strong and Bradley

Justices Bradley and Strong took their seats in the midst of the Legal Tender controversy when four justices struck down the law responsible for financing the Civil War.[28] Justice Grier's subsequent retirement and passage of the 1869 Judiciary Act opened two vacancies on the Court just as pressure built for rehearing the Legal Tender cases. In 1870 the two newest justices joined three Lincoln appointees in upholding the act and overruling a one year precedent.[29]

Grant was accused of appointing Strong and Bradley to specifically overrule the legal tender case but both justices were chosen before the case was decided. The two justices also disagreed on major economic issues of the time, suggesting their vote in the Legal Tender decision was not certain. In the Slaughterhouse cases, Strong voted with the majority that rejected the liberty to contract argument while Bradley joined the dissenters in supporting the economic arguments. Four years later in Munn, Bradley provided the reasoning for Chief Justice Waite's opinion while Strong joined Justice Field in dissent, arguing in favor of the liberty to contract.

Sitting in the Louisiana circuit, Bradley had first hearing of reconstruction cases then voting on those same cases as a justice. The first federal judge to consider the Slaughterhouse cases, Bradley struck down the Louisiana monopoly law then watched his colleagues overturn his decision.[30] Bradley refused to apply the 1871 Civil Rights Act to the Grant Parish Massacre in the Cruikshank case and was upheld by his colleagues.[31]

Bradley also composed memorable decisions within the Court. In *Bartemeyer v. Iowa*, he upheld a state law prohibiting the sale of alcohol, ruling there was no liberty right to operate a saloon.[32] Bradley concurred in Justice Miller's denial of a woman's right to become a lawyer, composing his own treatise on womanhood declaring "man is... woman's protector and defender," and "the natural and proper timidity and delicacy which belongs to the female sex evidently unfits it for many of the occupations of civil life."[33]

Bradley wrote one decision and joined the majority in several civil rights cases during the 1879 term that interpreted the scope of earlier civil rights laws. He ruled in Ex Parte Seibold that Seibold, a state election judge had interfered with federal election monitors, an act the federal government could prosecute under its authority to enforce nondiscriminatory election laws.[34]

Bradley composed a much different opinion hamstringing the 1875 Civil Rights Act. Writing for eight justices, he ruled the Fourteenth Amendment banned only state discrimination. Bradley struck down the public accommodations section, finding the law reached private discrimination which was outside federal authority under section five of the amendment. Bradley believed state governments were responsible for preventing such discrimination. Another eighty one years would pass before a major civil rights bill would be passed and upheld by the Court.[35]

While Munn, Cruikshank and Bartemeyer are lost in history, Bradley's participation in the 1877 Electoral Commission has attracted new interest after the 2000 disputed election.

## Electing a President

The 1876 centennial election was to mark a Democrat revival after sixteen years in the presidential wilderness. The party focused on reasserting political control of the South as military rule faltered in the region. Violence and corruption plagued the election in Florida, South Carolina and Louisiana, delaying the electoral vote count.[36] The controversy stretched out over months as Samuel

Tilden teetered one electoral vote short of the White House. An electoral commission was formed with an equal number of senators and congressmen of both political parties and five Supreme Court justices, two democrat, two republicans and a single independent, David Davis.

When Davis was elected Illinois senator by Democrats eager to curry his favor, he resigned from the Court. Justice Bradley was chosen to replace him and he proceeded to grant every contested electoral vote to Rutherford Hayes.[37]

Bradley's votes outraged Democrats who burned him and his republican colleagues in effigy.[38] Justice Field, one of two Democrat justices on the commission; spread the rumor Bradley switched his vote after meeting with prominent Republicans.[39]

The disputed election may have represented the height of Bradley's public stature but it did not end his influence. In *Boyd v. United States*, Boyd was being investigated for avoiding federal tariff laws, with his personal papers being seized by the government and used against him in his trial. Boyd appealed his conviction, claiming the seizure of his property was an illegal search. Bradley agreed, finding that the government's warrantless search violated the Fourth Amendment and in forcing Boyd to turn over evidence the government violated his Fifth Amendment protection against self incrimination. Bradley went further declaring the use of illegally obtained evidence in trial was unconstitutional a recognition of what would become the exclusionary rule. [40]

Four years later Bradley penned *Hans v. Louisiana*, interpreting state sovereign immunity under the Eleventh Amendment. Hans sued the state of Louisiana for interest owed on state bonds. Taking his suit to federal court, he was denied access under the Eleventh Amendment which forbade citizens of one state from suing another state in federal court. Hans argued as a Louisiana citizen he was not covered by the amendment. Bradley disagreed, noting a simple reading of the amendment produced the "anomalous" effect of non citizens denied access to federal courts while citizens of a state could sue in those same courts. According to Bradley the result was "absurd on its face" and undermined the intention of the framers of the Eleventh Amendment.[41] The Hans doctrine remains central to the Eleventh Amendment and its interpretation in the twenty first century.

## William Strong

Justice Strong's career was quieter than Bradley, his most productive term being his last in 1879. During the term, the Court interpreted the scope of the civil rights acts passed during the Grant Administration. Strong was responsible for three critical opinions the best known being *Strauder v. West Virginia*.[42]

The West Virginia constitution expressly forbade blacks from serving on juries. Strauder was convicted of murder by an all white jury and claimed the exclusion of black jurors violated the Fourteenth Amendment's equal protection clause. Strong and the Court agreed a race based ban on jury service constituted state action prohibited under the Fourteenth Amendment.

In *Ex Parte Virginia* tackled the issue of a state judge accused of manipulating the jury selection process to prevent black jurors from serving. Strong found that while there was no law banning black jurors, the judge was a state official whose actions represented official discrimination. Strong's opinion represented the high point of federal civil rights enforcement. [43]

Rives contended his right to a fair trial was violated because no black jurors had ever served in his Virginia county. [44] Narrowing his Virginia decision, Strong discerned no discrimination from the stark statistic, ruling absent a clear showing of state law or official action, there was no proof of constitutional violation.

Strong resigned in 1880, his departure prompted by the excessive workload as three of his colleagues, Justices Clifford, Swayne and Hunt, were unable to write opinions, their workload falling upon Strong and others. Tiring of the excess work Strong left once able to collect his full pension, leaving the Court further shorthanded.[45]

## The Conkling Justice

While Waite, Strong and Bradley suffered the slings and arrows of the political era while writing memorable opinions, Grant's third Court choice, Ward Hunt, has sunk into historical obscurity. A close ally of New York senator Roscoe Conkling, Hunt was selected based on his connections and his strong support of reconstruction and civil rights, key issues for Conkling.[46] Hunt served six cognizant years, suffering a stroke in 1879 but held the seat until Rutherford Hayes, a Conkling critic, was replaced by Chester Arthur, a Conkling ally. [47]

Hunt dissented as the Court backed away from civil rights enforcement. In *U.S. v. Reese*, Hunt was alone in criticizing the Court for limiting civil rights protections.[48] His one footnote in history involved women's rights. Sitting as a circuit judge Hunt presided over the trial of Susan B. Anthony, charged with voting in the 1872 election. After a short trial Hunt found Anthony guilty and handed down a hundred dollar fine.[49]

Hunt did provide key votes in economic rights cases, providing the fifth vote in the Slaughterhouse cases. Though opposing a broad based liberty to contract right, Hunt favored corporations in railroad bond cases, joining decisions granting railroads protection against municipalities suing them to collect on bonds.

## Grant's legacy

Ulysses Grant's four Court appointments enhanced his legacy more by sheer accident than presidential design. Filling four vacancies required eight appointments with three of his choices, Strong, Bradley and Waite neither his first nor his second choices while Ward Hunt was a suggestion from one of his closest Senate allies. At times it appeared the Senate controlled the nomination process with the president advising and consenting. With an administration tarred with scandal, incompetence and economic depression, Grant improved his legacy in appointing four men who composed some of the more consequential opinions of the period, earning him a ranking far above his administration.

## Warren Harding

Warren Harding's rise to the presidency was as unexpected as it was sudden. A man of moderate wealth, he achieved prosperity through marriage, serving as publisher of the Marion Star before his 1914 Senate election. After a single term in office he was ready to return to central Ohio and continue his career as a newspaperman but first made a quixotic snatch at the presidency.

Harding entered the 1920 Republican convention as a dark horse candidate barely winning his home state primary.[50] A deadlock among a less than stellar Republican field led to one of the more dramatic, if not entirely true, scenes in American politics as Republican leaders met in a "smoke filled room" and hashed out their choice for president. Harding easily dispatched Democrat James Cox to the status of footnote.[51]

Harding entered the White House with a light resume and lacking a clear ideology or program. The president displayed snatches of good judgment, choosing such luminaries as Charles Evans Hughes, Andrew Mellon, Will Hays and Herbert Hoover to serve in the cabinet and gaps in that same judgment with choices such as Albert Fall and Harry Daugherty. Harding also tried to calm the chaos that had enveloped the late Wilson years, cutting taxes and pruning much of the government created during World War I.[52] He faced a severe post war depression, the first engineered by the Federal Reserve, though by 1922 the economy was starting to recover. His signature foreign policy achievement was the 1922 Washington Naval Conference which saw the naval buildup reversed.[53]

But even with these achievements, Harding would be brought down by scandals, both administrative and personal. Worse for the president his sudden death prevented him from acting against the guilty and asserting his own innocence while preserving his legacy. A series of books in the 1920s cast Harding as a corrupt womanizer and an intellectual weakling who stood by as his Ohio friends robbed the government blind.[54] Harding's reputation would never recover though some neutral biographers attempted a revival.[55]

With nowhere to go but up, Harding's reputation experienced a significant improvement when his four Supreme Court choices were considered. While ranked near the bottom among administrations, Harding rose to a position of respectable mediocrity, falling just below Andrew Jackson but above Harry Truman.[56] While Taft and Wilson appointees dominated the Court in 1920, illness, death and disgruntlement created four vacancies for Harding.[57] His choices moved the Court to the right, refocusing decisions on the protection of property rights and the scrutinizing of state and federal economic regulation.

As with his cabinet and sub cabinet appointments, Harding's schizophrenic selections continued in his Supreme Court choices. His first two appointees, William Howard Taft and George Sutherland, earned plaudits while his next two appointees, Pierce Butler and Edward Sanford, were panned by historians.

Having won the Republican nomination as part of a convention day compromise and winning the general election in a walk, Harding had not considered the type of justice he would appoint. He would be granted little time to consider names as the ailing Chief Justice Edward White died in spring 1921. Former president William Howard Taft was the most often mentioned replacement—usually by Taft himself—and seen as a safe choice.

Taft had openly pined for a seat on the Supreme Court but refused appointment in 1906, under the urging of his wife, who preferred the title First Lady to wife of the chief justice.[58] During the eight years of the Wilson Administration, Taft maintained the hope the president would reach across the aisle and select him but Wilson chose three Democrats.

With the republican Harding as president, Taft's hopes were renewed. His supporters lobbied the president elect as Taft visiting Harding in Ohio before the inauguration. When Chief Justice White died, Harding forced Taft to wait a few months before choosing him over one of his campaign advisors, former senator George Sutherland. With an overwhelmingly Republican Congress, Taft had no difficulty in being confirmed.

During his nine years as chief justice, Taft revitalized a flagging and divided Court, using consensus, persuasion and hard work to influence his colleagues.[59] Taft's good nature smoothed over differences, both personal and legal, while his willingness to shoulder extra opinion writing emphasized the teamwork he preached to the justices. Taft was not beyond criticizing his colleagues, goading three ill and underperforming colleagues from the bench.[60] Taft improved the institution, pushing Congress to grant the Court greater control over its docket while lobbying for a new and separate Court building.

Harding's next Court appointment, George Sutherland, was a former Utah senator who exuded traditional Republican values and had been a Taft supporter during the battle over 1912 nomination.[61] Sutherland strengthened his conservative credentials when he defended his colleague, Utah senator Reed Smoot, from charges he was a polygamist.[62] Defeated in Woodrow Wilson's 1916 sweep of the western states, Sutherland remained in Washington and served as an advisor to Harding's presidential campaign. Sutherland had been Harding's first choice for the Court but the president chose Taft as chief justice.[63] When Justice Day resigned in 1922, Sutherland joined the Court and began a sixteen year career that saw him author some of the most consequential opinions of the era.[64]

A few months before his death in August, 1923, Harding appointed Pierce Butler and Edward Sanford, neither of whom added to his reputation for Court appointments. Butler's confirmation is one of the closest studied in the Court's history. Justice Day's resignation in 1922 set off a search for his replacement with the chief justice and Justice Van Devanter vetting their preferred candidates for the seat.[65] Taft and Van Devanter were turned down by several candidates including a governor, appeals court judges and Democrat John W. Davis.[66] Their next choice was Minnesota lawyer Pierce Butler, who was asked about his willingness to be nominated. When Butler approved, the two justices launched a public relations blitz on his behalf, seeking the support of lawyers, judges, politicians and the Catholic Church to lobby Harding.[67]

The president conferred with his advisors while considering the justices' recommendation. Butler was nominated though because of Harding's wishes rather than Taft and Van Devanter's efforts. Butler's qualifications were scant. A railroad lawyer, Butler's political experience was limited to low level positions and serving as a delegate to Democrat presidential conventions.

As a Democrat chosen by a Republican president, Butler had bipartisanship working for his confirmation but it ran into difficulties. As a member of the University of Minnesota's Board of Regents, Butler seized the role of chief enforcer against war dissenters. One of his targets was William Schuper, a political science professor fired after admitting he opposed American involvement in the war. Butler dominated the hearing against Schuper, challenging the professor for his imprecise answers and voting with the board to dismiss Schuper.[68]

When the Senate received Butler's nomination, Schuper became a useful tool for fringe elements of the Republican Party including Senators Robert La Follette and George Norris. Their opposition proved to be more sound than fury but Schuper testified before the Judiciary Committee, accusing Butler of being a closed minded conservative.[69] Few senators were swayed and the committee supported the nomination. In the full Senate a small group of senators sought to slow the process but were outnumbered and Butler was confirmed.

Harding's selection of Edward Sanford added little to his appointment legacy. Sanford was a long serving federal judge chosen for his political connections. Taft barraged Harding with suggestions about the appointment but the president followed his attorney general's advice and picked Sanford.[70]

A resident of Tennessee, Sanford represented a region still struggling for full acceptance in national policy. The new justice's benign nature ensured his confirmation without the political attacks suffered by Butler. But unlike Butler, Sanford proved to be a follower rather than a leader, his almost fanatical devotion to Chief Justice Taft saw him join his colleague's opinions at nearly a one hundred percent rate.

## The Chief

Two more oppositely inclined men could not be found than President William Howard Taft and Chief Justice William Howard Taft. Taft's single term was unmemorable, his desire to leave reflected in his ineffectual reelection campaign.[71] But a lack of interest in the presidency ran counter to his intense desire to serve on the Supreme Court.

For the nine years as Chief Justice, Taft reveled in his duties, herding his sick, contentious, stubborn, incompetent and bigoted colleagues toward institutional decision making, discouraging dissenting opinions and complaining when justices ignored his advice. Taft's legacy as chief was twofold, part intellectual leader, writing more opinions than any of his colleagues and part political leader as he strengthened the Court by pushing bills through Congress. Taft fit snugly within the Court's mainstream, enhancing his effectiveness as chief justice. Suspicious of government economic regulation, he consistently voted against state labor and wage laws but his most cited opinions dealt with presidential authority and the Fourth Amendment.[72]

When Woodrow Wilson fired the postmaster Myers in defiance of the Tenure in Office Act, Myers sued claiming his firing was illegal. The dispute offered Taft an opportunity to remove the strictures on this central executive power. Taft's magnum opus was a two hundred page opinion detailing the presidential appointment power from Washington through Wilson that concluded any limit on a president's removal authority was unconstitutional. The opinion was controversial, drawing dissents from usual Taft allies, Justice Sutherland and McReynolds and would be severely limited by a 1935 Sutherland opinion.[73]

If Myers had a limited shelf life, two of Taft's criminal justice opinions would last longer. Prohibition and the federal income tax had transformed federal law responsibilities and techniques. Wiretapping of phones was one of the new methods of crime detection and in *Olmstead vs. U.S. Taft* set the standard for considering warrantless wiretaps.[74] Olmstead's phone line had been tapped without a warrant and he claimed the tap was an unconstitutional search. Narrowly reading the Fourth Amendment's scope, Taft ruled the tap occurred outside Olmstead's residence and did not require a search warrant. Olmstead lacked an expectation of privacy in his phone conversations, allowing warrantless wiretaps to become a much used federal method of crime detection. Olmstead would be overruled forty years later when wiretapping became a controversial issue in official Washington.[75]

A more durable Fourth Amendment decision came in *Carroll vs. U.S.* as Taft upheld a warrantless search of a car netting illegal alcohol.[76] Taft ruled cars were different than permanent structures because cars could be moved and evidence destroyed. The chief's car search exception remains a durable Fourth Amendment doctrine even as it has been modified to require reasonable suspicion for a search.

The chief also revived a property rights agenda that had been allowed to dwindle during the White Court. He rekindled the liberty to contract doctrine even as he dissented in his first major liberty to contract case, *Adkins v. Children's Hospital.*[77] In his dissent, Taft reminded his colleagues that the Washington D.C. wage and hours laws was similar to state laws upheld in the past while dismissing Justice Sutherland's contention that the introduction of a minimum wage would lead to the imposition of a maximum wage.[78]

But Adkins was an anomaly as the chief struck one of Wilson's favored laws, the child labor tax act. In *Bailey v. Drexel Furniture*, the chief narrowly interpreted federal taxing power, limiting it to raising revenue or prohibiting inherently dangerous products such as margarine. Taft did not consider furniture made by child labor to be inherently dangerous, making the tax a labor rather than a safety issue, with labor laws the province of the states.[79]

Taft also joined other liberty to contract decisions, placing him firmly within the Court's dominant conservative bloc. With his intellectual leadership moving the Court to the right, Taft used his administrative and political skills to strengthen the institution's independence. The last major reform of the federal judiciary occurred in 1891 when Congress created an intermediate Court of Appeals and ended circuit riding. By 1921 the federal judiciary was in disarray as clogged dockets and overworked judges led to delayed trials in some districts while judges in other districts worked part time. Taft's lobbied Congress to allow chief district judges to transfer federal judges to districts where cases were backlogged. Congress passed the reform in 1922, creating much needed flexibility in federal courts.[80]

A backlog had also formed in the Supreme Court as a variety of writs including the writ of error mandated the Court hear minor cases lacking legal or constitutional importance. After lobbying from the chief justice, Congress passed the 1925 Judiciary Act eliminating many of the Court's mandatory appeals and made the Writ of Certiorari the centerpiece of the Court's authority to hear cases. The Act allowed the justices to focus on the most important constitutional issues.[81]

Taft's final lobbying effort would be for a separate facility to house the Court. Throughout its history the justices depended upon the kindness of Congress for their facilities, using a basement room during the first half of the nineteenth century then the old Senate chamber after 1860. But the justices lacked offices and a proper law library and Taft wanted a new Supreme Court building. Fortunately he lobbied during the flush times of the 1920s, convincing Congress to appropriate money for a building directly across from the capitol. The project continued during the Depression and was finished in 1935 under budget five years after Taft's death.[82]

## George Sutherland

In sixteen years on the Court Justice George Sutherland recognized government zoning powers, applied the right to counsel to the states, expanded presidential foreign policy powers, limited presidential appointing authority and revived the liberty to contract. Though commonly recognized as the most talented of the Four Horsemen, Sutherland has been labeled a reactionary unable to meeting the challenges of the Great Depression and driving the Court into the greatest political crisis since Dred Scott.

Sutherland's economic libertarianism flowered in his first term in *Adkins v. Children's Hospital.*[83] In Adkins Sutherland reversed fifteen years of decisions upholding minimum wage and working hours laws for women and minors. The justice swept away the reasoning in Muller and Bunting, finding that the paternalistic approach was unnecessary after passage of the Nineteenth Amendment. According to Sutherland women had been empowered by the right to vote, and no longer required special legislation but should be considered equal citizens.[84] Sutherland also revived the Lochner doctrine, denouncing the immorality of forcing employers to pay a government mandated wage. Adkins became the first case in Sutherland's revival of the liberty to contract and the striking of federal and state economic regulation.[85]

Four years later, Sutherland challenged the "clothed in the public interest" doctrine created by Chief Justice Waite in Munn. In *Tyson v. Banton*, Sutherland struck down an ordinance limiting prices for theater and entertainment tickets sold by brokers, finding that ticket brokers were not engaged in a business clothed in the public interest. [86] Sutherland also struck a blow to labor union power in the Bedford Cut Stone decision, ruling forms of secondary boycotts represented an illegal restraint of trade.[87]

The Taft Court was the pinnacle of liberty to contract as the Great Depression ended public fears of creeping socialism. States and the federal government enacted new regulations to curb the depression's effect including moratoriums on mortgage payments, these laws challenged as a violating the ban on the abrogation of contracts. When a Minnesota mortgage moratorium law was upheld in 1934, Sutherland dissented and reminded his colleagues the Contract Clause and the constitution were not intended to change with the times, good or bad.[88]

Two years later Sutherland struck the Guffey Coal Act, a New Deal measure targeting excess coal production and falling prices by limiting production, setting minimum prices and raising miners' wages through collective bargaining. [89] Sutherland had little difficulty striking the act, ruling the taxes used in the regulatory scheme were used to control production rather than raise revenue. He denied that coal mining affected interstate commerce and that labor relations were a purely local issue under the Tenth Amendment. Sutherland joined the Court in striking other New Deal measures but after Justice Roberts'1937 switch, he was he was forced into dissent, warning of dire consequences created as old doctrines were swept from the law books.

Sutherland's liberty to contract and general hostility to economic regulations did not foreclose all government regulation of property, including the zoning laws upheld in *Euclid v. Amber Realty*.[90] When Euclid, Ohio restricted the use and height of new construction, Amber Realty's plans to use property for industrial purposes were blocked by the regulation requiring a mixed residential and industrial use of the land. Amber sought compensation under the Takings Clause because the zoning regulation depreciated property values.

Sutherland upheld zoning regulations under the common law of nuisance allowing government to regulate property to protect citizens' health, safety and welfare. Sutherland offered one caveat to zoning regulations, requiring government to demonstrate a nexus between the zoning regulation and harm it was intended to prevent. [91]

The Court packing conflict overshadowed Sutherland's efforts limiting presidential appointment power while granting nearly unrestrained foreign policy authority. Sutherland had dissented from Chief Justice Taft's Myers decision granting president plenary authority to fire executive employees. When Franklin Roosevelt seized on the Myers' reasoning to fire a member of the Federal Trade Commission (FTC), Sutherland took the opportunity to write his dissent into law.

The FTC was an independent entity, and the president could appoint members but not remove them without showing cause. When William Humphrey a Hoover appointee, refused to leave the commission, Roosevelt fired him without cause. Humphrey's heirs sued for back pay, setting the stage for a drastic revision of the Myers' doctrine of a unitary executive.[92]

In Humphrey's *Executor v. United States* Sutherland found that the president's power to remove was not absolute. Sutherland differentiated Humphrey from Myers ruling the removal power was vested in the president for purely executive agencies. The FTC was a quasi executive, quasi legislative body that made and enforced rules. In delegating rule making to the commission, Congress retained the right to limit presidential removal power. After Humphrey Congress established independent boards and commissions outside the direct authority of the executive, a sore point for Roosevelt's succesors.[93]

But where Sutherland limited executive domestic power, he granted power in foreign policy. The Curtiss Wright munitions company was charged with violating an arms embargo imposed by President Roosevelt. The company charged the embargo limited international trade which was part of Congress' authority to regulate foreign commerce, a power improperly delegated to the president.

In *U.S. v Curtiss Wright*, Sutherland ruled national sovereignty had been vested in the British monarchy before falling to the national government after American independence. According to Sutherland sovereignty existed separate from the constitution with its written limits on executive power. Sutherland ruled that Roosevelt could impose an arms embargo under the sovereign power to make foreign policy decisions while ignoring the non delegation doctrine which applied to domestic policy.[94]

In a second case Sutherland defined the scope and constitutionality of executive agreements. Upon entering office the Roosevelt Administration established diplomatic relations with the Soviet Union. Under an executive agreement with the Soviets, the United States government seized Russian companies' assets and released them to the communist government. A New York bank refused to hand over assets claiming the agreement violated the Fifth Amendment Takings Clause. In *United States v. Belmont* Sutherland dismissed the bank's argument, equating executive agreements with ratified treaties. According to Sutherland an executive agreement which was not covered under Senate ratification enjoyed the same constitutional authority as a ratified treaty and therefore could override the Fifth Amendment's Takings Clause.[95]

Curtiss Wright and Belmont came in the midst of the Court Packing crisis as Sutherland and his colleagues were under attack for an overly restrictive view of presidential and federal power. Yet Belmont and Curtiss Wright vastly expanding executive authority over foreign policy and would be used by Roosevelt and his successors during the Cold War.

Sutherland's influence extended to the doctrine of selective incorporation of the Bill of Rights. *Powell v. Alabama* mixed rabid southern racism and due process violations in Alabama courts. After a group of black youth were arrested on rape charges they were tried and convicted in a trial a few days after the arrest, required only a few hours and saw little or no defense on their behalf. Sentenced to death, the Scottsboro boys lost their appeal to the Alabama Supreme Court.[96]

The rapidity of the trial and the lack of a vigorous defense in a capital case raised due process questions and whether the right to counsel was to be applied to the states. Joined by six justices, Sutherland ruled the defendants were too young and ignorant to understand the complex trial procedures and lacked competent counsel.[97] Though Sutherland tailored his decision to the facts of the case, the region, the crime and the defendants, Powell established precedent for required counsel in capital cases, a right that would be expanded over three decades.

Sutherland's final years were marked by physical but not mental infirmities. Much of his final term was spent at his home, his rare visits to the Court marked by his assistants aiding him in moving from room to room.[98] After his retirement Sutherland was appointed in 1940 to hear the appeal of federal district judge Martin Mantin, convicted on corruption charges. The panel upheld the conviction, Sutherland authoring the opinion for himself, Justice Stone and another district judge.[99]

## Pierce Butler

Warren Harding's rise from failure to respectability is attributed to his selection of William Howard Taft and George Sutherland as his choices of Pierce Butler and Edward Sanford added little to the Court or the country. The least memorable of the Four Horsemen, the quirky Butler had unusual habits including a refusal to join opinions citing law review articles, leaving him to concur and dissent without opinion. Among his few consequential opinions was a dispute over the technical issue of diversity of citizenship in federal courts.

Dating from the Taney Court, when citizens of two states were involved in a lawsuit, a federal judge heard the dispute a applied federal common law. By the twentieth century the diversity claim had become a favorite tactic of business seeking to challenge state economic regulations. Corporations used their status of citizen of many states to have a dispute sent to federal court where they would receive a more sympathetic hearing.

Such a maneuver was the central issue in *Black and White Taxi Co. v. Brown and Yellow Taxi Co.*[100] The Brown and Yellow Taxi Co. had an exclusive contract with the Bowling Green train station to carry packages and passengers from the station. When the Black and White Co. sued under Kentucky law to have the contract struck down, Brown and Yellow reincorporated in Tennessee to create diversity of citizenship, moving the case to federal court. The Black and White Taxi Co. claimed the diversity was contrived to shift jurisdiction to the more sympathetic federal courts and should be rejected.

Butler upheld the diversity claim by ignoring Brown and Yellow's maneuver. The justice declared the contract valid, refusing to defer to state court interpretation of state law and replacing that interpretation with federal law. [101] The Black and White decision would be overturned by Justice Brandeis in 1938, prompting a Butler dissent.

In the midst of the New Deal crisis, Butler authored *Morehead v. Tipaldo*, which revived the liberty to contract doctrine. In Tipaldo, Butler struck down a New York minimum wage law applied to laundry workers. Butler leaned heavily on Sutherland's Adkins decision and cobbled together a majority with Justice Roberts the key vote. Tipaldo may have been the final provocation for the Roosevelt Administration, which offered its Court Packing Plan less than a year later.

Though a strict economic conservative, Butler was an independent voice on other issues. He dissented from Taft's Olmstead decision, fearing excessive police power to conduct warrantless wiretaps. In a similar vein, Butler dissented in Myers, another Taft expansion of executive power. Butler joined Justice McReynolds in not acceding to a unitary executive bearing unrestrained removal authority. Butler also dissented in Buck v. Bell, his Catholic beliefs placing him foresquare against Justice Holmes' eugenics philosophy and forced sterilization. [102]

An unusual Butler dissent was published in Hansen v. Haff as the justice struggled to define concubinage. Hansen was a Danish citizen having an affair with a married American man. Returning from a foreign trip she was arrested and accused of being an alien engaged in immoral activities. On appeal the Court ruled she was not covered the under the act. Justice Butler dissented, denouncing Hansen as a concubine who should have been excluded from the country. [103]

In *U.S. v. Schwimmer* a Hungarian refugee applied for U.S. citizenship but refused to take the oath promising to defend the country. Butler rejected Schwimmer's claim the oath was unconstitutional, finding that pacifism was frequently a shield used by opponents of war to convince others not to fight. The opinion had echoes of Butler battling Professor Schuper as the justice found Schwimmer lacked concrete attachment to her country, including a desire to defend it. [104]

The 1937 judicial revolution consigned Butler and the conservatives to dissenting in Laughlin and West Coast Hotel. After Justices Van Devanter and Sutherland retired, he joined Justice McReynolds dissent in *Mulford v. Smith*, upholding the second Agricultural Adjustment Act. Butler also dissented in *Erie v. Tompkins*, the decision overruling Black and White Taxicab. Butler's last consequential opinion came in Breedlove v. Suttles upholding Georgia's poll tax from a challenge that it violated the equal protection clause. Butler died in 1939, leaving McReynolds to carry on the conservative standard for another two years.[105]

Edward Sanford was William Howard Taft's most consistent ally. Appointed in 1923, Sanford served seven years, dying on the same day as Chief Justice Taft. Sanford left a spare record, a consistent conservative vote though he dissented in liberty to contract cases such as Adkins and Banton. His most quoted opinion came in *Gitlow v. New York.*[106] Gitlow was the leader of a radical leftist group that mailed literature espousing the group's views. Charged with violating the state's criminal anarchy law, Gitlow was convicted and appeared a sure loser as the Court had never applied the free speech right to the states. Sanford broached this obstacle in an offhand manner declaring speech as a liberty right protected under the Fourteenth Amendment's due process clause.[107] Sanford then retreated, refusing to overturn Gitlow's conviction and ruled the New York law had not violated his newly discovered free speech rights. While Gitlow lost, Sanford triggered the process of selective incorporation.

In *Whitney v. California*, Sanford offered his gloss on the clear and present danger test. Whitney was prosecuted under California's anti syndicalism law, the state claiming she was a member of the communist party and participated in a conspiracy to overthrow the American government. Sanford upheld the California law and Whitney's conviction, denying her speech was protected by the First Amendment as it was part of an antigovernment conspiracy representing a clear and present danger.[108]

Sanford solved a nettlesome separation of powers issue, writing the definitive opinion on congressional recesses and their effect on the pocket veto.[109] When Calvin Coolidge pocket vetoed an Indian Claims bill during the 1926 congressional recess, several tribes claimed the bill was law because Coolidge had not officially vetoed it. The dispute focused on the meaning of congressional recesses and in the instant case Congress was not in session when the ten day signing period passed. The tribes backed argued the vetoed bill could be debated and an override vote held when Congress returned in December. Sanford disagreed, finding that the constitution required Congress to remain in session, receive a vetoed bill, record the president's objections in the daily journal and vote on override immediately after the objections were noted.[110] If Congress did not want the president to pocket veto a bill, it would have to remain in session until the ten day period passed, forcing him to issue an official veto. Sanford's opinion continued the Taft Court's expansion of executive authority which began in Myers. Within a year, the justice would be dead, his brief career adding little to Warren Harding's legacy.

## Harding's Legacy

Warren Harding is commonly remembered as a scandal plagued president whose death prevented him from mounting a defense of his administration. William Howard Taft and George Sutherland rank in the higher tier of justices.

Taft's leadership propelled him among the second tier of chief justices, while Sutherland's cogent and seminal opinions made him the one member of the Four Horsemen not condemned as a failure. Taft's and Sutherland's appointments overshadow the weaker choices of Pierce Butler and Edward Sanford much as Franklin Roosevelt's choices of Hugo Black and Felix Frankfurter overshadowed his selections of Stanley Reed and Frank Murphy. The two justices also raised Harding's standing, removing him from the failures to a more respectable mediocrity when considering his Supreme Court appointments.

## Notes

1. Smith, Jean Edward, *Grant* ( New York: Simon and Schuster, 2001), 550-551.

2. Smith, 554.

3. Murray, Robert *The Harding Era* (Newtown Ct: American Biography Press, 1969), 83-84.

4. In the poll Grant was rated nineteenth and Harding twentieth, above Jefferson (24th) and Truman (26th).

5. Smith, 93. Grant's financial problems dogged him into his retirement as during his last days his family teetered on bankruptcy, saved only his dramatic push to complete his memoirs before dying of cancer.

6. Trefousse, Hans, *Andrew Johnson* (New York: WW Norton, 1989), 245-247.

7. Smith, 457-458

8. Abraham, Henry, *Justice, Presidents and Senators* (New York: Rowman Littlefield, 2008),102.

9. Smith, 506-507

10. Fairman, Charles, *Reconstruction and Reunion Part 1* (New York: MacMillan, 1971), 731-733.

11. Jordan, David, *Roscoe Conkling of New York* (Ithaca, New York: Cornell University Press, 1971), 201-202. Conkling also worried about releasing his political hold over New York and knew he could never run for president, as Chase had, from the chief justice position.

12. Smith, 560; Maltese, John, *The Selling of Supreme Court Nominees* (Baltimore MD: Johns Hopkins University Press), 94-95.

13. Cushing has been selected for an ambassadorship by President John Tyler, the nomination rejected three times in the same day.

14. Smith 561-562

15. Trimble, Bruce, *Chief Justice Waite* (Princeton NJ: Princeton University Press, 1938), 158- 159, 250. In 1875 the Court was five hundred cases behind in their docket andby 1888 the Court was in arrears fifteen hundred cases.

16. 94 U.S. 113 (1877)

17. Whiteside, Ruth Ann, *Justice Joseph Bradley and the Reconstruction Amendments* (Dissertation Rice University, 1981), 183.

18. *Tyson v. Banton* 273 U.S. 418 (1927)

19. *United States v. Cruikshank* 92 U.S. 542 (1876)

20. 912 U.S. 214 (1876)

21. 95 U.S. 485 (1878)

22. *Minor v. Happersett* 88 U.S. 162 (1874)

23. 88 U.S. 162, 178

24. 98 U.S. 145 165 (1879)

25. 98 U.S. 145, 168

26. *Telephone Patent Cases* 126 U.S. 1 (1888)

27. Most U.S. volumes hold at least thirty cases and occasionally twice that number.

28. *Hepburn v. Griswold* 75 U.S. 603 (1869)

29. *Knox v. Lee* 79 U.S. 457 (1870)

30. Whiteside 183

31. Whiteside, 176

32. 85 U.S. 129 (1874)

33. *Bradwell v. Illinois* 83 U.S. 130, 142 (1874)

34. 100 U.S. 371 (1880) This was a broad interpretation of the Fifteenth Amendment, which allowed Congress to pass laws enforcing the amendment and his prohibition against voting discrimination based on race.

35. *The Civil Rights Cases* 109 U.S. 3 (1883) The lone dissenter in the case was John Marshall Harlan, oddly enough the only sitting justice to have owned slaves.

36. Fairman, Charles, *Five Justices and the Electoral Commission of 1877* (New York: MacMillan, 1988), 40-42.

37. Fairman, 95

38. Swisher, Carl Brent, *Stephen Field* (Washington D.C.: The Brookings Institution, 1935), 278.

39. Swisher, 278-279

40. 116 U.S. 616 , 639(1886)

41. 134 U.S. 1, 11, 16( 1890)

42. 100 U.S. 303 (1880)

43. 100 U.S. 339(1880)

44. *Virginia vs. Rives* 100 U.S. 313 (1880)

45. Kutler, Stanley "William Strong" in Leon Freidman and Fred Israel *The Justices of the United States Supreme Court 1789-1969* (New York: Chelsea House Publishing, 1969), 1161.

46. Fairman, 27

47. Jordan, David, *Roscoe Conkling of New York* (Ithaca NY: Cornell University Press, 1971), 416.

48. Whiteside, 227

49. Fairman, 224-225

50. Murray, 29. While Harding was not defeated in Ohio, he was unable to gain asignificant victory against his main opponent, Leonard Wood.

51. Murray, 37-39.While the room was smoky it was not filled with conspirators seeking to place a pliable Harding in the White House. Instead most of the Republicans wanted to escape from the torturous summer heat with the best available candidate, who appeared to be Harding.

52. Murray 171-173

53. Murray, 153-154

54. Trashing Harding would become a cottage industry during the roaring twenties with speculation about his personal life and death along with criticism of his economic and military policies.Among them were: Britton, Nan, *The President's Daughter* (New York: The Elizabeth Ann Guild, 1927). Britton claimed to be Harding's teenage mistress and the mother of his illegitimate daughter. Means, Gaston, *The Strange Death of President Harding* (New York: Guild Publishing, 1930) Means claimed Harding was poisoned, possibly by his wife.Russell, Francis, *The Shadow of Blooming Grove* (New York: McGraw Hill, 1968) Russell dug deep into Harding's personal life and professional scandals, describing hotel assignations that likely never occurred. White, William Allen, *Masks in a Pageant* (New York: MacMillan Press, 1928) White created the image of the Ohio Gang with its drinking and poker parties.

55. Murray, *The Harding Era*; Ferrell, Robert, *The Strange Deaths of President Harding* (Columbia MO.: University of Missouri Press, 1996).

56. Among the best known of the presidential rankings, Harding regularly battled with Ulysses Grant, Franklin Pierce and James Buchanan for the dubious ranking of the worst of the worst.

57. His four Court appointments in two and a half years was the highest proportion for any president.

58. Pringle, Henry, *William Howard Taft* .(Newtown CT: American Political Biography Press, 1998)

59. Steamer, Robert, *Chief Justice* (Columbia SC: University of South Carolina Press, 1986), 174-175.Taft is recognized as one of the top tier chief justices.

60. Murphy,184-185. Taft nearly ran McKenna from the Court, repeatedly seeking advice from the justice's physician on whether McKenna should continue then lobbied McKenna's children to convince the old man to retire.

61. Pascal, Joel, *Mr. Justice Sutherland* (Princeton N.J.: Princeton University Press, 1951), 105.

62. Pascal ,49-53.

63. Pascal, 113

64. Murphy, 167-168

65. Danelski, David, *A Supreme Court Justice is Appointed* (New York: Random House, 1964), 39-45.

66. Danelski, 53
67. Danelski,57-58; Murphy, Walter "In his own Image" *Supreme Court Review* 1961 159-193
68. Danelski, 100-103
69. Danelski, 102
70. Murphy 177-179
71. Taft received the lowest percentage of the popular vote, twenty three percent, and the fewest electoral votes, eight, of any sitting president.
72. Steamer, 184-185
73. 272 U.S. 52 (1926)
74. 277 U.S. 438 (1928)
75. *Katz vs. U.S.* 386 U.S. 954 (1967)
76. 267 U.S. 132 (1925)
77. 261 U.S. 525, 564 (1923)
78. 261 U.S. 525, 564-565
79. 259 U.S. 20 (1922)
80. Pringle, 995-996
81. Pringle 998-100
82. Steamer, 170-171
83. 261 U.S. 535 (1923)
84. 261 U.S. 535, 554
85. 261 U.S. 525, 549, 559
86. 273 U.S. 418 440-442 (1927)
87. *Bedford Cut Stone v. Journeyman Stone Cutters* 274 U.S. 37 (1927)
88. *Home Building and Loan Association v. Blaisdell* 290 U.S. 398 450-451 (1934)
89. *Carter v. Carter Coal Company* 298 U.S. 238 (1936)
90. 272 U.S. 365 (1926)
91. 272 U.S. 365, 389,396
92. Leuchtenberg, William, *The Supreme Court Reborn* (London:Oxford University Press, 1996), 62-64.
93. 295 U.S. 602 (1935)
94. 299 U.S. 304, 316-318 (1936)
95. 301 U.S. 324 (1937)
96. 287 U.S. 45 (1932)
97. Arkes, Hadley, *The Return of George Sutherland* (Princeton NJ: Princeton University Press, 1994), 265-266. Sutherland included a natural law definition of due process that went beyond the text of the constitution and included many unwritten requirements for a trial to be considered fair.
98. Newman, Roger, *Hugo Black* (New York: Pantheon Books,1994), 619
99. Borkin, Joseph, *The Corrupt Judge* (New York: Clarkson and Potter, 1962), 81.
100. 276 U.S. 518 (1928)

101. 276 U.S. 518, 530-531

102. Holmes produced less than his usual felicitous opinion, warning that the Virginia law was preventing the country from being "swamped with incompetence" and that it would be better for the state to resort to sterilization than "waiting to execute degenerate offspring for crime." 274 U.S.200, 206. (1927)

103. 291 U.S. 559 (1934)

104. 279 U.S. 664,653 (1929)

105. 302 U.S. 277 (1937)

106. 268 U.S. 652 (1925)

107. 268 U.S. 652, 667 Sanford declared "For present purposes we may and do assume that freedom of speech and of the press-which are protected by the First Amendment from abridgment by Congress-are among the fundamental personal rights and 'liberties' protected by the due process clause of the Fourteenth Amendment from impairment by the States."

108. 274 U.S. 357, 380 (1927) Whitney was a unanimous decision, both Justices Brandeis and Holmes joining the opinion. Whitney would stand for forty two years until overturned in *Brandenburg v. Ohio*. 395 U.S. 444 (1969)

109. *The Pocket Veto Case* 279 U.S. 655 (1929)

110. 279 U.S. 655, 684-685

## Chapter 11

# William Howard Taft (12) Richard Nixon (14)

William Howard Taft and Ri6chard Nixon left the White House in defeat and disgrace. Taft received the smallest percentage of the popular vote, twenty three, and the fewest electoral votes, eight, of any president running for reelection. Richard Nixon was forced to resign after the Watergate scandal. Both men are rated as below average or failures but enjoyed some success in their Supreme Court nominees, choosing several who were ranked among the near greats or above average.

William Howard Taft and Richard Nixon presided over polar opposite presidencies. Nixon spent his political career obsessed with power, seemingly every action planned for maximum political benefit. His desire to reach the White House overrode his ideology as the conservative Republican visited Communist China, signed arms control agreements with the Soviet Union and imposed wage and price controls, all during an election year. Nixon's paranoia and vengefulness destroyed his presidency as he tried to cover up what could have been contained as a minor scandal.

William Howard Taft never wanted the presidency. A judge at heart he was prodded to run for office by his ambitious wife. Taft was miserable during his four years in the White House and as his administration struggled, his chances for a second term dwindled. Taft's weak reelection campaign was diametrically opposite of Nixon's slash and burn strategy.[1]

Both Nixon and Taft were considered failed presidents, Nixon for his hubris, Taft for his passivity and both men spent their post presidency attempting to rehabilitate their legacies. Faced with the more difficult task of the two,

Nixon sought the role of elder statesman working behind the scenes and offering advice to Presidents Reagan, Bush senior and Clinton.[2] He wrote a host of books on foreign policy and traveled around the world to meet with foreign leaders. By the time of his death, nearly twenty years after his resignation, Nixon would be recognized by even his worst enemies as a first rate mind who disgraced the office.[3]

Taft revived his career by reaching the position he craved, chief justice. Taft proved a more capable chief than president, convincing Congress to build a separate Supreme Court building and lobbying to give the justices control over their caseload. By the time of his death in 1930 Taft had rehabilitated his name and career, his presidency more an aberration than a reflection of his talents.[4]

Taft and Nixon were ranked as below average or among the presidential failures but had their standing rise when their Court selections were considered.[5] The two presidents had ample opportunity for influencing the institution. Nixon's four appointees diluted Warren liberalism while Taft's six choices turned the Court from its controversial conservative agenda. Of Nixon's four appointees, only one—William Rehnquist – was the type of conservative justice promised by Nixon. Taft appointed competent justices, with two, Edward White and Charles Evans Hughes, producing consequential opinions. Even with their limitations, both men influenced the Court they inherited.

## William Howard Taft

During the Supreme Court's history several justices have yearned to live in the White House and used their judicial position as a launching pad toward the presidency. Yet only one president has wished to sit on the other end of Pennsylvania Avenue, William Howard Taft. Born into an Ohio political family, Taft's father was War Secretary and Treasury Secretary under Ulysses Grant while Taft was the father of a Senate majority leader and great grandfather to a twenty first century Ohio governor. Taft served as Secretary of War for Theodore Roosevelt after a brief stint as solicitor general and a federal appeals judge. Appointed governor of the Philippines he discovered he preferred judicial work to executive power. Returning to Washington in 1906 he was offered a Supreme Court seat but at the behest of his wife—who preferred the title of first lady to the nondescript role of a judicial wife—turned down the offer.[6]

Taft rode to the presidency on Roosevelt's coattails in 1908 but once in the White House he was unable to please the former president or his progressive supporters. Taft's administration proved to be a disaster and as Roosevelt had engineered his victory in 1908, he drove Taft to defeat in 1912 by challenging him in the Republican primary then in the general election.

During his one term Taft filled six Court vacancies, more than any other single term president. Those appointments saw the president remake the Court, moving it from decisions such as Lochner to a moderate conservatism with justices who upheld economic regulation and created the federal exclusionary rule.

Taft entered office disdainful of the Fuller Court, describing conservative justices as "those old fools."[7] During 1909-1910 Taft replaced this conservative core Justices Peckham and Brewer and Chief Justice Fuller died.

With three nearly simultaneous appointments, Taft remade the institution. Though he publicly favored youth on the Court, Taft chose men in their sixties while ignoring party considerations by selecting three Democrats, the most by any Republican president. His six choices are more easily analyzed when broken into trios of justices. The first trio, Justices Lurton, Lamar and Pitney, had little effect on the Court and left little imprint on Taft's legacy. The second trio, Justices White, Van Devanter and Hughes had a significant impact.

## Horace Lurton

As the only president to serve as a federal judge, Taft made his first choice one of his former colleagues from the Sixth Circuit Court of Appeals. Horace Lurton was one of those rare judges who had fought to overturn the constitution then later took an oath to uphold and defend it. A native Tennessean, Lurton joined the Confederate Army, fighting in the early battles along the Cumberland River. He was captured, escaped and joined the irregular cavalry force of John Morgan where he was again captured. Contracting tuberculosis Lurton was freed only by a personal appeal to President Lincoln from his mother.[8]

After the war Lurton earned a law degree and rose through the ranks of the state court system until he was appointed to the Sixth Circuit Court of Appeals, serving with two future justices, William Howard Taft and William Day.[9]

Lurton's close working relationship with Taft on the appeals court nearly earned him a Court appointment in 1906 when Lurton was recommended to Theodore Roosevelt to replace Justice Henry Brown. But the Democrat Lurton was opposed by Massachusetts Republican Senator Henry Cabot Lodge, who preferred a justice from his own party.[10]

Taft remembered his colleague, choosing Lurton to replace the Justice Peckham in 1909. The appointment of a southerner and Democrat raised questions among Republican senators as did Taft's breaking of his own promise to replace the old men on the Court with young men. Lurton was sixty six at the time of his appointment, the oldest of any nominated justice and in an era of limited life spans unlikely to serve an extended term.[11]

The Democrat started the Court's move to the left under the influence of Taft and Roosevelt appointees. Yet Lurton authored no profound or memorable opinions, his vote more important than his pen. Lurton served two full terms and struggling through two others, racked by illness. His four years left little impression and the justice is one of those barely recognized faces staring back in pictures of the Court usually seen in the biographies of more illustrious colleagues.

## Lamar

Taft's appointment of southern Democrats did not end with Lurton. The death of Roosevelt's appointee William Moody in 1910 created a vacancy that Taft filled with a member of the Georgia gentry, Joseph Rucker Lamar. Having married into the prominent Rucker family, Lamar used his connections to gain a spot on the state supreme court where he focused on administrative duties including setting rules for entry into the state bar and rewriting the state legal code.[12]

Lamar joined the opinions expanding federal commerce power and reinvigorating antitrust law. Lamar never composed an opinion whose name easily rolls from the tongue. His singular decision of importance came in *U.S. v. Grimaud.*[13]

The advent of federal regulatory agencies operating within the executive branch but assigned the task of creating regulations with the force of law presented the justices with the question of whether a hybrid agency, part legislative and part executive, could exist. A 1905 law granted the Secretary of Agriculture the authority to make rules that would protect the national forests. One of those rules was a ban on sheep grazing in the forest land. When Grimaud was prosecuted for grazing his sheep on public lands and appealed, arguing the secretary was making law rather than enforcing it. Lamar upheld the secretary's authority, finding the regulations banning sheep comprised law enforcement rather than legislating. The department could write rules as long as they were related to the congressional goal, in this case, protecting national forests.[14] Grimaud remains an obscure opinion in the important debate on executive power and Lamar's contribution to the debate also remains unknown. A safe, stolid justice, he lasted a bit longer than Lurton, dying in 1916 and leaving a seat that Taft yearned to be appointed to by Woodrow Wilson.

## Mahlon Pitney

A former New Jersey congressman, Mahlon Pitney was a judge at heart, earning a seat on the state supreme court then serving as chancellor, where he oversaw the entire state court system. Taft plucked him from that job to fill the vacancy created by the death of John Marshall Harlan.[15]

The nomination ran into problems as Taft's political capital had all but disappeared after the disastrous 1910 midterms. Pitney became the target of Democrats and progressives, who accused the judge of being too close to business and hostile to labor. Pitney was Taft's second choice after his first, Judge William Hook, saw his chances vanish after persistent progressive opposition to his economic decisions. Much of the opposition to Hook and Pitney hinged on concerns about pending railroad rates. Harlan usually voted against the railroads and his replacement represented a swing vote on the issue. But Taft prevailed and with his sixth appointment set the record for most choices by a one term president.[16]

Replacing a justice who was a legend in his own time, Pitney proved to be no Harlan. Criticized for writing confusing and barely coherent opinions, he managed to compose two memorable decisions. During his first term, Pitney revived the liberty to contract doctrine, which some thought had been dealt a fatal blow in the Muller decision. In *Coppage v. Kansas*, Pitney struck state ban on the so called yellow dog contract in which employees agreed not to join a union as part of their employment contract. Kansas had attempted to bolster union membership by outlawing these devices but Pitney rejected the law. He found the state law interfered with the liberty to contract and that an employer could require their employees to agree not to join unions.[17]

Coppage was denounced by progressives and Pitney was labeled antiunion. Yet Coppage was consistent with the Court's previous rulings, placing Pitney within the mainstream of the political system. Three years later Pitney authored *Frank v. Mangum.*[18] Leo Frank was convicted of the murder of a girl near Atlanta, Georgia. Frank was Jewish and his arrest excited considerable interest. The trial was conducted in an atmosphere of tension, with protesters outside the courthouse baying for blood and being heard inside the courtroom during the trial. Frank was convicted, though he had not been in the courtroom during the reading of the verdict, providing an avenue of appeal.[19]

The Frank case focused on the authority of federal courts to issue writs of Habeas Corpus in state cases where defendants claimed their constitutional rights had been violated. In 1915 federal judges usually deferred to state court decisions except in the most egregious violations. Pitney's opinion in Frank followed this tradition, rejecting the appeal and the authority of a federal judge to rule on his claims. While the Frank decision is held up by modern lawyers as an example of the Supreme Court refusing to correct an injustice—Frank was later proven innocent—it was simply one of a series of cases where the Supreme Court refused to apply federal constitutional standards to state courts.[20] Pitney's opinion was not out of the mainstream at the time but would not be fondly remembered. Pitney would be struck down by a stroke and arthritis, his last years on the Court spent in bed unable to function and he retired only after Chief Justice Taft convinced Congress to grant him a special pension.[21]

## Hughes

Charles Evans Hughes was one of only two men twice appointed to the Supreme Court and prove to be one of the more effective chief justices.[22] By far Taft's best nominee, Hughes accepted the Court nomination under the implicit promise that he would replace the aging Melville Fuller as chief justice. Hughes would be passed over for the promotion, seemingly ending his inevitable rise through the political system from New York governor to national office.[23]

Hughes was soon overwhelmed by the job with the daily grind of unending petitions and cases. Pushed to an emotional edge, Hughes resorted to electric shock treatments to treat his encroaching depression. Eventually he snapped free from the illness and his name became a hot topic for the 1916 presidential election. Hughes' nomination in the summer of 1916 would make him and Thomas Eagleton the only major party candidates on a national ticket to undergo treatment for mental illness.[24]

Even with his admitted difficulties, Hughes fit in well with Taft's moderate nominees, strengthening the majorities that cut back on the opinions of the "damned fool" justices Taft wanted to replace. Struggling with opinion writing and the crushing workload, Hughes was able to author two opinions of note in his six years. In *Bailey v. Alabama* he dusted off the Thirteenth Amendment to strike down a peonage law. The state allowed farmers and others to pay the fines of poor felons then force those felons to work off those fines as the twentieth century model for indentured servitude. Peonage laws targeted blacks and poor whites and Hughes ruled they were a form of involuntary servitude forbidden by the Thirteenth Amendment.[25]

Hughes not only struck a blow at the segregated south but also placed his imprint on the Commerce Clause. The *Shreveport Railway Case* saw the railroads and the federal Interstate Commerce Commission square off intrastate railway rates. Hughes found that interstate commerce included any commerce within a state that had a close and substantial effect on commerce between the states.[26] The close and substantial effects test would be the grounding for interpreting the Commerce Clause starting in the 1940s and would be the basis for cases upholding civil rights acts as regulations of commerce during the 1960s.

Hughes bolstered his progressive credentials in dissents in Frank, joining joined Justice Holmes in finding the trial lacked due process guarantees.[27] Hughes' dissent in Coppage took issue with revival of the liberty to contract.[28] Hughes also struck down a nativist Arizona law limiting non native born citizens to less than twenty percent of any business' workforce.[29]

The justice's six years as an associate foreshadowed his future. When Hughes left the Court in July 1916 he appeared headed to the White House as an unpopular Woodrow Wilson limped through a reelection campaign. Hughes' stunning defeat, he lost all but three states west of the Mississippi appeared to end his political career. A return to the Supreme Court came with his appointment by Herbert Hoover to lead the Court in the midst of the Great Depression. Once again the man and his moment met in American history and Hughes was able to guide the institution through one of its direst periods.

## Willis Van Devanter

Hughes' two terms as justice included the unusual event of his serving with three justices during both periods. Justices James Clark McReynolds, Willis Van Devanter and Oliver Wendell Holmes knew Hughes as both an associate and chief justice. The more obscure of these, Van Devanter was appointed to fill the vacancy created by Edward White's promotion to chief justice. The only Wyoming native to serve on the Court, Van Devanter served on the Eighth Circuit Court of Appeals and was known as a skilled legal draftsman.[30] Van Devanter was responsible for the Wyoming law code and aided in composing the 1925 Judiciary Act. In his twenty seven year tenure, Van Devanter struggled to write opinions, serving terms where he did not compose a single Court opinion while writing only four dissents during his career.[31] His struggles were referred to as "Pen Paralysis" by his colleagues and attributed it to an excessive attention to detail that prevented him from issuing opinions without months of work.[32]

Though Van Devanter's lack of productivity increased the workload on his colleagues, he was well liked and respected. William Howard Taft admitted leaning on Van Devanter for his cogent arguments during the justices' weekly conferences.[33] Unfortunately Van Devanter's efforts were unseen, his influence behind the scenes, contributing to his being ranked as a failure. Only his work for the 1925 Judiciary Act was a concrete accomplishment to judge Van Devanter as he lightened the Court's workload and allowed justices to focus on important issues.[34]

Van Devanter managed a few opinions of note including his 1913 decision officially ending the congressional reconstruction era by striking down the remaining section of the 1875 Civil Rights Act. In *Butts v. Merchants and Miners Transportation Corporation* he upheld a steamship company's separate but equal policy creating segregated seating for black passengers. The 1875 Act banned discrimination on the high seas and Van Devanter ruled the section was not severable from the sections banning private discrimination at the state level, which had been struck down in 1883.[35] While Butts limited federal power to prevent private discrimination, Van Devanter was not hostile to enhanced congressional authority to question witnesses.

In *McGrain v. Daugherty* Van Devanter upheld the Senate investigation of Warren Harding's former campaign manager and attorney general, Harry Daugherty for corruption and its subpoena of Daugherty's brother Mally.[36] After ignoring the subpoena and being charged with contempt of Congress, Mally appealed, claiming the investigation and subpoena were unconstitutional. Van Devanter rejected the claim, recognizing Congress had broad powers of investigation and oversight as part of his legislative power. Investigating Daugherty and executive corruption was part of that oversight duty and the power to subpoena witnesses was critical to uncovering wrongdoing. McGrain would become controversial when Congress began investigating domestic communism and was attacked for using subpoena power to embarrass leftists.

The *Prohibition Cases* entangled Van Devanter in the question of whether a constitutional amendment was unconstitutional. The Eighteenth Amendment was ratified to solve the interminable dispute of regulation of alcohol by state and federal government. The amendment granted power to Congress, which promptly passed the Volstead Act prohibiting production, sale and use of alcohol. Challenging the act Rhode Island claimed Congress lacked authority to ban alcohol throughout the nation. In a bulleted opinion that read more like a shopping list than a Court decision, Van Devanter dismissed Rhode Island's arguments and ruled the Eighteenth Amendment granted Congress plenary authority over alcohol.[37]

Van Devanter, dismissed as a failure performed one act of self sacrifice for his institution, retiring in April 1937 just as the Court Packing controversy reached a frenzied finale. His leaving the Court was attributed to political pressure on the Court but more likely caused by the financial inducement that was part of the Court packing plan. Passed in 1937 the bill restored full retirement benefits for judges past seventy who had served at least a decade as a federal judge. Full retirement benefits had been reduced by Congress to save money, an ironic testament to the free spending New Dealers who needed to spend a small amount to remove an obstacle to their plans.

Van Devanter's departure may have been time with two Roosevelt capitol hill critics, senators Burton Wheeler and William Borah. As always Borah had a variety of contacts in the capital, including Van Devanter who made no secret of his desire to retire. In the midst of the congressional debate over Roosevelt's plan, Borah may have convinced the justice his departure would help defeat the bill. Van Devanter's resignation reached the president's desk on the same day the bill was defeated in the Senate Judiciary Committee.[38]

## Chief Justice White

With only eight men having served as chief justice prior to 1909, the choice to fill that position would be one of Taft's most important. The chief not only has his name attached to the Court, he is expected to fulfill the role as social and intellectual leader. Taft's choice, Edward White, was the first associate justice to be promoted to the center chair and was the third Democrat chosen by Taft. White was originally appointed by Grover Cleveland, who after two defeated nominations turned the Senate's arcane rules against it and nominated Senator White of Louisiana. With the twin strategies of exhaustion and senatorial courtesy working for him, White was easily confirmed.[39]

During his sixteen years as an associate justice, White played the role of foil for some of his more conservative colleagues, dissenting when they struck down the federal income tax and weakened the Sherman Antitrust Act. He silently agreed to the separate but equal doctrine in Plessy, which upheld separate railway cars in his home state.[40] He also acquiesced in the liberty to contract doctrine created in *Allgeyer v. Louisiana*.

White authored few important decisions early in his career but at the turn of the century left his imprint in two areas, antitrust law and the reach of the constitution into overseas territories.

White settled an argument in antitrust law that split the Court since the 1890 Sherman Act. The act prohibited trusts that restrained trade. White's more libertarian colleagues including Justices Peckham and Brewer, sought to prohibit all monopolistic practices, including price fixing and bid rigging that undermined competition.[41] White disagreed, seeking a more nuanced approach that allowed some restraints on trade. Peckham and his followers won early battles, striking at what they perceived as anti competitive practices including price fixing.[42] But as the Peckham's allies departed White proffered a new interpretation. In his first term as chief justice, White created the rule of reason in *Standard Oil v. United States*[43] and *United States v. American Tobacco.*[44] White ruled the companies had technically restrained trade but that the restraints were a reasonable part of business and not an antitrust violation. The rule of reason became the Court's favored interpretation of antitrust law even as it was criticized as blatant legislating.[45]

After the seizure of overseas territories including the Philippines and Puerto Rico, the Court faced a series of cases seeking to apply constitutional rights to these new territories. Starting in 1900 the *Insular* cases focused on the question of whether the constitution followed the flag and American military into overseas territories.

Justice White led a bloc argued for plenary congressional power to pass laws for the new territories avoiding constitutional constraints reserved for American citizens. Opposing White's interpretation a bloc of four justices ruled the constitution followed the flag and those living in American possessions enjoyed full constitutional rights. The swing justice was Henry Brown, his vote deciding which bloc of justice's spoke for the Court. By 1905 White's bloc was in control, ruling the right to a jury trial or indictment by grand jury was not required in territories and some tariff laws applied to goods shipped from territories to the continental United States.[46] White's views in the Insular Case were in line with Taft's policies when serving as Philippines' governor, earning him the trust of the future president.[47]

## Chief Justice of the United States

Taft faced a difficult choice after the death of Melville Fuller. The job for which he yearned was open but he was forced to fill it with someone else. While Charles Evans Hughes believed he had been promised the center chair upon Fuller's death, there is some belief that Taft did not want a young man filling the job as Taft sought the center chair for himself. [48] White survived Woodrow Wilson's two terms and after the Warren Harding's election in 1920 had the good grace to die and allow Taft to assume the center chair.[49]

White proved unequal to the task of chief justice, unable to lead his colleagues even as he authored some of the era's more important decisions. In *Guinn v. U.S.* he struck Oklahoma's reconstruction era law limiting voting to white residents. The literacy test and grandfather clause portions of the law had been passed while the state was a territory. White rejected the argument the law did not discriminate based on race because it treated all races equally. Instead he found the Oklahoma law perpetuated race-based voting restrictions prohibited by the Fifteenth Amendment.[50]

The chief justice also turned back a Thirteenth Amendment challenge to the World War One draft law. [51] White faced a clash between the draft clause found in Article One Section Eight granting Congress authority to force military service and the Thirteenth Amendment's ban on involuntary servitude. The chief justice composed a rambling opinion noting demands of citizenship including mandatory military service in times of crisis and the history of the draft dating back to colonial times. Focusing on citizenship he brushed aside the contention of involuntary servitude with barely an argument.[52] Though not among his best, Arver protected the draft against future Thirteenth Amendment challenges.

White's tenure as chief is easily divided according to the Court's membership, marked by the departure of Charles Evans Hughes in 1916. When Hughes was serving the Court functioned at its most efficient, refraining from the conservative activism favored by Taft's "old fools." White mustered a moderate majority of Roosevelt and Taft appointees in creating new doctrines on the Commerce Clause and the Fourth Amendment. The Close and Substantial doctrine granted broader congressional commerce regulation while the Exclusionary Rule applied Fourth Amendment law to the federal government. In an unusual turn of events, the departure of two progressive justices, Hughes to run for president and Horace Lurton, who died, and their replacement by two even more progressive justices, Louis Brandeis and John Clarke, split the Court, strengthening the conservative block which revived liberty to contract and Tenth Amendment doctrines used to strike state and federal economic regulation. Even the chief justice grew more conservative, providing the critical fifth vote in *Hammer v. Dagenhart*, striking a federal ban on child labor using the Tenth Amendment.[53] The disarray that marked the White Court may have well influence one of White's successors. When faced with an offer to be promoted to chief justice by Richard Nixon, Justice Potter Stewart declined, noting the problems of the White Court as a warning against promoting a sitting justice to the center chair.[54]

Much like Taft's other appointees, White did not fulfill the high hopes of the president who appointed him. Instead of driving in a clear direction, the White led Court tended to drift, sometimes rejecting the doctrines of the past other times adding to the opinions so criticized by Taft and other progressive Republicans.

## The Nixon Court

If the first half of the twentieth century was dominated by political leaders such as Woodrow Wilson and Franklin Roosevelt, the honor for the second half of the century must be granted to Richard Nixon. From the start of his political career Nixon evoked radically different reactions from political partisans. Republicans worshiped him; Democrats loathed and feared him. The Alger Hiss case, a successful 1950 Senate run and rise to the vice presidency at the age of thirty nine hardened perceptions of him.[55]

His 1960 presidential defeat and disastrous 1962 race for governor of California seemed to mark the end of his political career. But Nixon won the 1968 election partly because of his focus on domestic issues such as law and order and the role of the Warren Court in the criminal justice process. His attacks on the Court implied he would replace aging liberal justices with a band of strict constructionists.[56]

Nixon's chance to remake the Court came immediately. Chief Justice Warren had conditionally resigned in the spring of 1968 but Lyndon Johnson bungled the appointment. Warren's resignation letter then passed to Nixon who faced a Republican judicial bench limited in qualified nominees. During the thirty six years prior to Nixon's election, there had been only eight years of Republican rule of the White House. Most of the prominent judges in the federal system were Democrats and unlikely to agree with Nixon's agenda. Nixon settled on Warren Burger, a night school law graduate and veteran of the D.C. Court of Appeals. While competent Burger was a disappointment to conservatives who hoped for a wholesale repudiation of Warren, but his nomination was an early political victory for Nixon as Burger was easily confirmed. A second vacancy came after the sudden resignation of Justice Fortas, his controversial promotion to chief justice defeated in the waning days of the Johnson Administration.[57]

With Republican charges echoing from the Fortas debacle, Democratic senators rejected two Nixon selections, North Carolinian Clement Haynsworth and Floridian Harrold Carswell.[58] With his strategy of appointing southern justices defeated by the Senate, Nixon chose Harry Blackmun, a Minnesotan close to Burger, having served as best man at Burger's wedding, their friendship earning the men the moniker, the Minnesota Twins.[59] The resignations of Justice Black and Justice Harlan opened two Court vacancies and Nixon made his two best selections, Lewis Powell and William Rehnquist. Their confirmation proved easier though not without difficulties.

Powell faced minimal resistance but Rehnquist withstood a barrage from Senate liberals, who criticized his defense of Nixon's war policies and accused him of racism. One of their weapons was a memo Rehnquist authored while serving as clerk to Justice Robert Jackson in 1953 while the Court was considering the Brown decision. Digging through Court records, liberals discovered one of Rehnquist's memos to Jackson defending the Plessy decision and segregated schools. Rehnquist defended the memo as a request by Justice Jackson for a summary of the pro segregation position but few believed the explanation. Rehnquist survived confirmation only because Nixon paired him with the amiable Lewis Powell.[60]

## The Burger Court

The Burger Court proved a disappointment for Nixon's strongest supporters as it trimmed rather than overruled the Mapp and Miranda criminal rights decisions while recognizing new rights under its abortion and affirmative action decisions. For every step forward the justices followed with a step backward in an oddly choreographed dance two step that cast doubt on the Court's leadership in the person of Chief Justice Burger.

Much has been written of Burger's leadership style, little of it positive. The chief has been portrayed as bumbling, pompous, bullying, distracted and inept.[61] Burger's strained relationship with the news media—including a physical confrontation with a news camera—did not aid him on the public relations front. The sharp divisions among the justices and Burger's lax management style worked against consensus as the Court's conferences descended into chaos.[62]

Burger's influence was strongest in judicial administration. His proposal for an intermediate court of appeals to remove the burden of a growing caseload for the justices was rejected by Congress. The chief did convince Congress to appropriate more money for law clerks and new equipment including a copier machine that brought the Court bravely into the 1960s. His most controversial creation was the cert pool in which all cert petitions were divided among clerks in all of the chambers. The clerks composed summaries of the petitions, distributing them to all of the chambers. Some justices feared the chief was seeking control of the Court's paper flow and refused to participate but the process improved efficiency by allowing justices to ignore scores of frivolous petitions.[63]

Burger's limited administrative success was matched by legal achievements during his early years. In his first four years he rewrote obscenity law, allowing states and localities to enforce obscenity statutes based on community standards.[64] Burger also pruned at the Miranda and Mapp decisions. In *Harris v. New York* Burger upheld the use of illegally obtained confessions to impeach an defendant's testimony. The chief ruled the Miranda decision could not be intended to protect perjury by excluding evidence that the defendant was lying under oath.[65]

Another of Burger's innovations on the Miranda ruling came in a pair of cases, six years apart, *Brewer v. Williams*[66] and *Nix v. Williams*.[67] Both cases focused on Williams who was arrested for killing a minor girl. During an extended drive the police elicited a confession from Williams while discussing the search for the victim's body. Williams directed the police to the girl's body and was subsequently convicted of murder. The conviction was overturned as five justices tossed out the confession as illegally obtained. Burger dissented, charging the Court with throwing out an uncoerced confession.

Nix was Williams' second appeal to reach the Supreme Court. Williams was retried, the evidence obtained from his confession used in the second trial under the doctrine of inevitable discovery. Burger took his cue from the trial judge and introduced an inevitable discovery doctrine, allowing police to use illegally obtained evidence if it would have been found using other methods of detection. Though Nix was a Fifth Amendment case, the doctrine was used in illegal searches.

Burger followed an incremental strategy in search and seizure law. In *South Dakota v. Opperman* the chief allowed police to use the inventory process to search impounded cars without a warrant and use evidence obtained from those searches.[68] In *California v. Carney*, Burger extended warrantless searches of cars to include motor homes.[69] In *California v. Ciraola*, the chief upheld the police use of an airplane to conduct aerial surveillance of a backyard where marijuana was being grown.[70] By 1986 Mapp and Miranda were riddled with exception. .

The Chief struggled to untangle the Court's confused Establishment Clause rulings. Instead his creation of the aptly named Lemon Test exacerbated the confusion and eventually forced Burger to abandon it in favor of new standards of tradition and secularism.[71]

Burger's most consequential opinion came in *United States v. Nixon.* The Watergate scandal had been bubbling in Washington D.C. for two years when it reached the Supreme Court in the summer of 1974. A special prosecutor had subpoenaed audiotapes of Oval Office conversations, some of which were about the Watergate burglaries. Nixon refused to produce the tapes, claiming executive privilege as the conversations included details about national security and law enforcement subjects. An outcry erupted from congressional Democrats, who argued for the sanctity of the office of special prosecutor and denounced Nixon for refusing to cooperate. [72]

The Court split along partisan lines as Burger struggled to build a consensus around a narrowed executive privilege. The chief limited claims of executive privilege to instances of national security or advice from counselors. In defining executive privilege, Burger sought to revive presidential authority, weakened during the Nixon Administration. [73]

In reviving executive power, Burger took aim at the one house legislative veto in *INS v. Chadha.*[74] When the attorney general refused to deport Chadha, the House of Representatives utilized a legislative veto to override the executive branch and order Chadha's deportation. When Chadha appealed his deportation, Burger framed the dispute as a separation of powers issue. The chief stuck down the one house legislative veto, finding that the House had made law when ordering Chadha's deportation. Laws could only be made by passage through both houses of Congress and presentment to the president. Under Burger's interpretation, the one house legislative veto violated the presentment clause.

The Chadha strengthened executive authority at the expense of Congress, the same result at Burger's opinion in *Bowsher v. Synar.*[75] During the budget battles of the mid 1980s, Congress passed the Gramm – Rudman Act granting the comptroller general Charles Bowsher, authority to cut spending. But because Bowsher could be removed by Congress, Burger ruled he was a legislative officer and thus could not perform executive acts, such as cutting spending.[76] Both Chadha and Bowsher represented Burger's attempt to regain executive authority over the budget and execution of the laws. Both decisions opened new avenues for challenging congressional authority and differed from Burger's other major opinions on integration and busing.

The school integration battles in the south had been fought and won by the Court by 1969 but upon entering office, Burger faced new issues. In *Swann v. Charlotte Mecklenburg*, Burger upheld busing as a means for a school district to integrate.[77] But faced with a busing plan in Detroit, Burger led five justices in retreating from the sweeping Swann decision and ruled de facto segregation could not be remedied through forced busing.[78]

Burger added his voice to job discrimination law, broadening the definition of discrimination to also ban employment policies with a disparate impact on minority hiring.[79] This turned discrimination law on its head, requiring business to prove its hiring policies were not discriminatory but rather based on business related issues. Burger's Griggs' opinion did not extend to the issue of affirmative action. Eight years later the chief dissented in *USW v. Weber* which upheld a corporate affirmative action program favoring promotion of black steelworkers ove white steelworkers.[80] In 1980 Burger wrote the decision upholding the federal policy of racial set asides for contracts.[81] Four years later Burger joined *Firefighters v. Stotts* which weakened Griggs by allowing seniority to override racial preference in dismissing firefighters.[82] Stotts would later be overruled by the 1991 Civil Rights Act.

The Burger Court proved a disappointment to conservatives who expected the Nixon appointees to overrule Warren Court decision. Instead Court observers described the Court as a "mosaic"[83] or as "pragmatic"[84] and an institution engaged in a "rootless activism."[85] Publication of the 1979 Bob Woodward expose, *The Brethren*, exacerbated doubts about the chief justice, who was portrayed as a pompous, intellectually light chief with a love for ceremony and little influence with his colleagues. As one Court employee put it, "when Burger retired it was just like Christmas morning."[86]

## Harry Blackmun

Harry Blackmun reached a narrowly divided Court and assumed the role of swing vote on critical constitutional decisions.[87] Derided as a clone of Warren Burger, Blackmun's reputation as a judicial conservative was quickly dispelled after he authored Roe v. Wade beginning a twenty year journey to the left.

Blackmun has been portrayed as a weak minded justice easily manipulated by the slick talking Justice Brennan. While Blackmun would never be mistaken as an intellectual giant, it is more likely he was not as conservative—read dangerous—as early opponents claimed.

Blackmun's entry into the liberal pantheon may well have come with the Bakke decision. A confusing and oddly divided case, Blackmun joined Justices Brennan, Marshall and White, in approving affirmative action programs at universities.[88] They joined Justice Powell's opinion—a majority of one—that supported affirmative action in some limited cases. After Bakke, Blackmun became a reliable vote in favor of social rights ranging from procreation to speech and religious rights and civil rights cases. Only when considering the rights of criminal defendants, the overarching issue of Richard Nixon's 1968 campaign, did Blackmun vote with the government's position.

Blackmun composed what might be the two worst opinions of the 1980s, *Garcia v. San Antonio*[89] and *Allegheny County v. ACLU.*[90] Garcia was the climax of a nearly ten year odyssey to define what state powers existed beyond the control of Congress. The search began in *National League of Cities v. Usery*, a dispute over paying a federal minimum wage to local government employees.[91] Blackmun provided the deciding vote striking down the federal minimum wage for state and local government. The Court recognized states enjoyed sovereign powers constitutionally protected from federal regulation, including wages paid to their employees After Usery the justices failed to identify another other sovereign powers in a series of cases in the early 1980s.[92] In 1985 the Garcia case triggered another debate over state sovereign powers with Blackmun's opinion the judicial equivalent of "no mas."

Justice Blackmun flip flopped from his Usery vote, admitting the search for state sovereign powers was difficult and too subjective.[93] The surprising admission that a legal problem was too difficult for the justices to untangle led Blackmun to overrule Usery and reject the view that states enjoyed sovereign powers separated from federal regulation.

In Allegheny County the ACLU challenged placement of a nativity scene along with a Christmas tree and Menorah in the county courthouse. In a split decision Blackmun upheld the Christmas tree display and the Menorah but not the nativity scene, ruling it represented an establishment of religion. Blackmun found that inclusion of religious symbols such as a creche violated the separation of church and state but that the inclusion of the Menorah did not as it was an historical not a religious symbol.[94] In ignoring the obvious religious connotations of the Menorah, Blackmun only added to the Tower of Babel that was the Court's Establishment Clause cases.

## Roe v. Wade

*Roe v. Wade* has been praised and panned by all sides of the ideological spectrum.[95] The abortion issue was raised just as the Court was considering gender discrimination issues under the Fourteenth Amendment's Equal Protection Clause and Congress was ratifying the Equal Rights Amendment.[96]

The abortion issue was dodged by the justices during the 1960s as liberalized abortion laws were signed by such unlikely supporters as Governor Ronald Reagan. By 1972 a majority of justices prepared to confront abortion in *Roe v. Wade*. The abortion decision was issued the day after Richard Nixon's second inaugural, a presage of a tumultuous and truncated second term and was controversial from its start. Writing for the Court Blackmun struggled to nail down the precise location of the abortion right, quoting the Ninth and Fourteenth amendments. Blackmun created a three trimester system, balancing state and individual interests by prohibiting abortion restrictions prior to the third trimester. Several concurrences were attached to Blackmun's opinion with Justice Douglas arguing for a broader interpretation of liberty, Justice Stewart defending the use of substantive due process in Roe and the chief justice missed the point, declaring the abortion right was not as sweeping as everyone thought.[97]

Blackmun was unprepared as former allies criticized Roe and compared it to Dred Scott. Much of the opposition clustered around an article from the dean of the Stanford Law School, John Hart Ely. In a Yale Law Journal article, Ely took aim at the fundamental weaknesses of the Roe decision. He found Roe was not a coherent decision when it identified abortion as a fundamental right and was not constitutional law because it was not based on a clear concept or text of the constitution.[98]

Those who had opposed Blackmun's confirmation suddenly brimmed with praise. A private man, Blackmun sought solace among his new Court allies including Justice Brennan who fulminated with praise for Blackmun as he shored up his crumbling liberal coalition. Abortion would become an obsession for the justice. When a random gun shot hit his house in Washington D.C., the incident was initially blamed on an unknown anti abortion protestor. This provided fodder for the pro abortion movement and its assumptions that the anti abortion movement was born of violence. Later the shooting was found to be random, a not unusual occurrence in an increasingly violent city.[99]

An unexpected backwash from the Roe decision came two years later in *Bigelow v. Virginia*.[100] A New York clinic challenged a Virginia ban on advertising for abortion services. The clinic claimed the ban violated its right to free speech and the seven justices of the Roe majority agreed. Blackmun's opinion changed the issue from abortion to free speech rights even as it focused on the right of women to know about abortion services. Known as the initial commercial speech case, Bigelow was followed in 1976 by another Blackmun opinion establishing the right of business to advertise their goods and services.[101] By 1980 a full fledged doctrine and four part test was created by Justice Powell, though Blackmun concurred in the decision, his ardor for speech rights cooled by the absence of abortion.

## A Judicial Smack Down

Blackmun's final years on the Court were spent mostly in dissent as he was relegated to leadership of a bloc of two justices which included Justice Stevens. He was left bemoaning the rightward turn of the Court, warning of his impending retirement and the devastating consequences it would have for his magnum opus, *Roe v. Wade*.[102] Blackmun's dissent in *Planned Parenthood v. Casey*, was the closest thing to a judicial endorsement of Bill Clinton and his pro abortion stance.[103]

Yet Blackmun remained loyal to Richard Nixon's law and order campaign, joining Court rulings against criminal defendants' rights including his dissent in Furman striking the death penalty and his joining of Gregg in reinstating the death penalty. He provided key votes in Nix v. Williams, *U.S. v. Leon* which created exceptions to the Mapp and Miranda decisions. But as retirement beckoned and the Court became more conservative, Blackmun performed his last switch, arguing against the death penalty.

His forum was the Court's decision to deny the appeal of a death row inmate.[104] Dissenting from the denial of cert, Blackmun criticized capital punishment, claiming he no longer wanted to "tinker with the machinery of death."[105] In his dissent, Blackmun traced his own capital punishment rulings, claiming he had not changed his personal opposition to capital punishment, but only his willingness to impose his views on the political system. According to Blackmun his switch could be attributed to the Court reducing the number of appeal options for death row inmates.[106] Blackmun's flip flop may have been triggered by *Herrera v. Collins*, where some justices suggested the wrongful execution of a defendant would not be cruel and unusual punishment.

But this time an anti death penalty diatribe would not go unanswered as Justice Scalia challenged Blackmun's attack on capital punishment. In the judicial equivalent of a legal smack down, Scalia ridiculed Blackmun, reminding the justice of the horrific details of the murder committed and the plain fact that murder victims receive many fewer appeals for their life than do those convicted of a capital crime.[107]

## Lewis Powell

All those who knew Lewis Powell described him with a single word, courtly. One of the last southern gentlemen in Washington, Powell served in the midst of the maelstrom that was social integration. As president of the Richmond School Board, Powell faced the choice of resisting integration or accepting the rule of federal courts. He chose moderation in guiding the school district toward desegregation absent the violence that raged through the south in the 1950s and 1960s.[108] As president of the American Bar Association Powell was an early critic of the Warren Court. For Richard Nixon, Powell represented a progressive southerner who accepted integration while adhering to a law and order credo. Nixon would later declare "ten years of Lewis Powell is worth thirty years of most (justices)."[109]

Appointed to fill Justice Black's seat, Powell proved to be more difficult to predict than Nixon had believed. In *United States v. U.S. District Court* struck down part of the 1968 Omnibus Crime Act which allowed the attorney general to wiretap without a search warrant. The decision was unusual for a law and order justice.[110]

Powell dissented in *Furman v. Georgia* striking down the death penalty. Four years later Powell led a trio of justices in *Gregg v. Georgia* reinstating the death penalty.[111] Joining Justices Stewart and Stevens, Powell rewrote capital punishment law, mandating a bifurcated process that had juries rendering a verdict then holding a separate sentencing hearing to determine whether the death penalty would be applied.

Powell also contributed to the paring of the Exclusionary Rule. In *Stone v. Powell*, the justice limited federal appeals for death row inmates, creating a cost benefit analysis in Fourth Amendment cases.[112] Powell found that a federal judge striking down a search years later provided little benefit but exacted considerable cost by freeing a convicted criminal.[113] This overturned Warren Court precedents extending opportunities for judges to overturn death sentences. Powell would join his fellow Nixon appointees in further limiting the rights of criminal defendants.[114]

While a conservative on criminal justice issues, on social issues Powell followed his Democrat heritage in favoring affirmative action and abortion. Powell authored the first affirmative action case in *Bakke v. Regents*. A majority of one, Powell ruled race could be a factor among many in determining college admissions. No justice joined all of Powell's opinion creating a decision that resembled a jigsaw puzzle as different groups pieced together different interpretations to form the law. Bakke was not the Court's proudest moment as it dodged a critical constitutional issue and left the law muddled. [115]

Powell also joined Roe yet his support of abortion rights weakened with the issue of public funding. In *Maher v. Roe*, Powell upheld a Connecticut regulation allowing Medicaid funding of abortions only when those abortions were medically necessary. Powell declared the state could make the value judgment favoring birth over abortion by using public money to favor birth and not fund abortions.[116] Powell joined Justice Stewart's opinion in *Harris v. McRae* upholding the federal Hyde Amendment ban on federal Medicaid funding of abortion.[117] Yet in a sign of his influence and swing status on the abortion issue, Powell was chosen to compose the opinion in one of the closest abortion cases of the 1980s, *Akron v. Akron Center*.[118] In Akron Powell struck down a series of limited regulations on abortion including an ordinance requiring an aborted child be disposed of humanely.

Powell's dedication to a constitutional right to privacy began and ended with abortion. *Bowers v. Hardwick* was the first challenge to sodomy laws heard by the Supreme Court. Bowers split the Court, with an initial vote to strike the law but a wavering Powell was tugged back into the conservative fold after an aggressive lobbying campaign mounted by Chief Justice Burger. In a concurring opinion Powell tried to have it both ways, joining Justice White's opinion upholding sodomy laws but wondering aloud if a twenty year sentence for sodomy was cruel and unusual punishment.[119]

Powell proved more skeptical when the Court sought to extend other social rights. He refused to give Justice Brennan a fifth vote in making gender a constitutionally protected class.[120] In *San Antonio v. Rodriguez* he declined to make wealth a constitutionally protected class, refusing to require states to fund school districts equally using income taxes rather than property taxes.[121] In *Warth v.*

*Seldin*, Powell refused to allow low income litigants to sue government and force it to build low income housing.[122] In both cases he slowed the progress of the substantive equal protection movement that sought to force equal treatment by government in the economics' sphere.

Powell's last years on the Court were his most difficult. Beset by health problems he missed much of the 1985 term then in his last term had to face the voluble Justice Scalia. The quiet Powell was put off by his boisterous colleague and with his health remaining tenuous he resigned in 1987.

## William Rehnquist

Richard Nixon's fourth and final Court choice was a dyed in the wool conservative who used his thirty three year career to shift the institution decisively to the right. William Rehnquist had been part of the conservative movement begun by Senator Barry Goldwater which sought to sweep the Republican Party clean of liberal "Rockefeller Republicans." Upon reaching the Court, it seemed as if Rehnquist was determined to perform the same cleansing ritual to constitutional law.

Having served as Justice Robert Jackson's law clerk for two terms, Rehnquist was imbued with suspicion of judicial activism, preferring instead to defer to legislative judgments and only overturning laws if they clearly violated the constitution. For Rehnquist there seemed few if any examples of such laws.[123]

The justice was accused of holding reactionary views, seeking to turn back the Court's clock to the pre 1937 period but Rehnquist was not a traditional conservative. He did not rail against government economic regulation and throughout his career warned his liberal colleagues their activism could be turned against them by a new crop of conservative justices.[124]

In most disputes Rehnquist favored government, taking issue with many of the Warren Court innovations. The justice challenged Establishment Clause ruling, refuting arguments that the separation of church and state was a constitutional doctrine. Rehnquist advanced his views in solo dissents in *Stone v. Graham*[125] and *Larkin v. Grendel's Den*,[126] where he argued fore greater church/state cooperation. Later he would join Chief Justice Burger's attempts to rewrite the Lemon test in 1983 and 1984.

In criminal defendants' cases, Rehnquist proved unwilling to second guess juries and trial judges, his near perfect support of prosecution over defendants meticulously documented during the hearings over his promotion to chief justice.[127] Rehnquist contributed new law in the area, finding a public safety exception to Miranda warnings in *New York v. Quarles*, granting police authority to ask questions of suspects without Miranda warnings if the public safety was in question.[128]

## The Lone Ranger

The Burger Court may have had the greatest ideological divide of any Court as the civil libertarian William Douglas lined up on the ideological left against the pro government conservative Rehnquist. Much like Douglas, Rehnquist found few followers in his crusades though the new justice's influence was building while Douglas' was waning. Seemingly isolated on the right, Rehnquist wrote mainly in dissent, offering arguments that the dominant constitutional doctrines of the era were flawed.

Those dissents included Furman, Roe and Bakke, generally considered the most liberal opinions of the Burger era. In each Rehnquist aimed his fire at judges who replaced the judgment of legislators with their own. Rehnquist preached judicial restraint to a doubting audience, even going so far as to vote against his conservative allies in upholding the Federal Election Act in *Buckley v. Valeo.*[129]

Although alone in his sentiments, Rehnquist earned the respect of conservatives, who saw him as the one voice of reason in the institution. Half jokingly dubbed the Lone Ranger by his law clerks, Rehnquist seemed poised for a career in obscurity, composing lone dissents quickly forgotten. Ronald Reagan's election shifted the tide in Rehnquist's favor as a popular conservative president used executive resources to argue conservative doctrine. No longer a tinny voice relegated to the Court's far right, Rehnquist began building coalitions with the chief justice, Justice O'Connor and the increasingly conservative Byron White. By 1986, Rehnquist's star burned brightly and his ideas had become part of the mainstream.[130]

Even as he preached judicial restraint, Rehnquist dabbled in activism, seeking to rebuild the wall of separation between state and federal power. Federalism had fallen out of favor in the 1940s but three decades later Rehnquist revived the Tenth and Eleventh Amendments which had been relegated to the role of a musty anachronism taught by law professors to fill out the empty days of their constitutional law courses.

In *Edelman v. Jordan* the state of Illinois was accused of not following federal regulations when dispensing social welfare payments. Jordan sued the state demanding Illinois follow federal regulations and demanded the state pay him benefits he had been denied. Illinois claimed immunity under the Eleventh Amendment on the claim of back benefits. Rehnquist agreed and cobbled together a majority of five extending state immunity to cases involving payment of previous benefits. Though an obscure ruling, Edelman removed the profit from lawsuits demanding back payments as a portion of those payments would go to lawyers challenging the state. With only future benefits considered, such lawsuits became less profitable. Edelman returned the Eleventh Amendment to constitutional relevance. [131]

Rehnquist revived the Tenth Amendment in *Usery v. National League of Cities.*[132] As part of the Great Society push for economic equality, Congress began requiring state and local governments to pay their employees the federal minimum wage. The angst suffered by state and local officials led them to challenge the law as an intrusion on their authority to set their own budgets. When presented to the justices, Usery appeared to be a simple case. Since the 1940s, the Court had upheld nearly every federal regulation of commerce, including those affecting state authority. But Rehnquist's opinion sent shockwaves through the federal system.

In Usery he carved out an exception to commerce regulations, forbidding those that intruded upon traditional state functions including but not limited to state employee salaries. Congress had overstepped its authority in ordering states to apply the federal minimum wage and for the first time in nearly forty years the Supreme Court limited federal commerce powers.[133]

Usery sent attorneys scrambling to take advantage of the new doctrine. The nine years between the Usery decision and its being overturned in Garcia witnessed renewed action in states' rights cases.[134] But Rehnquist's traditional state functions' doctrine was never used in a second case. It would not be until he was chief justice that Rehnquist would have his views enacted into law.

Reaching the Supreme Court just as it reached its liberal apogee, William Rehnquist spent much of his fourteen years as associate justice dissenting and playing the role of judicial Jeremiah warning his liberal colleagues of future reckoning.

## The Nixon Court Legacy

In his eulogy for Richard Nixon, President Bill Clinton expressed the belief the former president would be remembered for more than the Watergate Scandal. As the twenty first century began, two of Nixon's foreign policy achievements continued to bear fruit, casting a different light on his administration.

Closer ties to communist China and the country's leaders' decision to throw off deranged communist ideology and practices produced a worldwide economic impact. Nixon's decision to take the United States off the gold standard and create a floating currency system sped the globalization process. One of his domestic successes, four Supreme Court nominations, continued paying dividends for the Republican Party. Chief Justice William Rehnquist was the guiding force behind the decision on the 2000 disputed presidential election. It was the highlight of Rehnquist's career that he witnessed his lonely dissents become law in the U.S. reports. Though Nixon's other three selections would be remembered less readily, they did resemble the Nixon Administrations' confused policies as the justices lacked an ideological compass and failed to turn the institution in a conservative direction.

## The Taft and Nixon Justices

Few observers of the presidency will recall the Taft or Nixon Administrations fondly or hold them up as examples of success. Their Supreme Court appointments, though, were recognized as positive achievements, their justices a mix of liberal and conservative, distinguished and obscure. Taft and Nixon spend their post presidencies trying to revive their reputations, their Supreme Court appointments enhanced their legacies and aided in that revival.

## Notes

1. Pringle, Henry F, *William Howard Taft* (Newton, CT: American Political Biography Press, 1998), 834-837.

2. Crowley, Monica, *Nixon in Winter* (London: I.B. Taurus, 1998) Nixon conducted a one man crusade for Alexander Haig as secretary of state in the Reagan Administration, ranting against another Reagan choice, George Schultz, as a "candy ass." Cannon, Lou, *Role of a Lifetime* (New York: Simon and Schuster, 1991) 79-80. In 1992Nixon offered asolution to the Russian financial crisis by holding a conference without seeking the advice of then President Bush, Crowley, 83-85. Nixon alsooffered Clinton advice on Russia, 128-130.

3. Black, Conrad, *Richard Nixon, a life in full* (New York: Public Affairs Press, 2007); Reeves, Richard, *President Nixon: Alone in the White House* (New York: Simon and Schuster, 2001).Both of these excellent biographies portray Nixon in more complex terms.

4. Steamer, Robert, *Chief Justice* (Columbia: University of South Carolina Press, 1986), 173-177.

5. Nixon was ranked fourteenth in the survey, just above his old competitor, Lyndon Johnson. In most presidential polls Nixon is ranked among the worst, rarely rising above the bottom ten.

6. Pringle, 313

7. Bickel, Alexander and Benno Schmidt, *The Judiciary and Responsible Government1910-1921* (New York: MacMillan, 1984), 7. Taft portrayed Chief Justice Melville Fuller as senile and Fuller's colleagues as deaf and infirm.

8. Watts, Jr. James, "Horace Lurton" in Leon Friedman and Fred Israel *The Justices of the United States Supreme Court 1789-1969* (New York: Chelsea House Publishing, 1969), 1851-1853.

9. Bickel and Schmidt, 335-339

10. Abraham 130

11. Bickel and Schmidt 42-43

12. Friedman and Israel 1976-1978
13. 220 U.S. 506, 515,523 (1911)
14. 220 U.S. 506, 515, 523
15. Bickel and Schmidt 327-328
16. Bickel and Schmidt 320-323,331-332
17. 236 U.S. 1 (1915)
18. 237 U.S. 309(1915)
19. Oney, Steve, *And the Dead shall rise again* (New York: Pantheon Books, 2003), 464-467.
20. Oney 467
21. Even as ill health descended upon him, Pitney continued his assaults on unions. In *Truax v. Corrigan* 257 U.S. 312 (1921) the justice upheld an injunction against an Arizona union which picketed and boycotted a restaurant that hired non union workers.
22. William Cushing would be the other, first resigning as an associate justice then earning a recess appointment as chief justice before his nomination was rejected by the Senate.
23. It was Theodore Roosevelt, who had some influence with Taft and the Republican Party who opposed Hughes' promotion to the center chair. Bickel and Schmidt 59, Abraham 134
24. Bickel and Schmidt399
25. 219 U.S. 219(1911)
26. *Houston, East & West Texas Railway Co. v. United States* 234 U.S. 342 (1914)
27. 237 U.S. 309 , 346
28. 236 U.S. 1, 28
29. *Truax v. Raich*239 U.S. 33 (1915)
30. Bickel and Schmidt, 45
31. Friedman and Israel, 1952
32. Pringle, 971
33. Pringle, 971
34. Pringle, 998-1000
35. 230 U.S. 126, 134 (1913)
36. 273 U.S. 135 (1927)
37. *Rhode Island v. Palmer* 253 U.S. 350, 388 (1921)
38. Alsop, Joseph and Turner Catledge, *The 168 Days* (New York: DeCapo Press, 1973), 206-207.
39. Highsaw, Robert, *Edward Douglass White* (Baton Rouge: LSU Press, 1981), 53-54. Cleveland initially nominated William Hornblower, whose nomination was defeated by the Senate, possibly saving the Court some embarrassment in the future at using the Hornblower doctrine or serving in the Hornblower Court.Cleveland followed this rejection with the nomination of Wheeler

Peckham, who would also be defeated by the Senate though his brother's nomination was approved the next year.

40. White was never known as a racial progressive. As a southern Democrat he had fought with the confederacy, was rumored to have been a member of the Klu Klux Klan and generally accepted segregation of the races in public life.

41. Bork, Robert, *The Antitrust Paradox* (New York: Free Press, 1993), 8.

42. White dissented in *U.S. v. Trans Missouri* 166 U.S. 290 (1897) which dealt with price fixing and the Sherman Act. He took issue with the majority opinion which struck down a combination of railroads that attempted to set freight prices to maximize profits.

43. 221 U.S. 1(1911)

44. 221 U.S. 106 (1911)

45. Highsaw, 96

46. Highsaw, 172-173

47. Highsaw, 58-59

48. Hughes received considerable political support for promotion to the chief justice position which may have had the opposite effect on Taft as he rejected the man favored by many of his political opponents, Bickel and Schmidt, 62.

49. Highsaw, 187

50. 238 U.S. 347, 364 (1915)

51. *Arver v. United States* 245 U.S. 366 (1918)

52. 245 U.S. 366, 389

53. 247 U.S. 251 (1918)

54. Woodward and Armstrong, *The Brethren (*New York: Avon Books, 1979), 11.

55. Morris, Roger, *Richard Milhous Nixon* (New York: Henry Holt, 1991), 335-337, 618-620.

56. Reeves, 44

57. Maltz, Earl, *The Chief Justiceship of Warren Burger* (Columbia: University of South Carolina Press, 2000), 9.

58. Maltese, John, *The Selling of Supreme Court Nominees* (Baltimore: John Hopkins University Press, 1993),73-74.

59. Woodward and Armstrong, 87

60. Savage, David *Turning Right* (New York: John Wiley and Sons, 1992), 41- 43.

61. Woodward and Armstrong, 108

62. The direction that the Court was headed became apparent in 1971 in *Byers v. California* 402 U.S. 424. Byers challenged California's hit and run law which made it illegal to leave the scene of a car accident without providing personal information including name and address. Byers claimed the law forced people to incriminate themselves.Three of eight justices agreed that it was the responsibility of accident victims to find those who had hit them and provide

evidence of the accident in court.Four justices disagreed, ensuring that the public highways would not become the newest forum for a demolition derby.

63. Maltz, 10

64. *Miller v. California* 413 U.S. 15 (1973)

65. 401 U.S. 222, 226 (1971)

66. 430 U.S. 387 (1977)

67. 467 U.S. 431 (1983)

68. 428 U.S. 364(1976)

69. 471 U.S. 386 (1985)

70. 476 U.S. 207 (1986)

71. *Marsh v. Chambers* (1983). Burger composed the decision upholding legislative prayer for the Nebraska general assembly with the finding that the First Congress, which had ratified the First Amendment, had also begun its day with a prayer.In *Lynch v. Donnelly* (1984) Burger found that the inclusion of a religious creche among secular Christmas display on public property was part of the city's strategy to attract visitors to the downtown area to promote Christmas shopping.The decision created the infamous "reindeer rule" in which religious symbols were constitutional if surrounded by secular symbols such as Santa Clause and his reindeer.

72. 418 U.S. 683 (1974) Many of the same Democrats would be singing a different tune during the impeachment of Bill Clinton after an independent counsel collected evidence of perjury and obstruction of justice.

73. 418 U.S. 683, 707-708

74. 462 U.S. 919 (1983)

75. Two supporters of presidential power, Justices' White and Rehnquist, dissented in Chadha

76. 478 U.S. 714 (1986)

77. 402 U.S. 1(1971)

78. *Milliken v. Bradley*418 U.S. 717 (1974)

79. *Griggs v. Duke Power* 401 U.S. 424 (1971)

80. 443 U.S. 193 (1979)

81. *Fullilove v. Klutznick* 448 U.S. 448 (1980)

82. 467 U.S. 561 (1984)

83. Maltz, 13

84. Schwartz, Bernard, *The Burger Court:Counter Revolution or Confirmation* (New York: Oxford University Press, 1998),26

85. Blasi, Vincent, *The Counterrevolution that wasn't* (New Haven CT: Yale University Press, 1986), 17

86. Jefferies, John C, *Justice Lewis F. Powell, Jr.* (Charles Scribner's Sons: New York, 1994), 545.

87. Blackmun was derided by some clerks at "hip pocket Harry" because of his tendency to vote with Burger during his first years as a justice,Woodward and Armstrong, 122

88. Jefferies, 489-490
89. 469 U.S. 528(1985)
90. 492 U.S. 573 (1989)
91. 426 U.S. 833 (1976)
92. 456 U.S. 742 (1982), 455 U.S. 678 (1982), 452 U.S. 264 (1981)
93. The oddest portion of the opinion was Blackmun's litany of the Court's previous failures to untangle the difficulties of state and federal relations with the conclusion that accepting failure was the better part of valor.For the list of failures see 469 U.S. 528, 540-547.
94. Blackmun goes into a detailed discussion of the historical aspects of Hannukah and how it does not represent a fully religious holiday 492 U.S. 573, 585-587.
95. *Roe v. Wade*410 U.S. 113 (1973)
96. *Reed v. Reed* 404 U.S. 71 (1971)
97. Stewart denied that the economic due process eliminated in the 1930s had been revived with the abortion and privacy cases 410 U.S. 113, 169; while Burger cast doubt on the importance of Roe, 410 U.S. 179, 209.
98. Ely, John Hart "Wages of Crying Wolf" 82 *Yale Law Journal* 920, 94
99. Greenhouse, 182-183. As the only major biography of Blackmun, Greenhouse's work further exhibited the importance of abortion in Blackmun's legacy as there were fifteen mentions of abortion and Blackmun in the index out of approximately eighty five mentions of the justice, 259-261.
100. 421 U.S. 809 (1975)
101. *Virginia Pharmacy Board v. Virginia Citizen's Consumer Council* 425 U.S. 748 (1976)
102. *Planned Parenthood v. Casey* 505 U.S. 833 (1992) In his Casey dissent, Blackmun's apocalyptic language warned of the "darkness of the plurality" or those who wanted to overturn Roe, 923 and that he "fear(ed) for the darkness as four justices anxiously await the single vote necessary to extinguish the light," 924. Equating his colleagues and their anti abortion views with the dark ages was a desperate attempt to rally pro abortion opinion even further against the Court.
103. Blackmun described it as a "choice between two worlds," 505 U.S. 833, 926.
104. *Callins v. Collins*510 U.S. 1141. (1994)
105. 510 U.S. 1141, 1145.
106. 510 U.S. 1141, 1146
107. 510 U.S. 1141, 1148
108. Jefferies,142-143
109. Jefferies, 535
110. 407 U.S. 297 (1972)
111. 408 U.S. 238 (1972)
112. 428 U.S. 465 (1976)

113. 428 U.S. 465, 492-494

114. He joined pro-government cases such as *South Dakota v. Opperman, Texas v. Brown, Michigan v. Long, and California v. Carney, Wainwright v. Sykes, Rakas v, Illinois, Browder v. Director* and *U.S. v. Payner.*

115. 438 U.S. 265 (1978)

116. 432 U.S. 464, 471 (1977)

117. 448 U.S. 297(1980)

118. 462 U.S. 416(1983)

119. 478 U.S. 186, 198 (1986). Powell alluded to a Warren Court case, *Robinson v. California* 370 U.S. 660 (1962) where the justices found that drug addiction could not be treated as a crime because it was an involuntary act. Comparing homosexuality with drug addiction did not earn Powell many friends in the gay community Jefferies, 516-52, 523-524.

120. Woodward and Armstrong 302

121. 411 U.S. 1 (1973)

122. 422 U.S. 490 (1975)

123. Rehnquist was active in limiting habeas appeals in *Wainwright v. Sykes* 433 U.S. 72 (1977) and *Illinois v. Gates* 462 U.S. 213 (1983) while reinterpreting the Fourth Amendment to limit the Exclusionary Rule in cases such as *U.S. v. Ceccolini* 435 U.S. 268 (1978) and *Rakas v. Illinois* 439 U.S. 128 (1978)

124. See *Roe v. Wade* 410 U.S. 113, 177 (1973)

125. 449 U.S. 39 (1980) Rehnquist took issue with the Court striking down a Kentucky program in which the ten commandments were posted in public classrooms.In his dissent, Rehnquist argued that his colleagues should accept that laws could have both a secular and religious purpose and not to dismiss such laws as an automatic violation of the Establishment Clause.

126. 459 U.S. 116 (1982). The justice tweaked his colleagues for accepting a "silly case" that struck down a zoning law allowing schools and churches to oppose and prevent liquor licenses for businesses within 500 feet of either. Most distressing for Rehnquist was the Court finding that church involvement in political debates supposedly promoted sectarianism – Baptist churches supporting liquor licenses for members of the Baptist church while reflexively opposing licenses for Methodists based on some unknown theological interpretation, 130-131.In Larkin Rehnquist put his finger on the issue most disturbing to religious groups, the elimination of the right of churches to participate in public debate for fear of religion entering the public sphere.

127. Savage, 21

128. 467 U.S. 649 (1984)

129. 424 U.S. 1(1976)

130. Savage, 10

131. 415 U.S. 651, 677 (1974)

132. 426 U.S. 833 (1976)

133. 426 U.S. 833, 850

134. See *Hodel v. Virginia Surface Mining and Reclamation Association* 452 U.S. 264 (1981), *Transportation Union v. Long Island Railway Co.*455 U.S. 678 (1982), *FERC v. Mississippi* 456 U.S 742 (1982), *EEOC v. Wyoming* 460 U.S. 226 (1983)

# Name Index

# Supreme Court Case Index

www.ingramcontent.com/pod-product-compliance
Ingram Content Group UK Ltd.
Pitfield, Milton Keynes, MK11 3LW, UK
UKHW041103150926
475561UK00001BA/23

9 780761 853732